THE MURDER BOOK
EXAMINING HOMICIDE

Kim Davies
Associate Professor
Augusta State University

PEARSON

Prentice
Hall

Upper Saddle River, New Jersey 07458

Library of Congress Cataloging-in-Publication Data

Davies, Kim (Kimberly A.)
  The murder book : examining homicide / Kim Davies.
    p. cm.
  Includes bibliographical references and index.
  ISBN-13: 978-0-13-172401-3
  ISBN-10: 0-13-172401-0
  1. Murder. 2. Homicide. 3. Criminal psychology. 4. Criminal justice, Administration
    of. I. Title.
  HV6515.D36 2008
  364.152—dc22

                                                            2007033888

Editor-in-Chief: Vernon R. Anthony
Senior Acquisitions Editor: Tim Peyton
Editorial Assistant: Alicia Kelly
Marketing Manager: Adam Kloza
Production Liaison: Joanne Riker
Cover Design Director: Jayne Conte
Cover Design: Bruce Kenselaar
Cover Illustration/Photo: CORBIS
Full-Service Project Management/Composition: GGS Book Services

Pearson Education LTD.
Pearson Education Singapore, Pte. Ltd
Pearson Education, Canada, Ltd
Pearson Education—Japan

Pearson Education Australia PTY, Limited
Pearson Education North Asia Ltd
Pearson Educación de Mexico, S.A. de C.V.
Pearson Education Malaysia, Pte. Ltd

ISBN-13: 978-0-13-172401-3
ISBN-10:   0-13-172401-0

For my family, my friends, and my students

CONTENTS

PREFACE

The number of students declaring criminal justice and criminology as majors continues to increase. Classes on murder are more popular than ever. Majors and others flock to such classes across the United States. Unfortunately, however, almost no current comprehensive textbooks focus on homicide, although interesting and valuable books are available on different aspects of homicide and there are important monographs on the subject. Yet I was unable to locate a book that had the depth of important research and the breadth of topics I cover in my murder class. I was encouraged to write my own text, and here it is. I hope you find it valuable and important and that it has the depth and breadth you hope to find in your textbooks. I enjoyed writing it and I hope you enjoy reading it. More importantly, I hope it makes you think and that you learn.

I could not have written this book alone. I am greatly indebted to many individuals for helping me complete this work and make it so much better than it would be without their help. Most generally, I greatly appreciate the support and knowledge of the many wonderful criminal justice professionals and academic specialists in many disciplines whose curiosity and scientific research make a book such as this possible. Moreover, I thank the many wonderful individuals who together make up the Homicide Research Working Group (HRWG), a remarkable organization that brings practitioners and academics together in a supportive environment so important information and research may be shared in hopes of improving our knowledge about and our effectiveness in preventing homicide.

This book has also benefited from a variety of individuals who have read it in whole or in parts throughout my writing process. I was very lucky to have students give me feedback and encouragement on several chapters as I began the process of writing. Thank you and wishes of continued success to these students: Dee Dee Elam,

Tanginikki Grant, Heather Leviness, and Bronwyn Van Emmenis. I will always be indebted to the reviewers: Garry L. Boyer Sr., Dabney Lancaster Community College; Stephen Brodt, Ball State University; William Ralph Garris, University of SC Lancaster; Eric W. Hickey, California State University, Fresno; Craig W. Laker, Tri-State University; and Elizabeth E. Mustaine, University of Central Florida who provided many important points and suggestions, most of which I took to heart. Thank you, Elizabeth Mustaine, for generously sharing your syllabus when I first taught a course on murder. It helped focus my class and ultimately helped guide me in writing this book. Thanks to Margaret Lannamann for all her editorial guidance and to Suganya Karuppasamy and Anne Lesser for their attention to detail.

On a more personal note, I have been incredibly lucky to have so many people support me in my academic endeavors to this point that I cannot possibly include them all. Thus I name but a few here. Many thanks to the incredible faculty members who taught me during my time at The Ohio State University, and special thanks to those who influenced me so greatly: Ruth Peterson, Joseph Scott, Richard Lundman, and the late Simon Dinitz. It is very important that Susan Beauchamp, although we have never met in person, know how vital her encouragement was in helping me believe I could write my own textbook. Susan, without you I might still be thinking about it. Finally, I cannot thank my wonderful family and friends enough for all their support and their belief in me. Carla Corroto, you are the greatest friend one could ever hope to have. Lorraine, words cannot express how important your support has been to me.

Kim Davies
Augusta State University

Chapter 1

INTRODUCTION

Murder is intriguing. We only need to look around to see that people find murder interesting. An incredible number of popular books, television programs, and films have as their focus the killing of one human being by another. The norm in the U.S. news business is "if it bleeds, it leads." Leadoff stories on nightly newscasts and the leading stories of both local and national papers are often about murder. Some homicide cases receive national and even international attention, such as the murder of Laci Peterson and her unborn son Conner at the hands of her husband Scott Peterson. Although some cases disappear quickly from the headlines, others, such as the murders of Jon Benét Ramsey and the "Black Dahlia" and the murders by "Jack the Ripper," continue to garner airtime.

If popular culture is not enough to demonstrate that homicide is interesting, professors who offer courses on homicide could testify that it certainly attracts students. Across the United States, an open seat is rarely to be found in courses about homicide. It seems that no matter how high the course limits are set, the seats fill with students who have a variety of majors. Moreover, many of these students have been educating themselves about murder for years through true crime novels, Internet sites, and television newsmagazines. They have signed up for the course ready to learn the truth about homicide and, in all likelihood, the grisly details of it all.

What is the fascination with such a terrible phenomenon? Perhaps it is the sense of mystery—being clever and solving the case holds an appeal. Maybe it is linked to a sense of our own immortality and the fear of our deaths. For some, the fascination may be the inexplicableness of homicide. How could one person kill another? Still for others it is dark and intriguing because it is foreign and removed from the reality of their lives. Tragically, for others, it is the reality of murder that brings on or intensifies an interest in the subject. There is a need to understand why a loved one was murdered or even how someone we know could commit such a horrendous act.

Homicide is also an academic interest for scholars in various disciplines, including criminal justice, criminology, history, political science, psychology, public health, and sociology. In this book, the work of many scholars in these various disciplines are brought together in what is intended to be a fairly comprehensive overview of the scholarly study of murder. The goal is to provide a broad and rigorous academic treatment of homicide that is accessible and interesting to upper-division undergraduate students and lower-division graduate students enrolled in courses about homicide specifically or crime generally. This book takes students beyond what they learn about murder through popular media presentations on murder. Those who read this text will be exposed to the scientific study of different types of homicide, theories about homicide, and homicide law, as well as details about how homicide cases are worked by investigators and how murder cases are dealt with in the courts. Extraordinary murders featured in other popular texts are included as examples in this book, as are lesser known homicide incidents. Many cases are included throughout the book to make the reading interesting to students but also to clarify the scholarly work on homicide.

The manifest goal of this book, as I have noted, is to provide a broad treatment of the academic study of homicide. But I also hope that those who read this text will become more critical of media representations of homicide. Much false information about homicide exists in popular culture. This text is an academic treatment of the topic. The information presented here comes from studies completed by academic scientists in the biological and social science fields and, where appropriate, from criminal justice practitioners. The goal of much of this research is to prevent homicide or at least to reduce the occurrence of thousands of needless deaths each year. The aim is not sensationalism, and as such, the scholarly work on homicide, especially taken as a whole, gains us a more realistic view of what is, admittedly, an intriguing subject.

THE ORGANIZATION OF THE BOOK

Although the chapters are independent enough so they may be read in most any order, the intention was to provide a general foundation for the study of homicide by explaining definitions, data sources, and theories before moving on to specific types of homicide. Then, in the latter chapters, the text turns to what may be called a criminal justice view of murder where homicide investigation, the courts, victimization studies, and efforts at stopping murder are covered. In all, 18 chapters are included.

Chapter 2 provides relevant definitional and legal distinctions among the different types of homicide, including the differences among murder, manslaughter, justifiable homicide, and vehicular homicide. Chapter 3 includes an in-depth description of sources commonly used in homicide studies, including the FBI's Supplementary Homicide Reports, the National Center for Health Statistics mortality files, and the newer National Incident-Based Reporting System as well as other data sources that criminologists use to study homicide. Common homicide typologies used by criminologists in their studies of homicide are also included in Chapter 3. In Chapter 4, U.S. data on homicide overall and as related to sex, race, age, and place are reported. Attention is also given to cross-national comparisons and historical patterns.

Chapter 5 is the first of two theoretical chapters and covers early criminological explanations for homicide, including biological explanations (classical and positivist theories) as well as psychological explanations, including antisocial personality disorder and psychopathy. Chapter 6 is an overview of social and cultural explanations for homicide. It includes a variety of perspectives as they pertain to explanations of homicide, including deterrence and rational choice theories, social disorganization and anomie, differential association theory and social control theories, culture of violence, culture of honor and feminist explanations including possible ties between violence and gender or masculinity. A discussion of several correlates of homicide (i.e., class, race, gender, and alcohol use) and the relevance of social stratification are also included in this second theory chapter.

Chapters 7 through 13 each focus on a particular type of homicide. Confrontational homicide, defined as an altercation that grows out of a confrontation of some sort, is the most common type of homicide and the subject of Chapter 7. Chapter 8 on intimate partner homicide provides information on homicide between former and current spouses and sexual partners including same-sex couples. Chapter 9 is about children who kill and includes sections on patricide (the killing of a parent), gang killings, and school shootings. Chapter 10 looks at the killing of children by parents, stepparents, and others. Mass and spree murder, including workplace violence, family violence, terrorism, and corporate murders, are the subjects of Chapter 11. Chapter 12 is about serial killing, and Chapter 13 looks at murder as hate crime.

Chapter 14 takes a criminal justice turn as it focuses on solving homicides, the personnel and technology involved, and a realistic picture of how often homicides are easily solved. The subject of Chapter 15 is homicide in court. It includes an overview of defenses to criminal homicide including the insanity defense, as well as detailed information from the trial of a serial killer that helps illuminate what is permitted to be presented in court. Chapter 16 discusses the impact of homicide and focuses on the impact murder has on victims' families and the families of those who kill (although sometimes these are the same people), on those who serve as jurors, and on society in general.

In Chapter 17, the prevention of and punishment for homicide are discussed, including controversial approaches such as capital punishment and gun control. Finally, Chapter 18 is called the "Future of Homicide in the United States." It serves as a conclusion to this book at the same time it includes predictions for the future with regard to homicide trends, criminal justice responses to homicide, and future studies of homicide.

A Word or Two Before You Turn to the Other Chapters

I do not always follow the rules of scientific writing. Although this is an academic text, I often address the reader as "you" and I often, as I am doing now, refer to myself in the first person. I did reduce the use of the first person from earlier drafts of this work where reviewers thought it might detract from the subject matter overall, but

I retained its use in other places for two reasons. First, students tell me that they learn from me because I engage them and because I am approachable. Knowing this, it is my intention that this book be engaging and approachable. I think the use of the first person helps me to engage you more. I am talking to you. I am writing for you. My second reason for using the first person is more political.

I believe it is important that we all realize someone writes what we read. Whether you are reading a biology textbook, a management textbook, or the newspaper, there is an author. Someone is the voice behind what you are reading. Information, although factual, can never be completely unbiased. It is reported from some point of view. When we do scientific studies, we work hard to avoid bias, and if we are good scientists, we are aware of and report any possible biases or limits to our studies. Nevertheless, individuals approach their subjects based on their place in the world. I am trained as a criminologist in the sociological tradition, and I was educated at a university that *really* valued quantifiable knowledge. As such, you will see that I give much credence to rigorous scientific studies. Of course I think this is good. But you should think critically as you process information that you learn in the world. Think for yourself and be aware that textbooks do not just appear; they have authors and those authors make decisions about what to include and what not to include. Writers are influenced by their place in the world and their training, as well as by their reviewers and editors. As such, I use the first person to help remind you that I am the author and I am writing this text. It is not magically appearing as fact.

On a somewhat related note, my place in the world is in the United States, which is true for many scholars who write about homicide. As such, much of what I know and what other scholars know about homicide, we know about homicide in the United States. However, scholars around the world study homicide, and scholarly information is available about homicide in many parts of the world. The information in each chapter of this book pertains mostly to the United States. However, I have made an effort to include valuable studies from other parts of the world because I think we can learn much in the United States when we make comparisons with other countries. Limited to studies written in English, most comparative information in this text is from other English-speaking countries such as Australia, Canada, and the United Kingdom.

Finally, two last points about word use. First, although the technical definition of "homicide" refers to the killing of one human by another and "murder" implies criminal intent, the words *homicide* and *murder* are used interchangeably in this text. I do this ideally to make the reading flow better for the reader. Second, like Heide in her book *Young Killers*, I intentionally use the words *reportedly* and *allegedly* when reporting cases that do not have a disposition at the time I am writing about them. I believe innocence until proven guilty is an important part of the American legal tradition that needs to be reinforced.

DEFINITIONS AND DEGREES

Snuggled on your sofa in front of *Law and Order*, you watch district attorney Jack McCoy offer a "deal" in which he will drop the charges from felony murder to "man one" if the accused pleads guilty and "gives up" the guy who actually planned the robbery. The defense attorney suggests that her client will plead to nothing more than manslaughter or she may even argue the case calls for negligent homicide at best. The television screen changes to your local newscaster who informs you that coming up at eleven they will be the only station that has coverage of an arrest of a local man who will be charged with malicious murder in the slaying of a pregnant woman. This may be a typical night of television watching for many people in the United States. But many of us do not know the difference between murder and manslaughter or felony murder and malicious murder. Furthermore, depending on where we live, there may be no such thing as malicious murder because the legislature has not defined any act as a "malicious murder."

Yet, as I have suggested, we hear words like *murder, manslaughter*, and *justifiable homicide* bandied about all the time on crime dramas such as *Law and Order*. And depending on where we live, we may hear about malicious murders or reckless homicide. Just what do all these terms mean? What is the difference between first- and second-degree murder? Is the difference just that one is voluntary murder and the other is involuntary manslaughter? Is a murder the same as a homicide? What is a felony murder? What is malicious murder? Why wouldn't all murders be defined as malicious?

Although it is likely you have a sense about which types of killing are seen as more heinous, by the end of this chapter, you should also be able to amaze and astound (or at least annoy) your friends and family as you watch your favorite crime dramas. When you finish reading this chapter, not only should you be able to explain what someone means when they say murder is a crime that is *mala in se*, but you should be able to enlighten your friends with the distinctions among crimes such as first- and second-degree murder and involuntary manslaughter and voluntary murder. In addition, you will learn why and how homicide definitions vary within the United States as well as a brief history of U.S. homicide law. You will be familiar with the U.S. Model Penal Code's definition of criminal homicide and the elements that make up the crimes of murder, manslaughter, and negligent homicide. Moreover, you may be able to impress others with your ability to explain what is meant by *premeditation*, *deliberation*, and *malice aforethought*.

U.S. LAW: A BRIEF HISTORY

Whenever studying, or even discussing, crimes in the United States, it is important to realize that what is, or is not, defined as a crime varies. Definitions vary by state and even by jurisdiction within particular states. Nevertheless, especially when we consider homicide law, we can generalize to a great degree because state laws about homicide are often quite similar. This is not surprising because although states are separate sovereigns with their own constitutions, U.S. state law throughout the United States, except in Louisiana that has a French tradition, is based on English *common law*. Moreover, as state legislatures enacted or updated their laws regarding homicide over the last half of the twentieth century, most have instituted homicide laws modeled on the Model Penal Code.

In the United States initially, the death penalty was a mandatory punishment for all cases of murder. To limit the use of the death penalty in 1794, the state of Pennsylvania enacted the first homicide statute in the United States. The statute divided murder into first- and second-degree murder. First-degree murders were defined as those that were either premeditated and involved malice aforethought (deliberation) or those committed during the commission of another felony. Other intentional killings were considered second degree. Today, a majority of states still use the Pennsylvania model as a way to distinguish between degrees of murder (Stacy, 2000).

Mala In Se and Mala Prohibita

Several distinctions are to be made among crimes. Probably the most basic way to differentiate crimes is to define them as crimes that are *mala in se* or *mala prohibita*. *Mala in se* is a Latin term that means "wrong in itself"; a translation of *mala prohibita* would be "defined as bad." In other words, crimes that are *mala prohibita* are crimes that exist because we have defined a certain behavior as illegal or bad. Jaywalking would be a crime that is *mala prohibita*. Most people would not define jaywalking as a particularly wicked act, nor would they define a jaywalker as evil because he or she crossed against a traffic light or outside of a crosswalk. In all likelihood, you know lots of people who are not particularly evil but who regularly commit crimes that are *mala prohibita*. Perhaps even you have occasionally driven faster than the speed limit, smoked in a nonsmoking building, or maybe you have violated a liquor law such as those that prohibit underage drinking.

In contrast, crimes that are *mala in se* are considered to be naturally evil or wrong. They are crimes that most of us would agree are morally wrong. The crimes of murder, rape, and the sexual molestation of children would fit into the category of *mala in se* crimes. Thus, when we discuss homicide, we are usually considering a crime that is said to be bad in and of itself, or *mala in se.*

FELONIES AND MISDEMEANORS

A second general distinction to be made among crimes is a division that is commonly made within the U.S. criminal justice system. That is, the distinction between felonies and misdemeanors. Typically, crimes that are more serious are included among those

---

BOX 2.1

Homicide Law Outside of the United States

Homicide law varies across the world. However, there are similarities across different countries. Canadian and French homicide law, for example, is very similar to many U.S. state laws. Canada distinguishes between murders that are premeditated (first degree) and those that are not (second degree) and those that are not intentional (manslaughter). Similarly, in England and Wales, there is a distinction between murder and manslaughter that is reflected in the laws of many U.S. states. In England and Wales to be found guilty of murder, intention must be proven. However, the intention does not have to be an intention to kill but an intention to harm. Thus manslaughter in England and Wales is a broad category that includes a range of death at the hands of another from accidental death to voluntary manslaughter in which it may be proven the killer was provoked. Italy also views murder in which a defendant killed to avenge his or her honor as less serious than other types of homicide.

In other countries, the cruelty involved in the killing is a distinction made among different types of killing. Murder that is called *Mord* in Germany is reserved for the premeditated killing of another person done for the killer's pleasure or satisfaction, in a cruel way or way that is dangerous to the public, or to cover up or help with another criminal offense. Finland is similar to Germany in that *murha* (murder) is defined as manslaughter when it is planned; done in a cruel way; or in a way that endangers public safety. In Japan, the harshest penalties for murder are given to those who kill a lineal descendent.

Unlike most homicide law in Westernized countries, under Islamic law murder is often treated as a civil infraction to be settled by the family of the victim. Retribution may be selected by the family of the victim or, especially in the case of accidental death; financial compensation is paid to the victim's family by the offender and his family.

Finally, in contrast to the United States, some countries, including the United Kingdom, Canada, Australia, and Israel, have infanticide as a category of murder. Infanticide is most often defined in these countries as the killing of an infant by his or her mother in the first year of life as a result of the effects of postpartum depression (Brookman, 2005; Canadian Department of Justice, 2007; Encyclopedia Britannica, 2007; Horder, 2007).

categorized as felonies, whereas less serious crimes are considered misdemeanors. Logically, then, *mala in se* crimes are usually felonies, and *mala prohibita* crimes are more often, but not always, classified as misdemeanors. Felony crimes are punishable by death or imprisonment of more than a year in a state prison or penitentiary. Those convicted of misdemeanors are penalized to a lesser extent than those convicted of felonies. Misdemeanants are often fined or imprisoned in jail for less than a year. Crimes are either defined as felonies by statute, or they are considered felonies because the punishment assigned by statute is more severe than a year of imprisonment (Klotter, 2001). Homicide, whether defined by statute or because of the punishment assigned to it, is usually a felony crime.

MODEL PENAL CODE

After more than a decade of work, the American Law Institute introduced the Model Penal Code in 1962. Their goal was to establish uniform rational definitions of criminal offenses and to generate consistency in understandings about general criminal concepts such as criminal intent (which we discuss later). Section 210.1 of the U.S. Model Penal Code defines criminal homicide as follows:

1. A person is guilty of criminal homicide if he purposely, knowingly, recklessly or negligently causes the death of another human being.
2. Criminal homicide is murder, manslaughter, or negligent homicide.

So much contained in the first sentence must be considered in determining whether an act is a criminal homicide and in the second sentence, we are introduced to three basic categories of criminal homicide. In the paragraphs to follow, we carefully examine what is included in the Model Penal Code definition, beginning with the three elements of homicide noted in the first sentence of the definition.

Although, as noted earlier, homicide statutes vary, the concepts of common law relating to homicide can be found in the elements of the various crimes of homicide (Klotter, 2001). According to the Model Penal Code, the elements of homicide to be proved are (1) *purposely, knowingly, recklessly* or *negligently* (2) *causing* the *death* of (3) another *human being*. It is important to consider each element of the criminal code for homicide.

The first element of homicide according to the Model Penal Code requires that a person does the act that kills purposely, knowingly, recklessly, or negligently. Note that the "or" indicates that to be convicted, it only must be proven that one has purposely or knowingly or recklessly or negligently caused the death of another. Thus one can *recklessly* cause the death of another human even though the person has not *purposely* caused that death. So what is meant by the terms *purposely, knowingly, recklessly,* and *negligently*?

Taking the example of shooting someone, we can see what is meant by these terms. To shoot someone *purposely* means to do it intentionally rather than to do it by accident. To do it *knowingly* means you are aware you are doing it; you are doing it consciously. *Recklessly*, in contrast, means to do it without regard for the possible consequences. For example, you are probably aware you could hurt someone by pointing at the ceiling and pulling the trigger. Even if not your intention, if you shoot the gun at the ceiling and the bullet ricochets and hits your roommate, we could say you were reckless. Finally, to act *negligently* is to act without concern or care. For example, a parent who fails to watch his or her child closely could be considered negligent in the death if the child wanders off and falls in a pond and drowns.

The second element in the Model Penal Code's definition of homicide requires the prosecution to prove that the actions of the accused *caused* the *death* of another. The prosecution must provide evidence showing the accused committed the act that caused another human's death or put into motion the means that resulted in the death of another.

Todd, who is having an affair with Lisa, for instance, might say to Lisa that he would marry her if his wife, Marge, were out of the picture. Lisa may take this as a request to kill Marge. Lisa could then convince her brother Bart to shoot Marge by promising him that she will get him a cozy job in her lover's firm once Marge is dead. Let's say then that Bart shoots Marge as requested by Lisa, but unfortunately for Bart, a security guard sees the shooting on a security monitor and acts quickly to capture Bart before he escapes. It should no doubt be easy for prosecutors to prove that Bart killed Marge as long as the autopsy shows she died of a gunshot wound that matches up with the gun Bart used to shoot her. However, to prove Lisa or her lover caused Marge's death will take more work. Bart may agree to testify for the state to save himself. If he gives convincing testimony to the fact that Lisa persuaded him to kill Marge, the prosecutors may be successful in proving that Lisa's actions caused Marge's death. But what about Marge's husband Todd? Did Todd's actions cause Marge's death? Todd said he would marry Lisa if Marge was no longer a concern. There may be many men who say similar things to their mistresses. Are they suggesting that their mistresses should kill their wives? Are they asking them to kill their wives? Following the second element of the Model Penal Code's definition of homicide, to find Todd guilty of homicide, it would have to proven that Todd put into motion the means that resulted in Marge's death. Even if the prosecutor could do that, she would still have to prove the other elements were present.

The third element of homicide according to the Model Penal Code stipulates that a killing of one person by another is unlawful unless it is justifiable or excusable. Note that the homicide code does not include the death of nonhumans, nor does it include the killing of a fetus. (See Box 2.3 to read about the killing of a fetus.) According to the Model Penal Code, a human being is "a person who has been born alive" (Klotter, 2001). Thus the prosecution, in proving a homicide took place, must show that a killing of a human being has taken place.

Murder, manslaughter, negligent homicide, first- and second-degree murder, and even justifiable homicide, all share one main fact. One human has caused the death of another human being. The distinction that is made among them has to do with *mens rea*, or the killer's mental state. A cold-blooded premeditated murder is considered more heinous than a hot-blooded impulsive murder. The Federal Bureau of Investigation (FBI) defines murder and manslaughter as "willful killings of one human being by another" (FBI, 2002).

Most of the time, it is fairly easy to prove a person has been killed, but at other times it is more difficult. An example of a real-life case in which it was a challenge to show a human being had been killed has come to be known as the *wood chipper murder case*. Helle Crafts disappeared on November 19, 1986, and although her husband Richard Crafts eventually became a suspect in her death, detectives could not locate Mrs. Crafts's body. Without a body, it was likely to be impossible to prove a murder had occurred. Eventually, however, with painstakingly detailed detective work, the Newtown Police Department in Connecticut was able to determine that Mr. Craft had rented a wood chipper at the time his wife disappeared. With the help of an eyewitness who remembered seeing a wood chipper near Lake Zoar, detectives were able to locate the location where they believed Mr. Crafts disposed of his wife's body. At this site, they found over 2,000 strands of blond hair, several slivers of human bone, a part of a human finger, five drops of human blood, two teeth, a fingernail, and part of a toenail (Gado, 2005; Lee & O'Neil, 2002). After one mistrial, a second jury found Mr. Crafts guilty of his wife's murder (Gado, 2005).

BOX 2.2

Corporate Homicide

On June 14, 1985, the Illinois Supreme Court handed down a landmark decision in which Steven O'Neil, Charles Kirschbaum, and Daniel Rodriguez were found guilty of murder for the death of Stefan Golab. What made this a landmark case is that the three defendants were corporate officers, and they were found guilty for the death of an employee who died of cyanide poisoning. The company did not have proper safety equipment, and they did not warn employees about the danger of working with cyanide. The case was reversed on appeal in 1990 and remanded for a new trial. The three defendants, who were also employees of Film Recovery Systems, pleaded guilty to involuntary manslaughter in September 1993 (Ross, 2004).

In another case, the owner of the Imperial Foods chicken-processing plant in Hamlet, North Carolina, pleaded guilty to involuntary manslaughter for the 1991 deaths of 25 workers. The 25 workers died, and 56 more were injured when they were unable to escape from an oil fire because the plant doors were locked. Mr. Roe paid an $800,000 fine and spent four years in prison (Malveaux, 2005).

In the United Kingdom, the House of Lords is discussing the introduction of a corporate homicide law. Noting that more than 200 workers and even more members of the public are killed each year in work-related incidents, the country's leaders argued that many of these deaths are the result of the way business is regularly conducted. Unlike previous cases in which an individual manager would have to be found negligent, the new law focuses on the way the business is run or organized. Corporations will be found guilty of corporate homicide if business is managed with a reckless disregard for the possible consequences (Shepherd & Wedderburn, 2006).

BOX 2.3

Is the Killing of the Unborn Murder?

With the debates over abortion in the United States, laws that define the killing of a fetus or an unborn baby as a homicide are very controversial, with pro-life and pro-choice supporters seeing these laws as steps toward making abortion illegal. In this box, I present a new federal law and a South Carolina case that involve this controversy. Consider your thoughts on the federal law and the South Carolina case and what each may mean for U.S. homicide cases. Do you make a distinction between the "killing" of an unborn child that is believed to be caused by someone trying to harm the mother and a case in which a child is not born alive because of something the mother did while she was pregnant? Does it matter if what the mother did was illegal or legal? What if the mother was diabetic or heavily overweight and these conditions could be linked to the fetus not surviving, even though these are well-known risks to unborn babies? Think about these complicated questions and issues as you read the information in this box.

The Unborn Victims of Violence Act

The Unborn Victims of Violence Act, also known as "Laci and Conner's Law," named after Laci Peterson and her unborn son Conner, was signed into law by President George W. Bush on April 1, 2004. The bill makes it possible for prosecutors to charge an offender for harming or killing an unborn child in addition to any charges stemming from harm to the pregnant woman during the commission of certain federal crimes of violence. Although this act only applies to federal crimes, 32 states (as of June 2005) have homicide laws that recognize unborn children as victims at some point during the pregnancy. For example, Louisiana recognizes a fetus as a victim at any stage in a pregnancy, considering the killing of an "unborn child" as first-, second- or third-degree feticide. Whereas states such as Nevada, Rhode Island, and Washington consider the killing of an unborn but viable child to be manslaughter (Findlaw.com, 2005; NRLC, 2005).

Woman Convicted of Murder for the Death of Her Stillborn Baby

In 2001, a jury deliberated less than 15 minutes in South Carolina before finding Regina McKnight guilty of murder for the death of her stillborn baby. Without any scientific research linking cocaine use to stillbirths, prosecutors argued that because of her cocaine abuse, McKnight was responsible for her daughter, Mercedes, being born stillborn. McKnight, a homeless seasonal tobacco farm worker with a tenth-grade education, was sentenced to 12 years in prison. A handful of women had pleaded guilty to involuntary manslaughter in similar cases, but McKnight was the first to be tried and convicted of murder (Aronson, 2001). The South Carolina Supreme Court ruling that the punishment was reasonable because McKnight should have known that using cocaine would harm her child was upheld by the U.S. Supreme Court in October 2003 when the court refused to review the case. Advocates for pregnant women argue that this is a dangerous precedent that could lead to the prosecution of women for otherwise legal acts if their babies are born in less than perfect health (Talvi, 2003).

MURDER

According to the Model Penal Code, murder in the first degree (also commonly known as aggravated or premeditated murder) is the (1) unlawful killing of (2) one person by another (3) with malice aforethought, and (4) with deliberation, purpose, design, or premeditation (Klotter, 2001). Murder in the first degree may further be divided into murder and voluntary murder as follows: Murder is the (1) unlawful killing of (2) one person by another (3) with malice aforethought. In contrast, then, voluntary murder is the (1) unlawful killing of (2) one person by another (3) intentional killing with adequate provocation and committed in the heat of passion.

With regard to murder, *Malice aforethought* is often defined as having the intent to kill. However, it may also include the intent to cause grave bodily harm, recklessness, or the intent to commit a felony. Malice is acting intentionally (purposefully or knowingly) or recklessly. Intentional means willful. A homicide is typically considered

---

BOX 2.4

Killing to Survive Is Not Necessarily Justifiable

Regina v. Dudley and Stephens English Case

In a case from England in 1884, three shipwreck survivors in a lifeboat decided to kill a fourth survivor who was younger and too weak to resist. Two of the survivors, Dudley and Stephens, agreed that the youngest survivor must be killed so the remaining survivors could eat his flesh for survival. After being shipwrecked on a raft for four days, the four survivors caught a turtle, which they ate. By the twentieth day at sea, however, they had nothing else to eat. Occasionally, the four men were able to collect fresh water from rain, but after five days without fresh water and seven days without food, the men were growing evermore desperate and famished. More than 1,000 miles from land on the eighteenth day, Dudley and Stephens talked to Brooks about the possibility of killing the fourth survivor to save their lives. Brooks did not agree with their plan, but Dudley and Stephens argued the boy had no children as they did and it was best to kill him so they could survive. With Brooks napping, Dudley cut the youngest survivor with a knife and the three other men survived on his body and blood for four days until they were rescued.

Once rescued, Dudley and Stephens faced charges of murder for the young man's death. The court was faced with the question of whether the need to survive justified the taking of another's life. Dudley and Stephens argued it was a necessity for them to kill in order to live. However, the court disagreed and noted that the argument of necessity only works when protecting oneself against another. In this case, the young man was not doing anything to threaten the other survivors killing him; he was not attacking them. Dudley and Stephens were found guilty and sentenced to death; however their sentences were later reduced to six months in prison (ICL, 2004; Katz, Moore & Morse, 1999).

"intentional" if the killer wanted to kill the victim or was fairly certain his or her actions would result in the victim's death.

MANSLAUGHTER

Manslaughter is the unlawful killing of a human being without premeditation. It is not a degree of murder but a distinct offense, although sometimes it is referred to as third-degree murder (Klotter, 2001). It is murder without the malice aforethought or intent to do injury. According to Stacy (2000), contemporary American jurisdiction uses two approaches in classifying intentional killings as murder or manslaughter. Most follow the common law, which reduces and intentional killing from murder to manslaughter when the killer is in the throes of an excusably provoked emotional state of passion. However, 11 states follow the Model Penal Code heat-of-passion provision for manslaughter.

In common law for a killing to be considered manslaughter instead of first- or second-degree murder, the malice aforethought would have to be lacking because of provocation. Provocation is considered an affirmative defense to a charge of murder. It must be proved by the defendant by a preponderance of evidence. In other words, the defense would have to prove that the killer, acting as any reasonable person would act, lost emotional control because of some provocation on the part of the victim. Furthermore, the killer could not have had time to cool off between the provocation by the victim and the killing. Note, however, that only a limited number of situations are considered provocation enough to provoke a killing. Insulting words and invasion of property are not sufficient provocations for a death to be considered manslaughter (Stacy, 2000). Rather, provocations for a killing to be deemed manslaughter include illegal arrest, adultery with the offender's spouse, physical injury, or mutual combat. Adultery in itself, however, may not be provocation enough for murder. The Court has found that infidelity by a girlfriend (not a spouse) is not enough to prove provocation, but finding a spouse in the act of adultery is likely to be considered sufficient provocation for killing one's spouse (Stacy, 2000).

BOX 2.5

Sticks and Stones Can Break My Bones But Words Can Never Justify Manslaughter

Taunting words, even those meant to cause anger, have been held not to constitute adequate provocation for a defense to murder. For example, Girouard was having an argument with his wife, at which time she told him she did not love him and wanted a divorce. She also noted in less than kind words that his sexual ability was lacking. Girouard fatally stabbed her. The court found that her words were not enough to establish provocation. Words, alone, are not sufficient provocation to consider a killing manslaughter rather than murder. Words threatening bodily harm may be sufficient. But words alone are not enough (Blatt, 2002).

TABLE 2.1
Common Law and Model Penal Code Definitions

Common Law Definitions	Model Penal Code Definitions
First-Degree Murder A killing that is intentional, premeditated, and deliberate	**Murder** A type of first-degree murder defined as the unlawful killing with malice aforethought
Second-Degree Murder A killing that is intentional but not premeditated or deliberate	**Voluntary Murder** A type of first-degree murder that is intentional killing with adequate provocation and committed in the heat of passion
Voluntary Manslaughter A killing with no malice aforethought because of victim provocation (heat of passion)	**Manslaughter** A killing committed with a reasonable explanation or excuse such as duress
Involuntary Manslaughter A killing that is unintentional and without malice such as a careless driver	**Negligent Homicide** A death caused by negligence such as that by a careless driver

INVOLUNTARY MANSLAUGHTER

Although the Model Penal Code does not distinguish between voluntary and involuntary manslaughter, there is a distinction in common law (see Table 2.1). Following common law, involuntary manslaughter is an unintentional homicide. It is a killing committed without malice that is the result of the commission of an unlawful nonfelony act or a lawful act done negligently or from failure to perform a legal duty (Klotter, 2001:57). Thus involuntary manslaughter differs from voluntary manslaughter in that there is no intent and from murder in that there is no malice aforethought. Often manslaughter involves the killing of another through reckless and careless driving where the intent was not there but the negligent driving resulted in the death of another.

VOLUNTARY MANSLAUGHTER

In American common law, manslaughter is divided into voluntary and involuntary manslaughter. Voluntary manslaughter is a killing done in the heat of passion and thought to be provoked by the victim's actions. The killing of a human being is considered voluntary manslaughter if it is expected that a reasonable person would have acted rashly in the same circumstances. Every provocation by a victim is not considered equal, however. Common provocations accepted for categorizing a killing as

BOX 2.6

A Case to Think About: Voluntary Manslaughter

In 1994, Kenneth Peacock found his wife Sandra naked in bed with another man at approximately midnight. After chasing the man away, Kenneth drank for several hours and argued with his wife. Around 4 A.M., Kenneth killed Sandra with a hunting rifle. He pleaded guilty to voluntary manslaughter. His sentencing was questioned by many, especially legal experts on domestic violence and gender equality, because Judge Cahill of the Baltimore County Circuit Court sentenced Peacock to only 18 months in prison. Judge Cahill noted that he wished he did not have to send him to prison at all and he wondered aloud how many men married for four years would be able to walk away from their wife in bed with another without inflicting some corporal punishment (Lewin, 1994). States vary in how they define "heat of passion." In this case, Peacock did not kill his wife the instant he discovered her in bed with another man but several hours later. Furthermore, his first shot missed, and he had to reload the single-shot rifle before shooting her fatally with his second shot.

Until the 1970s in some states, a man who found his wife in bed with another and killed her was considered to have committed a justifiable homicide. The Peacock sentencing garnered attention across the country, especially after another Baltimore judge sentenced a woman to three years in prison who pleaded guilty to voluntary manslaughter for killing her husband who had abused her for 11 years (Corbin, 1995; Lewin, 1994).

What do you think about the Peacock sentence? In your opinion, what mitigates a murder to voluntary manslaughter? Is killing in the heat of passion for adultery sufficient for a killing to be considered voluntary manslaughter? Is the fact that a person abused by the killer for years a sufficient provocation for a killing to be considered voluntary manslaughter instead of a murder? What if the man who finds his wife in bed with another waits two hours or two days to kill his wife? What if a woman being abused waits until her partner passes out from drinking before killing him?

voluntary manslaughter would not include insulting words or gestures but may include spousal adultery, a violent assault, an illegal arrest, or mutual combat. If an individual uses excessive force in self-defense or when a person mistakenly believes self-defense is called for and kills someone, the killing would fall under the definition of manslaughter (Fox & Levin, 2001).

The Model Penal Code provision does not distinguish between voluntary and involuntary manslaughter, but it does expand beyond the common law definition to define a killing as manslaughter when "committed under the influence of extreme mental or emotional disturbance for which there is a reasonable explanation or excuse" (Model Penal Code 210.3, 1980). Those killings that would be considered manslaughter under the common law would also be considered manslaughter following the Model Penal Code. However, the Model Penal Code places fewer restrictions on the extenuating circumstances that mitigate murder to manslaughter. The Model Penal Code does not

---

BOX 2.7

Is It Manslaughter If You Fail to Save Someone?

Mr. Beardsley and his friend Ms. Burns spent the weekend drinking, and Burns took several tablets of morphine. Beardsley requested the help of a young man to help him move Burns to another apartment in their building so Beardsley's wife would not find Burns in their apartment. Beardsley asked the young man to look after Burns until she was sober enough to leave. The young man was worried about Burns's condition and eventually phoned a doctor who determined that she was dead. Beardsley was convicted of manslaughter. The prosecutor argued that he failed to perform his duty to care for Burns after she took a fatal dose of morphine. A person may be criminally liable if he or she fails to perform a legal duty and the omission causes harm; however in this case, the Supreme Court held that Beardsley had no legal duty to save Burns (Blatt, 2002). If you are a doctor or a babysitter, you may have a contractual duty to help another and thus if you do not, you could be found responsible or guilty. However, if there is no legal duty, your act of omission may not be counted against you (*People v. Beardsley*, 1907).

---

include the common law requirements of an immediate provocation, an excited emotional state, or a provocation by the victim. Instead, an extreme emotional or mental state can qualify a killing as manslaughter in the Model Penal Code as long as there is some reasonable explanation or excuse to explain it. The Model Penal Code thus focuses on reasonableness, whereas the common law focuses on whether there was provocation.

NEGLIGENT HOMICIDE

As noted earlier, the Model Penal Code does not include involuntary manslaughter as a crime. However, there is a provision for negligent homicide, which, like involuntary manslaughter, is the least serious of homicides. Negligent homicide is defined as a criminal homicide committed negligently. In other words, a person may be responsible for causing the death of another if he or she fails to perform some duty. For example, if a child dies of malnutrition in the United States, his or her parent may be charged with negligent homicide.

DEGREES OF MURDER

Many states have modeled their homicide laws on the Model Penal Code. However, 13 states (AZ, AK, CT, FL, IN, MT, NH, NM, NY, PA, TX, UT, WA) maintain a difference between degrees of murder so a distinction exists for the death penalty (Klotter, 2001). For example, in California, first-degree murder is the killing of a police officer or killing while in custody, and second-degree murder in California is a homicide in which the offender has (1) reckless knowledge and intent, or (2) depraved indifference to human life and reckless conduct that creates a serious risk to another that results in death, or (3) is a death caused during the commission of a felony. Similarly, some of these same states are included among the 14 states (CT, GA, IL, IN, IA, KS, KY, MN, NM, NY, OR, SD, TX, WA) that divide manslaughter into degrees (Klotter, 2001). First-degree or capital murder, second-degree murder, and voluntary manslaughter are usually classified as intentional homicides. The difference between them is usually a matter of the perceived relative seriousness of each. The more serious homicides receive the more severe punishment, with first-degree or capital murder qualifying for the death penalty in states where capital punishment exists. In most jurisdictions, premeditation or the co-commission of a dangerous felony during a killing is defined as first-degree murder. First-degree murder (sometimes referred to as "murder one") is thought to be deliberate and premeditated.

In contrast, a killing that occurs in the throes of an understandable extreme mental or emotional state is more likely to be considered voluntary manslaughter, the least serious offense category (Stacy, 2000). Second-degree murder has been reserved for killings not accompanied by aggravating and mitigating circumstances, such as those noted earlier above that push the killing to first-degree murder (aggravating) or pull it into voluntary manslaughter (mitigating). In most states, murders that are intentional but lacking in premeditation and deliberation are defined as second-degree murders. Thus the difference between second-degree murder and voluntary manslaughter is the provocation that moves the killer to kill. In states that separate murder by degree, if one has only the intent to inflict grievous bodily injury but kills another, the killing is usually considered second-degree murder. Murders committed while a person is under the influence of alcohol or drugs are usually considered to be second-degree murders if the intoxication reduced the intoxicated person's capacity to act deliberately and premeditate the killing (Fox & Levin, 2001).

Tom Stacy, a law professor at the University of Kansas, noted that over the past few decades, many more aggravating and mitigating circumstances are taken into account in determining which level of murder to charge. Aggravating circumstances are those that make the murder seem worse, such as torturing the victim or killing several victims. Mitigating circumstances are those that make the murder appear less heinous such as when a killer is under the influence of a substance that may have contributed to the killing. In addition to premeditation, the co-commission of a felony, and distraught emotional states, Stacy notes that additional aggravating and mitigating circumstances such as whether the killer manifested extreme cruelty or whether the victim consented to the killing are now considered.

FELONY MURDER

If the death of a human occurs during a dangerous felony crime (arson, burglary, rape, or robbery), even if there was no specific intent to murder, a person may be held accountable for the murder. This is known as the felony murder rule. The intent to commit a felony is believed to constitute the implied malice required for a murder at common law. Although the Model Penal Code does not include the felony murder rule, most states have retained this rule.

In April 2001, Okuri Brown was charged with felony murder for the death of Demetric Edwards, who was killed by Okuri's brother Buck. The Brown brothers had paged Edwards and arranged to purchase marijuana from him. When Edwards arrived, Buck pointed his gun at him and told him he was going to rob him. Edwards turned over the marijuana, and Buck shot him several times. On appeal, the Georgia Supreme Court, quoting Georgia Code, noted, "Every person concerned in the commission of a crime is a party thereto and may be charged with and convicted of commission of the crime" (*Brown* v. *the State*, 2004). Importantly, unlike Brown's case, even if a person dies as the result of a heart attack during the commission of a felony, the persons involved in the commission of the crime may be charged with felony murder. One may not even be directly present, as in the case of a getaway driver waiting outside for an acquaintance who is robbing a bank. If a customer dies during the robbery, the getaway driver may be charged with felony murder. Finally, even if the robber himself is killed by the security guard, the getaway driver could be charged with felony murder for his death.

CAPITAL MURDER

Capital murders are those in which the punishment may be death. The federal government of the United States and 38 states allow for the punishment of death for murder. Although the law varies somewhat from state to state, a murder may be eligible for a death sentence in certain circumstances. First, if the murder victim is of a special class such as a correctional or police officer, the killing may qualify as a capital offense. Second, if the homicide meets "special circumstances," such as being one of a multiple murder or a particularly heinous nature, it may qualify as a capital murder.

In 2004, I observed the trial of Reinaldo Rivera, who was sentenced to death for murder. Rivera, who had admitted to killing four women in Georgia and South Carolina, was sentenced to death for the killing of army sergeant Marni Glista because of the special circumstances surrounding his crimes. On Monday, January 26, as an ice storm raged outside the Richmond County Georgia courthouse, prosecuting attorney Danny Craig argued that to sentence Rivera to death only one of the following statutory aggravating circumstances must be proved:

1. Murder happened when engaged in commission of another capital felony (rape in Rivera's case)
2. Murder committed while defendant engaged in aggravated battery
3. Murder outrageous or wantonly vile, horrible, or inhuman in that it involved torture, depravity of mind, or an aggravated battery to the victim.

Prosecutor Craig argued that the state had proven all three, and at 8:35 P.M., slightly less than 12 hours after Craig made his argument, the jury returned a sentence of death. In this case, although Rivera had not been found guilty of multiple murders because he was only tried with one, the murder of Glista was found to have occurred during an aggravated battery, during a rape, and in a vile, horrible, or inhuman way. Thus Rivera was sentenced to death and is currently awaiting his execution on Georgia's death row.

BOX 2.8

Homicide in Civil Court

You may recall that juries found O. J. Simpson and Robert Blake had intentionally caused the deaths of Nicole Brown Simpson and Bonnie Lee
Bakley, respectively, despite the fact that each of these men was found not
guilty of murder or manslaughter in criminal court. The double jeopardy
clause of the Fifth Amendment applies only to criminal cases and does not
extend to civil court. Thus when these two well-known celebrities were
found not guilty in criminal court, the families of the slain victims could
still file a wrongful death suit against them. Moreover, because of two
major differences between criminal and civil court rules, it is easier to find
someone responsible for a wrongful death than it is to find them guilty of
murder. First, in civil cases the burden of proof is lower, making it easier to
convince the jury that the plaintiff is responsible. In criminal cases the burden of proof is "beyond a reasonable doubt," whereas in a civil case the
burden of proof is a "preponderance of evidence." Second, in civil cases
where the plaintiff faces the possibility of paying damages, he or she must
take the stand and testify. In contrast, in criminal cases where the accused
is subject to the loss of his or her liberty, the person has the right not to
testify. Because of these differences in civil and criminal court, individuals
like Robert Blake and O. J. Simpson can be acquitted in a criminal court
and yet be found responsible for the death in a civil court.

VEHICULAR HOMICIDE

Vehicular homicide may be considered a negligent homicide in some states and
manslaughter in other states. However, most states have vehicle-specific homicide
statutes. For example, Ohio has not only negligent homicide but aggravated vehicular homicide and vehicular homicide. The distinction between aggravated vehicular homicide and vehicular homicide is that aggravated vehicular homicide
involves the reckless use of a motor vehicle, motorcycle, watercraft, aircraft, loco-
motive, or snowmobile. Prosecutors in North Carolina and Kentucky have charged
impaired drivers with capital murder. These states have not created new laws;
rather they have used the existing capital murder law and applied that law to the
facts of the vehicular homicide.

Some drivers who are under the influence of alcohol or another drug may use
their impairment as a partial defense to murder; it is not a complete defense. It is
likely that the crime will be mitigated to a lesser crime such as involuntary
manslaughter or negligent homicide. Often, prosecutors agree to charge the accused
with manslaughter if she or he pleads guilty. The prosecutor recognizes that the person who drove drunk and killed did not intend to kill in these cases. Nevertheless, the
driver is ultimately held responsible for the killing.

BOX 2.9

Can Medical Malpractice Be Murder?

On July 8, 1993, 8-year-old Richard Leonard died of a heart attack during a routine ear operation. Dr. Joseph Verbrugge, the anesthesiologist responsible for monitoring the boy's vital signs, was charged with two felonies in connection with the boy's death. Verbrugge fell asleep during the surgery and thus failed to notice that Richard's temperature and heart rate spiked dangerously.

Verbrugge was the first Colorado doctor to be criminally prosecuted for the death of a patient. He was charged with reckless manslaughter and criminally negligent homicide. In this 1996 trial, the jury was unable to come to any agreement on the two felony charges; instead they found Verbrugge guilty of the lesser offense of criminal medical negligence. Verbrugge's license to practice medicine was revoked in California and Colorado as a result of this conviction.

In December 1997, prosecutors tried Verbrugge again on the felonies (because the jury was hung on these charges in the past). This second jury acquitted him of both counts. Then, in 1999, the Colorado Court of Appeals overturned the 1996 conviction of criminal medical negligence because the prosecutors had failed to bring the charges within the 18 months that the law stipulated for such cases (Jackson, 2001).

JUSTIFIABLE HOMICIDE

Justifiable homicides are killings that are warranted. Killing during combat in a war and the execution of a condemned inmate are both justifiable homicides. Killings in self-defense (see Chapter 15) and killings by a law officer in the line of duty are considered justifiable. According to the FBI, when a private citizen kills a person who is committing a felony crime, the homicide would also be justifiable (FBI, 2002).

When law enforcement officers kill in the line of duty, the homicide may be ruled justifiable. Deadly force by police officers, however, is not automatically considered justifiable. Officers who kill while using more force than is ruled necessary to make an arrest or stop a suspect may be charged with criminal homicide (Adler, Mueller, & Laufer, 2006). In *Tennessee* v. *Garner* 1985, the Supreme Court ruled that the use of deadly force by police officers may only be used to prevent the escape of a suspect that the officer has probable cause to believe poses a significant threat of serious physical injury or death to the officers or others (*Tennessee* v. *Garner*, 1985).

In October 1974, the police responded to a break-in call. After a neighbor directed the police to a backyard, Officer Elton Hymon saw Edward Garner crouched by a 6-foot fence at the back of the yard. Hymon was fairly certain that Garner did not have a weapon. Hymon identified himself as a police officer and started toward Garner. Garner began to climb the fence. Convinced that Garner

BOX 2.10
Suicide by Cop

Suicide by cop is a term that has worked its way into the everyday lexicon. It refers to an incident in which a person deliberately threatens a police officer or another person in such a way that the police will have little choice but to shoot. The offender's intention is suicide, but instead of taking pills or shooting himself (or more rarely herself), the offender forces the police to take the fatal step. In a study of all officer-involved shootings investigated by the Los Angeles County Sheriff's Department from 1987 to 1997, researchers found that 11% of all the shootings could be categorized as suicide by cop. Only one of the 46 individuals who committed suicide by cop was a woman. Nearly 4 out of 10 had a history of domestic violence. Nearly half (48%) of the weapons used by the suicidal individuals were firearms, and 17% were replica firearms (Hutson, Anglin, Yarbrough, et al., 1998).

would escape if he got over the fence, Hymon shot him once in the back of the head. Garner, who had stolen $10 and a purse, died at the hospital shortly after he was shot (*Tennessee* v. *Garner*, 1985).

Hymon had followed Tennessee police procedure when he shot Garner. Tennessee statute allowed officers to shoot fleeing suspect after identifying themselves as officers and demanding the suspect stops. Hymon was found to have acted within the duty of his job by both the Memphis Police Department and a grand jury. After Garner's father brought suit, the case made its way to the Supreme Court. They ruled that the killing of a suspect was a seizure, and based on the Fourth Amendment, it must be reasonable. The Tennessee statute was found unreasonable because it did not distinguish between different types of felonies. Officers cannot use deadly force unless they have probable cause to believe the suspect has committed a felony and is a serious danger to others (*Tennessee* v. *Garner*, 1985).

YEAR AND A DAY RULE

One issue that may be important for determining whether one has caused the death of another in some jurisdictions is the length of time that exists between the injuries that cause death and the death. Many states that follow common law use what has come to be known as the "*year and a day rule.*" The year and a day rule stipulates that one is responsible for a death only if the victim dies within a year and a day of the act believed to cause the death. In other words, if a victim dies of serious injuries after a year and a day go by, the offender would not be charged with homicide, although the person may be found guilty of aggravated assault. However, if a victim died even on the year anniversary of an attack, that would qualify as a homicide because the victim had perished before a year and a day had passed. This rule does not apply in every jurisdiction though. In many jurisdictions, if it can be proven that an offender's actions caused a death no matter how long after the action, the offender may be charged with murder.

SUMMARY

In this chapter, you learned about the distinction between crimes that are *mala in se* and crimes that are *mala prohibita*, as well as crimes that are felonies and misdemeanors. After a brief explanation of the origins of U.S. homicide law, the chapter included an explanation of the definition of homicide according to the Model Penal Code and common law. The distinctions made in the Model Penal Code include those among murder, manslaughter, and justifiable homicide and negligent homicide. Among the common law definitions and distinctions are the difference between manslaughter and the more serious first or second degrees of murder as well as justifiable homicide. Because many states make distinctions in terms of degrees of murder so a distinction exists for the death penalty, the different levels or degrees of murder were also included in this chapter. Finally, you read about felony murder, capital murder, and vehicular homicide and the year and a day rule. Now, you are ready to move to Chapter 3, where you will read about how we determine how many homicides are occurring and the details about each.

CHAPTER QUESTIONS

1. Define and give an example of a crime that is *mala in se* and a crime that is *mala prohibita*.
2. How do punishments differ for those who commit misdemeanor crimes and those who commit felonies?
3. Except in Louisiana, which has a French tradition, what is most U.S. state law based on?
4. What is the Model Penal Code definition of homicide?
5. Name the three basic categories of criminal homicide contained within the Model Penal Code definition.
6. According to the Model Penal Code, what are the three elements of homicide that must be proved to establish that a person has committed homicide?
7. In the Model Penal Code, what is meant by the terms *purposely, knowingly, recklessly,* and *negligently*?
8. Must there be a dead body to prove there has been a murder?
9. What is *mens rea*?
10. Explain the difference between murder and voluntary murder.
11. Within common law, what must be missing for a killing to be considered manslaughter instead of first- or second-degree murder?
12. Give an example of a justifiable homicide. Can anyone commit justifiable homicide?

13. Which has more restriction on what can be considered extenuating circumstances for mitigating a murder to manslaughter; common law, or the Model Penal Code?
14. Explain the difference between involuntary and voluntary manslaughter.
15. In common law the least serious homicide is involuntary manslaughter. What is the least serious crime in the Model Penal Code?
16. What is first-degree murder, and how is it different from second-degree murder and manslaughter?
17. Explain what is meant by aggravating and mitigating circumstances.
18. Which type of murder can a person be found guilty of even if he or she is not the individual to pull the trigger?
19. What is capital murder?
20. What is the year and a day rule?

References

Adler, Freda, Gerhard O. W. Mueller, and William S. Laufer. 2006. *Criminal Justice: An Introduction.* Boston: McGraw Hill.

Aronson, Barton. 2001, June 1. "A South Carolina Conviction Based on a Pregnant Woman's Cocaine Use: Should We Criminalize Harm to Unborn Children?" Retrieved January 8, 2005, from findlaw.com: http://writ.news.findlaw.com/aronson/20010601.html

Blatt, Dana. 2002. *West Group High Court Case Summaries.* Eagan, MN: West.

Brookman, Fiona. 2005. *Understanding Homicide.* London: Sage.

Canadian Department of Justice. 2007. *Criminal Code.* Accessed online at http://laws.justice.gc.ca/

Brown v. the State. 2004. Georgia Supreme Court, 277 Ga. 573.

Corbin, Beth. 1995, January. "Maryland Judge Declares Open-Season on Women." Accessed online at www.now.org

Encyclopedia Britannica. 2007. "Homicide." Retrieved February 1, 2007, from Encyclopedia Britannica Online: http://search.eb.com/eb/article-9040889

Federal Bureau of Investigation. 2002. *Crime in the United States.* Retrieved January 9, 2005, at http://www.fbi.gov/ucr/cius_02/html/web/index.html

Findlaw.com. 2004. "Lace and Conner's Law (Enrolled as Agreed to or Passed by Both House and Senate)." Retrieved January 10, 2005, from http://news.findlaw.com/hdocs/docs/abortion/unbornbi1132504.html

Fox, James Alan and Jack Levin. 2001. *The Will to Kill: Making Sense of Senseless Murder,* Boston: Allyn and Bacon.

Gado, Mark. 2005. "The Woodchipper Murder Case," *CourtTV Crime Library.* Retrieved January 10, 2005, from http://www.crimelibrary.com/notoriousmurders/family/woodchipper_murder/index.html.

Horder, Jeremy. 2007. *Homicide Law in Comparative Perspective.* Oxford, UK: Hart.

Hutson, H. Range, Deirdre Anglin, John Yarbrough, et al. 1998. "Suicide by Cop." *Annals of Emergency Medicine,* 32(6): 665–669.

Incorporated Council of Law Reporting (ICL). 2004. "*R v. Dudley and Stephens* [1884] 14 QBD 273 DC Special Issue—135 Years of the Law Reports and the Weekly Law Reports." Retrieved January 9, 2005, from http://www.justis.com/titles/iclr_bqb14040.html

Jackson, Steve. 2001, July 26. "An Ugly Picture: The Colorado Supreme Court Gets Involved in a Child-Pornography Case." Retrieved January 16, 2006, from Denver Westword.com: http://www.westword.com/issues/2001-07-26/news/news.html

Katz, Leo, Michael S. Moore, and Stephen J. Morse. 1999. *Foundations of Criminal Law.* New York, NY: Foundation Press.

Klotter, John C. 2001. *Criminal Law.* Cincinnati: Anderson.

Lee, Henry C., and Thomas O. O'Neil. 2002. *Cracking Cases, the Science of Solving Crimes.* Amherst, NY: Prometheus Books.

Lewin, Tamar. 1994, October 20. "What Penalty for a Killing in Passion?" *New York Times,* p. A18.

Malveaux, Julianne. 2005, March 17. "Sweatshops Aren't History Just Yet." *U.S.A. Today,* p. 13A.

National Right to Life Council (NLRC). 2005, October 5. "State Homicide Laws That Recognize Unborn Victims." Retrieved January 8, 2005, from http://www.nrlc.org/Unborn_Victims/Statehomicidelaws092302.html

People v. *Beardsley,* 1907. 150 Michigan 206, 113 N.W. 1128.

Ross, Debra E. 2004. "Employee Safety." In Lawrence M. Salinger, ed., *Encyclopedia of White-Collar & Corporate Crime.* Thousand Oaks, CA: Sage.

Shepherd and Wedderburn Law Firm. 2006. *Corporate Homicide Legislation.* Accessed online at Hg.org http://www.hg.org/articles/article_1584.html

Stacy, Tom. 2000. "Changing Paradigms in the Law of Homicide." *The Ohio State Law Journal,* 62(3): 1–48; accessed online at http://moritzlaw.osu.edu/lawjournal/stacy.htm

Tennessee v. *Garner.* 1985. U.S. Supreme Court, 471 U.S. 1.

Chapter 3

MEASURING MURDER

You open the *USA Today* Web page, and the headlines indicate that murder is decreasing. Then you happen to catch your local paper's headlines that scream about soaring homicide rates. What is going on? Is homicide increasing or decreasing? It could be that where you live, homicide has increased since the previous year while at the same time it has decreased in the nation as a whole. Why do the rates vary in different places, and why are they increasing or decreasing? These are some of the questions that academics and criminal justice practitioners may ask about homicide. Moreover, instead of relying on our hunches, which have the potential to be incorrect, academics and many criminal justice professionals employ the scientific method to learn about homicide. In employing the scientific method to answer our questions (and to generate more questions), we use various data sources.

It stands to reason, then, that what we know about homicide is only as good as the data we have to study it. The importance of homicide data quality is true for academic criminologists as well as for criminal justice practitioners and the general public. In this chapter, we look at the data that criminologists commonly employ when studying homicide, which is often the same data that practitioners use to try to stop or prevent homicide. In fact, the data criminologists use to study homicide is often collected for practitioners rather than for academic criminologists, which sometimes makes the studying of homicide difficult.

In this chapter, you will read about various data sources. The chapter begins with a discussion of three sources for national homicide data collected by the Federal Bureau of Investigation (FBI). These three sources are the Uniform Crime Reports (UCR), the Supplemental Homicide Reports (SHR), and the newer National Incident-Based Reporting System (NIBRS). These FBI sources are followed by the National Center for Health Statistics (NCHS) National Death Index (NDI) mortality files. Next is an overview of various regional homicide data sources, including the Chicago Homicide Data and the Homicide Investigation Tracking System (HITS) data in Washington. The chapter also includes a review of other sources criminologists use to study homicide, including case studies of particular cases or offenders. Finally, the chapter concludes with a discussion of the typologies of homicide used by criminologists in their studies of homicide.

If you are going to study in the field of homicide, it helps if you become familiar with a whole host of initials that are commonly bantered around when professionals talk about homicide. It is not uncommon, for instance, to hear a member of the HRWG talking about a comparison between the rates of homicide as reported in the NIBRS and the SHR. Another HRWG member who works for ICPSR may mention that HITS is available from NACJD. So what are these people talking about and who are they? Well, the HRWG is the Homicide Research Working Group, an organization of homicide researchers from a variety of disciplines who network together to improve homicide research across the world. Among the many members of the HRWG are those who work at ICPSR, the Interuniversity Consortium for Political and Social Research. ICPSR manages the NACJD, which is the National Archive of Criminal Justice Data. As for NIBRS, SHR, and HITS, each of these are data sets that we discuss along with other data sources (with other initials) later.

UNIFORM CRIME REPORTS

As you may know from other criminal justice courses, the FBI has a crime reporting program known as the Uniform Crime Reports (UCR) that collects data from state Uniform Crime Reporting agencies. Each year, the FBI produces *Crime in the United States* in which they list the Part I crimes that have been reported to the

---

BOX 3.1

Felony Murders and the UCR

When an individual victim dies of a heart attack that is believed to be the result of severe stress caused by an offender who is committing a felony, the death may be classified by statute as felony murder and thus prosecuted as such. However, it is not recorded as a criminal homicide in the UCR. As noted in the 2004 UCR Reporting Handbook, "a heart attack cannot, in fact, be caused at will by an offender. Even in instances where an individual is known to have a weak heart, there is no assurance that an offender can cause sufficient emotional or physical stress to guarantee that the victim will suffer a fatal heart attack" (p. 6).

BOX 3.2

Canadian and British Homicide Data

Statistics Canada works very much like the FBI in the United States to collect data on homicide. Whenever a homicide occurs, the investigating officer must complete a homicide survey that contains three main questionnaires: (1) the Incident Questionnaire, (2) the Victim Questionnaire, and (3) the Charged/ Suspect-Chargeable Questionnaire. Statistics Canada started collecting information on all murders in 1961 and then added information on manslaughters and infanticides in 1974 (Statistics Canada, 2005). The process is very similar in Britain where the Research Development and Statistics Home Office collect and report data from the police about crime reported to the police.

police throughout the United States in the previous year. These Part 1 crimes, also referred to as *index crimes,* include murder, aggravated assault, robbery, rape, larceny, burglary, vehicle theft, and arson. The FBI also reports the number of arrests for 20 Part II offenses, including most every other crime, ranging from vandalism and public drunkenness to drug violations and simple assault.

In the case of homicide, the UCR program keeps track of all murder and nonnegligent manslaughter. Regardless of how the killings may eventually be defined in a court of law, the deaths are defined as a murder or nonnegligent manslaughter in the UCR data if the police have classified them as such based on their investigation. Because definitions may vary by jurisdiction, those who report to the UCR are advised to use the FBI's definition of murder and nonnegligent manslaughter, which is "the willful (nonnegligent) killing of one human being by another" (FBI, 2005).

The UCR program, which began in 1930, is voluntary on the part of law enforcement agencies. Still, in a typical year like 2002, over 17,000 city, country, and state law enforcement agencies reported data on crimes in their jurisdictions. Another way to think about the coverage of the UCR is that in 2002, 93.4% of the total U.S. population lived in jurisdictions that reported crime statistics to the FBI (FBI, 2005). Although the FBI report that the primary objective of the UCR Program is to "generate a reliable set of criminal statistics for use in law enforcement administration, operation, and management," criminologists often use the data as an indication of how much crime exists in the United States and also to test theories about crime and crime prevention (FBI, 2002).

SUPPLEMENTAL HOMICIDE REPORTS

In addition to the UCR reports, the FBI has been collecting the Supplemental Homicide Reports (SHR) since 1961 (Riedel, 1999). The SHR were last revised in 1976, and since then, the format has remained the same (Fox, 2003; Riedel, 1999).

TABLE 3.1
Supplemental Homicide Reports

The SHR includes information on the following for each homicide incident:

• Month	• Sex of offender
• Year	• Victim/offender relationship
• Age of victim	• Circumstance of the crime
• Race of victim	• Weapon used
• Sex of victim	• Number of victims
• Age of offender	• Number of offenders
• Race of offender	• Reporting agency

Although early SHR data may be less reliable than more recent data, the SHR provides the most reliable, detailed, and timely data on homicides across the United States (Riedel, 1999; U.S. Department of Justice, 2003). Still as we will see later, there is no perfect homicide data set. Table 3.1 lists the information included in the SHR that includes the date of the offense; the age, sex, and race of both the homicide victim and offender; the type of weapon used; the relationship of the victim to the offender; and the circumstance surrounding each homicide incident. In the later section on typologies, you will learn more about the different categorizations of the information provided in the SHR and other data sets.

NATIONAL INCIDENT-BASED REPORTING SYSTEM

It is an exciting time for those who study crime. The UCR program is undergoing a slow but important transformation. Gradually, crime data collection is changing from what is known as a "summary system" to an incident-based system. The National Incident-Based Reporting System, or NIBRS, collects data on each single crime occurrence. Unlike the UCR, which uses a summary system, NIBRS contains much more detail. Over 20 years ago in 1982, the FBI and Bureau of Justice Statistics (BJS) task force began systematically to study the best way to revise the UCR data collection system. In 1985, after several meetings, conferences, and input from criminologists, the FBI released recommendations for an improved UCR program that considered the needs of criminal justice practitioners and researchers (FBI, 2005; Riedel, 1999). This new NIBRS program is different from the UCR in that instead of focusing on the eight Part I index crimes, NIBRS focuses on 46 specific crimes called Group A offenses in 22 categories and 11 less serious Group B offenses. With regard to the focus of this text, the Group A offense category of homicide offenses is most important. The homicide offense group in NIBRS includes the crimes of murder and nonnegligent manslaughter, negligent manslaughter, and justifiable homicide.

More important for the study of homicide than the increased number of crimes that NIBRS includes is the details of how and what data is collected for NIBRS as well as the introduction of quality assurance checks built into the NIBRS system (Addington, 2003; FBI, 2005). With the NIBRS system, crime data is collected in much greater detail than it was with the UCR and SHR. Fifty-two pieces of information about each crime incident are collected in NIBRS (Riedel, 1999). In addition to the demographic information that is usually collected on both the victim and offender, NIBRS includes information on types of injuries, multiple weapons (instead of just one as was the case with the UCR), dates of arrest, resident status of the victim and offenders, and the disposition of arrestees younger than 18 years old (Riedel, 1999).

Moreover, and different from the UCR system, NIBRS does not use a hierarchy rule. The hierarchy rule is something that you may have heard about in your other criminal justice courses. It means that if several crimes occur in one incident, only the most serious crime is recorded. For example, if an offender robs three people, rapes one of them, and murders another, only the murder is counted in UCR statistics because it is considered the most serious of all the severe crimes that occurred. With NIBRS, however, each crime would be recorded and counted separately but in such a way that the files would be linked so studies could be performed on the entire crime incident.

The FBI began collecting NIBRS data in January 1989; however, the NIBRS program does not yet have nationwide participation. It is a voluntary program, and some states have been slow to switch to NIBRS or are reticent about switching because the NIBRS program involves some new costs and officer training. The South Carolina Law Enforcement Division was the first organization to use NIBRS in 1987. As of 2005, 26 state programs have been NIBRS certified (FBI, 2005). In addition, 12 states are involved in testing NIBRS and the District of Columbia and 8 state agencies are in the stages of planning and development (FBI, 2005). The data from the agencies in the 26 participating states account for 22% of the U.S. population (FBI, 2005). Does your state report NIBRS data? At the time this book went to press, the following states were participating in NIBRS: Arizona, Arkansas, Colorado, Connecticut, Delaware, Georgia, Idaho, Iowa, Kansas, Kentucky, Louisiana, Maine, Massachusetts, Michigan, Missouri, Nebraska, New Hampshire, North Dakota, Ohio, Oregon, Rhode Island, South Carolina, South Dakota, Tennessee, Texas, Utah, Vermont, Virginia, West Virginia, Wisconsin, and the District of Columbia.

The future of NIBRS, although not perfect, is promising. As Addington (2003) notes, NIBRS is not designed to solve all the problems with SHR. However, four changes are likely to make NIBRS an improvement over SHR: (1) computerized data submission that permits data edits and record updating; (2) better and more instructions for submitting data to NIBRS; (3) a new certification requirement for agencies before they are permitted to submit NIBRS data; and (4) regular quality assurance checks by the FBI for logical consistency and completeness (Addington, 2003).

NATIONAL DEATH INDEX

Although most criminologists rely on data collected by the FBI to learn about homicide, there are other valuable resources. The National Death Index (NDI) is part of the National Vital Statistics System collected by the Center for Disease

Control and Prevention's (CDC) National Center for Health Statistics (NCHS). Compiled from state data, the NDI is a computerized index of death record information. The NCHS compiles statistical information about deaths in the United States as a way to inform those who make health policy decisions. Although the focus of the NDI is all deaths recorded by medical examiners or coroners in the nation each year since 1933, it is still a valid source for information on deaths caused by homicide (Riedel, 1999).

Different from other sources of homicide information that rely on police agencies, the NDI data is compiled from death certificate information. Standardized death certificate information is completed by a medical examiner or coroner. The completed death certificates are then given to local registrars or county health officers who verify them and send copies on to the state's vital statistics office where they are again checked and then sent to the NCHS. At the NCHS, cases are classified according to the International Classification of Diseases (ICD) and then entered into the National Death Index data set (Riedel, 1999) (see Table 3.2).

Death certificate information may include details about the injuries and conditions that contribute to a victim's death. They may also include information about the manner of death including homicide (Barber et al., 2002). However, because the focus is not on crime, death certificate information does not include any information on the homicide offender or suspect. However, the NDI does include information that is not included in many crime databases, such as marital status and educational level of the victim (Van Court & Trent, 2004). Other information collected by the NCHS are as follows:

1. Age, race/ethnicity, and sex of the victim
2. Whether victim was in the armed forces
3. Victim's social security number
4. Victim's birthplace, occupation, residence, and place of death
5. Parents' names and addresses
6. Places and manner of disposition
7. Whether an autopsy was completed
8. Times, places, and causes of death
9. Indication of whether death occurred at work (Riedel, 1999)

The ICD coding system is used to assign a cause of death code for each death certificate based on what the coroner or medical examiner noted as cause of death. It may seem straightforward, but there is a reason to be cautious in interpreting these data. As noted by Barber et al. (2002), law enforcement personnel may define a homicide as murder, manslaughter, justifiable homicide, or accidental killing of one human by another. A more common understanding of the term *homicide* is that it is an intentional killing of one human by another. As a result, one coroner may record the accidental shooting of a hunting buddy on a death certificate as an accident, whereas another coroner may record it as a homicide.

TABLE **3.2**
ICD-10 Homicide Cause of Death Codes

Code	Cause of Death
U01.0	Terrorism involving explosion of marine weapons (homicide)
U01.1	Terrorism involving destruction of aircraft (homicide)
U01.2	Terrorism involving other explosions and fragments (homicide)
U01.3	Terrorism involving fires, conflagration, and hot substances (homicide)
U01.4	Terrorism involving firearms (homicide)
U01.5	Terrorism involving nuclear weapons (homicide)
U01.6	Terrorism involving biological weapons (homicide)
U01.7	Terrorism involving chemical weapons (homicide)
U01.8	Terrorism, other specified (homicide)
U01.9	Terrorism, unspecified (homicide)
X85	Assault (homicide) by drugs, medicaments, and biological substances
X86	Assault (homicide) by corrosive substance
X87	Assault (homicide) by pesticides
X88	Assault (homicide) by gases and vapors
X89	Assault (homicide) by other specified chemicals and noxious substances
X90	Assault (homicide) by unspecified chemical or noxious substances
X91	Assault (homicide) by hanging, strangulation, and suffocation
X92	Assault (homicide) by drowning and submersion
X93	Assault (homicide) by handgun discharge
X94	Assault (homicide) by rifle, shotgun, and larger firearm discharge
X95	Assault (homicide) by other and unspecified firearm discharge
X96	Assault (homicide) by explosive material
X97	Assault (homicide) by smoke, fire, and flames
X98	Assault (homicide) by steam, hot vapors, and hot objects
X99	Assault (homicide) by sharp object
Y00	Assault (homicide) by blunt object
Y01	Assault (homicide) by pushing from high place
Y02	Assault (homicide) by pushing or placing victim before moving object
Y03	Assault (homicide) by crashing of motor vehicle
Y04	Assault (homicide) by bodily force
Y05	Sexual assault (homicide) by bodily force
Y08	Assault (homicide) by other specified means
Y09	Assault (homicide) by unspecified means

Source: Compiled from World Health Organization data (World Health Organization, 2003).

> ## BOX 3.3
> ### Comparing Two Data Sources
>
> Barber and her colleagues at the Harvard Injury Control Research Center compared accidental deaths by another with a firearm as recorded in the 1997 SHR data and the 1997 NDI data. A total of 168 victims in the 1997 SHR data were recorded as having been accidentally or unintentionally shot and killed by another human. Barber et al. were able to find 140 of these victims in the 1997 NDI data. Of those 140 they found, 105 (75%) were coded as homicides in the NDI data, 32 (23%) were recorded as accidents, and 3 (2%) were recorded as undetermined deaths.

NATIONAL VIOLENT DEATH REPORTING SYSTEM

In 2003, the CDC introduced the National Violent Death Reporting System (NVDRS). Somewhat like the FBI's decision to improve on the UCR with NIBRS, the CDC's NVDRS is an improvement over the NDI. Like the UCR and NIBRS, the NVDRS is a nationwide state-based system. Like the NDI, data are collected from a public health perspective—the goal is to provide data that will aid in the development of prevention strategies. Unlike the NDI, however, demographic data on the perpetrators of violent deaths and the victim offender relationships are collected.

Again parallel to the NIBRS system, the NVDRS does not yet have national coverage but is being implemented slowly and carefully with training provided for the states that participate and regular monitoring of the data submission process. The first NVDRS data results were released in April 2005 and include information from the six states that participated in the NVDRS (MD, MA, NJ, OR, SC, and VA) in 2003. As of August 2004, the number of NVDRS participating states had nearly tripled to 17 states. These 17 stretch across the United States and include Alaska, California, Colorado, Georgia, Kentucky, Massachusetts, Maryland, North Carolina, New Jersey, New Mexico, Oklahoma, Oregon, Rhode Island, South Carolina, Utah, Virginia, and Wisconsin.

Because the focus of the NVDRS is violent deaths, in addition to data on homicide, information is also collected about suicides, deaths by legal intervention (excluding executions), unintentional firearm injury deaths, and those deaths for which intent is not determined. State agencies collect information on the circumstances of violent deaths that they obtain from the police, medical examiners, and coroners. Like the NDI, homicides circumstance categorizations are based on the ICD-10 (see Table 3.2).

CHICAGO HOMICIDE DATA

In addition to the national data sources already discussed in this chapter, some excellent smaller homicide data sets are available through the Interuniversity Consortium for Political and Social Research (ICPSR). Carolyn Rebecca Block of the Illinois Criminal

Justice Information Authority and Richard L. Block of Loyola University (1998) have worked with the Chicago Police Department for many years on the Chicago homicide data set. ICPSR reports that the Chicago data set is one of the largest, most comprehensive data sets on violence established in the United States. There are nearly 23,000 homicides and 115 variables included in this data set that includes every homicide in the Chicago police homicide files from 1965 to 1995. Like the SHR, the Chicago data set is structured so criminologists can focus on victims, offenders, or incidents. In addition to the information collected in the SHR, such as victim/offender relationship, type of weapon, and circumstance, the Chicago data set includes information about the offender's previous criminal record and geographic variables, including the census tract, community area, police district, and police area where the victim was found.

HOMICIDE INVESTIGATION TRACKING SYSTEM

Although criminals may cross boundaries in commission of their crimes, law enforcement is divided by federal, state, county, and city boundaries, and in large law enforcement agencies there are often divisions between investigative units such as the robbery and homicide divisions. Additionally, as is well known enough to be included in many crime dramas and mystery novels, there have often been clashes between different law enforcement agencies over who has jurisdiction in some cases. This lack of cooperation across jurisdictions has been blamed for slowing down the apprehension of criminals such as Ted Bundy who have crossed jurisdictions while committing their crimes (Headley, 2000; Keppel, 1995; Keppel & Weiss, 1993).

Those who commit crimes across many jurisdictions make it more difficult for law enforcement agents to link the crimes together and gather evidence to help them find the offenders. In response to murderers such as the Green River Killer Gary Ridgway and Ted Bundy, who were discovered to have crossed jurisdictional boundaries, former King County Detective Robert Keppel (1995) developed the Homicide Investigation Tracking System (HITS) with funding from the National Institute of Justice.

The attorney general's office in the state of Washington maintains the HITS database as a repository on crimes that occur in the state of Washington and, to some extent, in Oregon, Idaho, Alaska, and British Columbia. HITS data include a wealth of information designed to help police investigators link crimes and apprehend offenders. Victim and offender characteristics, weapon information, crime evidence, geographic locations, and even information about vehicles are included in HITS. In addition, known murderers and sex offenders living in the community are also tracked in HITS. Even though HITS was designed to help with the apprehension of offenders, it is used by those who study homicide from an academic perspective as well.

Similar to national data sets such as SHR and NVDRS, law enforcement agents, coroners, and medical examiners report HITS data voluntarily. Additionally, prosecutor's offices in each of Washington's 39 counties, the Washington State Association of Sheriffs and Police Chiefs Uniform Crime Reporting Unit, and the Washington

State Department of Vital Statistics submit data to HITS. The HITS computer system permits each agency to enter, search, and analyze their own information and compare the crimes they have discovered with crimes occurring in other areas. The attorney general's office has also graciously allowed crime researchers to use this data set.

OTHER DATA SETS

Dr. Eric Monkkonen (2001, 2005), a historian, contributed much to the study of homicide by constructing homicide data sets for New York City and California that include data for the years before the FBI began collecting UCR data in 1931. His New York City data set includes homicide data for 1797 to 1999, and his Los Angeles California data set covers 1830 to 2003. With the goal of obtaining the best estimates of annual homicide counts and the most detailed information on individual homicide cases, Monkkonen used various sources to build his data sets, including court records, coroner's reports, and newspapers. The data sets he built include variables found in other data sets, such as age, sex, and race of the victim and offender, the type of weapon used, and the date and location of the killing. In addition, like the public health data sets, he included the birthplace of the offender and victim. Moreover, in the New York data set, Monkkonen included information on arrests, trials, convictions, and executions of the offenders.

HOMICIDE DATA CONCERNS

Although there is much to learn from these data sets about homicide trends in the United States, theories of criminal offending and victimization, and even homicide investigation, the data sets are not perfect. Those who use these data sets and those who read the studies and reports based on these data sets should know about some of the problems. Two major concerns about homicide data sets are first, the problem of incomplete or missing data and second, the accuracy of the data. First, the fact that the editors of *Homicide Studies, An Interdisciplinary and International Journal* dedicated their entire August 2004 issue to the problem of missing data should make it clear that this is a serious concern for those of us who study homicide. However, as James Alan Fox (2004) noted in his article in the *Homicide Studies* journal, the concern about missing cases is less a problem for homicide researchers than those who study other crimes.

Although we can never be absolutely certain, criminologists are more confident that most homicides come to the attention of the police than they are that most larceny cases or even aggravated assaults are reported to the police. The fact that dead bodies are the result of homicides makes it more likely that the crime of homicide will be discovered. However, there are, of course, cases as discussed in the previous chapter in which bodies are never found, and there is also the possibility that a murder has been classified as an accidental death. Still, criminologists are generally more confident about homicide data than other crime data.

Missing Data

Fox (2004) and others in the special issue of *Homicide Studies* address the bigger issue of missing data for the study of homicide. Although the data sources may show there has been a homicide, details about a homicide may be missing. The circumstance or weapon information may be missing or, more likely, data about the offender may be missing. Although missing information about offenders, especially if the victim/offender relationship is that of a stranger, has been an ongoing challenge for homicide researchers, the problem may be increasing as the percentage of homicides that are solved has been decreasing in recent years (Riedel, 2003). Cases that have not been *cleared* (another term for solved) usually do not have information on the offender's age, race, and sex simply because the offender is unknown.

In the *Homicide Studies* journal, dedicated to the problem of missing homicide data, Lynn Addington (2003) compared the amount of missing data for murder and manslaughter characteristics in the SHR and NIBRS for 1999. She found that the NIBRS and SHR data sets are similar in that they both have little missing information for victim characteristics. For offender and victim/offender relationship information, however, Addington found that the NIBRS data is more complete than the SHR. In contrast, the data on weapons and murder circumstances in the SHR are more complete than the same information in the NIBRS.

Data Inaccuracy

Although the problem is not an insidious one, occasionally data are recorded inaccurately in the national homicide data sets. Fox (2003) provides an excellent example of data that have been inaccurately coded. He notes that in 1977, a woman killed her three stepchildren and her husband. Because the SHR allow only one relationship to be recorded, all four victims were coded as stepdaughters. However, in actuality, this was only accurate for two victims. The remaining two victims should have been coded as a stepson and as a husband (Fox, 2003).

Homicide data inaccuracies that may be more difficult to detect are those that have been reported by researchers who have compared police files to homicide data. For example, Riedel (1999) notes that comparison between police records and SHR data have found differences on all the variables including age. One reason for this may be that specific SHR data cannot be updated.

Bias

Although not exactly a problem of missing or inaccurate data, an important caveat about NIBRS data is that it may have a small agency bias. As noted in the section on NIBRS, the program is voluntary, and thus not all law enforcement agencies report. In fact, few large cities report to the NIBRS program. NIBRS-reporting agencies tend to be smaller rather than larger law enforcement agencies. Thus criminologists who use NIBRS to study homicide need to be careful about generalizing their conclusions. In other words, if we draw conclusions about homicide using NIBRS data, we must be careful not to assume that we can draw the same conclusions for large cities.

CASE STUDIES

To better understand and learn about the details of homicide and to test individual-level theories of homicide offending, criminologists often use the case study method. A case study is an intensive study of a single case or number of cases. Often psychological researchers take this approach, but others who study homicide also find this approach enlightening. For a homicide researcher, a case study might involve an in-depth interview with a homicide offender or it may involve collecting all the information possible on a particular homicide incident or a number of events. Those who use the case study method may conduct interviews with offenders, witnesses, and survivors; they may observe trials, examine police and prison files, and collect newspaper accounts of events. Researchers who use the case study method to study homicide gain rich details that may contribute to our understanding of other cases or they may help us generate theoretical understandings of homicide offenders. For example, Shipley and Arrigo (2004) employ the case study method in their examination of Aileen Wuornos.

Despite the value of individual case studies, researchers must not generalize particular cases to all cases. In other words, just because we seem to gain an understanding of one offender does not mean we will understand them all. Levin and Fox (1985) point out that we must be careful in accepting any theories of homicide offending that are generated from a study of one or a few cases. Often those killers who are studied are the particularly bizarre offenders who may be very different from other homicide offenders. For example, Levin and Fox (1985) discuss the use of the MacDonald triad in predicting violence. The MacDonald triad refers to three factors believed to be common in the childhood histories of homicide offenders: bedwetting, fire starting, and the torture of small animals. (See Chapter 12 for more information on the MacDonald triad.) Case studies of many homicide offenders find at least one element of the MacDonald triad. However, Levin and Fox (1985) note that many individuals who express all three aspects of the MacDonald triad do not become murderers. We can learn much from individual cases, but we must be particularly careful in the generalization of these cases, especially when generating policy.

TYPOLOGIES

Whereas in Chapter 2, I discussed the different legal definitions of homicide that include typologies based on intent, criminologists who study homicide often divide homicide into different types based on the relationship between the offender and the victim or the circumstances surrounding the homicide. The rationale for dividing homicides in these ways is that many homicide researchers have found that different types of homicides call for different theories or explanations. It probably seems logical to you that the theories regarding the killing of husbands or wives may be different than theories that explain the killing of an employer or a stranger. Likewise, a killing in a "drug deal gone bad" is likely to be explained differently than a homicide that occurs during a domestic dispute or a robbery.

Most large homicide data sets are set up so researchers can study particular homicide circumstances and relationships or so a criminologist can compare different

TABLE 3.3
SHR Homicide Relationship Codes

Code	Relationship of Victim to Suspect
1	Husband
2	Wife
3	Common-law husband
4	Common-law wife
5	Mother
6	Father
7	Son
8	Daughter
9	Brother
10	Sister
11	In-law
12	Stepfather
13	Stepmother
14	Stepson
15	Stepdaughter
16	Other family
17	Neighbor
18	Acquaintance
19	Boyfriend
20	Girlfriend
21	Ex-husband
22	Ex-wife
23	Employee
24	Employer
25	Friend
26	Homosexual relationship
27	Other—known to victim
28	Stranger
88	Not applicable
99	Relationship unknown

Source: Compiled from FBI Uniform Crime Reporting Program and Supplementary Homicide Report Data Standards or Guidelines.

circumstances and relationships. For example, in the SHR, in addition to an unknown category and a not applicable category, there are 30 relationship codes (see Table 3.3). It would seem to be a fairly complete list, but look at it closely. Think about how you would code the murder of 24-year-old University of Richmond senior De'Nora Hill. According to newspaper accounts, Hill was shot to death by her former boyfriend, Joe Casuccio, in December 2005 (Bowes & Holmberg, 2005). How would you code Hill's relationship to Casuccio? At one time, she was his girlfriend, but this was no longer the case. She filed a criminal complaint against him the week before she was killed, which in all likelihood indicated that they were no longer friends, and "acquaintance" does not seem to capture their relationship either. If a similar case were in the Chicago Homicide Data (CHD) maintained by Dr. C. Becky Block, the relationship would be categorized as ex-girlfriend. The CHD contains other relationships that are lacking in the SHR, including customer, drug pusher, proprietor, and homosexual domestic relationship.

Table 3.4 includes the SHR circumstance codes. Like the relationship codes, much is covered, and this data set has been very useful to hundreds of homicide researchers.

TABLE 3.4
SHR Homicide Circumstance Options

Code	Circumstances
2	Rape
3	Robbery
5	Burglary
6	Larceny
7	Motor vehicle theft
9	Arson
10	Prostitution and commercialized vice
17	Other sex offense
18	Narcotic drug laws
19	Gambling
26	Other felony type—not specified
32	Abortion
40	Lover's triangle
41	Child killed by babysitter
42	Brawl due to influence of alcohol
43	Brawl due to influence of narcotics
44	Argument over money or property
45	Other arguments
46	Gangland killings
47	Juvenile gang killings
48	Institutional killings
49	Sniper attack
50	Victim shot in hunting accident
51	Gun-cleaning death, other than self-inflicted
52	Children playing with gun
53	Other negligent handling of gun
59	All other manslaughter by negligence except traffic deaths
60	Other nonfelony-type homicide
70	Suspected felony type
80	Felon killed by private citizen
81	Felon killed by police
88	Not applicable
99	Circumstances undetermined

Source: Compiled from Center for Disease Control data (Center for Disease Control, 2004).

However, the categories are not what researchers call "exhaustive." In other words, they are not a list of every type of homicide circumstance that could happen. There is the category "circumstances undetermined" and a few "other" categories, which may technically make the categorization exhaustive. However, there are also circumstances that could be added to the SHR circumstances to make it a more complete listing in today's world. Take a close look at the list in Table 3.4 and see if you can think of any homicides that do not fit the circumstances listed. Did you think of the 9/11 attacks on the World Trade Center? Certainly the category of terrorism is one that unfortunately could be added. In January 1999, the NCHS began using the tenth version of the International Classification of Diseases (ICD–10) to code cause of death in the NDI. The ICD-10 homicide codes includes several for terrorism, as you can see in Table 3.2. The ICD-10 was the first to include deaths caused by terrorism. In addition to the other homicide causes of death already listed in the ICD previous to the tenth version, ten types of death by terrorism were included in this latest revision.

SUMMARY

This chapter provided an overview and comparison of different sources of U.S. national homicide data, including the FBI's Supplemental Homicide Reports, the FBI's relatively new National Incident-Based Reporting System, and the National Center for Health Statistics National Death Index mortality files. Additional data sources commonly used by homicide researchers to study homicide in particular parts of the United States, including Chicago, California, Washington, and New York, were also reviewed. The use of case studies by some homicide researchers and common concerns about homicide data were discussed. The chapter ended with a comparison of circumstances and relationships catalogued and not catalogued in these various sources.

CHAPTER QUESTIONS

1. What does *SHR* stand for?
2. What data are included in the SHR?
3. What does *NIBRS* stand for?
4. How is NIBRS different from the SHR?
5. Why is the NIBRS likely to be better than the SHR?
6. How many states are included in NIBRS?
7. How are the NDI and the NVDRS different from the other data sources included in this chapter?
8. List at least two U.S. homicide data sources that are state or city specific.
9. What does HITS stand for, and what was the impetus behind this data source?
10. What are the two main concerns about homicide data?
11. What is a case study?
12. What must we be cautious when we use case studies to theorize about homicide offending?
13. Name five relationship categories in the SHR.

14. What relationships are missing from the SHR?
15. Compare the circumstances listed for the ICD Death codes in Table 3.2 and that for the SHR in Table 3.4. How do the circumstances listed differ, and what might account for these differences?

REFERENCES

Addington, Lynn A. 2003. "The Effect of NIBRS Reporting on Item Missing Data in Murder Cases." *Homicide Studies*, 8(3): 193–213.

Barber, Catherine, David Hemenway, Jenny Hochstadt, and Deborah Azrael. 2002. "Underestimates Of Unintentional Firearm Fatalities: Comparing Supplementary Homicide Report Data With Vital Statistics," *Injury Prevention*, 8: 252–256.

Block, Carolyn Rebecca, Richard L. Block, and the Illinois Criminal Justice Information Authority. *Homicides in Chicago, 1965–1995* [Computer file]. ICPSR06399-v5. Chicago: Illinois Criminal Justice Information Authority [producer], 1998. Ann Arbor, MI: Interuniversity Consortium for Political and Social Research [distributor], 2005–07–06.

Bowes, Mark, and Mark Holmberg. 2005. "UR Student Killed by Ex-Boyfriend Gunman Kills Himself; Victim Detailed 2 Months of Torment." *Richmond Times Dispatch* On-Line. December 7, 2005. Retrieved September 3, 2005, from http://www.timesdispatch.com/servlet/Satellite?pagename=RTD/MGArticle/RTD_BasicArticle&c=MGArticle&cid=1128768573551

Centers for Disease Control and Prevention (CDC). 2004. "National Violent Death Reporting System." Retrieved September 3, 2005, from http://www.cdc.gov/ncipc/profiles/nvdrs/facts.htm

FBI. 2002. *Crime in the United States*. U.S. Department of Justice.

FBI. 2004. *Uniform Crime Reporting Handbook*, 2004.

FBI. 2005. *Crime in the United States*. U.S. Department of Justice.

Fox, James Alan. 2004. "Missing Data Problems in the SHR: Imputing Offender and Relationship Characteristics." *Homicide Studies*, February 1, 2006, 10(1): 55–73.

Headley, Bernard. 2000. *The Atlanta Youth Murders and the Politics of Race*. Carbondale: Southern Illinois University Press.

Interuniversity Consortium for Political and Social Research (ICPSR). 2005. National Archives of Criminal Justice Data. "Learn More About the Chicago Homicide Dataset." Retrieved September 3, 2005, from http://www.icpsr.umich.edu/NACJD/SDA/chd95d.html

Keppel, Robert D. 1995. *The Riverman: Ted Bundy and I Hunt for the Green River Killer*. New York: Pocket Books.

Keppel, Robert D., and Joseph G. Weiss. 1993. *Improving the Investigation of Homicide and the Apprehension Rate of Murderers in Washington State, 1981–1986* [Computer file]. Compiled by Robert D. Keppel, Washington State Attorney General's Office, and Joseph G. Weiss, University of Washington, Center for Law and Justice. ICPSR ed. Ann Arbor, MI: Interuniversity Consortium for Political and Social Research [producer and distributor], 1993.

Levin, Jack, and James A. Fox. 1985. *Mass Murder: America's Growing Menace*. New York: Plenum.

Monkkonen, Eric. *Homicides in New York City, 1797–1999* [Computer file]. ICPSR version. Los Angeles: University of California [producer], 2000. Ann Arbor, MI: Interuniversity Consortium for Political and Social Research [distributor], 2001.

Monkkonen, Eric H. *Los Angeles Homicides, 1830–2003* [Computer file]. ICPSR03680-v2. Los Angeles: University of California [producer], 2005. Ann Arbor, MI: Interuniversity Consortium for Political and Social Research [distributor], 2005–08–04.

Riedel, Marc. 1999. "Sources of Homicide Data: A Review and Comparison." In M. Dwayne Smith and Margaret A. Zahn, eds., *Homicide A Sourcebook of Social Research* (pp. 78–93). Thousand Oaks, Calif.: Sage.

Shipley, Stacey L., and Bruce A. Arrigo. 2004. *The Female Homicide Offender: Serial Murder and the Case of Aileen Wuornos*. NJ: Prentice Hall.

Statistics Canada. 2005. *Homicide Survey Webpage*. Retrieved January 15, 2006, from http://www.statcan.ca/cgi-bin/imdb/p2SV.pl?Function=getSurvey&SDDS=3315&lang=en&db=IMDB&dbg=f&adm=8&dis=2

State of Washington Office of the Attorney General's Homicide Investigation Tracking System. Retrieved September 3, 2005, from http://www.atg.wa.gov/hits/hitsov.shtml

Van Court, Jason and Roger B. Trent. "Why Didn't We Get Them All? Analyzing Unlinked Records in California's Linked Homicide File." *Homicide Studies*, 8(3): 311–321.

World Health Organization. 2003. *International Statistical Classification of Diseases and Related Health Problems 10th Revision*. Online version accessed August 27, 2005. http://www3.who.int/icd/v011htm2003/fr-icd.htm

Chapter 4

PATTERNS AND TRENDS

For many of us who live in the United States, the nightly newscast could serve as a partial preview of the week's local obituary page. The news reporters stand "at the scene" in front of yellow tape reporting about another murder in the area. In some cities, murders are more common, and the news reporters do not report from the scene; instead your friendly local news reader tells you about the latest fatality from behind a desk. Even sadder, in some larger cities, murder has become so ordinary that individual incidents do not rate airtime. The cases may be noted in a back page of a local newspaper, if at all. Unless, of course, the murder is seen as less ordinary because it involves a child or a celebrity or something else that makes it catchy news.

In this chapter, you will read about current homicide patterns and trends. Demographics including sex, race, and age will be revealed, and you will also learn about the most common weapons used to murder. Because homicide varies over space as well as over time, this chapter also includes information about urban/suburban/rural variation, regional variation within the United States, and variation across the world. Note, however, that homicides are not monolithic. There are differences by circumstance type and victim/offender relationship as well. Thus this chapter begins with an overview of current homicide data by circumstance and victim/offender relationship. Then, other trends are discussed; disaggregated homicide data (different types of homicide) are included as relevant and available. However, because data on particular types of homicide are also included in other chapters of this book, we will try not to be too bogged down with details in this chapter. Nevertheless, it is important to be well informed about the data overall so you can view the media portrayals and reports and everyday discussions about homicide with a realistic and ideally critical perspective. Finally, a word of caution as you read this chapter. The reasons for the homicide patterns related in this chapter are not explored here. For the most part, this chapter provides the data and patterns. In the other chapters, explanations for the patterns are presented and explored.

How Common Is Homicide?

It is likely you agree that even one incident of homicide is too much. When that one victim is someone you love, or even someone you know, you realize just how tragic that one homicide can be. Sadly, family members and friends of thousands of persons each year in the United States have to deal with the unexpected loss of a loved one through the horrific circumstance of murder. The FBI reported that in 2004, 16,137 individuals in the United States were murdered, leaving their loved ones to deal with the terrible reality of their tragic deaths. There is some positive news overall, however; the number of homicides in 2004 reflects a 2.4% decrease from the year before in 2003 when there were a reported 16,528 murders (FBI, 2006a). Unfortunately, however, preliminary FBI reports for 2005 indicated a 4.8% increase in homicide from the year 2004 (FBI, 2006b).

The population is always changing. The population increases as people are added through birth and immigration, and the population decreases when people die and emigrate out of a nation. As a result, a decrease or an increase in the absolute number of homicides does not necessarily result in a corresponding decrease or increase in the homicide rate. Thus it is important to look not only at the absolute numbers of homicide each year but to consider the rate of homicide as well. A comparison of the murder rates for 2003 and 2004 reflects the decrease we saw in overall homicide numbers in these two years. The U.S. murder rate decreased from a rate of 5.7 homicide victims per 100,000 in 2003 to 5.5 per 100,000 in 2004. However, the data also show a decrease of 0.8% from 2000 to 2004 while the number of homicides increased 3.5% during this same time period (FBI, 2006a).

BOX 4.1

Determining the Homicide Rate

The rate for homicide in the United States is usually determined per 100,000 people in a given population. Because population sizes vary, we determine a homicide rate that can be compared across jurisdictions. If we are comparing homicide in cities, for example, we would want to have a number that is comparable across cities of different sizes. So we construct a number that tells us how many people were killed out of every 100,000 individuals in the population. In essence, we are making the population equal for comparisons of the number of homicides that occur. The homicide rate is determined following this formula: Homicide rate = H/(P/100,000).

H = the number of homicides in a particular area

P = the population in the particular area

The number 100,000 is used to determine a rate per 100,000 persons. To determine a rate for another population size, you would use that number here.

HOMICIDE TRENDS

As you can see in Figure 4.1, the decrease in homicide numbers and the homicide rate that we see from 2003 to 2004 is part of a trend that has been occurring since 1991 when homicide reached a rate of 9.8 per 100,000 (24,703 victims). As Figure 4.1 also shows, this decrease since 1991 is unprecedented in the last 50 years. The number of homicides in the United States decreased 65.3% between 1991 and 2004, whereas the homicide victimization rate decreased 55% during this same time period (see Figure 4.2). The 24,703 homicides recorded in 1991 was a

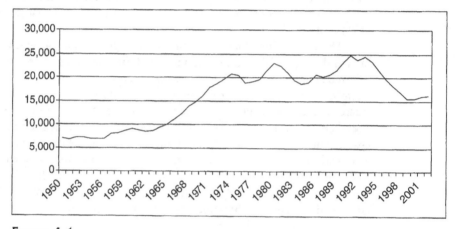

FIGURE 4.1
Homicides Known to the Police, 1995–2002
Source: Compiled from Bureau of Justice Statistics data (Fox & Zawitz, 2006).

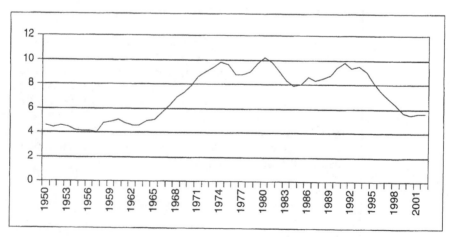

FIGURE 4.2
Homicide Victimization Rate per 100,000 Population
Source: Compiled from Bureau of Justice Statistics data (Fox & Zawitz, 2006).

record high for recorded homicides in the United States, but it was not the highest victimization rate. The victimization rate peaked in 1981 with a victimization rate of 10.2 per 100,000. Data from the Centers for Disease Control and Prevention (CDC) also indicate that homicide dropped in the rank of causes of homicide recently. Homicide was the 14th leading cause of death in 2002 but dropped to the 15th leading cause of death for the year 2003.

CIRCUMSTANCE TYPE

As reported in Chapter 3, most large data sets on homicide include details about each homicide. One of the details of homicide often recorded is the circumstance of the murder. The supplemental homicide data collected by the FBI show that the circumstances were known for 65% of homicides that occurred in 2004. As you can see in Table 4.1, homicides involving arguments were most common, making up 43.9% of the homicides in which the circumstances were known. Nearly a quarter or 22.8% of the known circumstances occurred along with another felony such as robbery or burglary.

It is likely, however, that the circumstance data presented in Table 4.1 underestimate some homicide circumstances. This is most obvious when you look at the number of homicides that appear to be linked to drugs or alcohol. Homicide data collected by the CDC may more accurately reflect alcohol and drug use involvement in homicide incidents. The National Violent Death Reporting System (NVDRS) data indicated that drugs were involved in approximately 16% of homicides in 2004 with known circumstances (NVDRS, 2005). Still, the role of alcohol or drugs in homicide may not always be clear, and the current homicide data for the United

TABLE 4.1
Known Homicide Circumstances, 2004

Circumstances	Number	Circumstances	Number
Rape	36	Romantic triangle	97
Robbery	988	Child killed by babysitter	17
Burglary	77	Brawl influenced by alcohol	139
Larceny theft	14	Brawl influenced by narcotics	98
Motor vehicle theft	38	Argument over property or money	218
Arson	28	Other arguments	3,758
Prostitution and		Gangland killings	95
commercialized vice	9		
Other sex offenses	14	Juvenile gang killings	804
Narcotic drug laws	554	Institutional killings	17
Gambling	7	Sniper attack	1
Others—not specified	324	Other—not specified	1,728
Felony type total	2,089	Nonfelony type total	6,972

Source: Compiled from Federal Bureau of Investigation Statistics Data (Federal Bureau of Investigation, 2006a).

States is limited in what it tells us about the connection among drugs, alcohol, and homicide. (See Box 4.6 on the role of alcohol and drugs in homicides in England and Wales.)

VICTIM/OFFENDER RELATIONSHIP

Figure 4.3 displays information about the relationship between the victim and offender in 2004. More than half of the victim/offender relationships, or 55.9%, were known to the police, and when they were known, acquaintances were the most likely offenders with 23% of victims killed by acquaintances. Nine percent were killed by their intimate partners, and 8% were killed by family members (not including spouses). Finally, 3% were killed by someone else the victim knew, such as a neighbor, employer, or employee.

In 1958, when Wolfgang published some of the first details about relationships in homicide cases, he noted that murder was most likely to occur between individuals who had some type of relationship. Further he found that when the victim knew the offender, it was most likely the offender was a member of his or her family (Wolfgang, 1958: 4). As you saw in Figure 4.3, this is no longer the case. The percentage of homicides committed by family members (including spouses) in the United States has declined steeply since 1966. The percentage of all homicide that are acquaintance killings has also decreased since the 1960s. Although the percentage of stranger killing increased until the 1970s, it decreased until the late 1970s to approximately 14%, where it has remained fairly stable for years. Homicides in which the victim/offender relationship is unknown, however, have increased greatly since the 1960s (Regoeczi & Miethe, 2003; Zahn & McCall, 1999). (See Box 4.2 on the increase in unknown victim/offender relationships.)

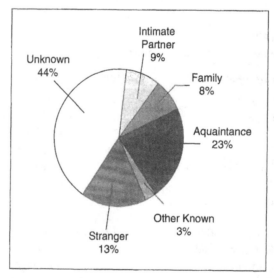

FIGURE 4.3
Murder and Nonnegligent Manslaughter by Victim's Relationship to Offender, 2004

Source: Compiled from Federal Bureau of Investigation Statistics Data (Federal Bureau of Investigation, 2006a).

BOX 4.2

Are Unknown Offenders Strangers?

The percentage of homicide cases in which the victim/offender relationship is unknown has increased remarkably since the 1960s. Some of those recorded as unknown may occur because the police had not made an arrest when the paperwork was submitted to the FBI for the Supplemental Homicide Reports (SHR). However, it is unlikely this would explain all unknown cases or the great increase in the unknown relationship cases. In a *Homicide Studies* article, Wendy Regoeczi and Terance Miethe (2003) studied whether and how homicide situations may have changed over time in ways that would explain the great increase in unknown relationship–type homicide. They also wanted to know if unknown relationship cases are just unsolved stranger cases. They found that unknown relationship cases changed over time. The unknown cases were more likely to involve white victims in the 1970s and African American victims in the 1990s. In the 1970s, unknown killings were likely to involve knifings, whereas in the 1990s, guns were most prominent among unknown offender cases. Regoeczi and Miethe also found that the most typical victim profile for an unknown case in the 1970s involved a white male victim who had been knifed, but females who were killed with a weapon other than a knife or gun were not uncommon. By the 1990s, there had been a shift in unknown relationship cases. The victims were mostly African American or another racial/ethnic minority who had been shot to death, and they were younger than the victims from the 1970s. The researchers concluded that unknown offender cases were reflective of all types of victim/offender relationship homicide cases, however; they were disproportionately more likely to be similar to stranger cases (Regoeczi & Miethe, 2003).

SEX

Homicide is predominately a male activity. More than three out of four victims, or 78%, of U.S. homicide offenders in 2004 were male. Similarly, when sex of the offender was known, 90% of homicide offenders were male. Moreover, greater than four out of five of the 11,932 known homicide offenders in 2004 were male. Logically then, as reflected in Table 4.2 and the pie diagrams in Figures 4.4 and 4.5, male

TABLE 4.2

Victim/Offender Relationship by Sex for Known Offenders

	Male Offender	Female Offender	Offender Sex Unknown
Male victim	4,488	488	74
Female victim	1,717	182	21
Victim sex unknown	41	10	18

Source: Compiled from Federal Bureau of Investigation Statistics Data (Federal Bureau of Investigation, 2006a).

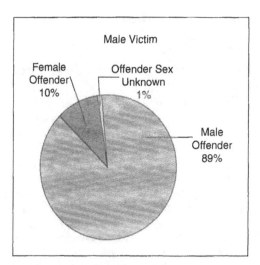

FIGURE 4.4
Sex and Victim/Offender Relationship (Male Victim)

Source: Compiled from Federal Bureau of Investigation Statistics Data (Federal Bureau of Investigation, 2006a).

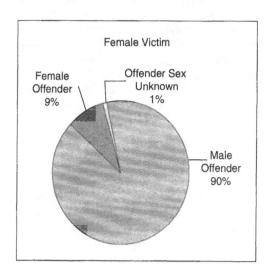

FIGURE 4.5
Sex and Victim/Offender Relationship (Female Victim)

Source: Compiled from Federal Bureau of Investigation Statistics Data (Federal Bureau of Investigation, 2006a).

offenders predominate as killers of both males and females. Eighty-nine percent of those who kill males and 90% of those who kill females are men (FBI, 2006a). The tendency of men to kill both men and women is also the case in Australia, where 83% of male victims were killed by men and 90% of female victims were killed by men (Johnson, 2005).

AGE

Just as with crime in general, homicide offending tends to be an activity that is committed most often by the relatively young. As you can see in Figure 4.6, the peak age for homicide offending in 2004 was 20 to 24 years. Moreover, those ages 17 to 29 accounted for the majority (57.6%) of homicide offending in which the age of the offender was known. Among offenders in 2004 whose age was known, less than 5% were older than 54 or younger than 17 years. Because males predominate as homicide offenders and victims, their age distribution is mirrored in the overall age distribution. Figure 4.7 shows that female victims and offenders tend to be adults between the ages of 20 and 54, and there is no age spike for females as there is for males.

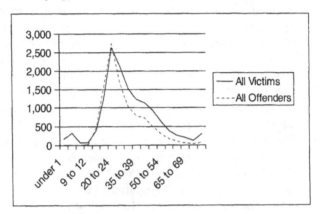

FIGURE 4.6
2004 Murder Victims and Offenders by Age

Source: Compiled from Federal Bureau of Investigation Statistics Data (Federal Bureau of Investigation, 2006a).

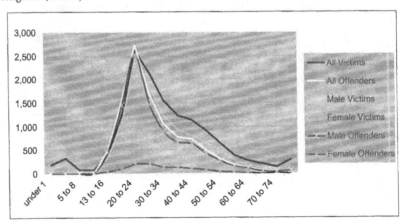

FIGURE 4.7
2004 Murder Offenders and Victims by Age and Sex

Source: Compiled from Federal Bureau of Investigation Statistics Data (Federal Bureau of Investigation, 2006a).

RACE

The 2004 homicide data show that among known offenders and victims, whites out-number African Americans but only by a small margin. In 2004, 48.6% of homicide offenders were white, 47.5% were African American, and less than 4% were categorized as another or unknown race. The victim data are very similar. Whites predominate as victims with 3,727 white victims (52.9%) in 2004. African American victims are a close second with 3,067 of the victims categorized as African American (43.6%). There were also 177 victims of other races and 68 victims for whom race was not known (FBI, 2006a).

We must be cautious about what conclusions we draw about race based on over-all numbers, however. Although the data show that whites outnumber African Americans, the rate of homicide is much higher for African Americans. The Bureau of Justice Statistics reports that in 2004, the rate of homicide victimization was six times higher for African American as compared to whites. Similarly, the rates of homicide offending for African Americans were seven times higher than the rates of offending in 2004 for whites (Fox & Zawitz, 2006).

Research by Martinez (1997) on homicide in Miami, a city with a large Latino population, is important for what it tells us about the two largest minorities groups in the United States. In his study of homicide in the 1990s, Martinez also found that African Americans were overrepresented among homicide victims and offenders. Although only 27% of Miami's population, 56% of Miami homicide victims were African American. Latinos made up 68% of the population but were underrepresented as homicide victims (38%). The rate of homicide per 100,000 in Miami for Anglos was 19.83, it was 21.66 for Latinos, and over three times as high at 73.49 for African Americans.

A look at who kills who in terms of race shows that white offenders tend to kill white victims, and African American offenders tend to kill African American victims. Of the 3,012 African American homicide victims who were known to be killed by an African American or white killer, 84.2% were killed by African American offenders.

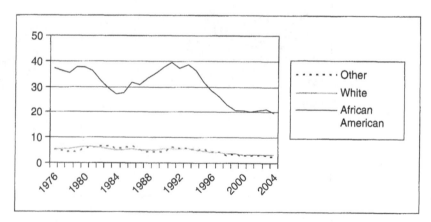

FIGURE **4.8**

Homicide Victimization Rate by Race, 1976–2004

Source: Compiled from Bureau of Justice Statistics data (Fox & Zawitz, 2006).

Again, based on the cases in which offender and victim race was known to be African American or white, the percentage of whites killed by whites was similar, at 85.7% (FBI, 2006a).

The good news is that official SHR data reveal declines in homicide victimization rates since 1976 among all races. As you can see in Figure 4.8, the decline in the homicide victimization rate has dropped precipitously for African Americans since the mid-1990s. The decline has been less for whites and others but a decline nonetheless. The gap in victimization rates between African Americans and other racial categories remains. However, because of the greater decrease in homicide victimization rates for African Americans as compared to other races, the gap has closed somewhat.

YEARS OF POTENTIAL LIFE LOST TO HOMICIDE

The National Center for Injury Prevention and Control provides a measure of premature mortality called the "years of potential life lost," or YPLL. In other words, if a man is murdered when he is 35 years old and the average life expectancy is 75 years, 40 years of potential life have been lost. Moreover, the NCIPC reports the YPLL to different causes such as heart disease, cancer, HIV, unintentional injury, and, relevant to this book, homicide.

Based on 2003 data, unintentional injury was the number-one cause of years of life lost in the United States before age 65. Unintentional injury was followed by cancer, heart disease, perinatal period deaths (immediately before or after birth), suicide, and then homicide at number six. Another way to consider this is that 18.5% of all the years of life lost were due to unintentional injury and 5% was due to homicide. After considering the data in this chapter about race and sex and homicide, it should be no surprise that the years of potential life lost vary by sex and race. Only 2.2% of the life years lost for white women were due to homicide. For white men, homicide was a larger contributor, with homicide responsible for 3.6% of the lost years. The figure grows to 4.3% for black females and 4.2% for Hispanic females. For Hispanic males, the percentage is considerably more, with 10.8% of all years lost due to homicide. Finally, the figure for black men is nearly five times higher than it is for white men. The number-one cause of years lost for black men is homicide, which is responsible for 15.4% of all the years lost for black men before age 65.

WEAPON USE

If you watched *CSI Miami* on November 14, 2005, you may remember that a woman was killed with a nail gun, and in the same episode Detective Ryan Wolf takes a nail to the eye. This may seem farfetched, but in 2001 a California man murdered his wife with a nail gun (as discussed in Chapter 8). Hardened homicide detectives will tell you there is no limit to what humans have used to murder. Guns, knives, and even clothing and cords for strangulation are fairly common. But you can probably think of other real cases in which the following have been used as weapons to murder others: Gatorade mixed with antifreeze or windshield wiper fluid, ice picks, iPods, cars, phone wires, and, of course, the hijacked airplanes used by terrorists on September 11, 2001.

The SHR categorize weapons into 16 different types (including 5 categories of firearms). It is clear in Table 4.3 and Figure 4.9 that guns predominate as murder

TABLE **4.3**

Weapons Used in 2004 U.S. Murders

Weapon	Number	Percentage
Total	14,121	100
Total firearms	9,326	66.0
Handguns	7,265	51.4
Rifles	393	2.8
Shotguns	507	3.6
Other guns	117	0.8
Firearm type unknown	1,044	7.4
Knives	1,866	13.2
Blunt objects	663	4.7
Personal weapons	933	6.6
Poison	11	0.1
Explosives	1	0.0
Fire	114	0.8
Narcotics	76	0.5
Drowning	15	0.1
Strangulation	155	1.1
Asphyxiation	105	0.7
Other or not stated	856	6.1

Source: Compiled from Federal Bureau of Investigation Statistics Data (Federal Bureau of Investigation, 2006a).

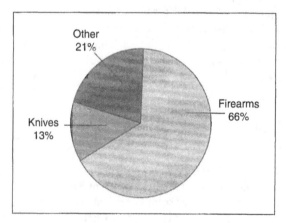

FIGURE **4.9**

Guns, Knives, and Other Weapons Used in 2004 Murders

Source: Compiled from Federal Bureau of Investigation Statistics Data (Federal Bureau of Investigation, 2006a).

weapons in the United States. Firearms were used as the murder weapon in 66% of all homicides in 2004, with handguns the most popular gun choice for homicide offenders. Knives (including other sharp instruments), personal weapons, and blunt objects were also common. When an offender uses his or her hands or feet to beat someone to death, it is categorized as a homicide by personal weapon. Hammers, bats, and pieces of wood are common blunt objects.

As discussed in Chapter 3, several data sources may be used by those who are researching homicide. Most of this chapter relies on data collected by the FBI. The CDC's National Center for Injury Prevention (NCIPC) data, however, may also be used to learn about weapon use in the United States. NCIPC data are categorized slightly different than FBI data. Nevertheless, the weapons used in 2003 homicides according to NCIPC data appear to be very similar to the weapons indicated in the 2004 FBI data. The NCIPC shows that firearms were used in 68% of homicides, cutting instruments were used in 15%, and other weapons were used in the remaining 17%. Table 4.4 includes the number of homicides and percentages for different weapons as categorized by the NCIPC.

BOX 4.3

Killer iPod

In March 2004, 23-year-old Arleen Mathers was arrested in Memphis, Tennessee, for first-degree murder. She allegedly bludgeoned her boyfriend with her iPod. After calling the police, Mathers showed the police the body of her 27-year-old boyfriend Brad Pulaski. He evidently died of internal bleeding after Mathers hit him repeatedly with the iPod after he apparently erased all of her music (Headlined News.com, 2004).

TABLE **4.4**
Weapons Used in 2003 U.S. Murders

Weapon	Number	Percentage
Total	17,732	100
Cut/Pierce	2,742	15.5
Drown	59	0.3
Fall	15	0.1
Fire	167	0.9
Firearm	11,920	67.2
Poison	81	0.5
Struck	222	1.3
Suffocation	670	3.8
Motor vehicle	51	0.3
Unspecified/Other	1,805	10.2

Source: Compiled from National Center for Injury Prevention and Control data (2003).

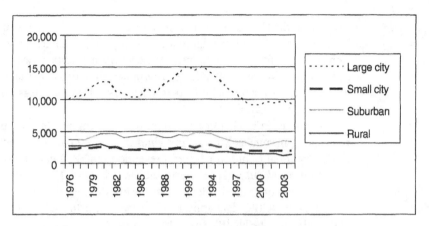

FIGURE 4.10
Homicide by City Size, 1976–2004
Source: Compiled from Bureau of Justice Statistics data (Fox & Zawitz, 2006).

COMMUNITY TYPES

The UCR also provides information about crime for different community types that range from the most densely populated Metropolitan Statistical Areas (MSAs) to less densely populated cities outside of MSAs, and the least densely populated areas known as nonmetropolitan counties outside of MSAs. Not surprisingly, most homicides and the highest rate of homicide occurred in the most densely populated areas. With 82.9% of the population in the United States, MSAs had 88.8% of the homicides with a rate of 5.9 per 100,000 residents. Ten percent of U.S. residents live in nonmetropolitan counties, and 10% of all 2004 U.S. homicides occurred in these counties for a rate of 3.6 homicides per 100,000 individuals. Finally, 6.8% of the U.S. population lives in cities outside of MSAs where 4.4% of U.S. homicides were committed in 2004. The rate of homicide at 3.5 per 100,000 residents in cities outside of MSAs was just under the rate for counties outside MSAs (Fox & Zawitz, 2004). The Bureau of Justice Statistics presents the data by city size (see Figure 4.10). The number of homicides in large cities drives the rate for the United States as a whole.

REGIONAL

Not only is homicide more common in cities, but it is also more common in the South. The Uniform Crime Report Program divides the United States into four regions to allow for crime comparisons across regions. Figure 4.11 shows the percentage of the U.S. population, the percentage of murders and nonnegligent manslaughters, and the murder rate for each region in 2004. As you can see, the

BOX 4.4

Most Murderous U.S. Cities*

What are your chances of being a murder victim or even a murder offender? Statistically, many variables affect the chances of any one individual being a homicide victim or offender. If we consider only the city in which you live, we might predict that your chances are greatest where the homicide rate is highest. In 2004, the 67 largest cities were ranked by homicide rate, and the top ten are as follows:

1. New Orleans
2. Baltimore
3. Detroit
4. Washington, D.C.
5. Saint Louis
6. Newark
7. Atlanta
8. Philadelphia
9. Oakland
10. Dallas

Criminologists Alfred Blumstein, Robert Friedman, and Richard Rosenfeld have created a formula that adjusts the city homicide rankings to account for the levels of poverty, racial disadvantage, economic instability, divorce, and other city-level measures believed to affect homicide rates. The idea behind the adjustment is to make the comparison across cities more equitable. Instead of comparing apples to oranges, the adjustment allows apples to be compared to apples. In this way, we may learn more about what policies and programs might be effective for decreasing homicide.

When the adjustments are made to the 2004 data, New Orleans, Baltimore, Washington D.C., Oakland, California, and Dallas remain in the top ten. However, cities such as Kansas City, Denver, Phoenix, Minneapolis, and San Francisco move up to the top ten. San Francisco makes the most dramatic climb from 30 in the unadjusted 2004 ranking to number 1 in the adjusted ranking. Atlanta has the most impressive descent, moving from number 15 to number 64 among the 67 large cities that are ranked. This means that San Francisco has a much larger rate than should be expected and Cleveland has a much lower rate than would be expected given the levels of poverty and other factors linked to homicide rates in those cities (Improving Crime Data Website, 2005).

*Cities ranked had populations of 250,000 or more.

Northeast is the least populous region of the United States, and it contributes least to the U.S. murder rate, and likewise the South is the most populous and contributes the most to the homicide totals. However, the rates for each region indicate that the South has more than its fair share of homicide. The murder rate for the Northeast

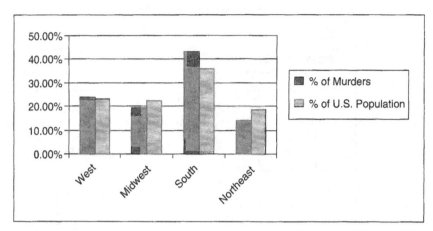

FIGURE 4.11
Population and Homicide Percentage by Region, 2004

BOX 4.5

Percentage Distribution of Homicide by Month in 2004

Homicide tends to follow seasonal patterns with a greater percentage occurring in warm months. You can see the percentages of homicide by month for 2004 in the table here. What do you think explains the greater percentages in summer months?

Month	Percentage
January	7.9
February	6.7
March	8.4
April	8.0
May	8.8
June	8.3
July	9.5
August	9.4
September	8.6
October	8.3
November	7.9
December	8.1

Source: Compiled from Federal Bureau of Investigation Statistics Data (Federal Bureau of Investigation, 2006a).

and Midwest were both under 5 per 100,000, and the rate in the West was 5.7 per 100,000 persons in 2004. The South, however, had a rare 6.6 per 100,000 in 2004. Possible explanations for the greater rates in the South are discussed in Chapter 7 in the discussion on confrontational homicide.

CROSS-NATIONAL COMPARISONS

In general, the numbers of homicides in a particular country are mostly static over time, although they vary by country (Johnson, 2005). Moreover, the homicide rate in the United States remains consistently higher than the homicide rate in many other countries. In Table 4.5, you can see the rates for several different countries. Australia's homicide rates, for example, varied between 1.7 and 2.0 per 100,000 between 1989 and 1999. Since 1989, the total number of homicide victims per year in Australia varied from a low of 297 in 1997–1998 to a high of 381 in 2001–2002, but because the Australian population is growing the rate never exceeded 2.0 per 100,000 with the 2001–2002 rate being 1.9 per 100,000 (Mouzos, 2000; Mouzos & Rushforth, 2003). Data from a 2001 report on international criminal justice statistics indicate that the average European Union homicide rate for the years 1999 to 2001 was 1.59 per 100,000. The rate in England and Wales was 1.61, the rate in Scotland was 2.16, and in Northern Ireland it was 2.65 per 100,000. Countries with notably low rates include Norway, Japan, Spain, Switzerland, and Denmark, with homicide rates between 0.95 and 1.12 per 100,000 (Barclay & Tavares, 2003).

TABLE 4.5
International Homicide Data for Select Countries

Country	Average Homicide Rate*	Country	Average Homicide Rate*
Norway	0.95	Australia	1.87
Denmark	1.02	Poland	2.05
Japan	1.05	Scotland	2.16
Spain	1.12	Hungary	2.34
Switzerland	1.12	Romania	2.41
Germany	1.15	New Zealand	2.50
Portugal	1.17	Czech Republic	2.52
Slovenia	1.18	Slovakia	2.55
Austria	1.26	Northern Ireland	2.65
Greece	1.38	Turkey	2.67
Cypress	1.39	Finland	2.86
Ireland	1.42	U.S.A.	5.56
Netherlands	1.51	Estonia	10.60
England & Wales	1.61	Lithuania	10.62
Malta	1.63	Russia	22.05
France	1.73	South Africa	55.86
Canada	1.77		

*Average homicide rate is measured per 100,000 population for the years 1999–2001. The homicide rates in different cities across the world also demonstrate the relatively high rates in the United States. At the low end, Ottawa, Canada had an average rate of 0.94, and Tokyo, Japan's rate was 1.21 for the years 1999–2001. In grave contrast, Moscow had a rate of 18.38 and Washington, D.C. had a rate of 42.87.

Source: Barclay and Tavares (2003).

BOX 4.6

Alcohol, Drugs, Mental Illness, and Homicide in England and Wales

An in-depth study of homicide data in England and Wales for the years 1996 to 1999 found that more than two out of every five offenders (42%) had a history of alcohol problems, and 40% had a history of drug problems. These histories were reflected in the study's finding that drug or alcohol misuse played a "contributory role" in 40% of all homicides. Drugs played a major role in only 6, or 1%, of the 1,594 homicides and a minor role in 14%; alcohol played a minor role in 6% and a major role in 14% of all homicides during the period studied. Fewer than 1 of 5 homicides (17%) was committed by individuals with severe mental illness and substance use problems. The authors of the study concluded that a public health approach to homicide should focus on alcohol and drug use over issues of mental illness (Shaw, Hunt, Flynn, et al., 2006).

Although the United States does not have the highest homicide rate in the world, it is in the top five for countries with viable data listed in Table 4.5. As you can see, the United States has a rate of 5.56 per 100,000. Estonia and Lithuania each have rates nearly twice that of the United States, and Russia's rate is nearly four times that of the United States with a rate of 22.05 per 100,000. Although the rate in these countries is very high, the rate in South Africa in 2001 was astronomical, at 55.86 per 100,000 (Barclay & Tavares, 2003).

SUMMARY

This chapter reviewed current homicide patterns and trends. Overall rates and trends that reveal that homicide is decreasing in the United States are covered before the chapter moves on to different categorizations of homicide. Because not all homicides are solved (see Chapter 14), the circumstances and victim/offender relationship are not always known. However, for homicides in which we know the circumstance, homicide involving argument are the most common. When the offender is known, it is most likely that the victim and offender know one another as acquaintances, intimate partners, or family members. In terms of sex, homicide is overwhelmingly a male activity with men making up the majority of both victims and offenders. Young people ages 17 to 29 years account for the majority of victims and offenders. Whites outnumber other races and ethnic groups as homicide offenders and victims. African Americans are close behind, and if homicide is measured as a rate, African Americans predominate as both victims and offenders. After the demographics are reviewed, the chapter included a section on years of potential life lost to homicide that reflects what the demographic data predict: the years of life lost because of homicide is highest among African American men. The chapter also includes a section on weapon use, and it is clear regardless of which data set is used that firearms are the most popular deliberate killing instrument in the United States. The chapter ends with information on the variance of homicide across community types, regions, and nations.

CHAPTER QUESTIONS

1. Has homicide increased or decreased in the United States in the twenty first century?
2. Why is it preferable to compare homicide rates instead of the number of homicides?
3. What does the trend in homicide look like since 1990?
4. What is the most common known homicide circumstance?
5. What is the most common known victim/offender relationship type for homicide?
6. Wolfgang noted that homicide offenders were most likely to be family members in his 1958 homicide study. Has this changed, and if so, how?
7. Are women or men more likely to be homicide offenders?
8. Are women or men more likely to be homicide victims?
9. What is the peak age for homicide offending?
10. Among known offenders, what racial group predominates as victims and offenders?
11. What do rates tell us about race and homicide?
12. What is meant by "years of potential life lost"?
13. As a percentage of all years of life lost, what group loses the most years to homicide?
14. What is the most common weapon used to commit homicide in the United States?
15. Where are homicide rates most likely in terms of community type, U.S. regions, and nations in the world?

REFERENCES

Barclay, Gordon, and Cynthia Tavares. 2003. *International Comparisons of Criminal Justice Statistics 2001*. London: United Kingdom Home Office, Research Development and Statistics Directorate (October 2004).

Blumstein, Alfred, and Richard Rosenfeld. 1998. "Explaining Recent Trends in U.S. Homicide Rates." *Journal of Criminal Law and Criminology*, 88(4): 1175–1216.

Federal Bureau of Investigation (FBI). 2006a. *Crime in the United States 2004*. Web version updated February 17, 2006. Retrieved March 24, 2006, from http://www.fbi.gov/ucr / cius_04/offenses_reported/violent_crime/murder.html

Federal Bureau of Investigation (FBI). 2006b. *Preliminary Annual Uniform Crime Report, 2005*. June 12, 2006. Retrieved September 30, 2006, from http://www.fbi.gov/ucr/2005preliminary/ index.htm

Fox, James Alan, and Marianne W. Zawitz. 2006. *Homicide Trends in the U.S.* Washington, D.C.: Bureau of Justice Statistics. http://www.ojp.usdoj.gov/bjs/homicide/tables/vracetab.htm

Headlined News.Com. 2004. "iPod Used in Domestic Homicide." *Headlined News.com.* Posted March 5, 2004, at http://www.liquidgeneration.com/rumormill/ipod_killing.html

Improving Crime Data Website. 2005. "City Homicide Rankings Adjusted for Differences in Crime-Producing Factors." Georgia State University Statistical Analysis Bureau. Accessed online at http://www.cjgsu.net/initiatives/ICD.htm

Johnson, Carolyn Harris. 2005. *Come with Daddy: Child Murder-Suicide After Family Breakdown.* Crawley: University of Western Australia Press.

Martinez, Ramiro. 1997. "Homicide Among Miami's Ethnic Groups." *Homicide Studies,* 1(1): 17–34.

Mouzos, Jenny. 2000. *Homicidal Encounters: A Study of Homicide in Australia, 1989–1999.* Canberra: Australian Institute of Criminology.

Mouzos, Jenny, and Catherine Rushforth. 2003. *Family Homicide in Australia.* Canberra: Australian Institute of Criminology.

National Violent Death Reporting System (NVDRS). 2005. *Homicides and Suicides—National Violent Death Reporting System, United States, 2003–2004.* Centers for Disease Control and Prevention. Accessed online at http://www.cdc.gov/mmwr/preview/mmwrhtml/mm5526a1.htm

Regoeczi, Wendy C., and Terance D. Miethe. 2003. "Taking on the Unknown: A Qualitative Comparative Analysis of Unknown Relationship Homicides." *Homicide Studies,* 7(3): 211–234.

Shaw, Jenny, Isabelle M. Hunt, Sandra Flynn, et al. 2006. "The Role of Alcohol and Drugs in Homicides in England and Wales." *Addiction,* 101(8): 1117–1124.

Wolfgang, Marvin. 1958. *Patterns of Criminal Homicide.* Philadelphia: University of Philadelphia Press.

Zahn, Margaret A., and Patricia L. McCall. 1999. "Trends and Patterns of Homicide in the 20th-Century United States." In M. Dwayne Smith and Margaret A. Zahn, eds., *Homicide: A Sourcebook of Social Research* (pp. 9–23). Thousand Oaks, CA: Sage.

Chapter 5

BIOLOGICAL AND PSYCHOLOGICAL EXPLANATIONS FOR HOMICIDE

The oldest explanations for homicidal offending are most likely supernatural explanations such as demonic possession or evil (Rasche, 1996). Even today we see some inkling of these explanations in the popular culture. One only needs to listen to how homicides are described by crime writers, newscasters, and others in various media outlets. For instance, in an article on Court TV's Crime Library Web page, Katherine Ramsland (2005) uses evil to explain a violent homicide that she describes as follows:

> To know evil, you have only to stand on the road in Jasper, Texas, where on June 7, 1998, three white men offered a ride to a 49-year-old black man, James Byrd Jr., who was on his way home from an anniversary party. Instead of taking him where he wanted to go, they beat, kicked, and tortured him merely for the color of his skin, and then spray-painted his face black before chaining him by the ankles to the back of their truck. As they sped down an isolated logging road, dragging him for nearly three miles, he tried keeping his head up, but his skin ripped off, his bones broke, and his elbows were shattered to the bone. When his head hit a culvert, it was ripped off, along with his right arm. What was left of his torso was dumped in front of a church for its black congregation to find.

Similarly, Jeffrey Dahmer, a serial killer who murdered 16 young men and dismembered their bodies, has been quoted as saying the following:

> Am I just an extremely evil person or is it some sort of satanic influence or what? I have no idea . . . do you? . . . from all that the Bible says, there are forces that have a direct or indirect influence on people's behavior (Masters, 1993: 112, as quoted in Mitchell, 1997).

61

There is no doubt that the crimes Ramsland describes and those committed by Jeffrey Dahmer are horrifically violent and disgusting. I remember feeling sickened when I first heard about Dahmer's crimes and those committed against James Byrd Jr. However, as with most scientists, I do not think we can explain the shockingly brutal murders of Byrd or of those young men cannibalized by Dahmer by saying that the offenders were evil. The field of criminology is based on the premise that crime and criminals can be studied scientifically. Granted, scientific studies and theorizing about criminals and crime is varied, with explanations ranging from those based purely on biological influences to those based entirely on environmental causes. As it turns out, few theories actually directly address homicide offending in particular. There are books and classes, however, dedicated to criminological theory. This chapter presents an overview of several theories or explanations of crime that have been or could be applied to homicide. It begins with an outline of early deterministic theories involving biological and physiological explanations. Then the discussions shifts to more modern biological and psychological explanations including personality disorders and psychopathy.

POSITIVISM

With the scientific discovery taking center stage in the eighteenth century, positivist explanations for crime came into favor. In direct contrast to classical thinkers who are discussed in Chapter 6, positivist theorists postulated that human behavior is influenced, if not caused, by factors that individuals cannot control. In other words, behaviors are determined. Humans do not have freedom of mind to decide whether they would do crime, but instead something about their makeup determines whether or not they would be criminals.

BIOLOGY, BODIES, AND OFFENDING

Cesare Lombroso (1825–1909) is sometimes credited with being the father of criminal positivism because of his dedication to the scientific study to criminality. In 1876, Lombroso wrote *The Criminal Man* in which he proposed the idea that some individuals are born to be criminals. Lombroso, a professor of psychiatry and anthropology, performed many postmortem examinations on convicts. The observations he made when he performed autopsies and his understanding of physiognomy (the study of physical appearance and behavior) and phrenology (the study of skull shapes) led Lombroso to begin to argue that criminals were physically different from noncriminals. Lombroso found that many of the criminals whose bodies he examined had physical deformities such as asymmetrical faces, flat noses, fleshy lips, unusual size ears, protruding jaws, and long arms. Influenced by the emphasis on scientific study of his time, he took careful measurements of convicted criminals to test and record his observations. His data led him to conclude that the physical abnormalities he witnessed in criminals were indicative of the relationship between biology and crime. Furthermore, likely influenced by Darwin's ideas, he proposed that criminals are biological throwbacks to an earlier evolutionary stage. He believed criminals to be more primitive and less highly evolved than their noncriminal counterparts. Lombroso used the term *atavistic* to describe these less evolved physically degenerate criminals (Fleming, 2000).

Lombroso, however, did not classify all criminals as atavists or "born criminals." He identified two additional types of criminals. The second group were the *insane criminals,* who, according to Lombroso, were idiots or imbeciles who had low intelligence and committed cruel, impulsive, and obscene acts. Lombroso called the third group criminaloids, who were not mentally ill but those who under the "right conditions" would commit crimes of passion including homicide (Meithe & McCorkle, 2001).

Lombroso's work on the biological criminal spawned much scientific work that attempted to test and build on his ideas. Among those who followed in Lombroso's footsteps are his students Raffaele Garofalo (1852–1934) and Enrico Ferri (1856–1928). Ferri introduced his own typology of criminals in which he too focused on their physical makeup. Ferri's (1917) classification included the insane, born, occasional, habitual, and passionate criminal. Garofalo (1914) was more psychological in his identification of criminals as murderers, violent criminals, criminals deficient in probity, and lascivious criminals.

Lombroso's work and those who followed him, although an important part of the history of criminology, have been greatly criticized because of their biased samples and lack of objectivity. Furthermore, these theories have not stood up to scientific scrutiny. Even as early as 1913, Charles Goring refuted the connection between physicality and criminal offending. In his book *The English Convict,* Goring found no support for atavism when he compared the measurement of 3,000 English prisoners and a control group. The idea that biology is related to criminality is still alive and well, but the belief that we can recognize criminals by their physical features has mostly died. Nevertheless, sometimes the public is still surprised to find that attractive individuals have committed heinous crimes. In fact, some offenders are believed to have used their attractiveness to ensnare their victims. Both Ted Bundy, who was executed in 1989 for the rape and murder of 28 women, and Dahmer, who killed at least 15 young men and cannibalized many of them, were thought by many to be attractive.

WILLIAM SHELDON AND BODY TYPES

Approximately 75 years after Lombroso first argued for a link between biology and criminal offending that was expressed in the physical makeup of criminals, Ernst Kretschmer (1888–1964) and then William Sheldon (1898–1977) classified those who did crime by their body type. Kretschmer studied over 4,000 criminals based on his classification of three body types including *leptosome* or *asthenic* (tall and thin), *athletic* (well-developed muscles), and (3) *pyknic* (short and fat). He found that violent criminals tended to be athletic, petty criminals were asthenic, and pyknics were most likely to be those who committed crimes involving deception and fraud. Thus, if this theory was valid, we would expect homicide offenders to be athletic.

> ## BOX 5.1
> ### Eugenics
> ___
> The term *eugenics* was introduced by Charles Darwin's cousin Sir Francis Galton. Originally introduced to describe the science of studying and improving on human genetics, eugenics is widely viewed negatively and not taken seriously today. Eugenics focuses on improving future generations of humans by encouraging only the most fit to procreate and limiting or preventing the less fit from having children. It is likely that whoever is in power will believe they and those like them are the most fit. The German Holocaust is one example of the introduction of eugenic principles in which we see one group, who defined themselves as Aryans, to be the most desirable humans.
>
> The belief that criminality is biological could lead to a eugenic-type approach to ending crime. If a society believes in eugenic principles, then whoever the powerful in society believe to be criminal may be prevented from procreating through severe birth control methods or even death (*Columbia Electronic Encyclopedia,* 2003).

It is likely that you have heard of Sheldon's classification theory because it is still used to describe body types in relation to exercise and body building. Sheldon argued there are three basic body builds or *somatotypes*: endomorph (fat and soft), ectomorph (thin and fragile), and mesomorph (muscular and athletic). Based on studies of juveniles, Sheldon and others found that mesomorphs were more likely to be criminals. Like Lombroso's studies, however, the theory that body type reflects criminality has been largely disproved, challenged for methodological failings, or avoided because of the controversial policy implications that may result from the belief that criminality is purely biological (Barkan, 1997; Glueck & Glueck, 1956; Sheldon, 1949). For more information, see Box 5.1 on eugenics.

HEREDITY AND GENES

Early studies about criminal families convinced some criminologists that the tendency toward crime was inherited. In his 1877 study, Richard Dugdale found six members of the Jukes family imprisoned in a New York county jail. Dugdale traced the Jukes family tree and found a great number of the family had been imprisoned over the past 200 years. Despite the fact that Juke family history failed to prove whether criminality or environment led to criminality, Dugdale's study was seen as support for the argument that deviance is genetically determined (Barkan, 1997; Hurwitz & Christiansen, 1983).

Similarly, Henry Goddard, an American psychologist, collected data on a family he called the Kallikaks. Seen as an improvement over Dugdale's Jukes study,

Goddard (1912) was able to compare the descendants of Martin Kallikak who fathered children both with his upstanding wife and with his "moronic" mistress. Because the descendants of the extramarital affair were more likely to be criminal and have other problems such as alcoholism as compared with the products of the legitimate union, it was believed "feeblemindedness" and criminality were the result of genetics. The fact that the "good" Kallikak descendants grew up in positive environments and had wealth, whereas the "bad" Kallikaks were impoverished, was overlooked by those who attributed the differences in the two lines to genetics (Barkan, 1997; Fishbein, 1996).

Much like these earlier studies on the Jukes and the Kallikaks, journalist Fox Butterfield has written about at least two families who appear to be passing criminal behavior from one generation to the next. In his book *All God's Children*, Butterfield (1996) traces the family history of Willie Bosket, one of New York's most dangerous criminals. From generation to generation, the young Bosket males find themselves in trouble with the police. Similarly, Butterfield wrote a cover story for the *New York Times* in 2002 on the family of Dale Vincent Bogle of Oregon, the patriarch of what appears to be a family of criminals. At least 28 members of Bogle's family had been convicted of crimes in Oregon. Bogle, who was known by the nickname "Rooster" before he died, has left a legacy of criminality. Tracey Bogle, Rooster's youngest son, has been convicted of crimes such as kidnapping and rape, and Tony, another son, has been convicted of murder in Arizona. The family penchant for crime goes beyond Rooster's sons. Rooster's wife, brothers, sisters, and grandchildren all have criminal records. Even Louis Bogle, Rooster's nephew, managed to rack up 25 convictions before he became paralyzed from the neck down as the result of an attack by a drug gang to whom he owed money (Butterfield, 2002).

The Bogles and Boskets are not the only modern families to share a history of crime. A 1991 U.S. Department of Justice survey of state prison inmates found that 37% of the inmates had an immediate family member who had also been incarcerated. Nearly a third (31%) had a brother who had served time, 6% had a father who had been imprisoned, and 4% of their sisters and 2% of their mothers had served time (Beck, Gilliard, Greenfeld, et al., 1993). These statistics, along with the case studies by Butterfield, support the veteran police officer's stance that criminality is often a family affair. However, whether the Bosket and Bogle families have passed their criminal tendencies on through their genes or their teachings or some combination is a much debated question.

TWIN STUDIES

Twin studies are believed by some to be the ultimate test of whether genetic or environmental factors best explain criminality (Hurwitz & Christiansen, 1983). Popular in Germany and Denmark, twin studies compare monozygotic (identical) twins and dizygotic (nonidentical, or fraternal) twins. Because twins raised together would share practically identical environments, a comparison of monozygotic and dizygotic twins would help discern how much behavior may be explained by genetics and how much is related to environmental factors. Because identical twins share 100% of their genetic makeup and dizygotic twins share as much genetically as any siblings, more similarities among monozygotic twins as opposed to dizygotic twins would suggest that genetics is more powerful than the environment in explaining behavior.

Dating back to the first systematic study of criminality in twins by German physiologist Johannes Lange in 1929, twin studies have measured the concordance rates of monozygotic and dizygotic twins separately to determine heritable components of crime (Hurwitz & Christiansen, 1983; Raine, 1993). A *concordance rate* is basically a measure that reflects the proportion (percentage) of twin pairs in which both twins have a particular trait such as criminal offending in common. To determine whether genetic influences or environmental influences explain the trait being studied, the concordance rates of the monozygotic and dizygotic twins are compared. Environmental factors would explain a trait if the rates of the trait were found to be similarly high among both identical and fraternal twins. However, if concordance rates are higher among the monozygotic twins as compared to the dizygotic twins, then genetic influences likely explain the trait in question (Raine, 1993). For example, in Lange's study of 30 pairs of twins, dizygotic twins had a concordance rate for criminality of only 11.8%, whereas monozygotic twins had a 76.9% concordance rate. In other words, among the 13 pairs of identical male twins, when one twin had been imprisoned, the other had been imprisoned in 77% of the cases. Among the nonidentical twins, when one twin had been incarcerated, the other had been imprisoned in only 12% of the cases. Thus Lange concluded that heredity is an important cause of crime (Hurwitz & Christiansen, 1983; Vold & Bernard, 1986).

Although studies with bigger samples than Lange's 30 have shown less difference in concordance rates between monozygotic and dizygotic twins, the evidence presented in twin studies still suggests that identical twins are more alike in their criminal offending than nonidentical twins, even same-sex fraternal twins (Farrington, 1998; Hurwitz & Christiansen, 1983). In a meta-analysis (a synthesis of several other studies), for example, Adrian Raine (1993) found that the concordance rate for identical twins was 52%, whereas it was only 21% for fraternal twins. Nevertheless, there are those who criticize the conclusion that twin studies prove that criminal offending, including homicide offending, can be explained by genetics. One criticism is that identical twins because they look more alike may be treated more alike and thus have a more similar environment than would dizygotic twins (Farrington, 1998). Other critics have noted that less than rigorous methods (whether the twins appeared identical) have been used to determine whether twins are monozygotic or dizygotic (Hurwitz & Christiansen, 1983). Still, twin studies consistently suggest there is likely some genetic predisposition for crime (Hurwitz & Christiansen, 1983; Farrington, 1998; Fishbein, 1996; Raine, 1993). However, it is important to remember that a predisposition is not the same as certainty and may only result in criminal offending under the right (or shall we say wrong?) environmental conditions. In fact, in a recent review of the history of twin studies, Rhee and Waldman (2002) concluded that genetic factors had a strong influence on whether individuals would engage in antisocial behavior. However, the influence of environmental factors was even stronger.

ADOPTION STUDIES

Adoption studies have also been a popular method used to investigate the link between biology and criminal offending. Adoption studies are based on the idea that a child raised by someone other than the biological parent(s) will share inherited genetic material with the biological parent but they will not be influenced environmentally (or socialized) by the biological parents. Likewise, they are environmentally influenced but not genetically influenced by the adoptive parent(s). Thus criminological researchers would expect children to be more similar to their adoptive parents in criminal offending if environment is more important than genetics for determining criminality. Conversely, if genetics is more causally related to criminality, it would be expected that adopted children would be more similar to their biological parent(s) as opposed to their adoptive parents.

The results of adoption studies are similar in their conclusions to the twin studies. Adopted children tend to commit criminal or deviant acts at rates more similar to their biological parent(s) and less similar to their adoptive parent(s) (Farrington, 1998; Raine, 1993). In one of the most discussed twin studies, Hutchings and Mednick (1977) studied all male adoptees in Copenhagen born between 1927 and 1941. As shown in Figure 5.1, they found that if only the boy's biological father had a criminal record, the boy was more likely to have a record (22%) than if only his adoptive father had a record (11.5%). Additionally, if both the biological and adoptive father had a criminal record, the boy was even more likely to have a record as well (36.2%) (Vold & Bernard, 1986).

Like twin studies, however, adoption studies have not ended the argument forever. As Farrington (1998) notes, some of the children had interactions with their biological parents before they were adopted and thus may have been environmentally affected by these parents. Additionally, adopted children possibly were labeled by their adoptive parents or others who knew of their biological parents' criminal behavior, and thus negative labeling could explain their offending behavior.

		Biological Father	
		Criminal Record	No Record
Adoptive Father	Criminal Record	36.2%	11.5%
	No Record	22.0%	10.5%

FIGURE 5.1
Hutchings and Mednick's Adoption Study Results Showing Percentage of Boys with Criminal Record

ADOPTED TWINS STUDIES

Ideally, the best study to determine the influence of genetics and environment on criminality would be an experiment in which we could compare a random sample of identical twins raised together to a random sample of identical twins in which the twins were separated at birth and raised apart. If environment is more important than genetics, we would expect twins raised together to be more similar than those raised apart. I hope you are thinking this would be a good test but an impossible one. We certainly would not want purposely to do an experiment in which we separated twins. Thus researchers must rely on finding cases where this has happened (rather than making it happen). And perhaps fortunately for many twin siblings, not enough twins have been discovered to have been reared apart for criminologists to come to any definite conclusions, but the studies that do exist suggest both genetics and environment are important in determining both our noncriminal and criminal behaviors.

A study by Grove and colleagues (1990), for example, suggests that genetics may be important in some behaviors that may be linked to criminality including alcohol and drug abuse/use. They compared 32 sets of adult identical twins who had been separated at birth or very shortly after birth and who were raised apart. They found that heredity could explain 41% of childhood conduct disorder and 28% of adult antisocial personality disorder (Farrington, 1998; Grove, Eckert, Heston, et al., 1990). Nonetheless, these are lower than expected based on other twin studies, making us very cautious about the results of other twin studies. Furthermore, as the authors note, their study is based on a few cases and on a young sample of individuals who still may develop alcohol or drug abuse problems.

An important point now argued by those on both sides of the issue—those who believe environmental factors are most important and those who believe genetics to be omnipotent in explaining criminal behavior—is that predispositions to certain behaviors may be influenced by environment. Just like height or weight, we may have the genes that should make us tall and wide, but our access to good nutrition (our environment) influences whether we meet our full potential (Farrington, 1998). Furthermore, even with the great progress made in genetic research with the genome project in which all the human genes were sequenced, scientific evidence suggests there is no one gene, or even a small number of genes, that predict criminality (Morley & Hall, 2003).

CHROMOSOMES AND XYY MALES

Crime has also been linked to chromosomal abnormalities. As you may remember from your biology or anthropology courses, we each have 23 pairs of chromosomes in the nucleus of our cells. The chromosomes carry our genes, which govern many of our characteristics such as our eye and skin color and our sex. The pair of sex chromosomes in most human females consists of two X chromosomes; most males have one X and one Y chromosome. Occasionally, a male child is born with an extra Y chromosome. Referred to as XYY males, research in the 1960s suggested these males were overrepresented in mental institutions and prisons and had a tendency to be violent (Jones, 2000). However, more recent studies reflect the current belief that XYY is not linked to violence including homicide offending or criminality. Young XYY males tend to be more energetic than XY males during childhood, and they may be, on average, slightly taller than XY males. Finally, despite earlier claims, XYY males are of average intelligence, stable workers, and they can father children with no risk to their offspring because the XYY syndrome is not heritable but a genetic abnormality (Nielsen, 1998; Raine, 1993).

HORMONES

Scientists have also studied the possible links between various hormones and violence including homicide. Although it is clear that an imbalance in hormonal levels may cause a variety of physical disorders such as the growth disorder called acromegaly, the connection between homicide and hormones is much less clear. Several studies find a correlation between levels of testosterone, adrenalin, estrogen, and progesterone and violence or homicide offending. However, as you will learn in the sections to follow, the links between hormones and homicide are uncertain.

Testosterone

The hormone testosterone is a steroid, produced naturally in the bodies of both males and females. However, testosterone is best known as the hormone that regulates the growth of male genitalia and male secondary sex characteristics, including muscularity, facial hair, and a deep voice. Based on the assumption that males are more aggressive than females, researchers have investigated whether testosterone may have something to do with violence. Olweus's studies of the effects of testosterone are often cited as supportive of such a link. Olweus and his colleagues (1986, 1988) found a connection between testosterone levels and self-reported aggression in adolescent males. Most of the studies like Olweus's studies that test the link between testosterone and aggressiveness or violence have examined males. However, a study in 1988 found that among women prisoners who were analyzed, those who had committed unprovoked assaults had higher levels of testosterone than those who were violent in response to a physical assault (Dabbs, Ruback, Frady, et al., 1988). Examining the relationship for testosterone and homicide specifically as opposed to the more inclusive category of violence, a study in 2001 found that inmates who had higher levels of testosterone were more likely to have killed an acquaintance and to have planned the action than those who had lower levels of testosterone (Dabbs, Riad, & Chance, 2001).

Although there does appear to be much evidence that suggest testosterone is linked to aggression, violence, and even particular types of homicide, Raine (1993) has emphasized that this is simply a link. We do not know the direction of the link. It could be that aggression causes testosterone levels to increase, and some evidence suggests that it does (Raine, 1993). As with other *biological* explanations discussed in this chapter, testosterone is only one of many factors that may be related to violence. Family support and living conditions have also been linked to hormonal levels, which in turn may sometimes be connected to violent behavior (Raine, 1993).

Adrenaline

Adrenaline, also known as epinephrine, is another hormone linked to violence. Like testosterone, you have probably heard of adrenaline. It is a hormone that usually increases when we are under stress. It causes our cortisol levels to rise, it makes our heart rate increase, it may make us perspire, and it increases our alertness. Unlike the positive relationship between testosterone and violence, the relationship between adrenaline and violence is believed to be a negative one. It is hypothesized that individuals who are violent may need higher levels of stimulation to arouse them (Mitchell, 1997). Thus those who commit criminal offenses may have lower levels of adrenaline than those who do not partake in criminal behaviors. Olweus (1987) found a negative relationship between adrenaline and aggression. Other studies, however, suggest that both alcohol and testosterone may interact with cortisol, making this relationship complex just as it is with testosterone. The experts agree and the research suggests again and again that there is no one cause for violence or homicidal offending in humans.

Premenstrual Syndrome

As I noted when discussing testosterone, most research exploring the connection between hormones and violence has focused on men. However, some research has explored the relationship between estrogen and progesterone levels and women's offending behavior. Parallel to testosterone, estrogen and progesterone are produced in both men's and women's bodies, although progesterone and estrogen are most closely linked to women's menstrual cycle and pregnancy. Further, some people have theorized there may be a link between fluctuations in estrogen and progesterone and other hormones linked to menstruation and pregnancy and women's offending behavior. Perhaps the most influential study supporting this notion was one conducted by Dalton (1961), who studied a sample of 156 newly convicted women in England. Dalton found that 46% of these women had committed their crimes either four days prior or four days after their menstrual cycle (Raine, 1993).

A tremendous amount of criticism has been leveled at connecting women's menstruation and their offending behaviors. First, it is well known that stress can influence menstrual cycles, and thus an increase in stress such as committing a crime or being arrested could impact on women's menstrual cycles. Just as with testosterone, the direction of any correlation found is not clear. Second, and particularly important for the study of homicide, the women in Dalton's study, as with most women arrested for crime, were arrested for nonviolent crimes. Third, as with studies that attempt to link race to crime, studies linking women's biology and negative behavior appear to receive more attention when women are making progress toward equality (Chrisler & Caplan, 2002; Faludi, 1991; see Box 5.2 about PMS and homicide). Fourth, women's experiences with menstruation appear to be influenced as much by culture as by hormones. The manifestations of any so-called symptoms

BOX 5.2

PMS and Homicide

In the late 1970s, women in many Western nations began to make strides toward equality in public life as a result of the women's movements in many countries. Women were working their way into public life, up the corporate ladder and into leadership positions. However, in the mid-1980s with Reagan leading the United States and Thatcher leading the United Kingdom (UK), conservatives began to chip away at the progress women were making (Faludi, 1991). In an intriguing paper, Chrisler and Caplan (2002) argue it is no surprise that biological explanations for women's behavior became popular again in the mid-1980s. Women's biology and the fact that many women can potentially bear children was used in the past as a reason for women not to participate in sports, education, and much of public life. In the 1980s, it was being used as an explanation for women's offending behavior, especially in the UK.

Two headline-grabbing murder trials in the UK riveted attention on Premenstrual syndrome (PMS) as an explanation for women's behavior. In the first, Craddock, a barmaid who had previous psychological problems and a history of violence, was arrested for killing a coworker by stabbing her to death during a disagreement. In the second case, a woman used her car to ram her married and abusive lover into a lamppost. The attorneys for both these women argued that they had killed because of their premenstrual hormonal fluctuations that "could turn placid women into dangerous criminals" (Chrisler & Caplan, 2002). In the first case, Craddock received a sentence of probation and court-ordered progesterone injections. In the second, the court reduced the charge to manslaughter because of exceptional circumstances, and she was also put on probation with restrictions such as no alcohol and the directive to eat well (Easteal, 1993).

Perhaps as a result of the publicity of these two cases, late luteal phase dysphoric disorder (LLPPD, the precursor to PMS) was added to the third edition of the *Diagnostic and Statistical Manual of Mental Disorders* (*DSM-III*). Interestingly, Paula Caplan reported being interviewed by a reporter who wanted to cover the debates over adding LLPPD to the *DSM-III*, and her editor told her he was not interested in the story. However, when it looked as if Kim Campbell would be elected to head the Progressive Conservative Party and become Canada's first woman prime minister, the editor decided to cover the story about LLPPD. Chrisler and Caplan (2002) report that this was an attempt to prevent the Progressive Conservative Party from winning the election by introducing the idea that women, including Kimberly Campbell, behave irrationally once a month and thus are not good leaders (Chrisler & Caplan, 2002).

The use of PMS as a defense has been used periodically in the United States, Australia, and the UK, but it has failed to catch on as a popular defense in the United States, perhaps because of the lack of medical evidence to support it. Even famed criminal attorney F. Lee Bailey noted that to use the PMS defense, a lawyer would need to be certain to have the medical evidence to back it up (Easteal, 1993).

associated with menstrual cycles are more likely in Western societies than in non-Western societies, and moreover, the symptoms vary by society (Chrisler & Caplan, 2002).

NEUROCHEMICAL AND HORMONAL FACTORS

Serotonin, a neurotransmitter or chemical stored in brain cells that carries information between these cells, has been found to be linked to offending. However, to measure serotonin a painful spinal tap is needed, so there are few studies that examine serotonin and criminal behavior and the ones that exist have small samples. One of the largest studies was done by Moffitt and colleagues (1997) in New Zealand. In this longitudinal study of over 1,000 children who were studied from the age of 3, the researchers found that at the age of 21 years, men who had been convicted of violence and those who self-reported high levels of violence had higher blood serotonin levels when they were younger than those who were less violent.

PSYCHOPHYSIOLOGICAL FACTORS

One area of criminological research that continues to flourish explores the connection between psychophysiological factors and crime. Psychophysiological measures of arousal and emotions such as heart rate, skin conductance, and electroencephalographic (EEG) activity have been linked to delinquent and criminal behavior (Farrington, 1998; Raine, 1993). Although not drawing a link directly between psychophysiological factors and homicide, in his review of the literature, Raine (1993) makes the argument that psychophysiological factors are correlated with antisocial and criminal behavior. Raine (1993) reports that skin conductance tests that use electrodes to measure the body's response to stimulation show that antisocial individuals (psychopaths) are underaroused by such tests in comparison to social or so-called normal individuals. Similarly, studies measuring heart rates find lower resting heart rates in "antisocials" (Raine, 1993: 190). EEG studies also suggest that antisocials are less aroused. EEG is recorded by placing electrodes on specific locations on the scalp that measure electrical activity in the brain. Although researchers suggest that violent offenders have abnormal brain patterns (electrical activity in the brain), there is still much inconsistency in the findings of this research, making it difficult to make any definitive conclusions.

Raine (1993: 166–172) notes, however, that one of the most replicable findings regarding biology and criminality is that antisocial or criminal people tend to have relatively low heart rates. Farrington notes this was true in his study of Cambridge youth where heart rate was measured at age 18. More than twice as many of the boys with low heart rate (65 beats or less per minute) were convicted for violence as compared to those with higher heart rates (Farrington, 1997). Importantly for our focus on homicide, Farrington (1997) also found that lower heart rates were also significantly related to self-reported violence and teacher-reported aggression.

Raine, Venables, and Williams (1990) also measured heart rate as well as skin conductance and EEG activity in 15-year-old boys and then they looked to see how many convictions these young men had up to the age of 24. They found that low heart rate, low skin conductance and low-frequency brain wave activity all predicted convictions. Importantly, low school achievement, low socioeconomic status, and living in a high-crime rate area also predicted convictions, although the biological variables were not found to be related to these environmental factors (Farrington, 1998). The research in this area continues, especially because much of it to date has suffered many of the same methodological flaws we saw in early positivist research. Many of the studies have been conducted on institutionalized populations, and longitudinal studies (long-term studies that help determine cause and effect) are missing (Raine, 1993).

NEUROPSYCHOLOGY AND BRAIN DYSFUNCTION

Neuropsychology is the study of the mechanisms that control behavior functions localized in certain areas of the brain. In particular, it is assumed that abstract reasoning, anticipation, planning, and inhibiting inappropriate behavior are located in the frontal lobe. Thus some experts argue that damage to the frontal lobe or a malformation of the frontal lobe can contribute to offending behavior including homicidal behavior.

Clear evidence indicates that damage to the brain can change one's personality. The story of Phineas Gage is often included in introductory psychology texts to illustrate how damage to the brain can affect an individual's personality. In September 1884, Gage was working on a railroad-building crew. Gage and his crew used dynamite to blast rock and prepare the land for laying down the track. Something went wrong with the rock blasting, and an iron rod approximately 3.5 inches long and over 13 pounds penetrated through Gage's head under his left cheekbone and exited through his forehead, piercing his frontal lobe. Amazingly, Gage survived. However, his personality changed greatly. Whereas in the past he was reliable and well liked, after the accident his coworkers and friends found him unreliable and mean. His change in personality helped us begin to learn about how different parts of the brain work. Further, because the damage to his frontal lobe appeared to change Gage's personality and reasoning abilities, medical science has continued to learn more about the brain and the connection between our brains and our behaviors (Fleischman, 2002).

A hundred years after Gage was injured, Lewis et al. (1986) investigated the link between homicide and head injuries. Lewis and her colleagues found that 90% of the 15 murderers they studied on Florida's death row had suffered severe head injury at some time in their life prior to committing a murder. Adrian Rain and his colleagues (1994) found that 50% of the murderers he studied had brain injury, whereas none of a comparison control group of nonmurderers had previous brain injury (Yaralian & Raine, 1999). It is logical to conclude, however, that head injury alone is not enough to explain why some people kill because many of us suffer some type of

---

BOX 5.3

Hypofrontality and Murder

As noted in Chapter 2, I observed the capital murder trial of Reinaldo Rivera, who allegedly killed four women in South Carolina and Georgia in addition to raping perhaps hundreds in Washington, D.C. Rivera was found guilty and sentenced to death for the murder of Sergeant Marni Glista, who he raped and strangled to death. In this case, Rivera's attorneys Jacque Hawke and Peter Johnson presented arguments that Rivera had a brain deficiency. Gerald Blanchard, who holds a master's degree in psychology and works as a licensed counselor in Wyoming, was presented as an expert for the defense. Based on two days of interviewing and testing Rivera, Blanchard presented a social history of Rivera including details of several head injuries suffered by him. Based on interviews with and tests of Rivera including a Sexual Addiction Inventory, the Millon Clinical Multiaxial III, and the Minnesota Multiphasic Personality Inventory-2 (measure of adult psychopathology), Blanchard testified that he suspected Rivera had a brain injury and especially a prefrontal brain injury. Thus according to Blanchard, he requested that Rivera have a hair mineral analysis, a spinal tap, and a positron emission tomography (PET) scan. Thomas Sachy, a neuropsychiatrist, was then called by the defense to testify that his diagnosis was that Rivera had antisocial personality disorder. Furthermore, in controversial testimony, Sachy argued that low activity in Rivera's frontal lobe, which he called "hypofrontality," was the cause of Rivera's psychopathy. Low activity in the frontal lobe could explain Rivera's behavior according to Sachy because this is the part of the brain responsible for impulse control. Sachy compared slides of Rivera's PET scans with slides of a "normal" PET scan. Sachy explained that what we were seeing was very little red color in the front of Rivera's brain as compared to a normal brain that showed more red color, indicating that Rivera had hypofrontality or low brain wave activity in his frontal lobe. Importantly, Danny Craig, the defense attorney, noted that Blanchard does not hold his doctorate in psychology, and much of what he testified about is not in the *DSM-IV*. Further, David Hess, a neurologist with the Medical College of Georgia, testified that he found Rivera did not have neurological abnormalities.

---

head injury in our lives whether through sports, car wrecks, or unfortunately, abuse, and we never commit murder. Nevertheless, this is likely to be an area where research continues (see Box 5.3).

NUTRITION

You may have heard that Dan White, who killed two public officials in San Francisco in 1978, received a lesser sentence because he ate too many Twinkies. Although the so-called Twinkie defense is largely a fiction created by the media

BOX 5.4

Critical Thinking: Corn Leads to Crime

Mawson and Jacobs (1978) found that countries that have significantly high homicide rates also have significantly high corn consumption. Does this mean corn causes crime? Is there something about corn that causes humans to do crime? Does the chemical makeup of corn interact with the chemicals in the human brain to cause humans to kill? Although it is important to take empirical findings seriously, we must be scientifically rigorous. In science, we are careful to follow the scientific method and not to come to conclusions hastily. In fact, it is rare in science that we can conclude causation exists. However, there are three basic criteria we follow to determine if we will conclude that causation is likely to exist. First, the cause must come before the effect. Second, the cause and effect must be correlated; they must appear to be related. Third, the relationship between the cause and effect must not be spurious. A relationship is said to be spurious when the relationship can be explained away by a third variable. For example, we know that when ice cream sales increase, homicide also increases. This relationship meets our second criteria of causation. But we cannot conclude a relationship between ice cream consumption and killing without considering the other two criteria. If the data show that ice cream sales increase first and then the number of homicides increase, the relationship would meet the first criteria of causation. And it very well may, but does the third criterion of causation hold up? Can anything else explain away the relationship between ice cream sales and homicide? Yes, in fact, the season or the weather can explain away the relationship. In the summer or when it is hotter, more ice cream is sold and people kill more often. Thus scientist have not demanded that we put warnings on ice cream cartons telling us that mint chocolate chip ice cream is dangerous to the health of those around us. Instead, scientists have concluded that the relationship between ice cream sales and homicide is spurious. There is no cause and effect.

So what may explain the relationship between corn consumption and homicide? Is there a cause-and-effect relationship? Using the three criteria for causation, think about whether you think this is a "real" relationship or not.

(see Box 5.5), the idea that nutrition may be linked to deviant behavior continues to circulate. Some research suggests that hypoglycemia (low blood sugar) may be connected to criminal behavior (Jeffery, 1990). For example, Fishbein (1982) found that placing a group of youths incarcerated in a juvenile center on a low sugar diet reduced their antisocial behaviors. Still, the evidence is not definitive; no clear link between nutrition and homicide (or even maladaptive behavior) has been found (Jones, 2000).

> ## BOX 5.5
> ### Twinkie Defense
>
> On November 27, 1978, Dan White, who was once a San Francisco city supervisor, shot to death San Francisco mayor George Moscone and city supervisor and gay activist Harvey Milk. Many thought that Dan White should have received the death penalty for this crime, but he was convicted of voluntary manslaughter. With time off for good behavior, he served just over five years in prison. At his trial, Dan White's attorneys put forth the argument of diminished capacity due to depression. In support of this argument, psychiatrist Martin Blinder testified as one of five therapists for the defense. During Blinder's testimony he noted that White's diet of junk food was indicative of his depression. Further, the junk food further contributed to White's depression. As a result of Blinder's testimony and a mention of the possibility that certain foods might affect one's behavior in defense attorney Smith's closing arguments, the defense's case became known as the "Twinkie defense." Satirist Paul Krassner, who covered the trial for the *San Francisco Bay Guardian* has been credited with introducing the phrase "Twinkie defense." *Newsweek* magazine picked up the phrase as did politicians and others who thought White should have received a harsher sentence for killing two government officials. In the 25-plus years since the trial of White for killing Moscone and Milk, many have speculated why White received the sentence he did. Some have argued that the jury was particularly conservative and that the fact that Milk was openly gay may have had something to do with it (Pogash, 2003).
>
> The case made sporadic appearances in the paper as the years went on. After getting out of prison, White committed suicide. The psychiatrist Martin Blinder was stabbed in October 2000. Police believed that his exwife Dorothy Braco may have been responsible for the stabbing. However, before she could be arrested, her body was discovered by a fisherman on the Esplanade Beach (Pervaiz & Martin, 2000).

LEAD

Most of the biological explanations that I discuss in this chapter have been tested with regard to maladaptive behavior, aggression, violence, delinquency, or criminal behavior. Scientific research that explores the link between different biological factors and homicide, in particular, is sparse. However, some evidence suggests that lead may be related to homicide offending. Interestingly, Stretesky and Lynch (2001) found a relationship between air lead concentrations and the incidence of homicide in U.S. counties. At the individual level in another remarkable study, Denno (1990) followed 987 African American children from birth to age 22. She found that lead poisoning is one of the best predictors of delinquency. Sociological explanations for crime are discussed more fully in Chapter 6. However, it is appropriate to note that lead poisoning is linked to poverty. Poor people are more likely to be subject to both airborne lead poisoning and lead paint in deteriorated housing.

ANTISOCIAL PERSONALITY DISORDER

We can not clearly label all theories or explanations for criminal behavior or homicidal behavior as either biological or social theories. Many psychological theories incorporate both biological and sociological explanations for behavior. One of the more popular psychological explanations for homicidal behavior labels the killer a psychopath. Antisocial personality disorder (ASPD), also known as psychopathy or sociopathy, is a persistent disorder or disability of the mind that results in abnormally aggressive or irresponsible behavior that is not the product of psychosis or other illness (Mitchell, 1997). Psychopaths may appear normal, and in fact they may be quite charming. Some have high intelligence; however, they do not appear to have the capability to be remorseful (Mitchell, 1997).

Dr. Robert Hare has developed what may be considered the industry standard, so to speak, for assessing and diagnosing psychopathy. Hare's checklist is believed to be the most reliable and valid for not only identifying psychopaths but also for predicting violence. Based on intensive reviews of files, hundreds of interviews, and years of experience and feedback from other professionals, Hare developed the Hare Psychopathy Checklist-Revised. This assessment instrument, which includes 20 items, aids mental health and criminal justice practitioners in determining whether an individual is a psychopath (Hare, 2006; Ramsland, 2006). An individual is scored for each of the 20 items. If the person does not have the trait, they receive a zero. If the individual definitely exhibits the behavior, the score is a two. As a result, an individual may score from 0 to 40 on Hare's scale. A score of 30 or higher would indicate an individual could be diagnosed as a psychopath (Ramsland, 2006).

Items on the checklist indicate the following characteristics, which are common among psychopaths: a lack of guilt or empathy, the manipulation of others, a focus only on oneself and minimization of other's suffering, shallow affect, grandiose senses of self-worth, lying, low frustration toleration, persistent norm violations, and high levels of impulsivity (Hare, 2006; Ramsland, 2006; Shipley & Arrigo, 2004). Importantly, all psychopaths are not believed to be killers, but many serial killers are believed to be psychopaths. There are psychopathic individuals who see no need to kill and find success in business or other pursuits, and there are serial killers who are not psychopaths. Some serial killers dehumanize their victims and thus are able to kill them without being psychopathic (Fox & Levin, 1999). Further, it must also be said that most killers are not likely to have antisocial personality disorder or any other mental illness. Most murderers, in fact, are "normal." They are found to be both legally sane and mentally healthy.

Scientists are still researching and debating what causes antisocial personality disorder. Similar to the work of Raine, Venables, and Williams (1990) on psychophysiological factors related to violence, discussed earlier, Hare has found that the brains of psychopathic individuals appear to work differently than nonpsychopathic individuals. The brains of nonpsychopathic individuals respond differently to emotional words and to neutral words such as *hat*. The brainwaves of psychopathic individuals, however, do not appear to view these words differently as measured by EEG activity. Whereas some scholars focus on the link between brain function and antisocial personality disorder (see Box 5.3), others focus on childhood abuse to explain the genesis of antisocial personality disorder (Shipley & Arrigo, 2004). Still others consider the relationship between brain function and environment. For example, those who believe suppressed activity in the frontal lobe is connected to psychopathic behavior in an individual may note the inactivity in the frontal lobe is the result of a traumatic brain injury suffered in childhood. Research about antisocial personality is likely to continue as the interest in serial killing, in particular, continues to grow (see Chapter 12).

SOCIOBIOLOGICAL THEORY AND HOMICIDE

The basic premise of sociobiological theory is based on evolutionary theory and the idea that genes are selfish. In other words, creatures adapt and evolve and make choices so their genes will continue on. Thus relative to homicide, we would expect that individuals are more likely to kill strangers than those related to them. Killing those related to them would decrease the chances that their genes would continue on. When Daly and Wilson (1988) tested this hypothesis, they found that victims were killed by "relatives" less than a third of the time. Furthermore, when individuals were killed by their relatives, it was far less likely that they were killed by consanguine (or blood relatives) than affinity (relatives through marriage) relatives.

BOX 5.6

Critical Thinking: Uxoricide, Stepchildren, and Sociobiology

Uxoricide is the killing of wives by husbands. Martin Daly, Karen Wiseman, and Margo Wilson (1997) studied the family situations of wives who were killed by their husbands between 1974 and 1992 in a Canadian city. Based on an examination of all 32 women who were killed by their husbands or male partners who lived with them (sometimes called common-law husbands) and a sample of the population at large, they concluded that having children from a former union increased the risk of homicide by a partner/husband. They found that women in their sample who were mothers were 12.7 times more likely to be killed by their current husbands/partners if the couple had children from her previous relationships who lived with them than those who had only the couple's children living with them. The authors also found that homicide risk was increased for those women attempting to leave their partners. The authors believe that a sociobiological perspective explains their findings.

1. How would a sociobiological perspective explain the findings of this study?
2. What else might explain their findings?
3. Do you think research on 32 women in Canada proves the sociobiology theory? Why or why not?

If you think about this, it may occur to you that many of us have a greater opportunity to kill or be killed by those who are related to us. Many of us live with at least one biological parent and often biological siblings when we are young, and then as adults there are good chances that we will be living with our biological offspring and maybe other biological relatives. As such, it may be just a matter of increased odds that we would kill or be killed by a biological relative. Knowing this, Daly and Wilson (1988) constructed victimization rates that distinguished between nonblood-related individuals that victims lived with and blood-related coresidents. Using 1972 Detroit data, they found that nongenetic coresidents were 11 times more likely to kill those living with them than genetically related coresidents (Daly & Wilson, 1988; Raine, 1993).

SUMMARY

This chapter focused on biological and psychological explanations for crime with an emphasis on homicide in particular when possible. Beginning with Lombroso's idea of the atavistic criminal, the discussion moved to Sheldon, who also postulated that criminality is biological. Evidence of the possibility that criminality might be an inherited trait was also included in this chapter. Early studies of families such as the Jukes and the Kallikaks that appeared to support this contention were included as were twin studies and adoption studies. The possible links between chromosomes, hormones, and crime were also reviewed. Then the connection between psychophysiological factors and crime as reported by Adrian Raine, who argues that people who are antisocial or criminal behavior tend to have low heart rates and have lower arousal compared with "normal" individuals, was discussed. Similarly, other researchers discussed in this chapter argue that depressed brain activity in the frontal lobe is associated with criminal activity. Finally, psychopathic personalities, which are believed to be common among serial killers, and an overview of sociobiological theory, which posits that humans will behave in ways that increase the chances that their genes will survive, round out this chapter.

CHAPTER QUESTIONS

1. What are atavists, and how are they related to crime?
2. Name and explain Lombroso's three types of criminals.
3. Name and explain Sheldon's three body types and note which is most likely to be criminal according to Sheldon.
4. Who are the Jukes and the Kallikaks, and what is their importance in the history of criminological theory?
5. What is a concordance rate?
6. What might we conclude from twin studies?
7. What do adoption studies tell us about crime?
8. What are XYY males, and what do we know about them today?
9. What are hormones, and how are they believed to be related to crime? What does the evidence suggest?

10. What are the arguments against the connection between women's menstruation and their offending behaviors?
11. What do EEG studies suggest about criminal behavior?
12. Who was Phineas Gage, and why is he important to the study of crime?
13. How might Twinkies and lead be linked with homicide? What does the evidence tell us?
14. What is a psychopath? Are all psychopaths killers? Are any?
15. According to a sociobiological theory of crime, who is more likely to kill a child—a parent, a stepparent, the father's brother, or the father's brother's wife? Why?

REFERENCES

Barkan, Steven E. 1997. *Criminology: A Sociological Understanding.* Upper Saddle River, NJ: Prentice Hall.

Beck, Allen, Darrell Gilliard, Lawrence Greenfeld, Caroline Harlow, Thomas Hester, Louis Jankowski, Tracy Snell, James Stephan, and Danielle Morton. 1993. "Survey of State Prisons Inmates, 1991." U.S. Department of Justice.

Butterfield, Fox. 1996. *All God's Children: The Bosket Family and the American Tradition of Violence.* New York: Knopf.

Butterfield, Fox. 2002, August 21. "Father Steals Best: Crime in an American Family." *New York Times,* p. A1.

Chrisler, Joan C., and Paula Caplan. 2002. "Strange Case of Dr. Jekyll and Ms. Hyde: How PMS Became a Cultural Phenomenon and a Psychiatric Disorder." *Annual Review of Sex Research,* 13: 274–306.

Columbia Electronic Encyclopedia. 6th ed. 2003. Columbia University Press. Licensed from Columbia University Press. Retrieved January 14, 2006, from www.cc.columbia.edu/cu/cup/

Dabbs, James M., Jr., R. B. Ruback, R. L. Frady, C. H. Hopper, and D. S. Sgoutas. 1988. "Saliva Testosterone and Criminal Violence Among Women." *Personality and Individual Differences,* 9: 269–275.

Dabbs, James M., Jasmin K. Riad, and Susan E. Chance. 2001. "Testosterone and Ruthless Homicide." *Personality and Individual Differences,* 31: 599–603.

Daly, Martin, and Margo Wilson. 1988. *Homicide.* New York: Aldine De Gruyter.

Daly, Martin, Karen Wiseman, and Margo Wilson "Women with Children Sired by Previous Partners Incur Excess Risk of Uxoricide" *Homicide Studies,* 1(1): 61–71.

Dalton, Katherina. 1961. "Menstruation and Crime." *British Medical Journal,* 2,1752–1753.

Denno, Deborah. W. 1990. *Biology and Violence.* New York: Cambridge Press.

Easteal, Patricia. 1993. "Premenstrual Syndrome in the Courtroom." In Patricia Weiser Easteal and Sandra McKillop, eds., *Australian Institute of Criminology Conference Proceedings,* Canberra: Australian Institute of Criminology.

Farrington, David P. 1997. "The Relationship Between Low Resting Heart Rate and Violence." In Adrian Raine, P. A. Brennan, D. P. Farrington, and S. A. Mednick, eds., *Biosocial Bases of Violence.* New York: Plenum.

Farrington, David P. 1998. "Individual Differences and Offending." In Michael Tonry, ed., *The Handbook of Crime and Punishment* (pp. 241–268). New York: Oxford University Press.

Ferri, Enrico. 1917. *Criminal Sociology.* Boston: Little, Brown.

Fishbein, Diana H. 1982. "The Contribution of Refined Carbohydrate Consumption to Maladaptive Behaviors." *Journal of Orthomolecular Psychiatry,* 11: 17–25.

Fishbein, Diana H. 1996. "The Biology of Antisocial Behavior." In John E. Conklin, ed., *New Perspectives in Criminology*. Boston: Allyn and Bacon.

Fleischman, John. 2002. *Phineas Gage: A Gruesome But True Story About Brain Science*. Boston: Houghton Mifflin.

Fleming, Rebecca B. 2000. "Scanty Goatees and Palmar Tattoos: Cesare Lombroso's Influence on Science and Popular Opinion." *The Concord Review*, 10: 195–217.

Fox, James Alan, and Jack Levin. 1999. "Serial Murder: Popular Myths and Empirical Realities." In M. Dwayne Smith and Margaret A. Zahn, eds., *Homicide: A Sourcebook of Social Research*. Thousand Oaks, CA: Sage.

Garofalo, Raffaele. 1914. *Criminology*. Boston: Little, Brown and Company.

Glueck, Sheldon, and Eleanor Glueck. 1956. *Physique and Delinquency*, New York: Harper Brothers.

Goddard, Henry. 1912. *The Kallikak Family*. New York: Macmillan.

Grove, William M., Elke D. Eckert, Leonard Heston, Thomas J. Bouchard, Nancy Segal, and David T. Lykken. 1990. "Heritability of Substance Use and Antisocial Behavior: A Study of Monozygotic Twins Reared Apart." *Biological Psychiatry*, 27: 1293–1304.

Hare, Robert. 2006. "Without Conscience." Accessed online at http://www.hare.org

Hurwitz, Stephan, and Karl O. Christiansen. 1983. *Criminology*. London: Allen and Unwin.

Jeffery, C. Ray. 1990. *Criminology: An Interdisciplinary Approach*. Englewood. Cliffs, NJ: Prentice-Hall.

Jones, Stephen. 2000. *Understanding Violent Crime*. Buckingham: Open University Press.

Lewis, Dorothy O., Jonathan Pincus, Marilyn Feldman, Lori Jackson, and Barbara Bard. 1986. "Psychiatric, Neurological, and Psychoeducational Characteristics of 15 Death Row Inmates in the United States." *American Journal of Psychiatry*, 143(77): 838–845.

Masters, Brian. 1993. *The Shrine of Jeffrey Dahmer*. London: Coronet.

Mawson, Anthony R., and K. W. Jacobs. 1978. "Corn Consumption, Tryptophan and Cross-National Homicide Rates." *Journal of Orthomolecular Psychiatry*, 7(4): 227–230.

Miethe, Terance, and Richard C. McCorkle. 2001. *Crime Profiles*. Los Angeles: Roxbury.

Mitchell, Edward W. 1997. *The Aetiology of Serial Murder: Towards an Integrated Model*. Masters Thesis, University of Cambridge, UK.

Moffit, T. E., A. Caspi, P. Fawcett, G. L. Brammer, M. Raleigh, A. Yuwiler, and P. Silva. 1997. "Whole Blood Serotonin and Family Background Relate to Male Violence." In Adrian Raine, P. A. Brennan, D. P. Farrington, and S. A. Mednick, eds., *Biosocial Bases of Violence*. New York: Plenum.

Morley, Katherine I. and Wayne D. Hall. 2003. *Is There a Genetic Susceptibility to Engage in Criminal Acts?* Canberra, Australia: Criminology Research Council.

Nielsen, Johannes. 1998. *XYY Males. An Orientation*. Published online by The Turner Center. Retrieved October 19, 2005, from http://www.aaa.dk/TURNER/ENGELSK/XYY.HTM#name

Olweus, D. 1986. "Aggression and Hormones: Behavioral Relationship with Testosterone and Adrenaline." In D. Olweus, J. Block, and M. Radke-Yarrow, eds., *Development of Antisocial and Prosocial Behavior: Research, Theories and Issues*. Orlando, FL: Academic Press.

Olweus, D. 1987. "Testosterone and Adrenaline: Aggressive Anti-Social Behavior in Normal Adolescent Males." In S. Mednick, T. Moffitt, and S. Stacks, eds., *The Causes of Crime: New Biological Approaches*. New York: Cambridge University Press.

Pervaiz, Shallwani, and Mark Martin. 2000, October 9. "Ex-Wife of 'Twinkie-Defense' Doctor Found Dead." *San Francisco Chronicle*. Retrieved January 11, 2006, from http://www.sfgate.com/cgi-bin/article.cgi?f=/c/a/2000/10/09/MN113889.DTL&hw=twinkie+defense&sn=004&sc=453

Pogash, Carol. 2003, November 23. "Myth of the 'Twinkie Defense.'" *San Francisco Chronicle*. Retrieved January 11, 2006, from http://www.sfgate.com/cgi-bin/article.cgi?file=/c/a/2003/11/23/INGRE343501.DTL&type=printable

Olweus, D., A. Mattesson, D. Schalling, and H. Low. 1988. "Circulating Testosterone Levels and Aggression in Adolescent Males: A Causal Analysis." *Psychosomatic Medicine*, 50:261–272.

Raine, Adrian. 1993. *The Psychopathology of Crime: Criminal Behavior as a Clinical Disorder.* San Diego, CA: Harcourt Brace.

Raine, Adrian, Monte S. Buchsbaum, Jill Stanley, Steven Lottenberg, Leonard Abel, and Jacqueline Stoddard. 1994. "Selective Reductions in Pre-Frontal Glucose Metabolism in Murderers." *Biological Psychiatry*, 36: 365–373.

Raine, Adrian, Peter H. Venable, and Mark Williams. 1990. "Relationships Between CNS and ANS Measures of Arousal at Age 15 and Criminality at Age 24." *Archives of General Psychiatry*, 47: 1003–1007.

Ramsland, Katherine. 2005. "Evil, Part Two: The Heart of Darkness—Reframing Evil." *Court TV Crime Library*. Accessed online at http://www.crimelibrary.com

Ramsland, Katherine. 2006, September 27. "Dr. Robert Hare: Expert on the Psychopath." *Court TV Crime Library*. Accessed online at http://www.crimelibrary.com.

Rasche, Chris E. 1996. "Theorizing About Homicide: A Presentation on the Theories Explaining Homicide and Other Crime." In Pamela K. Lattimore and Cynthia A. Nahabedian, eds., *Nature of Homicide: Trends and Changes, Proceedings of the 1996 Meeting of the Homicide Research Working Group* (pp. 23–34). Washington D.C.: U.S. Department of Justice.

Rhee, Sue H., and Irwin Waldman. 2002. "Genetic and Environmental Influences on Antisocial Behavior: A Meta-Analysis of Twin and Adoption Studies." *Psychological Bulletin*, 128(3): 490–529.

Sheldon, William. 1949. *Varieties of Delinquent Youth*. New York: Harper & Row.

Shipley, Stacey L., and Bruce A. Arrigo. 2004. *The Female Homicide Offender: Serial Murder and the Case of Aileen Wuornos*. NJ: Prentice Hall.

Stretesky, Paul B., and Michael J. Lynch. 2001. "The Relationship Between Lead Exposure and Homicide." *Archives of Pediatric Adolescent Medicine*, 155: 579–582.

Vold, George, and Thomas Bernard. 1986. *Theoretical Criminology*. 3rd ed. New York: Oxford University Press.

Yaralian, Pauline S., and Adrian Raine. 1999. "Head Injury." In Ronald Gottesman, ed., *Violence in America: An Encyclopedia*. New York: Simon & Schuster.

Chapter 6

SOCIAL AND CULTURAL EXPLANATIONS FOR HOMICIDE

Instead of looking to biological predispositions or psychological abnormalities to explain negative behavior, some criminologists employ a more sociological approach. In contrast to biological and psychological explanations for crime, these criminologists focus on factors outside of individuals to explain criminal behavior. They begin with the premise or assumption that our environment or social milieu influences our actions. Societies are structured differently and cultures vary. As a result, crime rates vary by place and over time. Moreover, there are patterns to criminal offending. Different groups within a society have different rates of criminal offending and victimization. Men are more likely than women to be both offenders and victims of homicide throughout the world. Within the United States, southerners have higher rates of homicide than northeasterners. African Americans and poor people are overrepresented as both homicide offenders and homicide victims. Criminologists who tackle the issue of homicide from a social or cultural perspective seek to explain these patterns through studying correlates of homicide at an aggregate level or by investigating the social histories of individual offenders and the context of criminal homicides.

This chapter includes a variety of criminological perspectives as they pertain to explanations of homicide. Although this chapter focuses on cultural and social explanations for homicide, the eighteenth-century classical school perspective as well as deterrence theory are also included. These theories are in this chapter because they are predecessors to more sociocultural views of crime and to the history of criminology. In addition to the classical school perspective and deterrence theory, social disorganization, differential association theory, social control theory, a general theory of crime, and neutralization theory are also covered in this chapter. These theories were developed to explain juvenile delinquency or criminal behavior generally rather than homicide specifically. Even so, these theories may be or have been used to explain homicide offending or particular types of homicide offending.

Criminologists have also proposed theories or explanations to account for the homicide patterns just discussed, such as the higher rates of homicide in the South. In this chapter, only brief reviews of two of these theories are included because they are explained more fully later in the text. The culture of violence and culture of honor explanations for homicide help explain confrontational homicide, and as such, these theories are expounded on more greatly in Chapter 7. However, other explanations postulated to explain homicide patterns, including lifestyle and routine activities theory, feminist perspectives on violence and masculinity, and sociological perspectives on social stratification are included in this chapter. Finally, this chapter explores what is known about the role of alcohol and drug use in homicidal behavior. Note that as you read this chapter, what you are reading are overviews of each of the theories and perspectives included, which ideally will serve as a simple refresher of theories you learned in your criminology theory course. For those readers who are not criminology majors, you may want to seek out more detailed examinations of some of these theories.

CLASSICAL SCHOOL PERSPECTIVE

Cesare Beccaria (1738–1794) is usually considered the father of what is known as the "classical perspective on criminology." In setting forth his ideas for reform in the Italian court system during the Enlightenment, Beccaria (1764/1986) argued that people are rational and hedonistic and that they possess free will. In other words, he believed that individuals make decisions about how they act. According to Beccaria, individuals weigh the costs and benefits of potential actions including criminal actions.

To joke around a bit, let's say you are studying diligently for your psychology midterm. As you are desperately trying to memorize what the hippocampus does, it occurs to you that you see your psychology professor every morning as you drive to school and if you ran over him, you would not have to take your exam. According to the ideas of Beccaria, you are rational. Thus you are capable of exercising logic, so you consider the consequences of running over your professor. Also according to Beccaria, you are hedonistic. You are motivated by your desire for pleasure and you attempt to avoid pain. Finally, you have free will—you can determine your own actions. There is not some greater force or something in your genes or the chemicals in your brain that leads you to act. You determine what you will do. So you decide you will keep studying because although the psychology exam may be painful, the pain you may experience if you kill your psychology professor will be far greater than the pain of the exam. Furthermore, if you study, you may actually do well, and then you will have the pleasure of telling your parents that you earned an A on your psychology exam. For you, the costs of not studying or, even worse, killing your professor is much greater than the pain you will experience from your parents' disappointment and the "strong arm of the law."

It is no surprise that many U.S. students find Beccaria's theory particularly appealing. In the United States, individualism is valued, and we often explain behavior in everyday situations at the individual level. Not surprising, then, criminologists today still find the premise of Beccaria's explanation for human behavior attractive, as seen in *rational choice theory* (Rasche, 1996). Rational choice theory also assumes that people are rational and they consider the risks involved in their actions before acting. Taking this a step further, however, rational choice theory, strongly associated with *deterrence theory*, posits that laws may have a deterrent effect on human behavior (Barkan, 1997). In other words, if the criminal justice system is set up in such a way that a person who violates a law is likely to be caught and punished, people will be less likely to commit crimes. After all, in their rational calculations they will decide that the punishment for a certain behavior is not worth doing the behavior. We see this logic reflected in some arguments for the death penalty, as discussed in Chapter 17.

SOCIAL DISORGANIZATION

Although not totally opposed to the idea of individual choice, social disorganization theorists introduced the ideas that crime is more complicated than individuals making choices. Taking a more sociological approach, early social disorganization theorists at the University of Chicago realized that crime was more prevalent in urban areas. Instead of assuming that something about the people who occupied the more crime-prone areas led them to commit crimes, social disorganization theories look to the structural causes for explaining crime. Studying crime in inner-city Chicago, in particular, Shaw and McKay (1942) found that regardless of who lived in what they called the "transitional zone" of the city; this zone had higher delinquency and crime rates. Shaw and McKay studied the city of Chicago over time and were able to see significant change in the population of the transitional zone. Importantly, they found that regardless of whether those who lived in the zone were of English, German, Irish, or African descent, this zone had the most delinquency. As a result, Shaw and McKay concluded it was not the people so much as the structural conditions of the area in which they lived that led to criminal behavior.

Shaw and McKay (1942) found that the transitional zone with the high crime rate had worse housing conditions than other areas. There were also higher rates of poverty and fewer intact families and less of a sense of community in the transitional zone than in other areas. They theorized that the zone was disorganized, leading to unclear norms and a lack of structure that helped keep individuals in line. Shaw and McKay's work was criticized for relying on official data because they are likely to be biased. If you think about this critique, it is quite logical. Police may look for crime more frequently in inner-city urban areas, and thus the rates will be higher there. Social disorganization theory was also criticized for failing to explain the fact that not everyone who lives in disorganized areas commits crimes, whereas some who live in nondisorganized areas do (Barkan, 1997).

Still, findings of recent homicide studies appear to support the basic ideas of social disorganization theory. For example, Krivo and Peterson (2000) find that greater economic disadvantage and low home ownership rates are correlated with higher homicide rates in 124 U.S. cities. Although Krivo and Peterson note that these factors operate somewhat differently for African American and white homicide rates because of the extreme economic disadvantage experienced by many African

Americans in the United States, their research still indicates the importance of structural factors for explaining homicide rates. Moreover, Krivo and Peterson are building on a rich tradition of homicide research that finds correlations between structural factors and homicide rates (e.g., Blau & Blau, 1982; Sampson, 1987; Shihadeh & Steffensmeier, 1994; Williams, 1984).

DIFFERENTIAL ASSOCIATION THEORY

Like social disorganization theory, Edwin Sutherland's *differential association theory* stands in sharp contrast to biological and psychological theories of crime. Influenced by social disorganization theory, Sutherland also set out to explain why crime was more common in poor areas (Barkan, 1997). However, Sutherland's theory (Sutherland & Cressey, 2006) could explain why not all people who lived in the inner city committed crimes and why some who did not live in high crime areas still did crime. Sutherland argued that crime is like everything else that humans do: We learn to do it. Basically, we learn how to commit crime and why we would want to commit crime from intimate others. Through family and peers we are exposed to ideas about laws. We learn that laws, or certain laws, should be followed and other laws are unimportant.

Differential association appears to explain some homicide better than other types. Gang killings, for example, are likely learned. Within the context of a gang, one

---

BOX 6.1

Stress or Training?: Explaining Murder by Military Men

In the summer of 2002, four military men stationed at Fort Bragg, North Carolina, killed their wives within a six-week period. The press who picked up on this story began to question whether the stress of combat was contributing to what appeared to be a rash of intimate partner homicide by soldiers. Three of the four soldiers had served in Afghanistan. However, according to news reports, officials at Fort Bragg indicated there was no "common thread among the cases" (Starr, 2002). Two of the soldiers allegedly shot their wives, another allegedly stabbed his wife, and the fourth strangled his wife. The military was considering ways to help those in the military deal with stress, and much of the talk around these cases dealt with the possible stress the soldiers faced as active duty soldiers (Starr, 2002). Stress is a likely culprit—at least a contributor. However, if we were to observe these cases through the lens of differential association, we might also conclude that something about the way these men are trained or about their learning in the military leads them to solve conflicts through violence. Still other theories might explain the pattern noted in the summer of 2002 as well as other data that suggest domestic violence is a problem for military families. Think about what other theories may explain domestic violence and intimate partner homicide by military men.

learns the value of violence and homicide for protecting one's territory or settling a score. There are many examples to be found of homicides that are the result of a gang initiation, which supports the idea that youth are learning to commit homicides from other youth. Take the tragic case that occurred in the Montbello High School cafeteria in January 2005. Seventeen-year-old Contrell Townsend died as the result of a fight. Townsend allegedly attacked 16-year-old Marcus Richardson as part of a gang initiation rite; however, Townsend ended up dead and Richardson was charged with second-degree murder (Pandratz, 2005). Also, as discussed in other chapters, studies of children who have killed, men and women who have killed their intimate partners, and even serial killers have found that exposure to violence during their childhood is common. This does not prove differential association theory, but it gives some credence to the idea that we learn violence.

SOCIAL CONTROL THEORIES

Social control theorists make an assumption that is radically different from the theorists discussed so far who think we must explain why people violate norms. Social control theorists assume people will commit crimes if left to their own devices, so to speak. Basically, social control theorists argue that something must exist to prevent people from doing crime. It may be a little farfetched—but maybe not—to think we would all commit homicide if something did not prevent us. It is likely you have heard someone express the sentiment that they were "mad enough to kill" or perhaps, even you have said, "I could kill him" or "her" or "my mother"—you get the picture.

So, what is it, according to social control theorists, that prevents us from committing crime? Well, it is our connection to conventional others. Durkheim (1893/1997), who you have probably heard about in your theory course, may have been one of the first control theorists, and his concept of anomie is very relevant here. According to Durkheim's theory of anomie, with industrialization and the increasing complexity and size of society, more deviance would be likely because family and community ties would be weaker and thus individuals would have less to lose if they did not conform. They would be less likely to have what Toby (1957) called a *stake in conformity*. Thus we would see more crime when people are less connected. In other words, you or I may be more likely to violate norms if we having nothing to lose by doing so. If we are not afraid of losing a job or of losing our standing in society, we might more seriously consider stealing or killing.

At a very basic level, this theory seems to make some sense for homicide. Where is homicide highest? Within the United States and other Western societies, homicides rates are highest in urban areas. According to Durkheim's ideas about anomie, we would expect more homicide in urban areas where people are believed to be less connected to other people. In smaller towns and rural areas, we may expect that individuals would be more likely to know others and may even be related to other people. Following Durkheim's ideas, then, it would make sense that there would be less law violation in nonurban areas, which is what we find: Homicide rates are lower in rural areas.

Travis Hirschi is the criminologist most associated with control theory. Hirschi (1969) proposed what is commonly referred to as social bond theory in his 1969 book *Causes of Delinquency*. According to social bond theory, the more we are connected to conventional others in society, the less likely we will commit delinquent acts. Furthermore, our bonds to society are formed through our socialization—especially socialization by parents and teachers. Hirschi, whose theory may be expanded to explain crimes as well as delinquency, explained that four major bonds connect individuals to society. The first bond of *attachment* reflects how close you are to conventional individuals. *Involvement*, the second bond, refers to how much time you spend doing legitimate activities. *Commitment* is like Toby's idea of stake in conformity. It is a measure of how dedicated you are to accomplishing your goals by following legitimate routes. In other words, are you willing to work hard in school and at a job? Finally, if you have a strong *belief*, you think the laws and norms of society make sense and should be upheld.

If any of these bonds are weak, delinquency or crime is likely. When these bonds are strong, violation of laws is less likely. Even though Hirschi (1969) proposed this theory to explain delinquency, social bond theory can be and has been used to explain all types of norm violation including crime. Using social bond theory to explain homicide, we would expect that individuals who are not bonded to others would be most likely to commit homicide. This certainly would work to explain some murders, and if you think about it, you have probably seen applications of this theory or ideas related to this theory.

When we know someone has committed murder, we look to their past. Was the person abused as a child? Is he or she a loner? If the answer to either of these questions is yes, we are less surprised than if the answer is no. When a murderer is married and has a good job, we are shocked. We look for something to explain the behavior. In these cases, we are using logic similar to the social bond theory. We expect that people who are doing well in society, who have something to lose by killing another, are less likely to kill. Sometimes this theory works, and sometimes it does not. Dennis Rader, the BTK killer, had a job and was connected to his church community, but he still killed. It seems he killed despite what appeared to be strong bonds from the outside. In contrast, Theodore Kaczynski, the Unabomber, had separated himself from others in society, and it would appear he had weak social bonds and thus his behavior would be more understandable from a social bond perspective.

A GENERAL THEORY OF CRIME

About 20 years after he postulated social bond theory, Travis Hirschi joined forces with Michael Gottfredson (Gottfredson & Hirschi, 1990) to propose the idea that it is a combination of low self-control and opportunity that leads to criminal behavior. Low self-control, according to Gottfredson and Hirschi, is the result of poor or absent parenting. With poor parenting, children do not learn to set goals and work for what they want, and they never learn to control their temper. As a result, they are impulsive and act without much thought as to how it will affect others. In terms of our focus on homicide in this text, Hirschi and Gottfredson's theory could explain spur-of-the-moment murders, but as with most theories, it may not explain all homicide. For example, a passion murder in which a man kills his wife for being in bed with another man could be explained with a general theory of crime. Likewise, we could use a general theory of crime to explain a killing by a young man who kills on the spur of the moment when a cashier does not hand over the cash during a robbery. A very carefully planned homicide in which a woman poisons her husband over time for the insurance money is more difficult to explain with the general theory of crime.

NEUTRALIZATION THEORY

Sykes and Matza (1957) originally proposed neutralization or drift theory to explain juvenile delinquency. When interviewing delinquent youths, Sykes and Matza found that the youths understood and knew the rules. In other words, they were not "all bad," but instead they *drifted* into and out of delinquent behavior. Sykes and Matza explained that the youth and others who partake in illegal or deviant behavior learned how to explain their situations in such a way that the delinquent or illegal act was justified. These explanations are called *techniques of neutralizations*.

Note that, according to Sykes and Matza, the transgressor employs these techniques of neutralization before the person violates the rules. Further, there are five typical techniques. The techniques are noted in the left column here, and in the right column is a quote that reflects the corresponding technique.

Technique	Corresponding Quote
Denial of Responsibility:	"It is not my fault"
Denial of Injury	"No harm is done"
Denial of a Victim	"They deserved it"
Condemnation of the Condemners	"They do it too or do worse"
Appeal to Higher Loyalties	"I had to do it for my family/wife/brothers"

To commit a delinquent act, Sykes and Matza explained that an individual would only have to employ one of the techniques of neutralization.

When I teach this theory in my course on social deviance, students do quite well in explaining how this theory may work for committing homicide. For example, using the denial of responsibility technique, a young woman may decide to kill her stepfather because he has abused her and her younger sister. She might think it is not her fault but his. He has essentially asked for his own death. A serial killer who seeks out prostitutes to kill may believe he is not causing any harm. In fact, he may believe he is making society better. He would be using the denial of injury. Those who commit hate crime murders may employ the denial of victim technique. They may kill others who they believe deserve to be killed, and thus they do not see the victim as a victim. A terrorist who kills may use the condemnation of condemner technique to commit murder. Terrorists may believe a government has done what they believe to be horrible acts, and thus they kill citizens of that particular country. The terrorists are acting under the belief that those who will condemn them (the leaders of the country whose citizens they have attacked) are no

---

BOX 6.2
College Students Kill Their Professors

In this chapter, I jokingly use an example in which you might consider murdering your professor. This is certainly no laughing matter to faculty colleagues, students, friends, and families of professors who were murdered by their students. Although a student killing his or her professor is more infrequent than high school and middle school students killing their teachers, it appears that graduate students are more likely to kill their professors than undergraduates. An article in the *Detroit Free Press* in 1998 relayed three incidents in which graduate students killed at least one professor:

- A student who received a failing grade on his master's thesis killed the three professors who served on his committee at San Diego State in 1996.
- A postdoctoral student at the University of Iowa who was angry about not winning a dissertation award shot three of his professors and two other people in 1991.
- Wlodzimierz Dedecjus, who was a graduate student at Wayne State University, killed Dr. Andrzej Olbrot, his doctoral adviser, in 1998. Dedecjus had done poorly in an independent study course he took with Olbrot.

Source: Anonymous (1999); Walsh-Sarnecki (1998); Zeman, Walsh-Sarnecki, and Helms (1998).

---

better and in all likelihood worse than the terrorists themselves. Finally, the appeal to higher loyalty technique may be used by someone who kills someone who has hurt a member of his or her family. A gang member who kills to protect the gang's turf may be using the appeal to higher loyalty technique as well. I have included just one or two examples for each technique. See if you can imagine other examples for each technique.

MURDER AS RIGHTEOUS SLAUGHTER

In his 1990 book *Seductions of Crime*, Jack Katz proposes an explanation for murder that seems in line with Sykes and Matza's techniques of neutralization. Katz argues that often when the killers and victims know one another, killers justify the crime in their own mind. They believe they are preserving what is good. This may explain a case like that of Joshua Torres, who killed Richard Tunley. According to police investigators, Torres allegedly walked in on 50-year-old Tunley as he was beginning to molest Torres's 2-year-old daughter sexually. Torres then killed Tunley (McGurk & Geller, 2004). In other situations, such as a husband who kills his wife who is cheating, we may be less sympathetic in agreeing with the offender's justification. Still, Katz (1990) makes the point that in the spur of the moment the killer believes he or she is justified in killing another. Using a phenomenological approach, Katz explains that the killer interprets the situation at hand as one in which the potential victim is doing something the killer cannot ignore. According to Katz, the killer turns personal humiliation into rage (Greek, 2005; Katz, 1990). Like those offenders who use the neutralization technique that Sykes and Matza call *denial of responsibility*, Katz argues that killers see themselves pushed by forces greater than themselves (Greek, 2005).

CORRELATES OF HOMICIDE

General theories of crime may or may not be helpful for explaining homicide in the United States. Furthermore, the theories may be better for explaining one type of homicide or another. Chapters 7 through 12 are dedicated to six types of homicide. In many of these chapters, theories relevant to the particular types of homicide are discussed. Within these chapters, important correlates of the specific types of homicide are also noted. In this chapter, however, several factors that may be pertinent to the development of or refinement of homicide theories are now discussed.

Homicide researchers know that anyone can be a homicide victim. However, as discussed in Chapter 4, the odds of being a murder victim are higher for some people and lower for others. Race, sex, social class, and where we live can affect our chances of being a murder offender or victim. Official statistics indicate that rates of homicide victimization and offending are highest among African Americans, southerners, men, lower-class individuals, and people who live in the United States (relative to other industrial nations). As a result, some criminologists have attempted to explain why factors such as race, region, sex, and social class are correlated with homicide. In the next few sections, explanations for these correlations are addressed. Lastly, the issue of relatively high homicide rates in the United States is discussed.

RACE AND HOMICIDE: THE CULTURE OF VIOLENCE

Writing approximately 30 years before Katz wrote about homicide as righteous slaughter, Marvin Wolfgang was a pioneer in the study of homicide. Wolfgang (1958) studied hundreds of cases of homicide in Philadelphia. He found that many of these cases involved young African American men who were involved in confrontations that ended in the death of one of them. Writing with Enrique Ferracuti in their book *The Subculture of Violence*, Wolfgang thus proposed a theory to explain the high number of homicides involving African American men. Wolfgang and Ferracuti postulated that a subculture of violence exists among African Americans. Those who grew up in this subculture learned that violence is an appropriate response in many situations. In fact, violence is required whenever one is challenged. A person, especially a young man, who backed down from a challenge or ignored a slight, would be violating the norms of the subculture of violence. Thus Wolfgang and Ferracuti (1967) explained that high homicide rates among young African American men were to be expected. Because violence was a norm, homicide was likely. (See Chapter 7 for critiques of the subculture of violence theory.)

REGION AND HOMICIDE: SOUTHERN SUBCULTURE OF VIOLENCE

Similar to Wolfgang and Ferracuti's subculture of violence theory, some scholars have argued that a southern subculture of honor among southern white men operates much like the subculture of violence among African Americans (Gastil, 1971; Nisbet & Cohen, 1996). Analogous to the subculture of violence explanation of higher levels of homicide among African Americans, the southern culture of honor was developed to explain higher rates of homicide in the southern United States. According to the southern subculture of violence theory, white men have learned that backing down is weak and unmanly. As a result, any affront to a southern man must be answered with violence. Thus, as with young men in Philadelphia, men in the South are expected to retaliate if insulted. These retaliations are often violent as required by the norms of the southern subculture, and thus homicide is more common in the South than in other areas of the country.

LIFESTYLE AND ROUTINE ACTIVITIES THEORY

The fact that the odds of being a murder victim are higher for some people and lower for others may be explained by lifestyle and routine activities theory. Because these theories both presuppose that the lifestyles and habits of both victims and offenders affect whether they will be involved in crime, the two are often discussed as one theory (Barkan, 1997). Lifestyle theory focuses on how the lifestyle of an individual may place him or her more at risk for becoming a victim. During the 1980s, for example, many homicide victims were believed to be young men involved in gangs and drug sales. Their involvement in the illegal drug trade increased their risk of homicide.

Similarly, according to routine activity theory, the routine behavior of individuals may increase or decrease their risk of murder (Cohen & Felson, 1979). Routine activity theory suggests that three elements are required for crime: a motivated offender; the availability of a suitable target; and the absence of effective guardians. Using routine activity theory, we can explain murder at both the macro and micro levels (Miethe & Regoeczi, 2004). Younger women as opposed to older women, for example, may be more likely to be raped and murdered because those motivated to do such crime are young men. Because younger women spend more time with younger men, we would expect them to be victimized at higher rates than older women (Mustaine, 1997; Mustaine & Tewksbury, 1999). Likewise, we might be able to explain higher numbers of homicide in certain neighborhoods because the neighborhoods are lacking in effective guardians. As such, stranger murders would be less likely in high-rise condominiums with security systems and security guards than in poorly maintained crime-infested high-rise public housing units like those that existed in Chicago's infamous Cabrini-Green public housing development.

MEN AND VIOLENCE: FEMINIST PERSPECTIVES ON MASCULINITY

Although feminist criminologists began to address the issue of gender in criminological research in the 1970s, it was not until the 1990s that criminologists really began to explore the connection between masculinity and violence (Brookman, 2000). With regard to homicide, one fact that appears to be true throughout time and across the world is that males are far more likely than females to commit homicide. This is a fact that has been taken for granted, and thus it has been largely ignored in theories of homicide offending. Although we know that all men do not murder and some women have murdered, the fact that nearly 9 out of 10 people who murder are men is important.

To understand "the links between men's use of violence and their perceptions and understandings of the functions that violence serves," Brookman (2000: 1) interviewed 20 men who had killed or violently assaulted other men. She found that the men used violence as a way to control others and to boost their masculine identity. It was important to these men for others to perceive them as tough because to be masculine is to be tough. Brookman (2000) is careful to note that some men are quicker to use violence than others. Moreover, drawing from Messerschmidt's (1993) work on masculinity and violence, Brookman points out that men's use of violence is likely related to the positions they hold in society. In other words, men who have alternative means to control others may not perceive the need to use violence. Either way, however, masculinity and control seem to be linked. Thus Brookman suggests there is a subculture of masculinity, and this subculture (discussed in Chapter 7) sometimes requires men to be violent.

SOCIAL STRATIFICATION AND HOMICIDE

Much research suggests a link between crime and economic conditions. With regard to homicide, data suggest that poor people in the United States and throughout the world are more likely to be found among homicide offenders and victims than are individuals in higher economic categories. As discussed by Shaw and McKay and other criminologists in the social disorganization tradition, crime rates, especially violent crime rates, tend to be higher in communities where people are economically disadvantaged. The reality of living a day-to-day existence in poverty is believed to be extremely stressful. For some people, the stress of living on the edge can push them to the brink, and thus violence may result. Additionally, growing up in an area where violence is common and where positive role models may be overshadowed by negative role models may help foster criminal ways among youngsters.

Along these lines, in his book *The Truly Disadvantaged*, William Julius Wilson (1987) made the argument that high levels of concentrated disadvantage and poverty generate high levels of crime including homicide (Krivo & Peterson, 1996). Further, this relationship is not simply a one-to-one relationship, but that communities with many people living in poverty are likely to have exponentially greater rates of homicide than those communities that are not saturated with poverty. Krivo and Peterson (1996)

BOX 6.3

Violence in the United States

Violence has always been an important part of U.S. history. Writing about American violence, Richard Maxwell Brown (1979) writes that this violence has been both negative and positive. Negative aspects include crime, political assassinations, and racial conflict. However, some of the most positive events in U.S. history have been very bloody. Beginning with U.S. independence, violence has led to what we see as important and valuable. The extremely bloody civil war preserved the nation and freed slaves. He ends his article by saying,

> Violence is clearly rejected by us as a part of the American value system, but so great has been our involvement with violence over the long sweep of our history that violence has truly become part of our unacknowledged (or underground) value structure. (Brown, 1979: 41)

What evidence is there that the United States values violence? What evidence is there that violence is not a value in the United States? Do you think violence as a value is related to homicide in the United States? Do you think there is a culture of violence or subculture of violence in the United States today?

---

examined neighborhood violent crime rates in Columbus, Ohio, where there are both black and white high poverty neighborhoods. Their findings support Wilson's ideas. They found that "extremely high disadvantaged communities have qualitatively higher levels of crime than less disadvantaged areas, and that this pattern holds for both black and white communities" (Krivo & Peterson, 1996: 640).

WHY DO WE KILL SO OFTEN IN THE UNITED STATES?

Despite the great amounts of wealth overall in the United States, those of us who live in the United States are at much higher risk for homicide than those who live in many other countries. As noted in Chapter 4 and seen in Table 6.1, the United States has one of the highest homicide rates in the world. In his textbook *Criminology*, Steven Barkan (1997) poses and gives possible answers to the question "Why is the United States more violent than other industrial nations?" (1997: 261). The first answer he discusses involves economic stratification. Barkan notes that studies indicate that countries with high income inequality have higher rates of homicide. In the United States we see great disparities between those at the top and those at the bottom of the economic ladder. Second, many people in the United States own guns, and assaults with guns may more likely end in death. Third, like the subcultural arguments postulated to explain high rates of homicide in the South and high rates of homicide among young African American men, some argue that we have a history and culture of violence in the United States.

TABLE 6.1
Number of Homicides (2000) and Average Homicide Rate (1999–2001) for Six
Highest Homicide Countries

Country	Number of Homicides, 2000	Average Homicide Rate per 100,000 population, 1999–2001
1. South Africa	21,683	55.86
2. Russia	31,829	22.05
3. Lithuania	398	10.62
4. Estonia	143	10.61
5. Latvia	150	6.47
6. U.S.A.	15,586	5.56

Source: Barclay and Tavares (2003).

BOX 6.4
Methamphetamine and Homicide

Toxicology reports during the first six months of 2005 indicated that a third of the 115 Phoenix homicide victims had ingested methamphetamines sometime near their death. Methamphetamines in the blood systems of murder victims is just one indication of what reporter Paul Rubin (2005) reported Phoenix police officers knew about homicide in their city. According to a report by Rubin, Phoenix police were seeing an increase in homicides linked to methamphetamines at the middle of the first decade of the twenty-first century. The police noted that alcohol was still very prevalent among both offenders and victims, and they still handled a case involving crack cocaine now and then as well as cases where no drugs or alcohol influences could be found. Police in Maricopa County, Arizona, however, were seeing increasing use of methamphetamines linked to all types of crime including homicide (Rubin, 2005).

THE ROLE OF ALCOHOL AND DRUG USE
IN HOMICIDAL BEHAVIOR

According to Parker and Auerhahn (1999), the role of alcohol and drug use in homicidal behavior has not been widely studied. Nevertheless, evidence suggests a strong relationship between homicide and alcohol or illegal drug use (Carcach & Conroy, 2001; Collins & Messerschmidt, 1993; Fagan, 1990). The evidence tends to show that over half of homicides involve offenders or victims that are under the influence of drugs or alcohol at the time of the homicide incident. However, note that alcohol is more frequently involved than illegal drugs (Parker & Auerhahn, 1999). The reason for the connection is not altogether clear, and theories are still being developed to explain the relationship. Nevertheless, Parker and Auerhahn (1999: 188) report that alcohol appears to be "a causal agent, albeit one among many, in the genesis of homicide." With regard to illicit drugs, Parker and Auerhahn (1999) report that the research does not yet explain the causal relationship, if any, between drugs and homicide. It could be that the connection between drug use and homicide is part of a generally violent lifestyle that may be explained by other theories. Although it could be that some combination of biological and environmental effects mix in the presence of illicit drugs to contribute to homicide.

SUMMARY

Most of the theories in this chapter postulate an explanation for crime that looks to structural or cultural explanations. The theories were presented somewhat chronologically beginning with the classical school perspective. Classical school criminologists began to see crime not as a result of biological or psychological abnormalities but as a consequence of a person's choice. As criminologists continued to study crime, they found that there were patterns to who was choosing to do crime and who was not. This observation led to social disorganization theory, which posits a link between environment and criminal offending. In time, Edwin Sutherland explained that the mechanisms by which we learn to commit crime is the same as how we learn anything. Social control theorist turned the questions about crime offending upside down by asking not why individuals do crime, but why don't we all do crime? Hirschi, a social control theorist, argued that bonds to society prevent us from doing crime. Later, however, with Gottfredson, Hirschi suggested that individuals with low self-control and opportunity are most likely to commit crimes. Similar to control theorists, Sykes and Matza argued that even if we know the rules or norms, we sometimes cross over the line. To cross the line, we use what they called techniques of neutralizations. These techniques allow offenders to justify their criminal acts before they do them. More recently, Jack Katz proposed the idea of righteous slaughter in which he postulates that some homicide offenders feel justified in killing another.

Following brief overviews of the major sociocultural explanations for crime and their application to homicide, common correlates of homicide including race, sex, social class and region as well as some of the theories postulated to explain these connections, including subcultural theories, were reviewed. Feminist explanations for masculine violence and William Julius Wilson's ideas about the truly disadvantaged as applied to homicide and class were also included in this chapter. Explanations for the high rates of homicide in the United States as compared to other industrial nations were noted. And finally, at the end of the chapter, a discussion on the unknown role of drugs and alcohol in homicidal behavior is included. In Chapter 7 and succeeding chapters, different types of homicide are reviewed. In some of these chapters, additional theories postulated to explain these particular types of homicide are included, and in other chapters, theories discussed in this chapter are expanded.

CHAPTER QUESTIONS

1. How are explanations for homicide in this chapter different from biological and psychological explanations for homicide?
2. How would Beccaria or another person using a classical perspective explain homicide?
3. Why does the transitional zone have the most crime according to social disorganization theorists?
4. Differential association theory postulates that crime is learned. Give an example of how homicide might be learned.
5. What do social control theorists ask with regard to crime?
6. List and explain Hirschi's four social bonds.
7. Can you imagine a case where all four social bonds are strong but a homicide still occurs? Explain.
8. How well do you think a general theory of crime explains homicide in the United States? Explain.
9. Give one example of homicide that might fit each of the techniques of neutralization.
10. What is meant by "murder as righteous slaughter"?
11. List at least three correlates of homicide discussed in this chapter.
12. Compare the subculture of violence and the subculture of honor.
13. According to lifestyle theory, why might women working in prostitution be overrepresented in homicide statistics?
14. What three criteria are necessary according to routine activity for crime to occur?
15. How are masculinity and homicide linked, according to feminists?
16. Discuss why homicide in the United States is relatively high compared to many other nations.
17. What theories in this or previous chapters might explain the high rates of homicide in the United States?
18. Which has a higher correlation with homicide, alcohol or illicit drugs?

REFERENCES

Anonymous. 1999. "Wayne State Professor Gunned Down in Class." *Chronicle of Higher Education*, 45(18): A8.

Barclay, Gordon, and Cynthia Tavares. 2003. *International Comparisons of Criminal Justice Statistics 2001*. London: Home Office.

Barkan, Steven. 1997. *Criminology: A Sociological Understanding*. Upper Saddle River, NJ: Prentice Hall.

Beccaria, Cesare. 1986. *On Crimes and Punishments*. Translated by David Young. Indianapolis: Hackett. (Original work published 1764)

Blau, Judith R., and Peter M. Blau. 1982. "The Cost of Inequality, Metropolitan Structure, and Violent Crime." *American Sociological Review*, 47: 114–125.

Brookman, Fiona. 2000. "Dying for Control: Men, Murder and Sub-Lethal Violence." In George Mair and Roger Tarling, eds., *British Criminology Conference: Selected Proceedings*. Vol. 3. Accessed online at http://www.britsoccrim.org/volume3/002.pdf

Brown, Richard Maxwell. 1979. "Historical Patterns of American Violence." In Hugh Davis Graham and Ted Robert Gurr, eds., *Violence in America: Historical and Comparative Perspectives*. Beverly Hills, CA: Sage.

Carcach, Carlos, and Rowena Conroy. 2001. "Alcohol and Homicide in Australia: A Routine Activity." Canberra: Australian Institute of Criminology.

Cohen, Larry, and Marcus Felson. 1979. "Social Change and Crime Rates." *American Sociological Review*, 44: 588–608.

Collins, Pamela M., and James J. Messerschmidt. 1993. "Epidemiology and Alcohol-Related Violence." *Alcohol Health and Research World*, 17: 93–100.

Durkheim, Emile. 1997. *Division of Labor in Society*. New York: Free Press. (Original work published 1893)

Fagan, Jeffrey. 1990. "Intoxication and Aggression," in M. Tonry and J.Q. Wilson, eds., *Drugs and Crime. Volume 13: Crime and Justice, A Review of Research* (pp. 241–320). Chicago: University of Chicago Press Journals.

Gastil, Raymond D. 1971. "Homicide and a Regional Culture of Violence." *American Sociological Review*, 36: 412–427.

Gottfredson, Michael R., and Travis Hirschi. 1990. *A General Theory of Crime*. Stanford: Stanford University Press.

Greek, Cecil. 2005. Seduction 1 Web page. Last updated November 22, 2005. Retrieved April 7, 2006, from http://www.criminology.fsu.edu/crimtheory/week12.htm

Hirschi, Travis. 1969. *Causes of Delinquency*. Berkeley: University of California Press.

Katz, Jack. 1990. *Seductions of Crime*. New York: Basic Books.

Krivo, Lauren J., and Ruth D. Peterson. 1996. "Extremely Disadvantaged Neighborhoods and Urban Crime." *Social Forces*, 75: 619–650.

Krivo, Lauren J., and Ruth D. Peterson. 2000. "The Structural Context of Homicide: Accounting for Racial Differences in Process." *American Sociological Review*, 65: 547–559.

McGurk, Joe, and Andy Geller. 2004, January 28. "NYPD: Dad Executes Paroled Sex Offender." *New York Post*. Retrieved April 7, 2006, from http://www.officer.com/article/article.jsp?id=9016&siteSection=1

Meithe, Terance D., and Wendy C. Regoeczi. 2004. *Rethinking Homicide: Exploring the Structure and Process Underlying Deadly Situations*. Cambridge: Cambridge University Press.

Messerschmidt, James W. 1993. *Masculinities and Crime: Critique and Reconceptuatlization of Theory*: Rowan & Littlefield Publishers, Inc.

Mustaine, Elizabeth E. 1997. "Victimization Risks and Routine Activities: A Theoretical Examination Using a Gender-Specific and Domain Specific Model." *American Journal of Criminal Justice*, 22: 41–70.

Mustaine, Elizabeth E., and Richard Tewksbury. 1999. "A Routine Activities Theory Explanation for Women's Stalking Victimizations." *Violence Against Women*, 5: 43–62.

Nisbet, Richard E., and Dov Cohen. 1996. *Culture of Honor: The Psychology of Violence in the South*. Boulder: Westview Press.

Pankratz, Howard. 2005, March 24. "Fatal Montbello Fight Described as Gang Rite." *Denver Post*, p. B-01.

Parker, Robert Nash, and Kathleen Auerhahn. 1999. "Drugs, Alcohol, and Homicide: Issues in Theory and Research." In M. Dwayne Smith and Margaret A. Zahn, eds., *Homicide: A Sourcebook of Social Research* (pp. 176–219). Thousand Oaks, CA: Sage.

Rasche, Chris E. 1996. "Theorizing About Homicide: A Presentation on the Theories Explaining Homicide and Other Crime." In Pamela K. Lattimore and Cynthia A. Nahabedian, ed., *Nature of Homicide: Trends and Changes, Proceedings of the 1996 Meeting of the Homicide Research Working Group* (pp. 23–34). Washington D.C.: U.S. Department of Justice.

Rubin, Paul. 2005, November 3. "Meth Fatalities: Methamphetamine Is Number-One with a Bullet When It Comes to Violent Death in Phoenix." *Phoenix New Times*. Retrieved April 21, 2006. http://www.phoenixnewtimes.com/2005-11-03/news/meth-fatalities/

Sampson, Robert J. 1987. "Urban Black Violence: The Effect of Male Joblessness and Family Dissolution." *American Journal of Sociology*, 93: 348–382.

Shaw, Clifford and Henry D. McKay. 1942. *Juvenile Delinquency and Urban Areas*. Chicago: Univ. Press.

Shihadeh, Edward S., and Darrel J. Steffensmeier. 1994. "Economic Inequality, Family Disruption, and Urban Black Violence: Cities as Units of Stratification and Social Control." *Social Forces*, 73(1): 729–751.

Starr, Barbara. 2002, July 22. "Fort Bragg Killings Raise Alarm About Stress: No Connection Established to Assailants' Afghanistan Duty." CNN.com. Retrieved April 22, 2006, from http://archives.cnn.com/2002/US/07/26/army.wives/

Sutherland, Edwin, and Donald R. Cressey. 2000. "Differential Association Theory." In Patricia and Peter Adler, eds., *Constructions of Deviance: Social Power, Context, and Interaction* (pp. 69–71). Belmont CA: Thomson.

Sykes, Gresham, and Matza, David. 1957. "Techniques of Neutralization: A Theory of Delinquency." *American Sociological Review*, 22(6): 664–670.

Toby, Jackson. 1957. "Social Disorganization and Stake in Conformity." *Journal of Criminal Law, Criminology, and Police Science*, 48: 12–17.

Walsh-Sarnecki, Peggy. 1998, December 12. "Instructors, Students Try to Gain Perspective After Murder." *Detroit Free Press*, p. 5a.

Williams, Kirk R. 1984. "Economic Sources of Homicide: Re-estimating the Effect of Poverty and Inequality." *American Sociological Review*, 49: 283–289.

Wilson, William Julius. 1987. *The Truly Disadvantaged: The Underclass and Public Policy*. Chicago: University of Chicago Press.

Wolfgang, Marvin. 1958. *Patterns in Criminal Homicide*. Philadelphia: University of Pennsylvania.

Wolfgang, Marvin, and Franco Ferracuti. 1967. *The Subculture of Violence*. London: Social Science Paperbacks.

Zeman, David, Peggy Walsh-Sarnecki, and Matt Helms. 1998, December 12. "Grad Student Faces Charges in Slaying of WSU Professor." *Detroit Free Press*, p. 1a.

Chapter 7

CONFRONTATIONAL HOMICIDE

As noted in Chapter 3, criminal justice researchers and practitioners categorize homicides in different ways. The next seven chapters are dedicated to different types of homicides. Because some of the categories are based on circumstances and others are based on victim/offender relationships, the categories are not necessarily mutually exclusive categories. In other words, a particular homicide could fall into more than one category. An adolescent boy, for instance, who goes into a murderous rage and kills his parents and then several of his schoolmates could appear in the chapter about children who kill as well as in the chapter on mass and spree killing. And, if he killed children in his school based on their race or religion, the incident could fit into the chapter on murder as hate crime. The fact that one case can fit in several chapters is something to keep in mind as you read the next several chapters. Nevertheless, these categories of homicide are often conclusive, and even if overlapping, they give us a place to start trying to understand why homicide happens and what we may do to prevent it. These categorizations also may help give us clues for solving homicide cases.

This chapter is about confrontational homicides, which may be the most common type of homicide throughout the world (Adler & Polk, 2001; Daly & Wilson, 1988). Although not always referred to as confrontational homicides, the types of homicides discussed in this chapter are those in which an altercation is viewed as a contest of honor by at least one of the participants. The altercation evolves into violence and ends in the death of a least one of the participants. This chapter includes an expanded explanation of confrontational homicide and recent real-life cases as well as important classical studies on homicide circumstances. Victim-precipitated homicide is explained in this chapter. Finally, the question of whether women take part in confrontational homicides is contemplated.

DEFINITION

Although some reference to confrontational homicide is made in criminal law discussions about self-defense law, Ken Polk seems to have introduced the use of the term *confrontational homicide*. In his 1994 book *When Men Kill*, Polk describes confrontational homicides as those that begin with a public altercation viewed as a contest of honor by at least one of the participants. The altercation then quickly evolves into violence and ends in death (Polk, 1994: 60). Also referred to as *honor contest violence*, confrontational homicides tend to occur in public places such as bars, parties, parking lots, or in nearby streets or alleys (Polk, 1994). The participants (victims and offenders) are often, but not always, intoxicated or under the influence of alcohol or illicit substances.

According to the literature, in confrontational homicides, both the offender and victim are most often male, and the incident that leads to the lethal violence is seen as a threat to the reputation of one of them. As noted by Polk (1999), the threat may be an insult, a bump, or some sort of nonverbal challenge. At the outset of these situations, there is no intention to murder. However, the original threat is followed by a verbal exchange in which one of the participants challenges the other, and the altercation quickly become physical. Sometimes one of the participants leaves the scene to return with a weapon, but often the situation escalates very quickly and the victim is killed with an available object (Polk, 1999). Sometimes the available object is a fist or a beer bottle, and sometimes it is a gun.

On November 9, 2005, an 18-year-old man in North Braddock, Pennsylvania, was playing a video game with friends when he allegedly shot two of his friends to death. According to newspaper accounts, 18-year-old Erskine Smith shot and killed Daniel Underwood, 17, and Jonathan Hutson, 19, after they argued during a PlayStation 2 football game (Belser, 2005). This homicide incident appears to encompass many of the components of a confrontational homicide. According to police detectives who investigated the incident, a squabble over a video game erupted quickly into a deadly situation. Both the victims and offender were male, and it did not appear the killing was planned but that it evolved out of some seemingly trivial incident.

GENDER AND CONFRONTATIONAL HOMICIDE

As you will see in this chapter, most studies of confrontational homicide have included men as both victims and offenders; others include women but only as victims. This is not surprising in some respects because women generally make up less than 15% of homicide offenders in any country where such statistics are kept. Furthermore, the theories that explain confrontational homicide often postulate either explicitly or implicitly some connection between masculinity and violence. Thus most of this chapter focuses on men as offenders and victims of confrontational homicide, and in most of the discussions both offenders and victims are referred to with male references. Nevertheless, in a study of homicide in Augusta, Georgia, that I did with Lori Scott, we found cases of homicide by women that could be classified as confrontational homicides. As a result, I include some examples of homicide in this chapter with female victims and female offenders. Then, toward the end of the chapter, once you are familiar with the theories, I return to the possibility that women can be involved in confrontational homicide as both victim and offender.

DATA ON CONFRONTATIONAL HOMICIDE

No official organization classifies homicides as *confrontational homicides*. Thus there is no way to be certain of how many homicides fit in this category. However, studies about this type of homicide give us some idea about the frequency of confrontational homicide. The FBI circumstance categorizations may also give us an approximation of the frequency of such homicides. Based on Wolfgang's (1958) classic study of homicide in Philadelphia, it may be surmised that around a third of homicides are confrontational homicide because Wolfgang found that 35% of the homicides he studied grew out of trivial altercations.

Polk (1994) found slightly fewer cases of confrontational homicide in his Victoria, Australia, study of homicide. He found that 22% of all homicides in Victoria could be classified as confrontational homicides. Importantly, confrontational homicide makes up the largest category in his study. Similarly, a review of 2004 homicide data from the FBI indicates that homicides resulting from arguments remain the most frequently cited circumstance for known circumstances (Fox & Zawitz, 2006). Nearly a third (29.8%) of homicides during 2004 were related to some type of brawl or argument. Although each of these 4,213 homicides may not fit exactly the definition of confrontational homicide, it is quite likely that many of them did. Furthermore, a portion of the remaining 9,908 homicides categorized as circumstances other than argument may have been confrontational homicides. For example, 97 homicides were classified as lover's triangle circumstances, and another 804 were categorized as juvenile gang killings. It is reasonable to believe some of these cases may also be categorized as confrontational homicides.

Figure 7.1 shows the percentage of homicide incidents that may have been confrontational homicides in 2000 to 2004. The figure shows the total number of homicides in each of these years that were classified as one of the following circumstances: romantic triangle, brawl due to influence of alcohol, brawl due to influence of narcotics, argument over money or property, other argument, or juvenile gang killing. Interestingly, these figures are practically the same as those found for homicides growing out of a trivial altercation in Wolfgang's classic Philadelphia study. Further, the percentage of these types of homicide does not vary significantly by year. In 2001, we see the highest percentage at 36.7%. The percentage dips in 2002 to 35.4% and rises again to 36.2% in 2004.

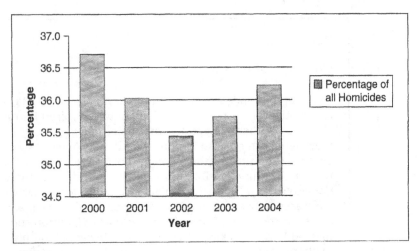

FIGURE 7.1
Percentage of Homicides Possibly Due to Confrontational Circumstances
Note: 2001 data does not include homicides due to the 9/11 terrorist attack.
Source: Compiled from Federal Bureau of Investigation Statistics Data (FBI, 2006).

HISTORY OF CONFRONTATIONAL HOMICIDE

Polk (1994) first discussed particular types of homicide scenarios as *confrontational homicides* fairly recently. However, these types of killings are not new. In fact, Mark Cooney (1997) argues that such killings have been quite common throughout history and across the world and among individuals at all levels of the social hierarchy. Although Cooney (1997, 1998) does not use the term *confrontational homicide,* he provides an overview of homicides that could easily be defined as confrontational. For instance, he discusses homicides that are the result of feuding, brawling, dueling, and lynching. In each of these forms, a homicide is the end result of a confrontation that begins when a man feels his honor is challenged. For example, Cooney (1997) notes that it is not uncommon for a chief among the Tauade of Papua New Guinea to kill another when he feels he has been insulted. Similarly, Cooney explains that it was common among elites in the sixteenth and seventeenth century to use their swords in situations in which they felt their honor was challenged.

Cooney (1997) also reports that beginning in the fifteenth century and lasting as late as the nineteenth century, dueling led to many homicides. Moreover, these duels were the result of some sort of an affront to a man's honor. You may even remember from your high school history class, as I do, that Andrew Jackson, the seventh president of the United States, shot and killed a man in a duel. Or perhaps you remember that Aaron Burr killed Alexander Hamilton in a duel (see Box 7.1). In both cases, the duels and the resultant homicides could be considered confrontational

---

BOX 7.1

Dueling Politicians

The duel that ended Alexander Hamilton's life on July 11, 1804, was the culmination of a long-standing feud between Aaron Burr and Hamilton. The two had been lawyers at the same time in Albany, New York, and they were both on Washington's staff during America's war for independence. At the time of the infamous duel, Hamilton was the secretary of the U.S. Treasury and Burr was the vice president of the United States. Hamilton was a Federalist and Burr was a Democrat, which was just one difference between them. They knew each other well, and each looked down on the other. During a dinner party, Hamilton supposedly disrespected Burr by talking about him negatively behind his back. Hearing of these remarks, Burr challenged Hamilton to a duel, and the two exchanged several letters. Hamilton refused to apologize, and eventually the two met at Weehawken to duel. They each drew their pistols and shot. Some speculate that Hamilton pulled his arm up to miss. Burr, however, hit Hamilton, who died the next day. Although a fairly common practice, dueling was illegal in New York during this time, and Burr was indicted for murder. Burr, however, was never tried for the murder of Hamilton. After spending a few months in Georgia, he returned to the nation's capital where he continued as vice president until his term ended in 1805 (Continetti, 2004).

---

homicides. The men in these cases dueled because one or the other said something that was seen as an affront to the other's honor. Although less formalized and more common among those of lower status than the duels of the past, men still kill each other in similar situations. Today, however, a man may kill because he feels he has been disrespected or "dissed." We rarely refer to such situations as affronts to one's honor nowadays.

A more recent homicide case than the duels of the eighteenth century that was widely covered by the press in England appears to be the result of a modern duel of sorts. Carl Morgan, a 24-year-old member of the rap group So Solid Crew, was given a sentence of at least 30 years in prison for murdering Colin Scarlett. Press reports indicate that Morgan killed Scarlett for disrespecting him. Apparently, Scarlett, who is referred to as Morgan's "love rival" by the press, was dating Morgan's ex-girlfriend, Elisha McFarlane (Bird, 2005). Morgan and McFarlane fought over McFarlane's relationship with Scarlett. This enraged Scarlett, who then beat Morgan as McFarlane watched. Morgan got a gun and set out to retaliate against Scarlett for the attack. Scarlett, who reportedly heard that Morgan was coming for him, acquired a gun as well. A modern-day duel ensued with both men drawing their guns. Scarlett fired seven shots that all missed Morgan. Morgan, however, appears to have been a better marksman. He managed to hit Scarlett in the neck, chest, and right hand with the four shots he fired (Bird, 2005).

VICTIM-PRECIPITATED HOMICIDE

In his 1958 study of homicide in Philadelphia, Marvin Wolfgang (1958) found it was not uncommon for the victim of a homicide to have been involved in the events that led to his death. In fact, sometimes the victim initiated the incident that resulted in his death. Wolfgang (1958) introduced the term *victim-precipitated homicide* to describe homicide incidents in which the victim was the first to employ "physical force against the subsequent slayer" (Wolfgang, 1958: 252). The concept of victim-precipitated homicide is very relevant for this chapter on confrontational homicides because, as should be clear; many cases of victim-precipitated homicide can often also be categorized as confrontational homicides. Moreover, victim-precipitated homicides and confrontational homicides often share many characteristics as seen in the following review of Wolfgang's Philadelphia data.

Wolfgang determined that 150, or 26%, of the 588 criminal homicides in Philadelphia he examined were victim-precipitated homicides. He found that the victims in victim-precipitated homicides were more likely to be male and African American than in non-victim-precipitated homicides. In the victim-precipitated homicides, 94% of the victims were male as compared to 70% in the non-victim-precipitated homicides. Further, nearly 80% of the victims were African American in the victim-precipitated cases in contrast to 70% in the non-victim-precipitated homicides. Different from what we have so far defined as confrontational homicides, however, women were found to make up a larger percentage (29%) of the victim-precipitated homicide offenders as compared with the non-victim-precipitated homicides (14%). It may seem that Wolfgang's finding that almost a third of homicide offenders who were provoked by their victims were women is in contrast to the notion of confrontational homicide. However, it is likely that many of these women were responding to men who initiated physical violence against them. Furthermore, it is possible that the men were violent toward the women because the men saw the women as challenging their masculinity or otherwise disrespecting them. As such, some of these homicides may very well be confrontational homicide. Certainly, all cases of women who murder men are not the result of a confrontation or domestic violence. Still as discussed in Chapter 8, many women homicide offenders kill their abusive husbands, former husbands, and boyfriends.

HOMICIDE AS A SITUATED TRANSACTION

Although Polk may have first used the term *confrontational homicide*, criminologists before him recognized the regularity with which homicide grows out of seemingly trivial altercations. In his 1977 study of homicide, Luckenbill (1977: 176) emphasized that homicide is often the result of seemingly inconsequential incidents that turn into "character contests." He explained that most homicides are the result of a contest in which adversaries interact in a way that at least one of them believed would keep him from looking weak. He called these interactions "situated transactions."

Luckenbill (1977) based his findings on an examination of police records for 71 homicides in a California county. The cases described by Luckenbill are very similar to the Australian cases that Polk described in his work on confrontational homicide. In both Polk's and Luckenbill's samples, most of the homicides occurred when the offender and victim were taking part in leisure activities such as dancing, partying, watching television, and, importantly, drinking alcoholic beverages. Thus it is not surprising that the majority of homicides occurred on the weekends and between the hours of 6 P.M. and 2 A.M. In Luckenbill's study, almost half the homicides occurred in a home, but notably, as Polk also found, taverns and street corners were also common locations for homicides. Luckenbill (1977) found that over 60% of the cases he studied involved victims and offenders who were either related or friends. However, in many cases the offender and victim were mere acquaintances or complete strangers before the tragic event of one of their deaths. Whether related or unrelated, enemy or acquaintances, Luckenbill noted that very often both the offender and victim had an audience of onlookers who knew either one or both of the men as lovers, friends, family, or coworkers.

Most importantly for this chapter on confrontational homicides, Luckenbill (1977: 177) found that these homicides followed a similar pattern in which the eventual offender and victim each played a role. Luckenbill described the six stages through which the homicide situation progressed beginning with the initial conflict and ending with the final move made by the offender after the death of his (or her) opponent. His stages appear to describe confrontational homicide.

Luckenbill refers to the first stage as the *opening move*. In the opening move the victim does something that is viewed as an affront by the offender. It could be that the victim makes a disparaging remark, such as calling the offender a wimp or otherwise challenging his manhood. Luckenbill found that the opening move by the victim varied, but three basic types of actions start the homicide transaction.

The most common opening move is a comment that the offender believes is offensive. Luckenbill found that 41% of the cases he studied fit this scenario. A homicide incident reported by the Associated Press appears to have begun with this first type of opening move. Travis Ault, a 17-year-old Spokane, Washington, youth, allegedly killed 18-year-old Wesley Myers and his 52-year-old mother Doreen Britt because Myers "bad-mouthed" one of his friends (Associated Press, 2005a). According to a witness quoted by the Associated Press (2005a), Ault stabbed Myers 16 to 17 times because "Wesley was talking trash to him."

The second most common opening move in a homicide transaction occurred in 34% of Luckenbill's cases. In these cases, a victim refuses to do what an offender wants. The offender interprets this refusal as a "denial of his ability or right to command obedience" (Luckenbill, 1977: 180). Although less typical because the offender is female, the 2002 homicide of school principal Norman Wicks in Vancouver provides an example of this type of opening move. Ian Mulgrew reported in *The Vancouver Sun* that Principal Wicks was stabbed by his lover, Teresa Senner, during a confrontation over his multiple infidelities. It is not the confrontation over Wicks's infidelity that makes this case fit the second type of opening move. Rather, it was that Senner killed Wicks because he said he would not leave his wife. Wicks would not comply with Senner's request, so she grabbed a large kitchen knife and killed him by stabbing him in the groin (Mulgrew, 2005).

In the third type of opening move, which described 25% of the cases that Luckenbill reviewed, the eventual offender finds a nonverbal gesture made by the victim to be personally offensive. Luckenbill indicated that often the offender believes this gesture is an insult to his sexual prowess. Scott Lemerond of Green Bay, Wisconsin, died as the result of an argument that appears to have started with the third type of initial move discussed by Luckenbill. Lemerond and Todd Charles, who were both 38 years old, fought at a party in Charles's living room. According to the Associated Press (2005b), Charles became angry with Lemerond when the latter took a bandana off Charles's head and began hitting him with it. In what clearly fits Luckenbill's third type of opening move, Charles reportedly said that Lemerond was trying to insult him in front of his girlfriend by hitting him with a do-rag. A fight between the two men began, and when it moved to the kitchen, Charles grabbed a grilling fork. It is not clear whether Charles stabbed Lemerond or whether he rolled on the fork in a struggle during their fight. Either way, Charles was charged with first-degree reckless homicide in the Brown County Wisconsin Circuit Court after Lemerond died as a result of the stabbing (Associated Press, 2005b).

The second stage of a homicide transaction, according to Luckenbill, is the interpretation of the event in the opening move as an affront. The offender views whatever the victim has done as offensive. It is not necessary that the victim meant it to be offensive; the key point of the second stage is the interpretation. Luckenbill acknowledges that in 60% of the cases in his sample, the victim or witnesses to the interaction helped the offender define the opening move as offensive. For example, in the case just noted above in which Charles allegedly stabbed Lemerond, Charles reportedly said that Lemerond was "trying to insult me in front of his girlfriend" (Associated Press, 2005b). Clearly, Charles saw Lemerond's actions as deliberately insulting and he found it offensive.

In the third stage, having determined that the victim has affronted him, the offender could excuse or ignore the insult. However, Luckenbill reports that in each of the homicide scenarios in his study, the offenders made a retaliatory move to save face and not sully their own reputation. The retaliatory moves, according to Luckenbill, are the opening moves for the offender in which he challenges the victim and in essence defines the situation as one in which violence may ensue. In the fork-stabbing case, the news report does not make it clear exactly what happened after Charles recognized Lemerond's actions as insulting. The reader is simply told that the men started fighting. It is likely that Charles responded to Lemerond's insult by moving into stage 3. In all likelihood Charles shoved, hit, or verbally challenged Lemerond, if not some combination of the latter.

Next, Charles and Lemerond most likely moved to Luckenbill's stage 4, at which point Lemerond's reputation would be on the line. Lemerond would have had to stand up to Charles and fought back, thus saving his own reputation at that point. Or he could have fled or apologized at the risk of being seen as weak by the other party guests, including his girlfriend. It seems that Lemerond made a move to save his own face during stage 4. Because, according to the witnesses, the men moved into stage 5.

Stage 5 is the "forging of a working agreement" at which time both victim and offender seem to be committed to battle (Luckenbill, 1977: 184). It is during this fifth stage that a weapon of some sort is brought in and the actual homicide occurs. Luckenbill notes that the offender may leave to get a weapon or may simply use something readily available as Charles did when he grabbed a fork. According to the

Associated Press report, as the men wrestled on the floor, Lemerond bit Charles on the leg. Charles reached into a kitchen drawer to grab a knife to use for intimidation or self-defense. He grabbed a fork instead of a knife, but it worked. After being stabbed with the fork, Lemerond clutched his chest and fell to the floor (Associated Press, 2005b) completing Luckenbill's stage 5.

Stage 6 is the final move by the offender. Luckenbill reports three general moves the offender may make in stage 6 following the homicide. Most often in Luckenbill's study, the offender fled the scene. However, in nearly a third of the cases, the offender remained until the police arrived, and in approximately one in five cases, the offender was held involuntarily by observers until the police arrived (Luckenbill, 1977).

As should be clear in the homicide involving Charles and Lemerond, confrontational homicides involve both the victim and offender. Luckenbill's work is important because he argues that the homicide is not a one-sided event with an unwitting victim assuming a passive role. Instead, Luckenbill views homicide as a "situated transaction" where each participant has an opportunity to stop the progression of the events but both, in an attempt to save face, keep moving forward. Luckenbill's work has been well received and is very important in emphasizing the role that the audience and victim may play in homicides.

Nonetheless, you can probably imagine or perhaps even know of a homicide—even a confrontational homicide that does not easily fit into Luckenbill's six stages. Polk (1994), for one, found that not all cases of confrontational homicide in his Victoria, Australia, sample fit easily into Luckenbill's six stages. Polk readily acknowledges that many cases do fit all of the stages, but in others it was difficult to trace all six stages. In some cases, according to Polk, the stages seem to be present but the victim who dies is not the individual who initiated in the escalation of the events.

It may also be that stage 1 is actually stage 3, and Luckenbill's scenario has started later than the actual transaction. For example, the homicidal transaction involving Charles and Lemerond may have actually started previously to what was described earlier as stage 1. As you can see in Figure 7.2, there could have been two or more stages before Lemerond removed the bandana from Charles's head and began hitting him with it. Charles may have looked at Lemerond's girlfriend in a leering way that Lemerond took to be an insult and an affront to his masculinity, and thus he began to hit Charles.

IMPORTANCE OF AUDIENCE

Luckenbill (1977) noted the importance of the audience, especially in stage 6, for determining the moves made by the actors in a homicide drama. Richard Felson (1982) and Mark Cooney (1998) have both made a point of studying and discussing the role of an audience or third party in either escalating or deescalating violence. Although they may not have focused only on confrontational homicide, their work is valuable for understanding confrontational violence. Felson (1982) interviewed over 500 individuals about disputes in which they had taken part in the past. Not surprising, in line with

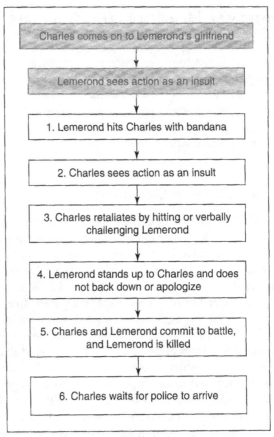

FIGURE 7.2

Luckenbill's Six Stages of Homicide as a Situated Transaction

Note: The steps in gray have been added to suggest the possibility that the transaction may have a longer history.

studies of confrontational homicide, Felson found that most interpersonal aggression was a response to a perceived rule violation and is thus justified by the aggressor. Further, males were more likely than females to express their anger when insulted, which may explain why confrontational homicide is more closely linked to males.

In relation to audiences, Felson determined that third parties (an audience) affected aggressive interactions. If third parties prompted the conflicts, the interactions tended to be more severe, which was particularly true when the participants were both male. However, if a third party mediated a conflict, the interaction did not escalate as much. It appears to be the case then that confrontations are more likely to end in violence when others are present who support the violent interaction in contrast to having someone present who tries to nullify the violence. This may seem obvious to any of you who have witnessed or been involved in a schoolyard brawl. If kids gather around and egg each other on, the violence often continues. When a playground monitor approaches, the fighting often slows or stops.

CONFRONTATIONAL HOMICIDE AND CULTURES OF HONOR

Crime statistics consistently show greater levels of violence and homicide in certain geographic regions or among particular people. Some criminologists who have attempted to determine why violence or homicide is concentrated in certain areas or among particular groups of people have postulated subcultural explanations. This section discusses two main subcultural explanations for violence that may have value for explaining confrontational homicide.

Subculture of Violence

In his 1958 study of homicide discussed earlier, in addition to the high number of victim-precipitated homicides, Wolfgang also found that African Americans were overrepresented as both victims and offenders of homicide in Philadelphia. African Americans made up only 18% of Philadelphia's population at the time, but Wolfgang found that 73% of homicide victims and 75% of homicide offenders were African American, and most of these were young men. To explain the high rates of violence among these young lower-class African Americans who lived in urban areas of Philadelphia, Wolfgang (1958) introduced the idea of a *subculture of violence*. Like Luckenbill's stages of homicide, Wolfgang found that much of the violence among the youth he studied was a reaction to some trivial matter and that a young man who did not respond to an affront with violence or aggression would be seen as weak. Writing with Ferracuti, Wolfgang argued there is a subculture of violence among lower-class males (Wolfgang & Ferracuti, 1967). They maintained that the norms among lower-class African American males were not completely different from the dominant culture. However, within the subculture where the young men grew up, they learned that the proper response to an insult was violence. In fact, a man's masculinity would be questioned as would his honor if he did not stand up for himself. And quite often, standing up for oneself demanded that one be physically violent.

In talking about the possibility that there may be a subculture of violence, Wolfgang (1958) wrote,

> There may be a sub-culture of violence which does not define personal assaults as wrong or antisocial; in which quick resort to physical aggression is a socially approved and expected concomitant of certain stimuli; and in which violence has become a familiar but often deadly partner in life's struggles. . . . Thus, altercations that lead to homicide become symptoms of unconscious destructive impulses laid bare in a subculture where toleration—if not encouragement—of violence is part of the normative structure. (p. 329)

According to Wolfgang, violence is seen as normal and expected in certain situations among African Americans, and sometimes this violence ends in death.

Although Wolfgang's theory is often cited, some critics argue that high rates of homicide among African Americans are not explained by a subculture of violence. Instead, structural factors are to blame for high rates of violence and homicide among minority group members. Using data from 158 cities, Shihadeh and

Steffensmeier (1994) found that inequality in those cities was much greater among African Americans than others in the cities studied. Thus African Americans had more economic hardships, and as such, Shihadeh and Steffensmeier argued that higher rates of violence among African Americans in urban settings are not necessarily the result of culture but because of structure.

The results of a study by Velez, Krivo, and Peterson (2003) also suggest that the higher rates of homicide among African Americans is more complicated than Wolfgang's subculture of violence suggested. These researchers studied what they call the black-white gap in killing. They used data from 135 cities with an overall population of at least 100,000 and an African American population of at least 5,000 to explore how social and economic circumstances influenced the level of homicide among whites and African Americans. Unlike other studies that suggest there may be different causes for homicides among African Americans and whites, Velez et al. (2003) found that the same structural explanations for homicide work for both African Americans and whites. As such, higher rates of homicide among African Americans are explained not only by greater levels of structural disadvantage among African Americans but are also a reflection of advantages that whites have over blacks in U.S. society. Among these advantages are higher home ownership rates, higher educational levels, and higher average household incomes.

Southern Subculture of Honor

The southern subculture of honor is similar to the subculture of violence in that both theories propose that high levels of violence among particular groups of people can be explained by a subculture that requires men to react violently to insults that could potentially damage their reputation. However, the southern subculture of violence explains violence by southern white men rather than violence by urban African American youth.

It is well known among criminologists that rates of homicide and assault have consistently been higher in the southern United States as compared to other parts of the country (see Table 7.1). As early as 1880, scholars such as H. C. Redfield began noting and exploring the variations in violent behavior between the North and the South (Redfield, 1880, as noted in Smith & Parker, 1980). The reason for the higher rates in the South, however, is contested (Dixon & Lizotte, 1987; Gastil, 1971; McNerlin & Davies, 1998; Huff-Corzine, Corzine, & Moore, 1986, 1991; Nisbet & Cohen, 1996; Smith & Parker, 1980). Similar to the contention over the explanations

TABLE **7.1**
Population and Homicide Distribution by Region, 2004

Region	% of Population	% of Murder and Nonnegligent Manslaughter
Northeast	18.6	14.1
Midwest	22.4	19.3
South	36.1	43.0
West	23.0	19.7
United States	100	100

Source: Compiled from Federal Bureau of Investigation Statistics Data (FBI, 2006).

for higher rates of violence among young African American males, some scholars argue that structural factors such as inequality and poverty explain the higher rates of violence in the south (Chu, Rivera, & Loftin, 2000). Still others use the culture of honor to explain the higher rates of violence in the South.

Nisbet and Cohen (1996) explain there is a "culture of honor" among white southern males. This culture of honor requires men to stand up to any affront to their honor. Thus a southern man is obligated to respond with violence to an insult aimed at him or his family. Nisbet and Cohen (1996) explain that this culture of honor has been passed down through generations of southerners. They argue that the culture of honor has developed in the South and not other parts of the country to the same degree because the southern United States was settled by Scott Irish herdsmen. This explanation may seem a bit odd at first. However, they make a convincing argument. They explain that herders make their living from their livestock and there is always the possibility that someone will steal their livestock. Because the South was a frontier region where herders had no police force or law officers to call in cases of theft, they needed to protect their property themselves. Thus they were required to always be ready to react violently to protect their livelihood. According to Nisbet and Cohen (1996), the herders who settled the southern United States passed this idea of self-protection down through the generations. Men learned that they needed to show no weakness. They needed to defend their honor and their family's honor or there would be great social costs to their reputations and ultimately their livelihood.

CONFRONTATIONAL HOMICIDE: IS IT A MAN'S WORLD?

Adler and Polk (2001) write that, "For the male players in the homicide drama, the challenge to manhood is far from a trivial matter" (p. 97). It does seem that, as Polk and others suggest, homicide is often the result of a character contest between men. Too frequently a man kills a stranger or someone known to him because he is afraid to be seen as unmasculine. It may be that another man is putting him down and he is afraid to be viewed as a "punk," so he strikes out with physical violence. Ultimately, especially perhaps among men in lower socioeconomic classes who have little power other than their physical prowess, violence is a way to prove one is a man. Indeed, many of the theories and discussions about homicide generally, and confrontational homicide specifically, focus on men as offenders and men as victims. Moreover, as noted in Chapter 4, men are far more likely than women to be both homicide offenders and homicide victims. Does this mean that women are not violent or that they do not participate in confrontational homicide?

In the late 1970s, the potential for violence among women became a focus of the media and criminologists. It was at this time that women began appearing on the FBI's most wanted list for the first time (FBI, 2006; see Box 7.2). There were also increases in the number of women being arrested. With the birth of the modern-day feminist movement and the increase in women's arrest, an interest in women as offenders began to surge. Before this time, little was written about women as criminals that did not rely on biological explanations for their behaviors.

During the 1970s as official statistics began to show increases in offending among women and the women's movement flourished, Fred Adler (1975) and Rita

BOX 7.2

First Women on FBI Most Wanted List

Only seven women have been on the FBI's Most Wanted List since the list began in 1950. A review of their crimes, however, reveals that confrontational homicide may not be common among women—at the very least; they do not end up on the most wanted list for confrontational homicide. **Ruth Eisemann-Schier**, who was placed on the list in 1968 for several crimes she committed with Gary Steven Krist including kidnapping and extortion, was the first woman to be placed on the list. Eisemann-Schier served a seven-year sentence for kidnapping student Barbara Mackle and burying her in a box. Eisemann-Schier, a native of Honduras, was deported back to her home country after her release from prison (Buchanan, 2002).

In 1969, **Marie Dean Arrington** was placed on the list after she escaped from a Florida correctional institute while awaiting execution for murder. The crime that led to Arrington's incarceration is more similar to confrontational homicide than other crimes committed by women on the most wanted list. Arrington killed June Ritter, the secretary of a public defender because she was angry with the public defender. In Arrington's mind, it seems, the public defender had not defended her sons well enough, and Arrington wanted revenge against him. She was rearrested in 1971 and is currently incarcerated in Broward County (per Florida Corrections Website, 2006).

In 1970, four women were placed on the FBI's most wanted list. During this turbulent time, many ended up on the list because of their politics or the acts they committed because of their politics. **Angela Y. Davis**, who is now a professor at University of California, Santa Cruz, was placed on the list because she was suspected of conspiring to free activist George Jackson from a courtroom in Marin County, California. She was acquitted eventually of all charges and remains an important political activist in the United States (Davies, 2004).

Bernardine Rae Dohrn, now an associate professor of law at Northwestern University and founder of the Children and Family Justice Center, also appeared on the most wanted list in 1970. She was taken off the list shortly after being placed on it, although she was still considered a fugitive. Wanted for alleged violent and subversive activities as a member of the Weathermen, a radical leftist group, she lived underground with her husband for 11 years. Once the couple surfaced, the charges against them were dropped because the government had used illegal methods in pursuing them. Dohrn, however, received three years' probation for a misdemeanor at a 1969 antiwar demonstration. Then, in 1982, she spent eight months in jail for refusing to testify before a grand jury about a Brink's robbery involving other members of the Weathermen (Guthmann, 2003).

Katherine Ann Power was placed on the list in 1970 for the murder of Boston police officer Walter Schroeder. As part of a plan to get funds for the Black Panthers, Power and four other members of a radical group planned a bank robbery in Massachusetts. During the robbery, Officer Schroeder was shot in the back by another police officer. Although Power

continued

did not shoot Officer Schroeder, she was charged with his murder because he died as the result of the felony she helped plan and for which she served as the getaway driver. Power was taken off the most wanted list in 1984 because there were no longer leads being generated from her appearance on the list (*New York Times*, 1984). In 1993, however, after 23 years of hiding, Power made international news when she surrendered to authorities. Power had been living as Alice Metzinger for years. She pleaded guilty and was sentenced to prison. Power was released after six years in prison.

Power's roommate **Susan Edith Saxe** was also a most wanted fugitive in 1970 for her role in the same bank robbery that cost Officer Schroeder his life. Saxe remained on the most wanted list for 4.5 years before being captured in Philadelphia. She served eight years for her crime and was released in 1982 (*New York Times*, 1982). She is now CEO of a Jewish Renewal organization.

Another woman did not appear until 1987 when **Donna Jean Willmott** was listed for crimes linked to her politics. Willmott is considered by some to have been a political prisoner for her support of the Puerto Rican independence movement. Others believe she is a terrorist. With Claude Daniel Marks she pleaded guilty in May 1995 to charges of conspiracy involving a plot to help Oscar Lopez escape from prison. In 1985, Marks and Willmott purchased more than 36 pounds of explosive from an undercover FBI agent, which they planned to use in the prison breakout. Now out of prison, Willmott works as an advocate for prisoners with children in San Francisco (Terrorist Research and Analytical Center, 1995).

Simon (1975) postulated links between the women's movement and women's offending behavior. Although Adler's theory, known as the masculinity theory, has received much attention, today most criminologists include it in their lectures about the history of criminology rather than as a viable theory. In essence, Adler postulated that the women's movement encouraged and allowed women to be more like men. Thus increases in women's criminal offending were not surprising. According to the masculinity theory, as women became more masculine because of the influence of the women's movement, their offending increased. In particular, as they became more masculine, women became more violent. With respect to confrontational violence, then, we would expect more cases of confrontational homicide by women. Although novel and popular, this theory has not proven to be the case. In places in the United States where women's status has improved, the number of women involved in homicide has not increased, nor has the quality or type of homicide committed by women changed.

Rita Simon introduced her theory at about the same time that Adler's theory was becoming popular. Similar to Adler's theory, Simon proposed a connection between increases in women's offending behavior and the women's movement as well. In contrast to Adler, however, Simon proposed that where women's offending increased it was not because they were becoming more "masculine" but simply that the women's movement had helped women gain more opportunity. The opportunity was both legitimate as in employment opportunities and it was illegitimate in that women who had gained in employment also gained greater opportunity for crimes such as embezzlement and fraud. Criminologists have focused less on Simon's predictions for women's violent offending. Simon hypothesized that the women's movement would, in fact, lead to fewer violent offenses such as homicide among women. She believed that as women gained greater economic opportunities they would have more opportunities to escape from situations in which they had been violent in the past: battering relationships. In other words, whereas before the women's movement, a woman may have had to result to homicide to escape from a relationship with a violent spouse or partner, with their employment and independence; women could escape battering situations without having to resort to violence.

More than thirty years after the masculinity and opportunity theses were first introduced; an examination of the data suggests that women's homicide offending has changed little. As can be seen in Figure 7.3, the rate at which women have committed murder has remained low. However, perhaps in support of Simon's opportunity thesis, homicide among women has decreased steadily, from 3.0 per 100,000 in 1976 to 1.2 per 100,000, where it has remained.

Still, this does not tell us about the character or circumstances of homicide by women. We do not know whether women have increased their participation in confrontational homicide. Certainly, women's participation is less than men's. Data from the California Department of Justice indicated that the most common circumstance listed for homicides committed by females in California in 2004 was argument (63.3%). For males, the most common circumstance was gang related (39.6%). However, for males the circumstances of argument was close behind, with 38.4% falling in this category. When thinking about whether these cases fit confrontational homicide, it is worth knowing that when the argument-type homicides were further disaggregated into domestic violence and all other arguments, it appears that a much larger percentage of women's offending as compared to men's offending involves

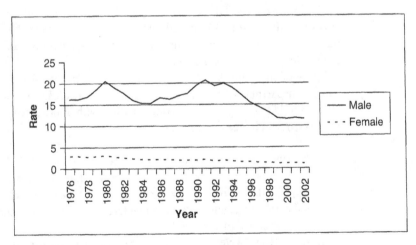

FIGURE 7.3

Homicide Offending Rate by Sex per 100,000 Population

Source: Compiled from Bureau of Justice Statistics Data and FBI Supplementary Homicide Reports, 1976–2002.

domestic violence. Nearly 2 out of 5 (38.7%) homicides committed by women involved domestic violence, whereas only 1.5% of men's homicide offending was categorized as domestic violence (Prasad, 2004). Although these data do not prove whether women commit confrontational homicides, it does suggest that confrontational homicide is not likely to be the most common type of homicide committed by women.

Nevertheless, my own research provides evidence that some women participate in confrontational homicide. Much like studies of male homicide offending by other criminologists, Lori Scott and I have found incidents of homicide among women that appear to arise out of seemingly trivial events that escalate into violence and end in homicide. When I recently reviewed the 41 homicide cases with female offenders in Augusta, Georgia, in the 1990s, I found that at least three incidents could potentially fit the definition of confrontational homicides as noted here from our case scenarios:

1. In 1995, three African American women ages 18, 19, and 22 were found guilty of murder malice in a drive-by shooting of a 14-year-old African American middle school student. The police believed the shooting was the culmination of an altercation that began the night before at a local pool hall.
2. In 1997, a 19-year-old African American woman and a 17-year-old white woman were arrested for killing a 24-year-old African American woman. A jury found the 19-year-old defendant who committed the stabbing not guilty because witnesses supported her story that she stabbed the victim to get her to stop beating the 17-year-old woman.
3. In 1997, a 31-year-old white woman killed her 47-year-old white male neighbor with her van. They had been feuding about the property line between their houses. She was found not guilty by reason of insanity.

These three cases did not involve masculinity as was significant in Polk's discussions of confrontational homicide. However, it is possible that the incidents fit Luckenbill's situated transactions. They may have grown out of seemingly trivial matters, and clearly they escalated.

More often in our data set, when the cases did not involve a woman killing her husband or partner (often, but not always, in self-defense), the women who killed appeared to kill as the result of a confrontation with another woman over a male in their lives, as can be seen in the following scenarios:

1. In 1990, an 18-year-old African American woman killed a 19-year-old African American woman. Apparently they had been fighting over a boyfriend. The offender was sentenced to 8 years in prison after pleading guilty to manslaughter after her first trial, in which she was charged with malice murder ended in a mistrial.
2. In 1991, a 24-year-old African American woman stabbed a 24-year-old African American woman in the neck, chest, and hip. They were arguing about a man whom they were both dating.
3. In 1992, a 17-year-old African American woman shot a 20-year-old African American woman in the chest with a .22-caliber revolver. The 17-year-old

offender went to her boyfriend's house where she found him with the victim. A confrontation ensued, and as the victim moved toward a knife, the defendant drew the gun she purchased the day before and shot the woman because "she was running her mouth off."

4. A 32-year-old African American woman pleaded guilty to voluntary manslaughter in the 1997 shooting of a 37-year-old African American woman who was dating the same man as she. The two women argued, and the defendant shot the victim with a .38-caliber handgun.

I need to emphasize that these confrontations over men make up only about 10% of the cases in our data set. We cannot draw any conclusions from them because our data set is limited, although we had all 41 cases in which a woman was believed to have killed another human being in three counties in Georgia in the 1990s. This is still a small number of cases in one particular geographic area. Furthermore, it may be worth noting that African Americans make up a larger percentage of the population of the counties in which we studied than is typical throughout the United States. Finally, although it may be somewhat typical of those who kill, most of those in our data set were poor—living on the margins and certainly not anyone who had obviously benefited much from the women's movement or any other movement (Scott & Davies, 2002).

It might be an interesting question to find out how typical it is for women to kill in confrontations over men in their lives. We know it will not be anywhere near the number of cases in which men kill in confrontational homicides because men kill so much more often than women. However, if men kill each other in an attempt to defend their masculinity, could it be that women might kill because of their femininity or because of what is valued about women in our society? Men are valued for being masculine, and part of being masculine is being violent. Women are valued as sex objects, and thus might they kill when their sexual appeal to a man is challenged by another woman and they strike out against this woman? This is not something that has been empirically tested at this point. Perhaps you will explore the possibility in class.

SUMMARY

In this chapter, confrontational homicide was defined as first discussed by Polk, who explained that it is essentially a character contest between men that ends in murder. Although no official statistics are kept on confrontational homicide per se, the data kept by the FBI on the circumstances leading to homicide may give some indication of the frequency of such homicides. Homicide involving arguments, brawls, and gang killings make up approximately a third of homicide cases in the United States in our recent history. However, as also noted in this chapter, confrontational homicide is not new or limited to the United States. As discussed by Cooney, homicide that results from feuding, brawling, dueling, and lynching may be considered confrontational homicide. Different concepts that are relevant to the study of confrontational homicide were also included in this chapter. First, although they did not call what they studied confrontational homicide, both Luckenbill and Wolfgang discussed homicide as the outcome of certain behaviors that fit to some degree with Polk's ideas about confrontational homicide. Wolfgang introduced the concept of victim-precipitated homicide in which the victim often initiated the situation that led to his death. Luckenbill discussed homicide as a situated transaction. His research indicated that homicide moves through six stages in which both the offender and victim played a role that included the acceptance of violence for resolving a conflict or dispute. Following a discussion of Luckenbill's work, both the subculture of violence and the southern subculture of honor were described. These theories are similar in that they were both developed to explain why a certain population has higher rates of homicide. Further, both contend that violence is seen in some cultures as a legitimate means for maintaining one's respect. Studies that support and go against these two theories were also included to encourage critical thinking about them. Finally, the chapter ended with a discussion of the possibility that women take part in confrontational homicide. Theories and data about women's homicide offending are included to help you consider this possibility and draw your own conclusions.

CHAPTER QUESTIONS

1. What is meant by the term *confrontational homicide*?
2. Who is most likely to take part in confrontational homicide, and why do you think this is the case?
3. Discuss Cooney's research as related to confrontational homicide.
4. Explain a victim-precipitated homicide.
5. What is meant by "homicide as a situated transaction"?
6. Outline Luckenbill's six stages of homicide as a situation transaction.
7. List and explain the three different opening moves according to Luckenbill.
8. How might an audience affect the outcome of a homicide?
9. Compare and contrast the *subculture of violence* with the *southern subculture of honor*.
10. Is confrontational homicide a man's world? Be sure to support your answer.

REFERENCES

Adler, Christine, and Kenneth Polk. 2001. *Child Victims Of Homicide*. Melbourne: Cambridge University Press.

Adler, Freda. 1975. *Sisters in Crime*. New York: McGraw Hill.

Associated Press. 2005a, November 22. "Court Records: Killings Apparently Triggered by Perceived Insult." Retrieved March 19, 2006, from LEXIS-NEXIS Academic Universe, News Articles.

Associated Press. 2005b, September 26. "Green Bay Man Charged with Murder by Fork." Retrieved March 19, 2006, from LEXIS-NEXIS Academic Universe, News Articles.

Belser, Ann. 2005, November 11. "2 Shot Dead in Flap over Video Game in North Braddock." *Pittsburgh Post-Gazette.* Retrieved December 10, 2005, from Post-gazette.com.

Bird, Steve. 2005. "So Solid Crew Gun Killer Gets 30 Years." *The Times.* Retrieved February 6, 2006, from http://web.lexis-nexis.com.bindery.aug.edu:2048/universe/document?m= 4d8571766f11f217e9ebfe15db20a5ad&_docnum=11&wchp=dGLbVtb-zSkVb&_md5= 39b84567084d75dd979b4d25a31cf643

Buchanan, Edna. 2002, September 15. "South Florida's Crimes of the Century Riveted the Nation." *Miami Herald.* Retrieved March 18, 2006, from http://www.miami.com/mld/ miamiherald/news/photos/4069377.htm

Chu, Rebekah, Craig Rivera, and Colin Loftin. 2000. "Herding and Homicide: An Examination of the Nisbett-Reaves Hypothesis." *Social Forces,* 78(3): 971–987.

Continetti, Matthew. 2004, December 13. "The 200-Year Duel; Two Centuries After Their Famous Forebears Met on the Banks of the Hudson, the Hamiltons and the Burrs Are Still at It." *The Weekly Standard.* Retrieved February 8, 2006, from http://web.lexis-nexis.com. bindery.aug.edu:2048/universe/document?_m=a336b84b8046d3bba76a38f4f251122a&_ docnum=1&wchp=dGLbVtb-zSkVb&_md5=ada402d3a2cc31f792b446a5c8f708f0

Cooney, Mark. 1997. "The Decline of Elite Homicide." *Criminology,* 35(3): 381–407.

Cooney, Mark. 1998. *Warriors and Peacemakers: How Third Parties Shape Violence.* New York: New York University Press.

Daly, Martin and Margo Wilson. 1988. *Homicide.* New York: Adline.

Davies, Kim. 2004. "Angela Y. Davis." In Mary Bosworth, ed., *Encyclopedia of Prisons and Correctional Institutions* (pp. 211–212). Thousand Oaks, CA: Sage.

Dixon, Jo, and Alan J. Lizotte. 1987. "Gun Ownership and the 'Southern Subculture of Violence.' " *American Journal of Sociology,* 93(2): 383–405.

Federal Bureau of Investigation. 2006. "The FBI's Ten Most Wanted Fugitives." Retrieved February 15, 2006, from http://www.fbi.gov/mostwant/topten/tenfaq.htm#10

Felson, Richard B. 1982. "Impression Management and the Escalation of Aggression and Violence," *Social Psychology Quarterly,* 45:245–254.

Florida Corrections Website. 2006. Retrieved March 18, 2006, from http://www.dc.state.fl.us/ oth/timeline/1966–1969a.html

Fox, James Alan, and Marianne W. Zawitz. 2006. *Homicide Trends in the U.S.* Washington, DC: Bureau of Justice Statistics. Accessed online at http://www.ojp.usdoj.gov/bjs/homicide/ tables/vracetab.htm

Gastil, Raymond D. 1971. "Homicide and a Regional Culture of Violence." *American Sociological Review,* 36: 412–427.

Guthmann, Edward. 2003, July 21. "For 11 Years, Bernardine Dohrn and Bill Ayers Were on the Run from the FBI. In The Film 'The Weather Underground,' The Anti-War Activists Explain Why They Fought the Law—and Why They Have No Regrets." *San Francisco Chronicle.* Retrieved March 19, 2006, from http://www.sfgate.com/cgi-bin/article.cgi? f=/c/a/2003/07/21/DD38016.DTL

Huff-Corzine, Lin, Jay Corzine, and David C. Moore. 1986. "Southern Exposure: Deciphering the South's Influence on Homicide Rates." *Social Forces,* 64(4): 906–924.

Huff-Corzine, Lin, Jay Corzine, and David C. Moore. 1991. "Deadly Connections: Culture, Poverty, and the Direction of Lethal Violence." *Social Forces,* 69(3): 715–732.

Luckenbill, David. 1977. "Criminal Homicide as Situated Transaction." *Social Problems,* 25: 176–186.

McNerlin, Christina, and Kim Davies. 1998. "Southern Belles or Steel Magnolias?: A Regional Analysis of Female Arrest Rates for Violent Crimes in the United States." Presented at the American Sociological Association Meetings, San Francisco.

Mulgrew, Ian. 2005, September 5. "Crimes of Passion Are Crimes." *The Vancouver Sun* , p. A13. Retrieved March 20, 2006. Available online at LEXIS-NEXIS Academic Universe, News Articles.

New York Times. 1982, May 9. "Headliners Susan Saxe Gets Out." Retrieved March 19, 2006, from http://query.nytimes.com/gst/fullpage.html?res=9A0DE2DB1438F93AA35756C0A964948260

New York Times. 1984, June 18. "Around the Nation; F.B.I. Drops Radical from Most Wanted List." Retrieved March 19, 2006, from http://query.nytimes.com/gst/fullpage.html?res=9400E7D61639F93BA25755C0A962948260

Nisbett, Richard E., and Dov Cohen. 1996. *Culture of Honor: The Psychology of Violence in the South.* Boulder, CO: Westview Press.

Polk, Kenneth. 1994. *When Men Kill: Scenarios of Masculine Violence.* Cambridge: Cambridge University Press.

Polk, Kenneth 1999. "Males and Honor Contest Violence." *Homicide Studies,* 3 (1): 6–29.

Prasad, Umash, ed. 2004. *Homicide in California 2004.* Sacramento: California Department of Justice.

Scott, Lori, and Kim Davies. 2002. "Beyond the Statistics: An Examination of Killing by Women in Three Georgia Counties." *Homicide Studies,* 6(4): 297–324.

Shihadeh, Edward S., and Darrel J. Steffensmeier. 1994. "Economic Inequality, Family Disruption, and Urban Black Violence: Cities as Units of Stratification and Social Control." *Social Forces,* 73(1): 729–751.

Simon, Rita J. 1975. *Women and Crime.* Lexington, MA: Lexington Books.

Smith, M. Dwayne, and Robert Nash Parker. 1980. "Type of Homicide and Variation in Regional Rates." *Social Forces,* 59(1):136–147.

Terrorist Research and Analytical Center. 1995. "Terrorism in the United States Webpage." Retrieved March 18, 2006, from http://www.fas.org/irp/threat/fbi_terror95/terrorin.htm

Vélez, María B., Lauren J. Krivo, and Ruth D. Peterson. 2003 "Structural Inequality and Homicide: An Assessment Of The Black-White Gap In Killings." *Criminology,* 41(3): 645–672.

Wolfgang, Marvin. 1958. *Patterns in Criminal Homicide.* Philadelphia: University of Pennsylvania.

Wolfgang, Marvin, and Franco Ferracuti. 1967. *The Subculture of Violence.* London: Social Science Paperbacks.

Chapter 8

INTIMATE PARTNER HOMICIDE

Prior to the mid-1970s, it was rare for those in the criminal justice system, and society in general, to take violence between spouses very seriously. Before 1974, for example, when a husband assaulted his wife, the assault was defined as a misdemeanor. To make this clear, if a man punched or beat up his neighbor or a stranger on the street, he could be charged with a felony. If this same man beat the woman he was married to in the same way, he would be charged with a misdemeanor. Domestic violence between spouses was considered a private matter (Browne, Williams, & Dutton, 1999). As a result, it is not surprising that criminologists failed to focus on intimate partner violence and homicide. In the 1980s, however, feminists and others in the battered women's movement began to bring the issue of domestic violence from behind closed doors into the public realm. Since that time, many studies have addressed domestic violence and intimate partner homicide.

In this chapter, you will read about what criminologists and criminal justice officials have learned from the many studies about intimate partner homicide. The first section presents relevant definitions. Then the data on intimate partner homicide in the United States and in other countries, including the differences with regard to gender in this type of homicide, are presented. In looking at the data, the trends and patterns of intimate partner homicide since the establishment of domestic violence shelters and mandatory arrest policies are considered. A discussion about the use of the battered women's syndrome in court cases involving women who have killed their intimate partners is included as well. Also importantly, not all intimate partner homicide is the result of battering or domestic violence situations. As such there is a discussion about the different motivations for intimate partner homicide. As in other chapters, the many examples will help make the theories and data more real to you.

DEFINITIONS

Intimate partner homicide is a term used to reflect the killing of a victim by an offender who is either currently or was formerly in a sexual relationship with the victim. In the past, different terms were used to describe such killings, but they often failed to include all the types of relationships encompassed in the more general term *intimate partner homicide*. Uxoricide, or wife killing, for example, leaves out the killing of former wives, homicides of those in de facto marital relationships, and the killing of males by their wives or other sexual partners. Similarly, spousal homicide, although sometimes the relevant focus depending on the question, again leaves out de facto marital relationships such as common-law marriages, same-sex relationships, and former spouses. Domestic homicide may be good for any sexually involved couples who are living together, but then again, it may be confused with any type of homicide that occurs within a family, such as the killing of one's children, parents, or sibling.

In this chapter, the more inclusive term *intimate partner homicide* is used to refer to the killing of one's current or former sexual partner. Married and unmarried as well as heterosexual or same-sex couples are included in this definition because research suggests these types of homicide have many commonalities. However, there is also research that suggests differences between ever-married couples and never-married couples. Thus, if the research or data presented in this chapter involves a different definition, I am careful to use the most exact term. So if you read about spousal homicide in the United States in this chapter, you may assume it refers to the homicide of a husband by a wife or a wife by a husband. If you read the term *intimate partner*, you know it refers to a person currently or formerly involved in a sexual relation with another.

DATA ON INTIMATE PARTNER HOMICIDE

Despite the fact that men are more often the victims of homicides than women, men are less likely than women to be killed by their intimate partners. Nearly a third of female homicide victims and only 5% of male homicide victims are killed by their intimate partners (Paulozzi, Saltzman, Thompson, et al., 2001). According to FBI data on homicides known to the police in 2004, 579 men murdered their wives, common-law wives, or ex-wives; 149 wives murdered their husbands, common-law husbands, or ex-husbands. Similarly, 445 men murdered their girlfriends, whereas 147 women murdered their boyfriends. Another way to think about this is to note that men in the United States killed their female intimate partners approximately 3.5 times as often as women killed their male intimate partners.

Although there are certainly enough similarities in the dynamics involved in different types of intimate partner homicides to include them in one chapter, it is also important to realize that homicides committed by intimate partners may vary by the type of intimate relationship. As such, several studies have looked at difference between married and nonmarried couples. These studies that compare ever-married couples (married, separated, and divorced) to nonmarried couples who live together (cohabitating) find that the risk of homicide is greater for nonmarried couples (Shackelford, 2001). In the United States, for example, the risk of intimate partner homicide for men in cohabitating relationships is 10 times greater than the risk for married men.

As with other types of homicide, however, the data indicate that there are also differences by race. Intimate partner homicide rates tend to be highest among African Americans as compared to other racial groups (Block & Christakos, 1995; Paulozzi et al., 2001). Rates among Native Americans, although lower than African Americans, are higher than whites, and Asians/Pacific Islanders have the lowest rates (Paulozzi et al., 2001). In Table 8.1, you can see these differences in rates between racial groups as well as the fact that the victimization rates were higher for women than for men. However, the data broken down by race and sex also show that African American males had the highest risk of being victims of intimate partner homicide in the years 1981 to 1998. The next most at risk in order were as follows: African American females, American Indian females, American Indian males, white and Asian females, and white and Asian males. Other data also suggest that the rates among Latinos are relatively low in comparison with African Americans as well (Block & Christakos, 1995).

Like other types of homicide, age is also relevant. Those in particular age groups appear to be at greater risk for both offending and for becoming victims of intimate partner homicide. Both victims and offenders of intimate partner homicide tend to be, on average, older than those involved in other types of homicide. Furthermore, likely reflecting the pattern of men marrying women who are younger than themselves, studies also tend to show that men involved in intimate partner homicide are older on average than women who are killed by or kill their intimate partners (Block & Christakos, 1995). U.S. data, for example, show that men are most at risk for intimate partner homicide victimization beginning in their late 30s and lasting through their 50s, whereas women's risk period was highest beginning in their 20s and lasting until they turn 50 years of age. Similarly, the peak ages for offenders of intimate partner violence was older for men. Chicago data show that the peak for male offenders was 35 to 39 years. For women in Chicago, the peak for offending by African American women was 25 to 29 years. The rates of intimate partner homicide offending for white and Latino women, however, was low at all ages without any discernible peaks (Block & Christakos, 1995).

TABLE 8.1
Intimate Partner Homicide Victimization Rates per 100,000 Population

Race	Women	Men	Total
African American	3.55	4.11	3.77
Indian American/Alaskan Native	2.26	1.20	1.79
White	1.11	0.49	0.81
Asian/Pacific Islander	0.92	0.19	0.57
Total	1.43	0.89	1.15

Source: Paulozzi et al's (2001) estimation of annual rates using SHR data from 1981 and 1998.

Differences in age between partners in intimate partner relationships also result in different rates of intimate partner homicide victimization. Intimate partners who are in relationships with greater age differences, for the most part, are more at risk for partner-committed homicide (Shackelford, 2001). In other words, men who married or live with much older women or much younger women are at greater risk for homicide than those who marry women close in age to themselves (Daly & Wilson, 1988; Shackelford, 2001). Data also suggest that married women are more likely to be killed by their partners when they are married to older men as opposed to younger men or men their same age (Shackelford, Buss, & Peters, 2000).

Even though we see that rate of intimate partner homicide varies by sex, age, and race, we also know that many nondemographic factors are associated with intimate partner homicide as listed in Box 8.1. As will be clear throughout the remainder of this chapter, previous violence or abuse within the intimate relationship is a very common factor in intimate partner homicide. Also important, and often linked to intimate partner violence, are the abuser's use of illicit drugs and (most often) his alcohol use. A study comparing the differences between battered women in fatal and nonfatal battering relationships found a strong relationship between the abuser's drug use and intimate partner homicide. The abuser's use of alcohol, however, was not related to intimate partner homicide. The victim's alcohol abuse and drug use were not associated with the risk of intimate partner homicide independent of other risks of being killed (Campbell, Webster, Koziol-McLain, et al., 2003).

BOX 8.1

Sex Ratio of Intimate Killing

SROK is an acronym for "sex ratio of intimate killings." Criminologists have been particularly interested in SROK since the late 1980s when Daly and Wilson (1988) first pointed out that the SROK was considerably closer than the overall ratio of female killing to male killing. For a number of years, women have accounted for approximately 14% of all homicides in the United States. However, many studies have indicated that in the United States (but not necessarily in other countries), the numbers of women who kill their intimate partners are more equal to the number of men who kill their partners. Gauthier and Bankston (2004), for example, reported that about 60 to 70 women kill intimate partners for every 100 men who kill their partners. Criminologists have also noted that the SROK differs by race and marital status and even between cities. The SROK in Chicago, for example, was a nearly even 1:1 (Block & Christakos, 1995), and incredibly, the ratio was 2:1 in Detroit where women were killing their partners far more often than men were killing their intimate partners. Based on everything you have read in this chapter (and in this book so far) and what you know about the United States, how might you explain this phenomenon?

U.S. TRENDS

There is some good news about intimate partner homicide in the United States. Between 1976 and 2000, the number of men murdered by their intimate partners dropped 68% from 1,357 men killed in 1976 to 440 male victims in 2000. The data regarding women also show improvements, but the news is not as good for women. Between 1976 and 1993, the number of women killed by their partners remained fairly stable, and then in 1993 the number began to drop. In 1993, 1,581 women were murdered by their partners, and in 2000 there were 1,247. Thus the number of female victims of intimate partner homicide decreased about 20%, reflecting a less dramatic drop for female victims as compared to male victims. Moreover, the number of women killed by partners remains higher than the numbers of males killed by their partners (Rennison, 2003). A section later in this chapter addresses possible explanations for the decline in intimate partner homicide.

COMPARISONS ACROSS THE WORLD

Data from other countries such as Australia show that intimate partner homicide is not uncommon in other countries. In fact, as a percentage of all homicides it may be higher in other countries than it is in the United States. However, this does not mean that the rate of intimate partner violence is lower in the United States. Instead, the higher percentage of intimate partner violence in other countries is the result of the higher incidents of other types of homicide in the United States. In 2000–2001 in

BOX 8.2
Dowry Death in India

An article appearing on the newswire on May 29, 2006, reported two dowry deaths in the previous 24 hours in different parts of India. "Dowry death" refers to the killing of a woman by her husband (and/or his family) when her family refuses (or cannot) pay the dowry demanded by the husband and his family. Dowry is a customary payment of cash and goods paid to the husband's family by the woman's family. The dowry, however, is not a one time payment but rather a continuation of payments through the first several years of marriage. Some have viewed the dowry as a "compensation for the cost of maintaining an economically unproductive human being" and thus a reflection of the inferior status of women (Prasad, 1994: 73).

According to the 2006 wire report, Sanjit Naskar was arrested for allegedly beating his wife Barnali Naskar and then hanging her. Sabir Ali, who had yet to be arrested, killed his wife Sabina Bibi by setting her on fire. As indicated by the fact that the term *dowry death* exists, these types of killing are not uncommon. Despite a Dowry Prohibition Act making dowry

continued

> deaths illegal in India, nearly 7,000 women were murdered in 2001 in what were recorded as dowry-related incidents. As in the murder of Sabina Ali, the method of death is often burning. "Bride burning," as it is called, is so common in parts of India that the burn unit in one Indian hospital reports admitting between 2 and 5 new bride burning cases each day, with as many as 70 of these women dying each month (Global News Wire, 2006; Tucker, 2006).

Australia, 22% of homicides could be classified as intimate partner murders (Mouzos, 2002). Likewise in Canada, one out of five homicides is committed by an intimate partner (Dawson, 2004). In the United States, about 10% of all homicides are intimate partner homicides (Rennison & Welchens, 2001).

Data from countries, including Canada, Australia, Scotland, England/Wales, and India, among others, also reveal another difference between these countries and the United States. In the United States, the numbers of women who kill their partners is closer to the number of men who kill their partners than in other countries (Block & Christakos, 1995; Lindgren, 2006; Mouzos & Shackelford, 2004). In other countries, men outnumber women in much greater numbers as offenders in intimate partner homicide. In a four-year period in Ontario, Canada, for example, men committed 94% of intimate partner homicides, and women were victims in 93% of the cases. In the United States, men commit closer to 80% of all intimate partner homicide.

GENDER DIFFERENCES IN INTIMATE PARTNER HOMICIDE

As noted earlier, a much large percentage of female homicide victims as compared with male homicide victims are killed by their intimate partners. Women in the United States, in fact, are more likely to be killed by intimate partners than by any other type of murderer (Campbell et al., 2003). Moreover, intimate partner homicides, including those in which women kill their male partners, are often linked to intimate partner abuse committed by males. As a result, much of the research about intimate partner homicide has focused on domestic violence and often on cases where men are the offenders and females are the victims. In the sections to follow, some of this research is discussed. We also look at the growing body of literature dedicated to explaining the declining rates of intimate partner homicide committed by both men and women. Most intimate partner homicides involve a single perpetrator and a single victim; however, a small number of individuals who kill their partners also kill one or more of their children and/or themselves in cases of familicide and/or homicide-suicide. These multiple killing cases are discussed here and to some extent in Chapter 11 on mass and spree killing.

Women are killed by their partners more often than men are killed by their partners, and research suggests that men and women kill their partners for different reasons (Websdale, 1999). Although not unheard of, it is extremely rare for a woman to kill her partner as an end to a long cycle of violence that she has perpetrated against her partner. Men, in contrast, quite often batter their partners for years before killing them (Websdale, 1999). Most male perpetrators of intimate partner homicide kill their partners in situations where the men are trying to control their intimate partner. As a consequence of this controlling behavior, which we do not see in the same way among women, men are also far more likely than women to kill an estranged partner. Men are also more likely to commit familicide or suicide than are women (see Chapter 11). In addition to killing their partners, when men find out their partners are cheating on them, they are also more likely to commit a double homicide by killing not only their partner but her paramour than are women to kill their partner and his mistress. Finally, women who kill their partners, often, but clearly not always, kill as a method of self-defense (Websdale, 1999).

It is rare that an intimate partner homicide is committed by more than one offender. In fact, it may seem impossible for an intimate partner homicide to be committed by multiple offenders because most of us have only one intimate partner, and it is difficult to imagine that even if a person had two partners, they would get together and murder the person they both considered to be their intimate partner. In reality, when there are two offenders of an intimate partner homicide, the second offender is usually an accomplice who has been brought in to help with or commit the murder. Women, in fact, are more likely than men to employ an accomplice in the murder of their intimate partner (Block & Christakos, 1995).

Such was the case in Ohio in 2001 when Donna Marie Roberts and Nathaniel Jackson plotted to kill Roberts's partner Robert Fingerhut. Jackson and Roberts were having an affair, and eventually they decided they wanted to be rid of Fingerhut. They surmised that if they killed him, they would stand to collect on a $550,000 insurance policy. Jackson was incarcerated for a short time, and while incarcerated he and Roberts wrote over 100 letters in which they discussed their plans to get rid of

---

BOX 8.3

Shania Twain, a Sexy Dance, and a Gun Lead to a Husband's Death

A story that captured the interest of the media in Great Britain was the killing of Gregory West by Linda West. The couple had only been married two months when Linda phoned 999 (Britain's equivalent of 911) and cried as she told the dispatcher that she shot her husband. At trial 49-year-old Linda West told the jury she was doing a sexy dance to Shania Twain's "Man! I Feel Like a Woman" song while holding a shotgun. At the end of the dance, she claims that she dropped the gun on the floor to take a bow. The gun, which had a defective safety, went off by itself when it hit the floor. The bullet struck West in the heart and killed him instantly.

Neighbors of the couple reported they had heard the couple arguing the same evening West was killed. Mrs. West, however, reported that they were having a "lovely evening" before West was shot. It appears that the jury believed neighbor's accounts more than they believed Mrs. West. After 8.5 hours of deliberation, the jury found Linda West guilty of murder. She was sentenced to life in prison by a judge, who noted that he did not believe the killing was planned. However, he believed that in a "short period of drunken madness" a crime did take place, and for that she would serve at least 16 years of a life sentence (Millar, 2006; Vasagar, 2006).

Fingerhut. Once released, the plan went forward, and Jackson shot Fingerhut to death. In separate trials, both Roberts and Jackson were found guilty of aggravated murder and sentenced to death for Fingerhut's murder (*State* v. *Roberts,* 2006). Following her 2003 trial, however, Roberts appealed, and in 2006 her conviction was affirmed by the Ohio Supreme Court. However, her sentence was overturned because the judge allowed a prosecutor to help prepare the sentencing decision, which is in violation of Ohio law. At the time of this writing, her new sentence has not been determined. However, the death penalty is still an option (Associated Press, 2006a).

EXPLANATIONS AND MOTIVATIONS

One way to categorize and explain homicides is to divide incidents into expressive and instrumental killings. Because the killing of a spouse is more often a spur-of-the-moment action in which one partner strikes out to try to hurt the other, intimate partner homicides are often classified as *expressive* killings. An *instrumental* homicide is a killing in which the offender is attempting to gain something with the killing. There are intimate partner homicides in which an instrumental goal is clear. Kelly Gissendaner, the only woman on death row in Georgia at the time of this writing, convinced her boyfriend to kill her husband for the insurance money they would gain. Other women and men involved in custody battles over their children have killed their partners to gain sole custody or to avoid paying child support or alimony.

Although it may make sense to say that intimate partner homicides are more likely to be expressive than instrumental, this may not be the best way to categorize such killing. When we really examine cases of intimate partner homicide, we will find that often it is difficult to determine whether a homicide is instrumental or expressive. If a man is upset because his wife is leaving him, he may react with anger and, in fact, kill her. This certainly fits the definition of an expressive killing. He has not plotted and planned to kill his wife. The man being left is angry, and he could be hurting his partner simply because she is hurting him. However, such a killing could also be viewed as an instrumental killing. The motivation may be to control his wife and keep her from leaving. Similarly, the killing of his wife could have been instrumental in that the goal was to keep her from being with anybody else.

Any categorization of motivations for intimate partner homicide may lead us to the same problems we have in attempting to categorize such homicides as expressive or instrumental. Producing mutually exclusive categories appears impossible. Intimate partner homicide may be motivated by sexual jealously, fear, greed, anger, and rage. The death of an intimate partner may evolve from a love triangle, a plot to obtain insurance money, or it could be a seemingly unavoidable end to a tragically violent relationship. Upon discovering an intimate partner homicide, investigators and prosecutors may piece together a story that involves several of these elements or only one.

In March 2006, Jeff Dennis, a police officer, was arrested for the shooting death of his wife Carli. Officer Dennis, who originally reported his wife's death as a suicide, gave many conflicting reports about where he was when his wife died. Moreover, none of Officer Dennis's accounts coincided with blood splatter found on his shirt that suggested he was facing his wife when she was shot. Investigators believed that Dennis killed his wife when he found out she was having an affair with one of her coworkers (Sweeney, 2006). Thus this case appears to be the result of a lover's triangle. It would seem that the motivation could have been anger, rage, sexual jealously, and fear that she was going to leave him. As is too often the case, he could have been acting on the premise that if he could not "have her, nobody could." At the time of this writing, the case remains to be tried.

Whereas Carli Dennis's homicide was somewhat of a surprise, the death of Norma Pescador was perhaps more predictable. After a history of domestic violence incidents, in December 2001, Manolito Pescador used a nail gun to kill his wife Norma Pescador. In this case, there was no doubt that the police were investigating an intimate partner homicide. Pescador clearly killed his wife. He called the police himself and admitted he had shot her nearly a dozen times in the head with a nail gun. When the police arrived, Pescador was covered with his wife's blood. Why would a man so brutally kill a person he had promised to love forever? In this case, Pescador told his adult son Jeffrey that he shot his wife because she was unfaithful and she was abusing one of the couple's younger children. Jeffrey, however, testified his mom was not having an affair or abusive and that his father was extremely jealous (*People* v. *Pescador*, 2004).

During the murder trial against Manolito Pescador, several witnesses testified that Pescador had a history of violence against his wife. In one incident Norma jumped from a speeding car because Pescador had threatened to kill both of them by crashing their car. Neighbors who testified at trial reported that Norma told them that Pescador had cut up her credit cards, constantly accused her of affairs, and that Norma believed that Manolito would kill her (*People* v. *Pescador*, 2004). In this case, we see a history of domestic violence, involving sexual jealously, anger, and what seems to be Pescador's obsessive need to control his wife leading to Mrs. Pescador's death.

The death of Norma Pescador is all too similar to so many other violent relationships that end with the death of one of the partners. Yet everyday women and men who are abused by their partners continue to live with these abusive partners. It is not uncommon for someone who has not been involved in a battering relationship to ask why a woman or man who is being abused by her or his partner does not leave the relationship. As we have learned more about battering relationships and intimate partner homicide, it has become clear that leaving or threatening to leave may actually increase the risk for homicide (Block & Christakos, 1995; Davies, Block, & Campbell, 2007). In their study of intimate partner homicides in Chicago, Block and Christakos (1995) found that a male offender was much more likely to murder his partner because she or he attempted or threatened to leave than for other reasons. In fact, it was the primary or secondary factor given for intimate partner homicide in Chicago for 13% of husbands, 4% of wives, 5% of common-law husbands, 3% of common-law wives; 9% of boyfriends, and 1% of girlfriends who killed their intimate partners (Block & Christakos, 1995).

Emile Durkheim, who you may remember for his study of suicide, has also contributed to our understanding of men who kill partners who are attempting to leave them. Durkheim noted that connections to family were related to lower suicide rates. Yet he also pointed out that family life sometimes increases the risk of homicide. When a marriage ends, for example, Durkheim (1897/1979) argued that the husband has more to lose than the wife, and thus men are more likely than women to kill their spouses as a result of the dissolution of a marriage. Although research suggests that divorced women fare much worse economically than divorced men, Durkheim may still have a valid point when we look at this in a social-psychological context. Durkheim could be getting to issues of control and status for men in patriarchal societies. Although there have been changes in U.S. society since Durkheim first wrote about suicide and homicide, we still live in a predominantly patriarchal society. Men are expected to be leaders and to be in control. In everyday life when men find they are not in control, some may strike out against their partners. When a woman is leaving her partner, this situation is particularly challenging to many men's sense of power and control. In fact, as noted earlier, a woman's leaving is often a trigger for intimate partner homicide; especially in relationships in which the man is already a batterer.

It is important to realize that in an abusive relationship, not only is the abused partner at greater risk for homicide but so is the abuser (Block & Christakos, 1995; Browne, 1986). On May 13, 2006, police responded to a 911 call in the Bronx where they found Juan Hernandez with two stab wounds to his chest. A kitchen knife was lying near his body. Juan's wife of 26 years, Gloria Hernandez, was outside the couple's apartment. She was wearing a nightgown that was soaked with blood and her thumb was cut. Police took both Mr. and Mrs. Hernandez to a medical center where Mr. Hernandez was pronounced dead. Mrs. Hernandez was arrested for the murder of her husband (Lowe, 2006).

Gloria Hernandez, unlike many other battered women who escape an abusive husband by killing him, was not prosecuted for her husband's murder. After hearing the evidence on May 19, 2006, a grand jury refused to indict Hernandez for murder or manslaughter. Mrs. Hernandez, who was 55 at the time of the stabbing, and her daughter from a previous marriage, 37-year-old Maria Diaz, testified that Mr. Hernandez regularly beat Mrs. Hernandez. Mr. Hernandez, who it was reported regularly used drugs, was angry at Gloria the night he died because she would not give him money for drugs. He attacked her with a knife and tried to choke her. However, she was able to take the knife from him and she stabbed him to save herself (Lowe, 2006).

One certainly would not want to argue that the Hernandez case ended well because Juan Hernandez lost his life. However, often the outcome is worse. A woman who has been abused for years is freed from her abuser but sent to prison or even sentenced to death. Such was the outcome of Frances Harrop's first trial in a Canadian court of law where she was sentenced to hang for the shooting death of her husband George. She had told police that she shot her husband twice as he slept. She then lay beside his body and slept for several hours before calling family members. She told the detective who investigated the case, "It was either his life or mine. My husband has threatened my life on several occasions. It was either me taking his life or him taking my life" (Holliday, 2006: C16). The couple's five sons testified that they hated their father, who often threatened to kill their mother. Other witnesses testified that Mrs. Harrop often had bruises on her body and Mr. Harrop used his wife as a punching bag. Mrs. Harrop thanked the prosecutor for the fair trial he conducted. Nevertheless, she was sentenced to hang for the killing of her husband.

However, she was eventually granted a new trial because it was determined that the justice (judge) failed to explain insanity fully to the jury. In the second trial, Frances Harrop was found not guilty due to insanity. Eventually, she was released after it was determined she was sane. Harrop was far luckier than other women who have spent years in prison after killing an abusive husband. However, scholars have noted that for a woman who kills her abuser to be found not guilty, she often must be proven insane. This is despite the fact that killing one's partner may be a sane response to an abusive situation. In 1940 when Harrop killed her husband, the "battered women's syndrome" was not known. Today, although battered women are still often found guilty for killing abusive husbands, there is the possibility that the defense can have an expert testify about battered women's syndrome, as discussed later in this chapter.

INSTRUMENTAL GAIN

As in the case of Manolito Pescador, the primary motive of most intimate partner homicides is to hurt or control the other person. These killings often occur in the context of a domestic violence situation. There are intimate partner homicides, however,

---

BOX 8.4

Warning Signs for Intimate Partner Homicide

Several studies have been conducted to determine how violent intimate partner relationships that end in homicide differ from those that have not ended in homicide (Campbell et al., 2003). The point of these studies was to determine what might be done to prevent intimate partner homicide. The researchers interviewed battered women who had been in violent relationships within the last year and relatives of women who were killed by their partners. Several factors were found to differentiate the relationships in which women were abused but not killed and those in which women were killed. These warning signs that a relationship may end with a murder in the United States and in other countries are as follows:

1. Prior history of domestic violence
2. Separation
3. Depression (his or hers)
4. His unemployment
5. Perpetrator threatens to hurt his or her partner
6. Victim believes that partner is capable of killing her or him
7. History of substance abuse and alcohol abuse
8. Stalking behavior
9. Escalating violence
10. Incidents of violence involving choking
11. Perpetrator who makes threats to hurt himself
12. Male partner who has been arrested for violent crimes
13. Male partner who is suicidal
14. Presence of a firearm in the home
15. Presence of the victim's children from a previous relationship

What would you do if your mother, sister, or friend came to you and indicated that some of these warning signs were happening in their life?

Source: Block and Christakos, 1995; Campbell et al., 2003; Davies, Block, and Campbell, 2007; Lindgren, 2006.

in which the goal is to gain money or property or perhaps even the custody of one's children.

Often it is clear to police investigators that they are dealing with an intimate partner homicide, but sometimes it is not immediately apparent. Such is the case of Piper Rountree, who killed her former husband Michael Jablin. Rountree and Jablin were married for 18 years and had two children before their divorce. Jablin, who lived in Richmond, Virginia, was awarded custody of the couple's three children. Rountree moved to Texas, where she had a license to practice law and where she was closer to her sister and other family members.

When Jablin was shot dead in the driveway of his Virginia home one Sunday morning as he walked outside to get his newspaper, the police did not immediately suspect his former wife. Because the killing had occurred outside the home and because Rountree lived so far from her ex-husband, she was not an immediate suspect. And even though men are more likely to kill their estranged partners than women are to kill theirs, police did not rule out Piper Rountree as the possible murderer. At first, no evidence indicated that Rountree had been in Virginia. However after a careful investigation of credit card purchases and flight logs, police built a case against Rountree that led a jury to convict her of first-degree murder. The prosecutors argued that Rountree wore a wig and used her sister's identification to fly from Texas to Virginia. Once in Virginia, they argued, she shot her former husband with a .38-caliber gun so she could gain sole custody of the couple's three children and avoid paying over $700,000 in back child support she owed. The jury found Rountree guilty of what appears to be an instrumentally motivated homicide and recommended that she serve a sentence of 20 years to life (CBS News, 2005).

WEAPON USE: HOW DO INTIMATE PARTNERS KILL ONE ANOTHER?

In comparison to other types of homicide, knives are more common in intimate partner homicide. Data for four years in Ontario, Canada, for example, reveal that knives or other sharp instruments stand out as the most common weapon used in intimate partner murder (33% of cases), but firearms were a close second with 28% of the deaths involving guns, and 15% of the victims were beaten to death and 13% were choked to death (Lindgren, 2006). Similarly, in Chicago, between 1965 and 1990, knives were the most common cause of death (37%) followed closely by guns (35%) (Block & Christakos, 1995). However, in the United States overall, data show that firearms are the most common weapon used by both men and women when committing intimate partner homicide. From 1981 to 1998, 59.1% of male victims and 64.1% of female victims of intimate partner homicide were killed with firearms. Knives were next most common, with 35.3% of male victims and 16.1% of female victims killed with a knife. It is believed that men were more likely to be killed by knives than women because their female partners use weapons of opportunity, which are more likely to be knives for women than for men. Moreover, when killing male partners, wives were more likely than girlfriends to use firearms (Paulozzi et al., 2001).

Although knives and guns may be most common, there are practically no limits to how intimate partners murder their partners. In 2006, Esad Lemo killed his estranged wife Jasminka with his car. Esad and Jasminka Lemo were living in separate apartments in Pennsylvania as their divorce was being processed. At this same time, according to newspaper reports, Lemo lost his job, became upset, and directed his anger at his estranged wife. Witnesses told police that Lemo jumped a curb with his car and drove across a grassy area before pinning his wife between his car and a building. She died of her injuries. As is often the case with intimate partner homicide, there was a record of domestic violence complaints involving Esad Lemos (Associated Press, 2006b). Unfortunately, Mrs. Lemo could not avoid her ex-husband, who was determined to hurt her.

THE POTENTIAL OF PUBLIC POLICY TO MAKE A DIFFERENCE

As noted earlier, over the past 25 years or so, intimate partner homicide has decreased considerably. What explains this decline? Could it be the increased attention to domestic violence in our society and the public policy responses to domestic violence, including increases in domestic violence hotlines and legal advocacy programs? Criminologists have asked these same questions, and their studies have provided answers that show the promise of public policy in decreasing violence and ultimately homicide. Nevertheless, the impact of these resources has not been exactly what domestic violence movement advocates may have hoped they would be. Positively, the studies have shown that resources for battered women are significantly associated with lower rates of women killing their husbands. It seems that legal advocacy and other resources for battered women have helped women see they have options beyond killing their partners to escape the violence (Browne & Williams, 1989; Dugan, Nagin, & Rosenfeld, 1999, 2003).

The availability of services for the victims of domestic violence, however, has not been as strongly linked to decreases in wife killing by husbands. Ironically, the public policy innovations put in place to protect battered women appear to have been more successful in saving the lives of abusive men than of battered women. Granted, the reduction in the number of homicides committed by battered women is beneficial because these men's lives are saved and a number of battered women may avoid incarceration. However, the smaller decrease in men killing their partners remains a curiosity.

Dugan and colleagues (2003) attempted to explain this curiosity by considering nonmarital heterosexual intimate partner homicide in addition to marital intimate partner homicide. As with the earlier studies, their study explored possible explanations for the decreases in intimate partner homicide. They found that for a majority (65%) of the 48 cities studied, more alternatives to living with or depending on an abusive partner coincided with lower levels of intimate partner homicide. However, there were some differences by relationship and by race. For example, as Aid to Families with Dependent Children (AFDC) benefits declined, more unmarried men were killed by their girlfriends, and African American men, in particular, were more likely to be killed. There were increases in men killing their African American girl-friends, but not white girlfriends, as AFDC benefits declined. Unmarried intimates were also less likely to be killed when domestic violence arrest policies were more aggressive, but aggressive arrest policies did not appear to affect intimate partner homicide by spouses. Legal advocacy was connected with fewer killings of white wives by their partners. Mandatory arrest policies were linked to fewer deaths of married women of all races, and warrantless arrest policies were associated with decreases in the killing of unmarried male intimates and unmarried white females. Education appeared to provide some protection against intimate partner homicide overall, but this did not hold true for African American intimates who were not married when these relationships were examined separately (Dugan et al., 2003). Research shows complications in drawing conclusions about what works in preventing intimate partner homicide. Nevertheless, this research demonstrates the impact that public policies may hold for reducing homicide.

INTIMATE PARTNER HOMICIDE IN COURT

In the past, there were rules that permitted a husband to beat his wife as long as the instrument he used had a circumference that was smaller than the circumference of his thumb. (This practice is the origin for the phrase "rule of thumb.") The killing of a wife by her husband was not seen as a horrible crime. In some places, in fact, if a man discovered his wife was having an affair and killed her as a result, the killing was viewed as justified and not always prosecuted. Today, such crimes are more likely to go to trial. But what happens in court? Are those who kill their intimate partner treated the same as those who kill strangers?

A study comparing intimate partner homicide and nonintimate partner homicide in Toronto, Canada, found that individuals accused of killing their partners were significantly more likely to be convicted than those accused of killing nonpartners. However, the author cautions that this finding is likely connected to other facts. First, individuals who kill their partners are less likely to be charged with first-degree murder than those who kill nonintimate partners. Secondly, and probably most important, those who are accused of killing partners are more likely to plead guilty than those who kill nonintimate partners. Nevertheless, for those who go to trial, individuals who are accused of killing their intimate partners are more likely to be found guilty than those charged with killing a nonintimate partner (Dawson, 2004).

BATTERED WOMEN'S SYNDROME IN COURT

In the United States, self-defense is an affirmative defense to murder. In other words, if defendants present convincing evidence that they killed another human being to protect their own life; the defendant will not be held responsible for the death. In most U.S. jurisdictions, the law of self-defense states that an individual may use reasonable force against another when the individual reasonably believes the other person is threatening her or him with imminent and unlawful harm. This definition may work well if you manage to bash a burglar in the head with a lamp and kill him while he is beating you with a golf club. It would seem that any reasonable person would believe you were protecting your own life. Hitting him with a lamp would appear to be reasonable force if he were hitting you with a golf club. Furthermore, it would be believable that the harm to you was immediate, and clearly it would be unlawful to beat you with a golf club.

When a woman like Francine Hughes, however, kills her husband by setting his bed on fire while he sleeps, a jury is not likely to see it as self-defense. After all, if you killed a person who was sleeping, it would be difficult to prove that you felt you were being threatened with imminent harm. Similarly, if a woman uses a gun to kill a man who is hitting her with his fist, some prosecutors and juries may not view her use of a gun as reasonable force because he was not using a weapon. With cases such as Francine Hughes's killing of her sleeping husband, immortalized in the book (and film) *The Burning Bed*, and Lenore Walker's groundbreaking book *Battered Woman*, criminologists and criminal justice professionals began to better understand the complications involved in a woman leaving her abusive partner (McNulty, 1989; Walker, 1980).

Battered women's syndrome is a psychological state akin to post-traumatic stress syndrome, which, in some cases, may explain why a woman kills her abusive husband. It is important to know that battered women's syndrome is not a defense to murder. However, as of 2004, more than 30 states have allowed expert testimony on battered women's syndrome to be introduced in court cases. This testimony does not work as a get-out-of-jail-free card. However, this testimony is sometimes introduced as mitigating circumstances that may explain why a woman would see no other option but to kill her partner. As a result, a jury may consider a woman's abuse in determining if she is guilty and what she is guilty of when she kills an abusive partner.

SUMMARY

This chapter focused on homicide that occurs between individuals who are or who have at one time been in a sexual relationship with one another. Throughout the chapter, much attention was given to the ways in which intimate partner violence by men and women differ. Although the data showed that men kill their partners more often than women kill their partners, it was also noted that the ratio of female-to-male intimate partner homicide was closer in the United States than in other parts of the world. The differences by age and race for intimate partner homicide were included. Good news about the decreases in intimate partner homicide was presented; although it was noted that the news may be better for men than for women. Explanations and motives for intimate partner homicide and the circumstances of intimate partner homicide were reviewed, including expressive and instrumental explanations. Much attention was also focused on domestic violence leading to intimate partner homicide by both men and women. A section about weapon use in partner-committed killing emphasized that knives are used more often in intimate partner–type homicide than in other types of homicide, although guns still predominate as killing instruments in the United States overall. The impact and potential for public policies to make a difference and intimate partner homicide in and outside court rounded out this chapter on intimate partner homicide.

CHAPTER QUESTIONS

1. How is "intimate partner" defined in this chapter?
2. Are men or women more frequently the victims of intimate partner homicide?
3. What group (by race and sex) are most at risk for intimate partner homicide?
4. Name some other factors by which intimate partner offending and victimization rates differ.
5. What is the SROK, and how does U.S. SROK compare to other countries?
6. Is intimate partner homicide decreasing or increasing? Does this vary by sex?
7. How does intimate partner homicide in the United States compare with intimate partner homicide in other countries?
8. How might you explain some of the gender differences in intimate partner homicide?
9. What explanations are discussed in this chapter to explain intimate partner homicide?
10. How does Emile Durkheim contribute to the understanding of intimate partner homicide?
11. What explains the decrease in intimate partner homicides that have been experienced recently in the United States?
12. According to the study in Canada, are those accused of killing their partners more or less likely to be convicted than those accused of killing nonpartners?
13. Do you think a study of U.S. courts would find the same results as the Canadian study on intimate partner homicide court?
14. What is the law of self-defense?
15. Is there a battered women's syndrome defense? Explain your answer.

REFERENCES

Associated Press. 2006a. "Ohio Voids Woman's Death Sentence." Accessed online at Los Angeles Times.com, http://www.latimes.com/news/nationworld/nation/la-na-death3aug03,1,2541320.story

Associated Press. 2006b, August 15. "Police: Suburban Pittsburgh Man Pinned Wife Against Wall with Car." *Associated Press State and Local Wire.*

Block, Carolyn Rebecca, and Antigone Christakos. 1995. "Intimate Partner Homicide in Chicago over 29 Years." *Crime & Delinquency,* 41(4): 496–526.

Browne, Angela. 1986. "Assault and Homicide at Home: When Battered Women Kill." In Michael J. Saks and Leonard Saxe, eds., *Advances in Applied Social Psychology* (pp. 57–79). Hillsdale, NJ: Lawrence Erlbaum.

Browne, Angela, and Kirk R. Williams. 1989. "Exploring the Effect of Resource Availability and the Likelihood of Female-Perpetrated Homicides." *Law & Society Review*, 23: 75–94.

Browne, Angela, Kirk Williams, and Donald G. Dutton. 1999. "Homicide Between Intimate Partners: A 20-Year Review." In M. Dwayne Smith and Margaret A. Zahn, eds., *Homicide: A Sourcebook of Social Research*. Thousand Oaks, CA: Sage.

Campbell, Jacquelyn C., D. Webster, J. Koziol-McLain, et al. 2003. "Risk Factors for Femicide in Abusive Relationships: Results from a Multisite Case Control Study." *American Journal of Public Health*, 93(7): 1089–1097.

CBS News. 2005, May 20. "Two Wigs, a Gun and Murder." Accessed online at www.cbsnews.com/stories/2005/05/19/48hours

Daly, Margo, and Martin Wilson. 1988. *Homicide*. New York: Aldine.

Davies, Kim, Carolyn Rebecca Block, and Jacquelyn Campbell. 2007. "Seeking Help from the Police: Battered Women's Decisions and Experiences." *Criminal Justice Studies*, 20(1): 31–57.

Dawson, Myrna. 2004. "Criminal Justice Outcomes in Intimate and Non-intimate Partner Homicide Cases." Research Report, rr04-6e. Ottawa: Department of Justice Canada, Research and Statistics Division.

Dugan, Laura, Daniel S. Nagin, and Richard Rosenfeld. 1999. "Explaining the Decline in Intimate Partner Homicide: The Effects of Changing Domesticity, Women's Status, and Domestic Violence Resources." *Homicide Studies*, 3(3): 187–214.

Dugan, Laura, Daniel S. Nagin, and Richard Rosenfeld. 2003. "Exposure Reduction or Retaliation? The Effects of Domestic Violence Resources on Intimate-Partner Homicide." *Law & Society*, 37(1): 169–198.

Durkheim, Emile. 1897/1979. *Suicide: A Study in Sociology*. Translated by John A. Spaulding and George Simpson. New York: Free Press.

Gauthier, DeAnn K., and William B. Bankston. 2004. "'Who Kills Whom' Revisited: A Sociological Study of Variation in the Sex Ratio of Spouse Killing." *Homicide Studies*, 8(2): 96–122.

Global News Wire. 2006. "Two More Killed over Dowry Dispute." *The Statesman LTD Source*. Accessed at http://www.thestatesman.net/page.arcview.php?clid=22&id=145506&usrsess=1.

Holliday, Bob. 2006, June 25. "Sentenced to Hang; Fearing for Her Life, Wife Killed Abusive Husband." *Winnipeg Sun*, p. C16.

Lindgren, April. 2006, June 21. "Domestic Violence Death Toll Remains High." *Kingston Whig-Standard*, p. 11.

Lowe, Herbert. 2006. "Jury Won't Indict Abused Wife: Bronx Woman Says Husband of 26 Years Tried to Stab Her First and She Killed Him in Self-Defense." *Newsday*, p. A18.

McNulty, Faith. 1989. *The Burning Bed: The True Story of an Abused Wife*. New York: Avon Books.

Millar, Chris. 2006, March 29. "Wife Shoots Her Husband Dead as she Dances to Shania Twain." *The Evening Standard*, p. 9.

Mouzos, Jenny. 2000. *Homicidal Encounters: A Study of Homicide in Australia, 1989–1999*. Canberra: Australian Institute of Criminology.

Mouzos, Jenny. 2002. *Homicide in Australia: 2000–2001 National Homicide Monitoring Program (NHMP) Annual Report*. Research and public policy series no. 40. Canberra: Australian Institute of Criminology. http://www.aic.gov.au/publications/rpp/40/.

Mouzos, Jenny, and Todd K. Shackelford. 2004. "A Comparative, Cross-National Analysis of Partner-Killing by Women in Cohabiting and Marital Relationships in Australia and the United States." *Aggressive Behavior*, 30: 206–216.

Paulozzi, Leonard J., Linda E. Saltzman, Martie P. Thompson, and Patricia Holmgreen. 2001, October 12. "Surveillance for Homicide Among Intimate Partners—United States, 1981–1998." *Morbidity and Mortality Weekly Report (MMWR) Surveillance Summaries*, 50: 1–16.

People v. *Pescador* 2004. Cal. App. 4th. No. C042759. Third District, June 8, 2004.

Prasad, Devi. 1994. "Dowry-Related Violence: A Content Analysis of News in Selected Newspapers." *Journal of Comparative Family Studies*, 25(1): 71–89.

Rennison, Callie Marie. 2003. *Intimate Partner Violence, 1993–2001.* Washington, DC: U.S. Department of Justice.

Rennison, Callie Marie, and Sarah Welchens. 2001. *Intimate Partner Violence.* Washington, DC: U.S. Department of Justice.

Shackelford, Todd K. 2001. "Partner-Killing by Women in Cohabitating Relationships and Marital Relationships." *Homicide Studies,* 5: 253–266.

Shackelford, Todd K., David M. Buss, and Jay Peters. 2000. "Wife Killing: Risk to Women as a Function of Age." *Violence and Victims,* 15(3): 273–282.

State v. *Roberts,* 110 Ohio St. 3d 71, 2006-Ohio-3665.

Sweeney, Rory. 2006. "Cop Killed Wife Over Affair." *The Times Leader,* March 11, 2006. Accessed online at http://www.highbeam.com/doc/1G1-143106530.html.

Tucker, Julie. 2006, February. "Bride Burning." *The Woman's Voice, 1.* Accessed online at http://www.womansvoice.ca/Issues/Feb2006/BrideBurning.php

Vasagar, Jeevan. 2006, June 24. "'Shania Twain' Shotgun Killer Is Jailed for Life." *Guardian.* Accessed online at http://www.guardian.co.uk/gun/Story/0,1804905,00.html

Walker, Lenore. 1980. *Battered Woman.* New York: Harper Paperbacks.

Websdale, Neil. 1999. *Understanding Domestic Homicide.* Boston: Northeastern University Press.

Chapter 9

CHILDREN WHO KILL

On March 22, 2005, 16-year-old Jeff Weise killed his 58-year-old grandfather Daryl Lussier and his grandfather's 32-year-old girlfriend Michelle Sigana before going to school where he killed seven additional people and wounded another seven. Like other school shooters before him, Weise stole the weapons he used, a pistol and a shotgun, from a relative. This time the weapons were believed to be his grandfather's police-issued weapons. Unlike other now infamous school shootings, the school in Red Lake, Minnesota, where Weise opened fire was equipped with metal detectors at the entryway and staffed by a guard. Weiss shot and killed the unarmed guard to make his way into the school. After entering the school, he killed five students and a teacher. Then, like other school shooters before him, Weise shot himself in the head. This school shooting, the nation's worst high school shooting since Columbine in 1999 where Dylan Klebold and Eric Harris killed 13 people and then themselves, was the first to occur on an Indian reservation. Young Weise was a member of the Ojibwa tribe (CNN, 2005).

Jeff Weise, Dylan Klebold, and Eric Harris and other young school shooters have dominated newspaper headlines in the United States. The idea that these angry boys and others like them may blow up at any moment and seek revenge in the sacred halls of our educational institutions is horrific. Despite the dreadful reality of the school shootings that dominated the nation's headlines in the 1990s and the scattering of school shootings since 2000 that have not received as much media attention, children kill far less often than adults. Nevertheless, there was an alarming increase in homicides committed by those ages 14 to 17 in the 1980s, which fortunately decreased in the 1990s but looks to be increasing again recently.

By the end of this chapter, you will be familiar with many of the issues involved in homicide by children and adolescents. The chapter begins with important terms in the study of homicide by those younger than 18 years. Then a couple of historic cases of homicide by children are reviewed to make the point that homicide by children is in no way a new phenomenon. As usual, data and trends are reviewed along with important and relevant demographic information about youth homicide. Within a section about those who children kill, there is a detailed discussion on parricide, or the killing of a parent, because this is a much studied phenomenon. Common circumstances and motives are also included for children who kill their parents and others. Finally, the chapter ends with a focus on the processing of young homicide offenders in the criminal justice system, including the practice of trying children in adult courts.

DEFINITIONS

The term *juvenile* is often interpreted to refer to children younger than 18 years; however, this term is not used uniformly across all jurisdictions (Heide, 1999). This chapter focuses on children younger than 18 years who have murdered. However, because there are differences between very young offenders and teen offenders, it is important to be clear about who we are studying when we look at children who kill. In this chapter, the terms *youth, juvenile,* and *children* are used to refer to people younger than 18 years. *Teen, teenager,* or *adolescent* is used to refer to children who are under 18 years but at least 13 years of age. Finally, those children under age 13 are called *preteens* or *preadolescents.*

BOX 9.1

Lizzie Borden: A Famous Case of a Child Who Killed Her Parents?

Lizzie Borden took an axe,
And gave her mother forty whacks,
When she saw what she had done,
She gave her father forty-one.

Chances are you have heard this nursery rhyme–like song about Lizzie Borden. The axe murder of Andrew and Abby Borden in Fall River, Massachusetts, continues to be an intriguing case more than 100 years after it occurred in 1892. Although it is true that this was a horribly violent murder, many of the details of the case are lost to those who only know the little ditty about Lizzie. First and importantly for this chapter, Borden was actually 33 years old at the time of the murder. She was not a child as many who recite the song may believe. Second, there were only 29 "whacks"—enough for very gruesome corpses but not the 81 whacks mentioned in the rhyme. Third, Lizzie Borden was found not guilty of the crime in an 1893 trial, although many continue to believe her guilty to this day. Finally, it was actually Borden's stepmother who was killed—a fact that may make some question her guilt even more (Linder, 2004).

HISTORY

Although much was made about children killing in the 1990s when we saw great increases in urban teen homicide and several school shootings, cases of children killing are not new. In 1874, 14-year-old Jesse Pomeroy was found guilty for mutilating and killing a 10-year-old girl and a 4-year-old boy in separate incidents (Gribben, 2006).

Girl murderers, although less frequent, are also not new. Eleven-year-old Mary Flora Bell was found guilty of the 1968 strangulation murders of 3-year-old Brian Howe and 4-year-old Martin Brown in New Castle, England (Sereny, 2000).

U.S. common law does not consider children younger than 7 years capable of mens rea. In other words, they are not believed to be capable of intending to commit a criminal act. Nevertheless, cases in which children younger than age 7 kill reintroduce the question as to whether young children can understand the gravity of the act they committed. Should we hold preadolescent killers responsible when they take the life of another human? Should they be tried for murder? It may seem that these are new questions that we must struggle with in what seems to be an increasingly violent society. Yet incidents of children killing, even young children killing with guns, are not new either.

In 1929 in Paintsville, Kentucky, 6-year-old Carl Newton Mahan killed his 8-year-old friend Cecil Van Hoose. Although younger than many of the boys involved in school shootings in the 1990s, it appears that this early twentieth-century killing involved bullying as many of the school shootings have. Carl and Cecil found a piece of scrap iron that could be sold to a metal scrap dealer. According to newspaper reports, Cecil hit Carl and took the scrap iron for himself. Carl ran home, where he stood on a chair to grasp his father's 12-gauge shotgun from above a door. He found Cecil and reportedly yelled, "I'm going to shoot you" before he shot his playmate (Tortora, 2000). The case against 6-year-old Mahan was heard in criminal court in 1929 shortly after Van Hoose's death. A jury heard the case and found Mahan guilty of the lesser crime of manslaughter. The judge sentenced him to 15 years in a juvenile reform school. The sentence, however, was not to be served. A mixture of appeals and public outcry combined, and a circuit court judge ruled that Mahan's case should not have been heard in criminal court. Cases against youngsters were supposed to be heard by a judge, not a jury. The attorney general of Kentucky made the final decision to allow Mahan to remain with his parents. Little is known about what happened to Mahan after he was released. There is no evidence that he continued on to be criminal. We know only that he died at the age of 35 in 1958 (Tortora, 2000).

BOX 9.2
The Crime That Shocked Britain

At 3.39 P.M. on Friday, February 12, 1993, a shopping center surveillance camera in a Liverpool shopping center captured images of Robert Thompson and Jon Venables walking hand in hand with 2-year-old James Bulger. This would be the last images of Bulger alive. James's mother took

continued

her eyes off him for just a few minutes, and he disappeared. She panicked. The police eventually were contacted, and photographs of Bulger were shown on the nightly news in hopes that someone had seen the cute 2-year-old. It was not until after midnight, however, that investigators found the blurry images of two 10-year-old boys walking Bulger out of the mall. However, the abductors were not identifiable on the tape. On Sunday afternoon, four boys found Bulger's badly battered body on railway tracks approximately 2 miles from the mall where his mother had last seen him. An anonymous caller suggested that Robert Thompson and Jon Venables might have something to do with the crime. Police were apprehensive, but with little to go on they picked up the boys. Eventually the boys confessed and were found guilty at trial. They were sentenced to indefinite sentences.

In 2001, Venables and Thompson were headline news again. They were to be released and their identities protected. Some were outraged, including many of Bulger's relatives. Others argued the boys were so young when they committed the crime that they did not understand the gravity of the offense they were committing at the time they committed it. What do you think? Do you think the boys should have been released? What would convince you they should be released or they should remain incarcerated? If you knew that both boys were considered delinquents and often caused trouble before they were apprehended for Bulger's killing, would it make you think differently? (Scott, 2005).

OFFICIAL DATA ON HOMICIDE BY CHILDREN

Although the number of children who kill is alarming, the data show that they make up a relatively small percentage of those who kill. As Table 9.1 shows, less than 10%, or 2,821, of those arrested for murder and nonnegligent manslaughter for the years 2002 to 2004 were younger than 18 years. Not surprising, as age increases, the number of arrests for homicide also increases. Only 3 children under the age of 10 were arrested in the years 2002 to 2004 for murder and nonnegligent manslaughter. Over 10 times as many children between the ages of 10 and 12 were arrested and even more, or 289, between the ages of 13 and 14 were believed to have killed in these years. Police arrested

TABLE 9.1

Arrests for Murder and Nonnegligent Manslaughter by Age for 2004, 2003, and 2002

Age in Years	2004	2003	2002	Total
Under 10	2	1	0	3
10–12	13	11	17	41
13–14	129	76	84	289
15	180	130	140	450
16	311	223	274	808
17	430	342	458	1230
18 and older	8,933	8,336	9,134	26,403
Total	**9,998**	**9,119**	**10,107**	**29,224**

Source: Compiled from Federal Bureau of Investigation Statistics data (FBI, 2003, 2004, 2005).

BOX 9.3

Eleven-Year-Old Charged as an Adult

The murder trial of Nathaniel Abraham in Michigan garnered national attention and much controversy in 1999. Abraham was arrested in October 1997 for the shooting death of 18-year-old Ronnie Greene Jr. Despite the fact that Abraham was only 11 years old at the time of Greene's death, he was charged with first-degree murder. Because of a law in Michigan allowing children under 17 years old to be charged as an adult for a serious crime, Abraham was charged as an adult. Prosecutors argued that Abraham, who had a previous arrest for burglary and who was suspected of several additional crimes, was the type of serious juvenile offender for which the Michigan law, which allowed prosecution of children in adult courts, was enacted. Defense attorneys and others in the media argued that Abraham did not have the mental faculties to kill another intentionally. They argued that in addition to his age, he had the mental ability of a 6-year-old (Robinson, 1999a). After three days of deliberation, the jury failed to find Abraham guilty of first-degree murder. However, he was convicted of second-degree murder and sentenced to juvenile detention until age 21 (Kennedy & Hunter, 2000; Robinson, 1999b).

To see the actual sentencing documents, visit http://www.courttv.com/archive/trials/abraham/sentence_text_ctv.html

---

450 15-year-olds, 808 16-year-olds, and 1,230 17-year-olds. Still, it is important to remember that children make up a small portion of those arrested for murder. In Table 9.1, for instance, 17-year-olds make up only 4.2% of all those arrested for murder.

Trends: Are Children Killing More Often or Less Often?

When we ask whether killing by children is increasing or decreasing, it is best to consider the question separately for adolescents and preadolescents because as shown in Figure 9.1, the rates are very different. In fact, the rates among those younger than 14 years are barely perceptible in the figure because they hover very close to a rate of zero. However, the Bureau of Justice Statistics reports that among preadolescents (under age 14), homicide commission began increasing in the late 1980s and continued to increase in the early 1990s. However, since it peaked in 1994 at a rate of 0.4 per 100,000 for preadolescents, it has decreased to the lowest levels ever. In 2000, 2001, and 2002, the rate of homicide commission among those 14 and younger was 0.1 per 100,000. Among those ages 14 to 17, there was a very rapid increase after 1985 when the rate was 10.5 per 100,000. The rate continued to increase to a peak rate of 31.3 per 100,000 in 1993. Since 1993, the homicide offending rate among 14- to 17-year-olds has plummeted to the lowest levels ever recorded. In 2002, the rate was 9.0 per 100,000.

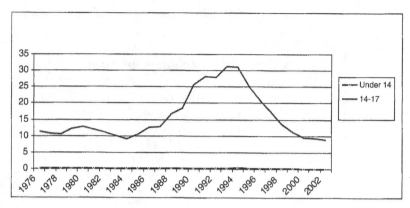

FIGURE 9.1

Homicide Offending Rates per 100,000 for 14- to 17-Year-Olds and Those Under 14 Years

SEX AND JUVENILE HOMICIDE OFFENDERS

When we discuss trends or statistics about homicide offending by those younger than 18 years, it is important to note the many differences found between female and male juvenile homicide offenders. First and foremost, males far outnumber females as juvenile homicide offenders. A 1999 National Study of Juvenile Homicide that examined FBI Supplementary Homicide data between 1980 and 1997 indicated that 93% of known juvenile homicide offenders were male. Furthermore, as Table 9.2 shows, at every age, boys are more likely to be arrested for murder and nonnegligent manslaughter than girls. Finally, when we look at the percentages for all three years totaled, it appears that as age increases, the percentage of males arrested also increases. However, the data for each year show this is not a stable relationship.

The data on homicide by juveniles also indicate that the number of female juvenile homicide offenders has remained fairly constant over the past 20 years, with about

TABLE 9.2

Percentage of Arrests of Males for Murder and Nonnegligent Manslaughter by Age for 2004, 2003, and 2002

Age in Years	2004	2003	2002
Under 10	50.0	100	0*
10–12	84.6	81.8	76.4
13–14	79.0	89.4	84.5
15	81.6	91.5	87.1
16	91.6	90.5	90.1
17	91.1	90.9	91.4
18 and older	88.4	89.5	89.1
Total	**88.4**	**89.6**	**89.1**

*No homicides

Source: Compiled from Federal Bureau of Investigation Statistics data (FBI, 2003, 2004, 2005).

130 girls committing homicide each year between 1980 and 1997. The numbers of juvenile male homicide offenders during this same period varied greatly with the number decreasing between 1980 and 1984 and then increasing greatly to over 2,500 in 1993 and 1994 before decreasing to approximately 1,500 male juvenile homicide offenders in 1997. Other differences between male and female children who kill, including the weapons they use and who they kill, are discussed in subsequent sections of this chapter.

RACE AND JUVENILE HOMICIDE OFFENDERS

The 1999 National Study of Juvenile Homicide, which revealed differences between female and male juvenile offenders, is also valuable for what it tells us about race and juvenile homicide offending. This study indicated that for every million juveniles in the United States, 56 were homicide offenders. The incidence, however, varies by race. Just over half (56%) of known juvenile homicide offenders between 1980 and 1997 were African American. The difference does not seem like much until the rates are considered, and then the differences are striking. Thirty of every million white juveniles; 34 of every million Native American juveniles, and 44 of every million Asian juveniles committed homicide as compared to 194 of every million African American juveniles. Furthermore, African American juvenile offenders used guns in 72% of their offenses; Asians used firearms in 67% of their offenses; whites used guns in 59% of their offenses, and only 48% of Native American juvenile offenders used guns (Snyder & Sickmund, 1999).

Youths were most likely to kill individuals of their own race, with 90% of whites killing whites, 76% of African Americans killing African Americans, 58% of Asians killing Asians, and finally 48% of Native Americans killing other Native American youth. As a percentage of all their victims, white and Native American youth killed their family members (16% and 17%, respectively) more frequently than did African American (7%) and Asian (7%) youth (Snyder & Sickmund, 1999).

CHILDREN IN OTHER COUNTRIES

The numbers of youth who commit homicide in the United States is much higher than the numbers of children who kill in other Westernized countries. Moreover, although not as drastically different, children in the United States made up a larger percentage of those arrested for homicide as well. In Australia in 2003–2004, 15% of homicide offenders were age 19 or younger. During the same years, in the United States, 22% of those arrested for homicide were under 20 years old (FBI, 2004, 2005; Mouzos, 2005).

Note, however, that the problem of juvenile homicide is not shared equally across the United States. Snyder and Sickmund (1999) reported that in 88% of the more than 3,000 counties that reported crimes to the FBI in 1997, not a single juvenile was known to have committed a homicide. Only one juvenile homicide offender was known to have committed a homicide in 6% of the reporting counties. In fact, over a quarter (26%) of juvenile homicide offenders in 1997 were located in the following eight cities, which together make up only 12% of the U.S. population: Baltimore, Chicago, Dallas, Detroit, Houston, Los Angeles, New York, and Philadelphia (Snyder & Sickmund,

---

BOX 9.4

Nevada Tan—The Japanese School Girl Killer

In June 2004, a 11-year-old Japanese girl used a box cutter to slash the throat of her 12-year-old friend, Satomi Mitarai. The murder took place in an empty classroom where the young offender, known as "Girl A," left Mitarai to bleed to death. The girls' teacher saw blood on the offender's clothes and realized Mitarai was missing. The teacher discovered Mitarai in the classroom. At her trial, Girl A was said not to have a psychiatric disorder; however, the judge reported she "was only capable of taking extreme measures—either suppressing her anger to avert a crisis, or attacking other people—as she was unable to appropriately deal with her anger" (Shimbun, 2004). Girl A reportedly killed her friend Mitarai because Mitarai had posted negative remarks about Girl A's weight on the Internet (Shimbun, 2004).

Girl A has since become somewhat of an icon on the Internet, where hundreds of images of her as a meme cartoon character can be found. According to information on at least one of these sites, a class photograph including Mitarai and the young girl who killed her was posted on the Internet (humblefool.net). In the photo, the young killer was wearing a blue hooded sweatshirt with the word "Nevada" emblazoned across the front. Not long after the photograph of "Girl A" first appeared, there was much talk about her on the Internet, especially on a Japanese website called 2channel. Girl A became known as "Nevada-tan," with "tan" being the way a small child might pronounce the honorific "chan." Thus Nevada-tan would basically translate into English as "Widdle Nevada" (humblefool.net). Many of the cartoon caricatures of her depicted on the Web show her in the blue Nevada shirt splattered with blood, and she is often depicted with a box cutter. The real "Nevada-tan" has been sentenced to a juvenile institution, but her Internet meme is still easy to find on Japanese and American fan pages and on image boards where many anonymous posters appear to be in competition to post the most horrific and sometimes pornographic cartoons of Nevada-tan as well as actual photographs and artwork by the young killer (humblefool.net).

1999). Large urban populations with all the problems associated with such cities experienced much higher juvenile homicide rates than less densely populated places.

VICTIM/OFFENDER RELATIONSHIP: WHO DO CHILDREN KILL?

Looking at Table 9.3, you can see that male juvenile homicide offenders and female juvenile offenders most often killed acquaintances. In fact, 54% of young male offenders killed their acquaintances, and 46% of female offenders killed their acquaintances. Boys, however, were more likely than girls to kill strangers. Thirty-four percent of male victims were strangers and 15% of female victims were strangers. Family members

TABLE 9.3
Homicide Type by Age, 1976–2002

	Victims				Offenders			
	Under 18 (%)	18–34 (%)	35–49 (%)	50+ (%)	Under 18 (%)	18–34 (%)	35–49 (%)	50+ (%)
All homicides	9.8	52.7	22.7	14.8	11.1	64.8	17.2	6.9
Victim/offender relationship								
Intimate	2.3	46.9	33.6	17.2	1.1	47.1	34.3	17.6
Family	19.2	32.6	26.5	21.7	6.1	49.5	27.8	16.6
Infanticide	100.0				8.3	81.3	9.4	1.1
Eldercide				100.0	10.5	50.2	18.3	20.9
Circumstances								
Felony murder	7.7	46.5	21.6	24.2	15.1	72.9	10.1	2.0
Sex related	19.8	45.2	16.2	18.8	10.8	74.1	13.0	2.1
Drug related	5.5	71.8	19.6	3.2	10.9	76.6	11.2	1.2
Gang related	25.4	7.4	5.9	1.3	30.4	67.7	1.6	.3
Argument	5.4	56.4	26.1	12.0	6.9	60.2	23.1	9.7
Workplace	2.1	28.6	30.7	38.5	5.0	53.3	26.6	15.1
Weapon								
Gun homicide	7.5	59.0	22.5	11.0	12.1	64.1	16.1	7.7
Arson	28.4	27.2	18.9	25.4	11.7	58.4	22.8	7.1
Poison	26.5	24.2	16.7	32.6	4.9	50.9	26.1	18.1
Multiple victims or offenders								
Multiple victims	18.6	45.9	19.0	16.4	9.7	65.9	18.6	5.9
Multiple offenders	11.3	55.2	19.7	13.7	18.7	72.8	7.3	1.2

Note: The victims of the 9/11 terrorist attacks are not included in this analysis.

Source: Compiled from Federal Bureau Investigation Statistics data and Supplementary Homicide Reports (FBI, 1976–2002).

made up only 9% of the victims killed by males, whereas 39% of those killed by female juvenile offenders were family members (Snyder & Sickmund, 1999).

Some of the differences in who male and female juveniles kill and in the weapons that they use may be explained by the fact that young girls are far more likely than young boys to kill their own infants. Eighteen percent of female juvenile homicide offenders killed victims under the age of 1 year. For male juvenile homicide offenders this figure was approximately 1%, although Snyder and Sickmund (1999) note that because there are so many more male juvenile homicide offenders, the annual number of infants killed by males and females was nearly equal each year between 1980 and 1997, with each sex killing approximately 25 infants each year.

Parricide

One particular type of killing by children has garnered much research attention. Just as we are stunned when a parent kills a child, we find it shocking when a parent is killed by his or her child. It is very likely that even if you were a small child in 1989 when they killed their parents, you know the names Erik and Lyle Menendez. In one of the first big cases covered on *Court TV* in 1993 and 1994, many watched as defense attorneys for the brothers explained that Erik and Lyle killed their parents, Jose and Kitty Menendez, after years of abuse. To save money, both boys were tried at the same time; however, each had a separate jury. Both juries and *Court TV* viewers watched months of testimony. The prosecution told how the brothers, who were 17 and 21 years old, respectively, at the time of their parent's murders, had broken into their own home and used shotguns to riddle their parents' bodies with bullets. The defense attempted to prove that the boys had been abused and were reacting against that abuse. Amazingly, to many, the juries could not agree whether the boys should be convicted for killing their parents. Because both juries were deadlocked, the judge had to rule a mistrial. District Attorney Gil Garcetti decided to proceed with another trial. Eventually, after many postponements, the boys were tried again in 1996. This time they were convicted. On March 20, 1996, a jury convicted Erik and Lyle Menendez of two counts each of first-degree murder for the murders of their parents. Both were sentenced to life in prison (Pergament, 2005).

Although *parricide* technically refers to the killing of a close relative, the term has come to mean the killing of one's parent. The killing of one's father is called a *patricide;* the killing of one's mother is called a *matricide.* Parricide is most often committed by an adult daughter or son. However, a small number of parricides are committed by offenders like Erik Menendez, who are younger than 18 years.

Kathleen Heide, who is one of the foremost experts on children who kill, has written extensively about parricide. Heide (1992) suggests that three types of children kill their parents. First, most common are severely abused children who, in a sense, feel they are trapped. They may be physically, emotionally, and/or sexually abused. Second are those children who are mentally ill. And third, according to Heide, are dangerously antisocial children. Heide's research has led her to the conclusion that children who kill their parents often have troubled family histories. It may not be surprising, if we think about it, but she has found that they often come from violent homes where alcoholism or heavy drinking is common. Often the children in Heide's research felt trapped and isolated, and although they may have attempted to run away, they had been unsuccessful.

Unlike other types of adolescent homicide offenders, more often than not, the parricide offender is a white upper-middle or middle-class male who does not have a juvenile record. More typical of other juvenile homicide offenders, the typical parricide offender is 16 to 18 years old (Hegadorn, 1999). Aaron Clark, who was sentenced to 15 years to life for stabbing his 48-year-old mother to death after they argued about his girlfriend, is typical in that he was 16 years old at the time of the killing (*New York Times,* 2005). However, unlike Aaron, adolescent parricide offenders are more likely to kill their fathers (Hegadorn, 1999).

Heide notes that her case studies of adolescent parricide offenders have found many of the offenders to be good students who were believed to be close to their family while living a secret life of abuse (Heide, 1992). Like young Aaron and the Menendez brothers, the child parricide offender tends to kill his parent in a very violent attack. The child's rage is reflected in the excessive number of wounds suffered by the parent whether the method of attack is a beating, a stabbing, or a shooting.

Frequently, as in some cases where battered women have killed their abuser, the child tends to strike out against his or her parent when the parent is not attacking the child (Hegadorn, 1999).

YOUTH GANG MURDERS

Parricide may attract much media attention but so have gang killings, especially during the 1990s. Those who study adolescent homicide and especially those who have focused on the great increases in homicide among those age 14 to 17 in the early 1990s have noted that much of youth homicide revolves around gang activity. To learn more about gang homicide, Klein (1995) compared gang and nongang homicide in Los Angeles. He found that gang homicides were more likely than nongang homicides to occur in the streets, involve autos, guns, and unidentified assailants. Injuries to those other than the homicide victim and fear of retaliation were also more common in gang homicides than in nongang homicide. Offenders and victims in gang homicide were more likely to be male and Hispanic than those involved in nongang homicide. Finally, on average, suspects in gang homicide were younger than those involved in nongang homicide. With respect to the point of this chapter, however, note that the average age of Los Angeles gang homicide suspects was 19.4 years of age. In other words, many but not all of the killings described by Klein (1995) would involve juveniles.

Still, the connection among gangs, drug trafficking, and murder is believed by many to be so strong that the considerable decreases in U.S. murder rates that occurred in the 1990s are attributed to changes in the crack cocaine market and the reduction of gang wars over territory. But scholars continue to explore the relationships among drugs, drug trafficking, murder, and other violent crimes. Goldstein (1985) proposed three probable relationships between drugs and violence. First, the "pharmacological" effects of drugs may contribute to violent behavior committed by the offender. Second, drug users may commit crimes so they can afford to buy illicit drugs, which are often expensive because of their illegality. Third, violence is commonly used by those in the illegal drug business to secure and maintain territory for drug sales or as a way of deterring those in the business from violating business norms.

It is the third connection between drugs and violence that many believe explains much of the youth homicide in a several large cities that drove the great increases in youth homicide during the 1980s and early 1990s (Block & Christakos, 1995). Although some studies fail to support the idea of strong relationships between gang-related homicide and drug trafficking, others have concluded that drug trafficking is directly related to homicide through drug market wars and indirectly related to homicide by bringing individuals from rival gangs together (Block, Christakos, Jacob, et al., 1996; Klein, 1995). Others have argued that firearm ownership is a stronger predictor of youth homicide than gang use and drug sales. Still, there is a strong connection among gun use, drug sales, and gang membership, making it difficult to determine whether one factor contributes more to youth murder than another (Moore, 1990).

WEAPON USE AND CO-OFFENDERS: HOW DO CHILDREN KILL?

Male juvenile killers are more likely to kill with firearms than are female juvenile offenders. Nearly three fourths of male juvenile offenders used firearms, whereas less than half (41%) of female juvenile offenders killed with guns. Boys used knives in 14% of the homicides they committed in comparison to girls who used knives in 32% of homicides they committed. More than a fourth (27%) of female juvenile offenders used other methods such as drowning, strangling, or beating their victims. Boys used other methods in only 14% of the murders they committed.

According to the data from 1980 to 1997, the number of juvenile offenders who had a co-offender increased with the offender's age. About half of juvenile homicide offenders age 14 to 17 killed with a co-offender. Children younger than 10 years who killed were far less likely to have a co-offender, with only 14% of children under 10 years killing with another. Approximately a quarter of 10-year-olds (28%) and exactly a quarter of 11-year-olds killed with a codefendant. Almost a third (32%) of 12-year-olds and 42% of 13-year-olds had co-offenders. Older juveniles were more likely than younger juveniles to kill with adults. Younger children who had co-offenders were more likely to

---

BOX 9.5

Six-Year-Old Kills at School

February 29, 2000, was the last day of 6-year-old Kayla Rolland's life. She was shot to death in her elementary school in Flint, Michigan. The shooter was a 6-year-old classmate who had brought a .32-caliber handgun to school. A teacher and other children witnessed the killing. The young boy shot only one shot, but it hit Kayla in the neck. After the shooting, he ran to the bathroom where he threw the gun in the trash can. Kayla was rushed to a hospital and died within the hour. The boy was not charged with the crime because as Genesee County Prosecutor Arthur Busch stated, "There is a presumption in law that a child . . . is not criminally responsible and can't form intent to kill" (BBC News Online, 2000).

The young shooter retrieved the gun from a bedroom where he lived. Some suggested that the house was a crack house and the child had to live there with a family member because his mother had been evicted. According to prosecutors, the gun belonged to 19-year-old Jamelle James. Prosecutors charged James with manslaughter for Kayla Rolland's death. They argued that he had shown off with the pistol in front of the young boy whose name was withheld for his protection. They also claimed that James kept the gun loaded in his bed making it accessible to the young shooter (Anonymous, 2000). James pleaded no contest to involuntary manslaughter and was sentenced to a prison term of 2 to 15 years (CBS News, 2000). Do you agree with the sentence James received? What do you think should happen to the young killer, if anything?

kill with other youngsters (Snyder & Sickmund, 1999). Heide (2003) has also reported that girls are more likely than boys to employ accomplices to kill the girl's family members (with the exception of their own infants). Fifteen-year-old Holly Harvey, for example, employed the help of her girlfriend Sandy Ketchum in the brutal 2004 stabbing murders of Harvey's grandparents Carl and Sarah Collier in Georgia (Shirek, 2004).

MOTIVE: WHY DO CHILDREN KILL?

An ominous foretelling of what would dominate news headlines in the 1990s occurred in 1987 when honor student Nathan Ferris responded to teasing with deadly violence. Ferris shot and killed a fellow student with his father's .45 caliber pistol, which he had brought from home apparently to use against children who teased him. Young Nathan was a loner and children often teased him. After shooting his classmate, Ferris shot and killed himself. Shootings like this one and the many well-publicized school shootings across the United States in the second half of the 1990s posed new questions about adolescent murderers. Many of the young school shooters who dominated the news at the end of the twentieth century did not kill for profit or out of passion. (See Table 9.4 for a list of school shooters.) They were not urban teenagers involved in gang violence. The young men who killed in school were mostly white suburbanite teens who came from seemingly good middle-class families. Moreover, these young boys often planned massacres with the intention of killing many of their classmates and teachers (Smith, 2000).

Research suggests that young people who kill do not kill out of the blue. Instead, many of these children have not only been exposed to violent and abusive environments, but often the children themselves have displayed aggression in the past (Dent & Jowitt, 2003). In a review of the literature in 2003, Kathleen Heide noted that studies indicate it may be important to differentiate between adolescent and preadolescent homicide offenders when attempting to determine why young people kill. Children under the age of 9 who kill may not understand the reality of death and fail to realize the irreversibility of their actions (Heide, 2003). Preadolescent killers tend to kill on impulse, whereas adolescent killers are apt to be influenced by their involvement in gangs or in response to particular situations, such as in confrontational homicide situations as discussed in Chapter 7 (Heide, 2003).

As with all homicide offenders, it is difficult to determine what factors lead the very few children who kill to kill. The theories in Chapters 5 and 6 may be used to explain homicide by some children. Often children who kill are found to be suffering from psychological disorders or more severe psychopathology such as psychosis (Heide, 2003). However, it is important to realize that many of the studies that report children who kill have mental disorders use convenience samples obtained by psychologists and psychologists. In other words, much of what we know about children who have killed has been learned from studying children who have been assigned to psychological or psychiatric treatment (Heide, 2003). Although it is not difficult to believe that many children who kill have mental problems of some kind.

Many studies, nonpsychological and others, have indicated that abuse is not uncommon in the backgrounds of adolescent and preadolescent homicide offenders.

TABLE 9.4
Student Fatal School Shooting* Incidents, 1990–2005

Date	Student Shooter(s), Age(s)	Location	Number of Fatalities
Jan. 18, 1993	Scott Pennington, 17	Kentucky	1 teacher, 1 janitor
Feb. 2, 1996	Barry Loukaitis, 14	Washington	1 teacher, 2 students
Feb. 19, 1997	Evan Ramsey, 16	Alaska	1 principal, 1 student
Oct. 1, 1997	Luke Woodham, 16	Mississippi	2 students (and his mother)
Dec. 1, 1997	Michael Carneal, 14	Kentucky	3 students
Mar. 24, 1998	Andrew Golden, 11, and Mitchell Johnson, 13	Arkansas	1 teacher, 4 students
Apr. 24, 1998	Andrew Wurst, 14	Pennsylvania	1 teacher
Apr. 28, 1998	Unidentified, 14	California	2 students
May 19, 1998	Jacob Davis, 18	Tennessee	1 student
May 21, 1998	Kip Kinkel, 15	Oregon	2 students (and his parents)
Apr. 20, 1999	Dylan Klebold, 17, and Eric Harris, 18	Colorado	1 teacher, 12 students, themselves
Apr. 28 1999	Unidentified, 14	Alberta, Canada	1 student
Nov. 19, 1999	Victor Cordova Jr., 12	New Mexico	1 student
Feb. 29, 2000	Unidentified, 6	Michigan	1 student
Mar. 16, 2000	Unidentified, 16	Germany	1 school director
May 26, 2000	Nathaniel Brazill, 13	Florida	1 teacher
Aug. 4, 2000	Unnamed, no age	Brazil	1 student
Sept. 26, 2000	Darrell Johnson, 13	Louisiana	1 student
Mar. 5, 2001	Charles Andrew Williams, 15	California	2 students
Mar. 30, 2001	Donald R. Burt Jr., 18	Indiana	1 student
Apr. 26, 2002	Robert Steinhaeuser, 19	Germany	13 teachers, 2 students, 1 police officer, himself
Apr. 29, 2002	Dragolav Petkovic, 17	Bosnia-Herzegovina	1 teacher, himself
Sept. 24, 2003	John Jason McLaughlin, 15	Minnesota	2 students
Jan. 13, 2004	Murati D., 17	Hague, Netherlands	1 deputy headmaster
Feb. 2, 2004	Unidentified	Washington, DC	1 student
May 7, 2004	Unidentified, 17	Maryland	1 student
May 21, 2004	Unidentified, 17	New South Wales, Australia	1 student
Jun. 1, 2004	Luis Quinones, 17	U.S. Virgin Islands	1 student
Sept. 8, 2004	Unidentified, 15	Argentina	3 students
Nov. 5, 2004	Unidentified, 18	South Africa	1 student
Mar. 11, 2005	Unidentified, 15	South Africa	1 principal
Mar. 21, 2005	Jeff Weise, 16	Minnesota	1 teacher, 5 students, 1 security guard, 2 relatives
Mar. 29, 2005	Unidentified; no age given	Turkey	1 teacher
Nov. 8, 2005	Kenny Bartley, 15	Tennessee	1 principal

*See these sources for a listing of other school shootings that were not fatal as well as for fatal killings that were not shootings, cases before 1990, and for those in which the offender was not a student at the school where the killings took place.

Sources: Compiled from Indianapolis Star.com, 2005, and the Angels of Columbine Website, 2006.

Additionally, many young homicide offenders have records, as do many of their parents (Holmes & Holmes, 2001). Gang affiliation, alcohol abuse, and educational problems are also often found to be common among juvenile homicide offenders (Busch, Zagar, Hughes, et al., 1990; Holmes & Holmes, 2001). Still others have noted that violence may be associated with early factors in children's development such as what one's mother ingested while pregnant, nutritional deficiencies, ineffective discipline, and even lack of consistency by caregivers (crimelibrary.com).

Although much excellent psychological research is available on children who kill, in her 2004 book about school shootings, Katherine Newman uses a sociological perspective to examine school shootings. Instead of focusing on the personalities and potential mental problems of the young boys who massacred others, Newman examines the culture and social structure of schools. Newman notes that media violence, gun culture, a culture of violence, family problems, peer relations, mental illness, bullying, demographic change, and copycatting have all been blamed for school shootings. She contends that all of these explanations hold some water. However, she believes that one reason alone does not account for murderous rampages by children. Instead, she proposes five causes that are necessary for such a killing to happen, although she notes that these are not sufficient causes (Newman, 2004). The causes are as follows:

1. The young shooters' self-perceptions are that they are marginal.
2. The shooters are experiencing psychosocial problems that make their marginality more extreme than it is in reality.
3. A cultural script of masculinity in our society suggests that shooting people will gain them the respect they desire.
4. The organization of public schools in the United States makes it difficult to recognize warning signs given off by the young killers. The signs are missed by teachers and administrators, and if recognized by peers, the children do not report to the administrators.
5. The easy availability of guns in U.S. society.

BOX 9.6

Media Violence and Children who Kill

In an article in Phi Kappa Phi's National Forum, West Point military psychologist Lieutenant Colonel David Grossman reports how amazing it is that 14-year-old Paducah, Kentucky, school shooter Michael Carneal was able to shoot eight classmates with only eight shots. After only a few practice shots with a stolen .22 pistol, Carneal made eight out of eight "kill shots;" five in the head and three in the chest. Grossman, who trains elite military forces and law enforcement agents, asks how a 14-year-old boy acquires "the skill and the will to kill" (Grossman, 2000). His answer is "video games and media

continued

violence." Grossman argues that most animals, including humans, have a "natural resistance to killing their own kind." In fact, he notes that the military has learned over time that most military recruits are resistant to killing others and must be trained to kill. The military, according to Grossman, uses "brutalization, classical conditioning, operant conditioning, and role modeling" to teach military personnel to kill. So what does this have to do with school shooters and other children who kill? Grossman argues that through a constant bombardment of media images of violence, children become desensitized to the reality of violence and death. The skills to be able to shoot "successfully" and, in particular, to shoot humans are learned through violent video games that teach children to kill with "military precision." Finally, children learn through watching their heroes kill in stylized violence sequences that killing others is a viable solution for dealing with problems.

Grossman uses scientific studies to back up his claims, but some will argue he is overexaggerating the connection between media violence, violent video games, and children who kill. What do you think? What arguments could you make to support him? What might you argue against him? What evidence might we use to support or oppose his claims? You may want to read Grossman's article for yourself; he has it posted on his "Killogy" site: http://www.killology.com/article_teachkid.htm.

CRIMINAL JUSTICE PROCESSING: WHAT HAPPENS TO CHILDREN WHO KILL?

With the introduction of juvenile court in Illinois in 1899, juveniles who committed crimes were viewed and treated differently from their adult counterparts. Many people believed that children, especially young children, did not possess the mental capacity that would make mens rea possible. Further, it was believed it was best not to label children as criminals but on occasion to intervene in their lives and help set them on a better path. Certainly, this approach worked for many children, but as conservatism grew in the United States and as violent juvenile crime increased in the 1980s and 1990s, legislatures began enacting laws that allowed juveniles to be treated as adults.

The Juvenile Offender Act of 1978 (also known as the "Willie Bosket Law") was introduced in New York in 1978. It allowed juveniles as young as 13 years old to be tried in adult courts. The law is named after Willie Bosket, who killed another young man in a fight and shot and killed two additional men on the subway in New York just because he wanted to see what it was like to kill another human (Butterfield, 1996).

As more attention was focused on juvenile crime in the 1980s and 1990s, more states followed New York's lead, and by 1999, juveniles could be tried as adults in all

50 states. Traditionally, the decision about whether a youth would stand trial in adult criminal court was left to a judge. However, between 1992 and 1997, 44 states added or amended their transfer provisions, making transfer to adult court more likely. In some states the decision is still at the discretion of a judge; in others, the judge must explain why he does not transfer the children, and in the most restrictive jurisdictions, the waiver to adult court is mandatory if the case and youth meet particular conditions such as age, criminal history, and seriousness of crime requirements (Snyder & Sickmund, 1999).

In many states, the prosecutor asks for a waiver so a child will be prosecuted in an adult criminal court; other states require the judge to initiate a waiver. Then it is usually the juvenile court judge who makes the decision about whether to waive jurisdiction. Typically, however, the judge is not totally free to make the decision to transfer a youth. Instead, in most cases, one or all three of the following criteria are required: the current crime for which the child is being charged must be serious (e.g., murder or manslaughter), he or she must be of a particular minimum age, and he or she must have a previous record of serious offending. Still, in all states, the juvenile court is required to hold a hearing in which the prosecution and defense may present evidence in support or in opposition to the waiver. Usually, for a juvenile to be waived there must be a preponderance of evidence in support of bounding the youth to adult court. Usually the Juvenile Court must consider not only the best interest of the public but what would be best for the youth, although the exact balance between the public and the youth's interest varies by state (Griffin, Torbet, & Szymanski, 1998).

The nation is still not at ease with bounding children over to adult courts, as exemplified in the case of Lionel Tate. At age 12, Tate killed Tiffany Eunuck, a 6-year-old neighbor girl whom his mother was babysitting. According to court testimony, Tate was imitating wrestling moves that he had learned while watching professional wrestling. Tragically, Tiffany died as the result of the Tate's actions. A jury in adult criminal court found Tate guilty, and he was sentenced to life in prison (Gaines & Miller, 2004). In 2004, his sentence was overturned in appeals court because it was ruled that the court had not determined whether Tate had the mental capability to understand the charges against him. In lieu of another court trial, Tate pleaded guilty to second-degree murder and was sentenced to time served plus a year of house arrest. Sadly, Tate continued on in crime, and by the age of 19 in 2006, Tate was sentenced to return to prison for 10 to 30 years for a parole violation. Tate had violated his parole by being in possession of a gun and allegedly robbing a pizza delivery man in 2005 (Skoloff, 2006).

In 2005, a case of a 7-year-old Florida boy reintroduced the question of what to do about youngsters who murder and especially the very young. According to newspaper accounts, the 7-year-old Florida boy beat his 7-month-old half sister to death with his hands and feet and a piece of lumber. In Florida where the murder took place, there is no age barrier for homicide cases. However, authorities were struggling with what to do, believing it would be very unlikely that the young boy had the mental capacity that would make criminal intent possible. However, to do nothing would be unfathomable (Dennis, 2005).

BOX 9.7
Should Parents Be Held Accountable?

Should parents be held responsible when their children kill or otherwise harm another person? What if a child kills with a gun found in his or her own home? Some states are holding parents responsible for their children's delinquency. The methods by which parents may be charged varies from legislation first initiated in Colorado in 1903 that made it illegal to contribute to the delinquency of a minor to laws in some states that require parents of children who get in trouble to attend counseling sessions. Some states now have laws that hold parents criminally or civilly responsible for their child's action. The penalties for failing to keep one's child out of trouble vary widely and include mandating parental participation in juvenile court proceedings and financial fines to cover court costs and any harm their child has done or for the treatment and detention of their child. Parents may also be required to attend parenting classes or if found negligent, they may be sentenced to jail (Office of Juvenile Justice and Delinquency Prevention, 1997).

The idea of holding parents responsible has gained public support, but the reality may be more difficult to enforce. Moreover, there is no research that considers whether it works or not. What do you think about holding parents responsible for their children's actions? What penalties would you support for a parent whose child commits murder? Do you think these laws are likely to prevent youth homicide?

SUMMARY

This chapter focused on children who kill, including historic and more recent cases that lead to many questions about how children who kill should be treated in the criminal justice system. Killing by youth has captured much attention in the United States with the great increases in the 1990s and the infamous school shootings whose aftermaths were broadcast on television screens across the nation. Nevertheless, in this chapter the data showed that children were arrested for less than 10% of all homicides in the first years of the twenty-first century. Still, the data show that youth in the United States commit hundreds of homicides each year, and relative to other counties, U.S. numbers are alarming. There is relatively good news, however: Juvenile homicide has been decreasing since 1993 with the lowest levels ever recorded in 2002. In this chapter, as in other chapters, we saw that homicide offending varies by both sex and race, and interestingly some places in some years have no youth homicide offenders at all. That children tend to kill acquaintances was noted, and special attention was paid to parricide and gang killings. Like adults, children who kill do so for various reasons. In this chapter, psychological and sociological explanations for such crime were reviewed. Finally, the chapter ended with a discussion about what happens to children who kill, with special attention to the relatively new process of bounding over children to adult courts.

CHAPTER QUESTIONS

1. Why are children under age 7 not always charged if they kill another person?
2. What percentage of those arrested for murder and nonnegligent manslaughter for the years 2002 to 2004 were younger than 18 years?
3. When did adolescent killing peak?
4. What are some of the differences between female and male juvenile homicide offenders?
5. How does adolescent homicide offending vary by race?
6. How does youth homicide in the United States compare to youth homicide in other countries?
7. Do juveniles tend to kill alone or with co-offenders?
8. Thinking about what you now know about the data on race and youth homicide and that youth homicide is more predominant in some cities, how might you explain the differences? How might the possible motives for such homicide help explain these differences?
9. Who do children kill?
10. What is parricide?
11. What are the most common weapons used by children to kill?
12. What are the different explanations given for why children kill? Which do you find most believable?
13. What are the five causes that Newman believes are necessary for a school shooting to occur?
14. When, if ever, do you think juveniles should be tried in adult courts?
15. What is the Willie Bosket law?
16. What do you think should be done about very young children who kill? Be sure to consider front door (before the crime) and back door (after the crime) solutions.

REFERENCES

Angels of Columbine Website. 2006. *School Violence.* Accessed online at http://www.columbine-angels.com/SV_Home.htm

Anonymous. 2000. "Six Year-Old Boy Shoots Classmates; Man, 19, Charged with Involuntary Manslaughter for Possessing the Gun." *Jet,* 97(15). Accessed at http://www.encyclopedia.com/doc/1G1-61487222.html.

BBC News Online. 2000, March 1. "No Charges for Schoolboy Killer." Accessed online at http://news.bbc.co.uk/1/low/world/americas/662183.stm

Block, Carolyn R., and Antigone Christakos. 1995. *Major Trends in Chicago Homicide: 1965–1994.* Chicago: Illinois Criminal Justice Information Authority.

Block, Carolyn R., Antigone Christakos, Ayad Jacob, and R. Przybylski. 1996. *Street Gangs and Crime: Patterns and Trends in Chicago.* Research Bulletin. Chicago: Illinois Criminal Justice Information Authority.

Busch, Kenneth G., Robert John Zagar, John R. Hughes, Jack Arbit, and R. Bussell. 1990. "Adolescents Who Kill." *Journal of Clinical Psychology,* 46: 472–485.

Butterfield, Fox. 1996. *All God's Children.* New York: Harper Books.

CBS News. 2000, September 11. "Jail Time for Letting Boy Get Gun." CBS News. Accessed online at http://www.cbsnews.com/stories/2000/09/11/national/main232396.shtml

CNN. 2005, March 23. "School Gunman Stole Police Pistol, Vest." CNN.com. Retrieved April 7, 2006, from http://www.cnn.com/2005/US/03/22/schoolshooting

Crimelibrary.com. "The List." Retrieved August 18, 2006, from http://www.crimelibrary.com/serial_killers/weird/kids1/index_1.html

Dennis, Brady. 2005, June 2. "What to Do If 7-Year-Old Boy Killed Half Sister?" *St. Petersburg Times* Online. Retrieved August 16, 2006, from www.sptimes.com

Dent, Renuka Jeyarajah, and Sharon Jowitt. 2003. "Homicide and Serious Sexual Offences Committed by Children and Young People: Findings from the Literature and a Serious Case Review." *Journal of Sexual Aggression*, 9(2): 85–96.

Federal Bureau of Investigation. 1976–2002. Supplementary Homicide Reports, 1976–2002. Washington, DC: Department of Justice. Accessed online at http://www.ojp.usdoj.gov/bjs/homicide/teens.htm

Federal Bureau of Investigation. 2003. *Crime in the United States 2002.* Washington, DC: Department of Justice.

Federal Bureau of Investigation. 2004. *Crime in the United States 2003.* Washington, DC: Department of Justice.

Federal Bureau of Investigation. 2005. *Crime in the United States 2004.* Washington, DC: Department of Justice.

Gaines, Larry K., and Roger LeRoy Miller. 2004. *Criminal Justice in Action: The Coree.* Belmont, CA: Wadsworth.

Goldstein, Paul J. 1985. The Drugs/Violence Nexus: A Tripartite Conceptual Framework. *Journal of Drug Issues*, 15: 493–506.

Gribben, Mark. 2006. "Jesse Harding Pomeroy." Retrieved August 18, 2006, from CrimeLibrary.com. http://origin-www.crimelibrary.com/serial_killers/ history/pomeroy/1.html

Griffin, Patrick, Patricia Torbet, and Linda Szymanski. 1998. *Trying Juveniles as Adults in Criminal Court: An Analysis of State Transfer Provisions.* Washington, DC: U.S. Department of Justice.

Grossman, Dave. 2000. "Teaching Kids to Kill." *Phi Kappa Phi National Forum.* Retrieved August 3, 2006, from http://www.killology.com/article_teachkid.htm

Hegadorn, Robert. 1999. "Clemency: Doing Justice to Incarcerated Battered Children." *Journal of the Missouri Bar,* 55(2): 61–116. Retrieved November 18, 2005, from http://www.mobar.org/journal/1999/marapr/hegadorn.htm

Heide, Kathleen M. 1992. *Why Kids Kill Parents: Child Abuse and Adolescent Homicide.* Columbus: Ohio State University Press.

Heide, Kathleen M. 1999, *Young Killers—The Challenge of Juvenile Homicide.* California: Sage Publications.

Heide, Kathleen M. 2003. "Youth Homicide: A Review of the Literature and a Blueprint for Action." *International Journal of Offender Therapy and Comparative Criminology,* 47(1): 6–36.

Holmes, Ronald M., and Stephen T. Holmes. 2001. *Murder in America.* Thousand Oaks, CA: Sage.

Indianapolis Star.com. 2005. "Timeline of Incidents: School Violence Around the World." Retrieved January 21, 2006, from www2.indystar.com

Kennedy, Aldina, and Latoya Hunter. 2000. "Abraham Sentenced to Juvenile Detention." CourtTV Online. Accessed online at http://www.courttv.com/archive/trials/abraham/011300_2ctv. html

Klein, Malcolm W. 1995. *The American Street Gang: Its Nature, Prevalence, and Control.* Oxford: Oxford University Press.

Linder, Douglas. 2004. "The Trial of Lizzie Borden." *Famous Trials Webpage.* Accessed online at http://www.law.umkc.edu/faculty/projects/ftrials/LizzieBorden/bordenhome.html

Moore, Joan W. 1990. "Gangs, Drugs, and Violence." In Mario De La Rosa, Elizabeth Y. Lambert, and Bernard Gropper, eds., *Drugs and Violence: Causes, Correlates, and Consequences* [Research Monograph No. 103, pp. 160–176]. Rockville, MD: U.S. Department of Health and Human Services, National Institutes of Health, National Institute on Drug Abuse.

Mouzos, Jenny. 2005. *Homicide in Australia: 2003–2004 National Homicide Monitoring Program (NHMP) Annual Report.* Canberra: Australian Institute of Criminology.

Newman, Katherine S. 2004. *Rampage: The Social Roots of School Shootings.* New York: Basic Books.

New York Times. 2005, September 8. "Metro Briefing New York: Mineola: Teenager Sentenced for Matricide." Retrieved November 13, 2005, from http://proquest.umi.com/pqdweb?index=1&did=893098471&SrchMode=1&sid=9&Fmt=3&VInst=PROD&VType=PQD&RQT=309&VName=PQD&TS=1138567766&clientId=30209while

Office of Juvenile Justice and Delinquency Prevention. 1997. *Juvenile Justice Reform Initiatives in the States 1994–1996.* Rockville, MD: Juvenile Justice Clearinghouse.

Pergament, Rachel. 2005. "The Menendez Brothers." Crime Library.com. Accessed online at http://www.crimelibrary.com/notorious_murders/famous/menendez/index_1.html

Robinson, Bryan. 1999a, September 19. "13 Year-Old—and Michigan Juvenile Law—Under Fire in Murder Trial." *Court TV Online.* http://www. courttv. com/archive/trials/abraham/101999_ctv. html.

Robinson, Bryan. 1999b, November 16. "13 Year-Old Convicted of Second Degree Murder." CourtTV Online. http://www.courttv.com/archive/trials/abraham/111699_verdict_ctv.html

Scott, Shirley Lynn. 2005. *The Death of James Bulger.* The Crime Library. Accessed online at http://www.crimelibrary.com/notorious_murders/young/bulger/1.html

Sereny, Gitta. 2000. *Cries Unheard: Why Kids Kill: The Story of Mary Bell.* New York: Owl Books.

Shimbun, Itsuki Iwata Yomiuri. 2004, September 21. "Sasebo Case Leaves Questions Family Court Ruling Does Little to Explain Why a Girl, 12, was Killed." *The Daily Yomiuri (Tokyo).*

Shirek, Jon. 2004. "Teenagers: Cold-Blooded Killers." WXIA-TV Atlanta. Accessed online at 11Alive.com

Skoloff, Brian. 2006, May 18. "Lionel Tate Sentenced to 30 Years in Prison for Gun Possession." *Associated Press Report.* Retrieved August 18, 2006, from http://lionel-tate-news.newslib.com/story/201–3137252/

Smith, Helen. 2000. *The Scarred Heart.* Knoxville, TN: Callisto.

Snyder, Howard N., and Melissa Sickmund. 1999. *Juvenile Offenders and Victims: 1999 National Report.* Washington, DC: U.S. Department of Justice National Center for Juvenile Justice. Retrieved July 27, 2007, from http://www.ncjrs.org/html/ojjdp/nationalreport99/toc.html

Tortora, Andrea. 2000, March 5. "Kentucky 6-Year-Old Tried for Murder." Cincinnati *Enquirer.* Retrieved August 16, 2006, from http://www.enquirer.com/editions/2000/03/05/loc_kentucky_6-year-old.html

Chapter 10

CHILD MURDER AND INFANTICIDE

When you think about the homicide of children, a few infamous cases probably come to mind. If you are a fan of true crime writings or serial killer websites, you probably think of John Wayne Gacy, the "clown killer" who raped and murdered more than 30 young boys during the 1970s and then buried many of his young victims under his home. The mysterious Jon Benét Ramsey case in which a 6-year-old pageant queen was found murdered in her family home may come to mind, especially with the 2006 attention shed on this 1997 case. You may also think of Andrea Yates, who drowned her five children in a bathtub in Texas. The memory of Susan Smith strapping her two young boys into their car seats and rolling the car into a lake in 1994 may quickly follow your thoughts of Andrea Yates. And then the more recent case of Lashuan Harris allegedly dropping her three young sons into the San Francisco Bay may occur to you. For those who have lived in the United Kingdom (or who have traveled there at a time when the press was focusing on this story as I have), the tragic and tortuous death of James Bulger at the hands of two 10-year-old boys may come to mind. Finally, even if you were not alive in 1966 when they disappeared, most anyone who has lived in Australia recalls the Beaumont children disappearance. The three Beaumont children ranging in age from 4 to 9 years old took a bus trip to the beach by themselves (a much more common and acceptable practice for children of that age in the 1960s) one January morning in 1966. The children never returned, but the case still remains in the public eye with the Australian police increasing the reward to $100,000 (in Australian dollars) for information leading to the offender as recently as June 2005 (Brown, 1999; *New Zealand Herald*, 2005).

These cases and just the idea that someone would murder a child continue to both horrify and capture the public's imagination. With 24-hour news stations such as MSNBC, CNN, and Fox News repeatedly broadcasting stories of missing children throughout the United States, the public is more aware than ever of the abduction and killing of children across the country and throughout the world. Moreover, cases of missing children commonly appear as entertainment in fictionalized television shows such as *Law & Order* and *Missing*. The AMBER Alert System, which began in 1996, also makes us immediately aware of the abduction of helpless children soon after an abduction has occurred. It is no wonder that the fear of child predators hunting down, kidnapping, and killing vulnerable children persists even if the reality of child homicide suggests that far more children are killed by their family members than by the strangers we fear.

Certainly, even one child abduction and murder is appalling, but the reality of approximately 2,000 children murdered in a single year in the United States in a variety of circumstances, including at the hands of their own parents, is dreadfully sobering. Although criminological studies about the homicide of children are relatively rare (Lord, Boudreaux, Jarvis, et al., 2002), in this chapter we review what is known about the homicide of children. As is the case throughout this book, I focus on the United States, but information from other countries, especially Australia and the United Kingdom, are also included. Beginning with a brief review of the history of child homicide, the chapter proceeds to the official crime data that tell us how common child homicide is and something about the victims. Then through a focus on the terminology used to describe different types of child homicide, victim/offender relationships, circumstances, and possible motives related to child homicide are explored. The chapter ends with a section about how the courts treat those who kill children.

HISTORY

The homicide of children is not new. As Coramae Richey Mann (1993: 227) has reported, it is an "age-old practice." Infanticide, the killing of infants, in particular, has existed throughout history. Infanticide is believed to have been practiced by primitive people and, to some degree, by nearly every culture and every class of people since primitive times. During the seventeenth and eighteenth century in France, fathers legally decided whether to let their children live or die. In 1741, in London, infanticide was so common that Thomas Coram established a foundling home to provide refuge for infants and young children cast away by their mothers because he found it disturbing to see babies dying in the gutters and rotting on trash heaps (deMause, 1988; Smith, 2006).

In the United States and other countries, now and in the past, unmarried women have killed their babies because of the stigma associated with having children out of wedlock. Infants have also been sacrificed for religious reasons, as a method of population control, or because their parents could not afford to raise them (Smith, 2006). At different times, it has also been acceptable to kill babies with birth defects or those who are female. In present-day China, for example, because females are culturally less valued than males, girl children are often killed.

Children of preschool age and older have also perished at the hands of their parents and caretakers as the result of abuse and neglect. But too, as portrayed in Euripides' play *Medea* written in 431 B.C.E., parents have deliberately murdered their own children as a way to hurt their child's other parent. Throughout time, across the world, and every day, children are killed at the hands of both their family members and strangers.

OFFICIAL DATA ON CHILD HOMICIDE

In most parts of the world, the murder of children is far less common than the murder of adults. For example, children make up 10% to 20% of all homicide victims in Australia, Canada, the United Kingdom, and the United States (Adler & Polk, 2001). Because of the relatively high homicide rates in the United States, however, the number of children killed each year is in no way insignificant. In fact, the estimates suggest as many as six children are murdered each day in the United States (Lord et al., 2002). In a study of 26 high-income countries during the early 1990s, the Centers for Disease Control and Prevention (CDC, 1997) found that the homicide rate for children (younger than 15 years) in the United States was five times higher than that for children in the other 25 countries combined (2.57 per 100,000 compared with 0.51). Although the rate of child homicides in most other parts of the world is much lower than it is in the United States, the number of homicides of children in some South American countries is far worse than it is in the United States. For example, an estimated six child homicides occur each day in the Brazilian streets of Rio—ironically, this is the same as that given for the United States (Jubilee Action, 2005). However, a comparison of the population size of Rio and the United States leads to the staggering reality that the child homicide rate in Rio is 47 times greater than the already high rate of child homicide in America.

Types of Child Killing

Perhaps because the killing of children has been unfortunately common or maybe because people find it so perplexing, several terms are used to categorize the various types of child homicide. Unfortunately, however, the categories sometimes overlap, as in the case of infanticide and filicide, which you will discover as you read. The sections to follow contain definitions and examples for the many different categories of child homicide.

Neonaticide is the murder of a newborn within the first 24 hours of his or her life. In October 2005, Holly Ashcroft, a 21-year-old architecture student at the University of Southern California was charged with one count of murder and one count of child abuse in the death of her newborn baby. A homeless man phoned the police after he found the body of a newborn baby boy in a dumpster he was rummaging through to find aluminum cans. Ashcroft, the young USC student from Billings, Montana, who allegedly abandoned her newborn in the dumpster, is similar in many ways to other women who have abandoned their newborn babies (Trounsen & Wride, 2005). Like most women who abandon their newborns, Ashcroft is young and single, and she appears to have concealed her pregnancy. Also like others who have committed neonaticide, Ashcroft appears to have given birth alone, she did not give birth in a hospital, and the father of the baby is absent from the picture (Meyer & Oberman, 2001).

Like other neonaticide deaths, the death of Ashcroft's baby boy appears to be relatively nonviolent. The baby died of exposure. Strangulation and suffocation are the most common methods of killing a baby within the first 24 hours of life with head trauma, drowning, exposure, and stabbing the next most common (Meyer & Oberman, 2001). Some other risk factors associated with neonaticide are less clear or unsupported by this case. Low birth weight of the child, late or no prenatal care, and social and economic stresses are thus far unclear in this case, but they are reported as risk factors for neonaticide in the criminological research (Meyer & Oberman, 2001). A final risk factor that appears to be absent in this case is that many mothers who commit neonaticide are lacking in formal education; Ashcroft was in her third year of college (Trounsen & Wride, 2005).

Neonaticide is far from uncommon. In fact, the Los Angeles police report that between 5 and 8 newborns are found in L.A. each year, and the Ashcroft baby was the fourth they had seen that year (Trounsen & Wride, 2005). In a study I did with Lori Scott, we found of the 44 women who had killed in a 10-year period in Augusta, Georgia, two had killed newborn babies by abandoning them. The women we studied in Georgia who committed neonaticide were not as attractive to the media as the young, attractive, and often middle-class women we see in the national media coverage of neonaticides. In the media, we see young women such as Melissa Drexler, the "prom mom" who pleaded guilty to killing her baby at her high school prom in 1997. Or we see Amy Grossberg, the former high school cheerleader who, with her boyfriend Brian Peterson, killed their newborn baby and deposited him in a trash can. And we learn about Holly Ashcroft, the young woman discussed earlier who is described as a "sweet young woman from Montana" (Trounsen & Wride, 2005).

Because neonaticide is seen as a common problem and perhaps because the cases we learn about are those with attractive middle-class teenagers, many states have adopted laws that allow young parents to leave their newborn child at a fire station, hospital, or police department without any penalties. In Michigan, the law is called the safe delivery of newborns law and it stipulates that a parent can anonymously leave a newborn with an emergency service provider, including police, firefighters, and hospital personnel (Sorbet & Schlinker, 2004). Between January 2001 and October 2004, 18 babies were turned over to emergency service providers in Michigan. In California, where they have a similar policy, 35 infants were left at hospitals and fire stations between January 2001 and October 2005 (Trounsen & Wride, 2005).

Infanticide is defined as the killing of an infant child who is generally less than 1 year old. In the United States, homicide ranks 15th on the list of leading causes of death for children in their first year of life. The risk for homicide is greater for a child in his or her first year of life than in any other year of life before the age of 17 years (Paulozzi & Wells, 2001). Moreover, the risk for infanticide is greatest during the first 4 months of life and is most likely on the first day of life. In their examination of U.S. homicide victimization during infancy for the years 1989 to 1998, Paulozzi and Wells (2001) determined that the homicide rate for the first day of life was ten times greater than the rate during any other time of life. For the period they studied, Paulozzi and Wells found that 7.3% of all infant homicides occurred on the day of birth and thus could be defined as neonaticides, as discussed in the preceding section.

In the United Kingdom and Australia, *infanticide* is defined within the law as a crime committed by the mother during the first 12 months of her infant's life; a father cannot by definition commit infanticide in these countries. Of course, fathers in all countries can and do kill children younger than 1 year. In the United States, infanticide is not necessarily defined as a crime apart from homicide, and in common usage the term *infanticide* refers to the killing of infants without regard to who the offender is or how the offender may be related to the victim. Data of infanticide in the United States indicate that both women and men kill infants. Infants, in fact, are most likely to be killed by their mother up until they are a week old and then they are more likely to be killed by a male—typically their father or stepfather (Overpeck, Brenner, Trumble, et al., 1998).

Emergency workers in Lawrence, Kansas, arrived at a residence early on Friday, October 14, 2005, to find 5-month-old Risha Lafferty nonresponsive. The child was not breathing and she had no pulse. After an autopsy on the infant indicated that she died of "traumatic injuries," Risha's father Jay Decker was arrested and charged with first-degree murder (*Lawrence Journal-World*, 2005). Decker's account to the police did not coincide with the injuries suffered by his daughter, so he was arrested and charged with his daughter's homicide. During Dent's subsequent trial, the prosecutors presented evidence that Risha's skull was fractured and she had been shaken. In addition to expert testimony, pieces of drywall from the family home showing a circular dent was presented as evidence that Decker had bashed baby Risha. In November 2006, Decker was found guilty of first-degree murder in the death of his daughter, and in January 2007 he was sentenced to life in prison (Belt, 2007).

Prolicide is the killing of one's offspring and includes both infanticide and the killing of a fetus in utero. A more common term for the killing of one's own children is *filicide*, which refers to the killing of one's own child (including a stepchild) and thus could include the killing of an adult child. More frequently, however, it refers to the killing of a minor child and thus could include both neonaticides and infanticides. Thus we could describe both the alleged neonaticide by Holly Ashcroft and the alleged infanticide by Jay Decker as filicides because they are believed to have killed their own children.

As seen in Figure 10.1, children in the United States, especially young children, are far more likely to be killed by their parents than all other categories of perpetrators added together. From 1976 to 2002, 61% of child homicide victims younger than 5 years were killed by their parents, 23% were killed by male acquaintances, 6% were killed by other relatives, and only 3% were killed by strangers (Bureau of Justice Statistics, 2003). Data from the UK and Australia indicate the same pattern with the highest percentage of perpetrators among parents even if the overall number and rates of killing in the UK and Australia are much lower as compared to the United States (Browne & Lynch, 1995). Anecdotal evidence on the killing of street kids by police in some developing countries, however, suggests that parents may not be the most likely offenders in those child homicide cases (Browne & Lynch, 1995).

There are several well-known cases of filicide in the United States, including the three drowning homicide incidents in which Andrea Yates, Susan Smith, and Lashuan Harris each killed more than one of their children by drowning them. Although these three well-known drowning cases involve mothers killing children, fathers also kill their own children. For example, 22-year-old Ronnie Paris Jr. was sentenced to 30 years in prison for killing his 3-year-old son, who was also named Ronnie. The 3-year-old died as a result of injuries to his head inflicted by his father, who roughly played with

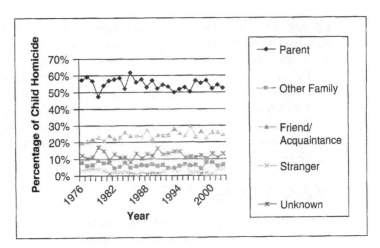

FIGURE 10.1

Relationships of Perpetrator to Victim in Child Homicides for Victims Younger Than 5 Years

Source: Compiled from FBI, *Supplementary Homicide Reports,* 1976–2002.

his young boy as a way to make the boy tough because he feared his namesake would be a "sissy" and grow up gay. The boy's mother, Nysheerah Paris, who was 20 years old at the time of her son's death, will also face charges for child neglect; she may receive a sentence of up to 15 years in prison (Montgomery, 2005).

Answering the question as to whether mothers or fathers are more likely to kill their own children is difficult. It depends on how we break down the data. If we consider children under 5 years of age only, as shown in Figure 10.1, fathers (including stepfathers) make up a slightly higher percentage (31% vs. 30%) of killers than do mothers (including stepmothers) (Bureau of Justice Statistics, 2003). However, mothers commit neonaticide more frequently than fathers. Data from Chicago for the years 1965 to 1995 are illustrative. During this 30-year time period in Chicago, 32% of infants were killed by their fathers, 44% were killed by their mothers, and 1.3% were killed by both parents who acted together. For toddlers and preschoolers, the gap closes with 20% killed by their fathers, 21% by their mothers, and 1.3% by both parents (Vogt & Block, 2003).

Data from countries other than the United States do not show a clear pattern either. Data from Australia indicate that biological mothers have been more likely to kill their children than biological fathers. However, if we focus just on children under 1 years old who were killed by their biological parent in Australia, 55.8% were killed by their fathers (Mouzos, 2000). In Canada, however, children younger than 1 year are equally likely to be killed by their mother or their father (Correctional Services of Canada, 1995). Interestingly, in Fiji, the difference is much greater, with biological mothers the perpetrator in 75% of the 49 child homicide cases between 1982 and 1994 in which a biological parent was responsible for the crime (Adinkrah, 2001).

Most criminologists have not attempted to determine whether there is a difference in filicide between parents and stepparents. However, using Canadian data, Wilson and Daly (1988) found that stepchildren are victims more often than expected. They are not saying that more stepchildren are killed. Instead, they argue that stepchildren are overrepresented among child victims. Essentially, they consider how many stepchildren there are who reside with a stepparent and determine that the ratio of stepchild homicides to stepchildren is much higher than the ratio of biological child homicides to biological children. It is rarer, however, to learn about stepmothers killing their stepchildren than stepfathers killing their stepchildren. This may be because fewer stepchildren live with stepmothers. However, if we compared biological mothers and fathers only, the data may show that biological mothers edge out biological fathers among filicide offenders.

Filicide-Suicide

Some children are killed by their parents as part of a murder-suicide; otherwise known as filicide-suicide. Filicide-suicide cases tend to share some commonalities regardless of whether the perpetrator is a father or a mother. First, child victims of filicide suicide and the parent offenders tend to be older than children and parents, respectively, in other filicide cases. Second, it is also far more likely that the offender is a biological parent than a stepparent in filicide-suicide cases. Third, the perpetrators tend to kill all of their children rather than leaving any of them alive. Finally, parents who kill more than one of their children are more likely to commit suicide than those who kill only one of their children (Adler & Polk, 2001; Johnson, 2005; Oberman, 2002; Shackelford et al., 2005).

In November 2005, Edward McGuffey, a 37-year-old Indiana man, killed his 4-year-old son Jason. Newspaper reports about the incident indicated that McGuffey and his wife had separated approximately 2 weeks prior to the killing and he feared losing his son. McGuffey sent e-mail to about 80 individuals in which he explained why he had killed his son and was preparing to kill himself. One of the first people to receive McGuffey's e-mail called the police, who arrived at the McGuffey house to find both the 4-year-old boy and his father dead of apparent gunshot wounds (WRTV Indianapolis, 2005). The following excerpts from McGuffey's e-mail were printed on INDYSTAR.com (2005), an Indianapolis media site:

> I was going to try to fight this legally, but I have almost no chance of winning. The mother automatically gets the benefit of the doubt as being the most important parent when the child is age 8 and under—the "tender years." I would have to show that she is not fit to be a parent in order to gain custody.
>
> So my other option is to move out East. To take my entire life—my job, house, church, all my friends and family, everything I know—and throw it in the trash can. To take a huge financial loss on the $70,000 room addition that I just spent countless hours working on.
>
> Now, please don't feel bad for Jason. He is young and innocent, so he will surely go to heaven to be with the Lord. There is no question that he is better off now. The big question is what he would have accomplished in his lifetime.

Filicide-suicides by mothers and fathers share some commonalities, but criminologists have also reported differences in filicide-suicides committed by mothers and by fathers. The McGuffey tragedy, in which young Jason was killed by his father, is a fairly typical case of filicide-suicide committed by a man. Fathers who commit suicide-filicide often kill their children within the context of marital separation or a child custody

BOX 10.1

Oyako-Shinju

Oyako-shinju is the Japanese term for parent-child suicide. As you may have detected from the name, it is less stigmatized in Japan than in the United States. In the United States, we usually refer to the killing of one's child and oneself as a murder-suicide rather than as a parent-child suicide. Parent-child suicides in Japan are often viewed with sympathy because the parents are viewed as having no other option but to kill their child when they kill themselves. Because the parents' dedication and responsibility to their children is so strong, a suicidal parent, especially a mother, would have difficulty leaving her child because it would be seen as wrong to leave a child alone in a world that the parent has left by suicide.

Boshi-shinju, mother-child suicide, is more common than *fushi-shinju*, father-child suicide, and the motives for the two are different. *Boshi-shinju* is usually believed to be the result of a psychiatric disorder or family conflicts including marital infidelity by the husband/father, whereas financial problems and physical illness are often given as the motive for *fushi-shinju*. They also differ in that fathers more often kill older children; mothers more often kill preschool age children. In both *boshi-shinju* and *fushi-shinju*, however, the suicide is seen as a way to deal with stigma whether the stigma was caused by a cheating husband or a failing business.

In 1985, the meeting of Japanese and U.S. culture clashed when Fumiko Kimura attempted to commit *oyako-shinju* in Santa Monica, California. Upon discovering that her husband had a mistress, Japanese immigrant Fumiko Kimura attempted to drown herself and her two children. She was successful in killing her children, but bystanders rescued Kimura before she drowned. She was charged with first-degree murder in California. Attorneys for Kimura attempted to defend her by explaining she was following her native culture and would not have been punished had she performed these same acts in Japan. In the end, however, she plea-bargained to voluntary manslaughter and was sentenced to five years of probation and one year of jail time, which she had served while awaiting her trial. Her light sentence likely reflects the judge's understanding of the Japanese cultural practice of *oyako-shinju* (McLean, 2000; Takahashi & Berger, 1996).

disagreement with the child's mother (Adler & Polk, 2001). In contrast, mothers who commit filicide-homicide tend to kill their children because they fear their children will not have anyone to care for them once the mother commits suicide. Not surprising, then, the suicidal filicide mothers that Adler and Polk (2001) studied in Victoria, Australia, were more likely to have tried to get psychiatric treatment than suicidal-filicide fathers.

Jennifer Ann MacNeil, who killed her 4-year-old twin girls in British Columbia in October 2004, appears to be fairly typical of mothers who kill their children and then commit suicide. MacNeil, a 30-year-old single mother, used a vacuum cleaner hose to direct carbon monoxide from the exhaust pipe of her car to the passenger compartment where she sat with her two girls as they all perished. There was no indication that the twin girls' father had ever been a part of their lives. One of MacNeil's friends was reported to have said that MacNeil had been depressed during the previous three years. Still, family and friends reported being shocked by the news that she killed herself and her two children (Lazaruk, 2004).

A final characteristic that most strongly distinguishes filicide-suicides by men and women is that fathers who kill their children and themselves are far more likely than suicidal homicidal mothers to also kill their spouses (Adler & Polk, 2001; Wallace, 1986). Although the reasons are not clear, David McGowan became one of these men who killed his wife, his children, and himself in the spring of 2005. A 911 dispatcher answered the phone in the early morning hours of May 10, at which time a gunshot was heard followed by the sound of what was believed to be McGowan and the phone falling to the floor. McGowan apparently called the police after shooting his 42-year-old wife, his 75-year-old mother, and his three children, age 8, 10, and 14. McGowan, a 44-year-old investigator for a district attorney's office in California, used his service weapon, a 9-mm Smith and Wesson semiautomatic handgun, to shoot each of his victims and himself in the head. Although financial or marital problems are often associated with mass family killings like this one, authorities knew of no such problems (Downey, 2005).

Because McGowan killed his wife and his children, this suicide-homicide event may also be called a *familicide*, which sometimes refers to the killing of a whole family. However, familicide is more often used to define a multivictim homicide in which the offender kills his or her spouse or former spouse and at least one or more of either of their children (Wilson, Daly, & Daniele, 1995). Despite the fact that when women kill they are most likely to kill their partners or their children; they rarely kill both their children and their spouse in one incident (Adler & Polk, 2001; Oberman, 2002; Wilson et al., 1995). Daly and Wilson (1988), in fact, have noted that familicide is a very uncommon crime among men and almost unheard of among women offenders. Adler and Polk (2001) also found this to be true in their study (1985–1995) of child homicides in Victoria, Australia. They found no women in their study who had killed both their husband or former husband and their children. Similarly, in her study of mothers who killed in Chicago, Oberman (2002) did not have any cases of mothers who killed their partners and their children.

In addition to being committed more often by fathers, data from England, Wales, and Canada suggest that the percentage of children killed by gunshot is higher in familicides than the percentage of children killed by their parents or stepparents in nonfamilicide incidents (Wilson et al., 1995). This is likely because many children who are killed by their parents in these countries are beaten to death or otherwise die at the hands of their parents as opposed to the parents using a weapon, as discussed in the next section about weapons used to kill children.

WEAPON USE: HOW ARE CHILDREN MURDERED?

The weapons most commonly used to kill children in the United States changes from personal weapons such as hands, feet, and fists to firearms as the age of the children increases. Many young children who are killed die as the result of child abuse by their

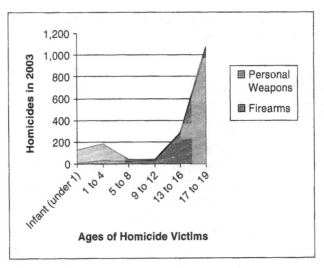

Figure 10.2
Personal Weapon and Gun Homicides of Child Victims in the United States, 2003

Source: Compiled from FBI, *Crime in the United States,* 2003 [*N* = 1,755].

caretakers. As seen in Figure 10.2, then, victims younger than 5 years were most often killed by personal weapons, such as the killer's hands, feet, or fists. However, as children age, their risk for homicide by those other than their parents also increases, and we see that the most frequent weapon used to kill those ages 5 to 8 were firearms (29.3%); still, 17% in this age group were killed by personal weapons. Among those age 9 and older, the most common weapon of death was a firearm, and as age increases so does the percentage killed by firearms. Slightly under half (46.3%) of those ages 9 to 12 were killed with firearms. Strikingly, firearms were used in 74.8% of the homicides of those ages 13 to 16, and 80.8% of those in the 17- to 19-year-old category. Children in each age category were also killed with knives, blunt objects, fire, and by asphyxiation. However, in 2003, only three children were poisoned; two in the 1- to 4-year-old category and one in the 17- to 19-year-old category. Finally, although no children ages 9 to 12 were known by the FBI to have been strangled to death in 2003, one child or more in every other age group was strangled.

Overall, when a child is killed in the United States, it is most likely that he or she was killed with a gun (FBI, 2003). Firearm-related homicide for children younger than 15 years is far higher in the United States than in other countries. In a CDC study (1997) of the 26 wealthiest nations, the U.S. non-firearm-related homicide rate was found to be nearly four times the rate of all of the other 25 countries combined (1.63 vs. 0.45) in the early 1990s. However, the difference for firearm-related homicides was even greater, with the U.S. rate nearly 16 times higher than all the other 25 countries (0.94 vs. 0.06). Even so, firearms were the primary cause of child homicide in Australia, Finland, Germany, Israel, and Italy. However, in what seems amazing to any of us who live in the United States, ten countries (Denmark, Hong Kong, Ireland, Japan, Kuwait, Netherlands, New Zealand, Scotland, Singapore, and Taiwan) had no firearm-related child homicides during the time period studied by the CDC. Importantly, during this same study period, a total of 957 child homicides involving firearms occurred in the United States.

KILLING TIMES AND SEASONS: WHEN ARE CHILDREN KILLED?

The peak time of the day for child homicide is different than the peak time for adults. Child homicides are higher during daytime hours compared to nighttime hours, and they tend to peak on weekdays as opposed to adult homicides that are higher on the weekends (Chew, McCleary, Lew, et al., 1999). It may be surprising until you think about it, but the season in which child homicide peaks does not exactly follow the adult pattern of higher rates in the summer. In fact, the homicide of children varies by age of the child victim. Winter is when we see increases in the homicide of children who are younger than 2 years. In contrast, the homicide of children ages 5 to 14 is higher in the summer (McCleary & Chew, 2002). Children of school age are likely to have increased risk for homicide in the summer because they are out of school and have more opportunity to be victimized by both strangers and family members. For infants, the winter months may be more stressful for parents (those most likely to kill infants), who are more likely to be feel trapped alone in the house with their small children and perhaps even with small children who are suffering from winter colds and thus less pleasant to be around than usual.

AGE, SEX, AND RACE: WHO IS KILLED?

Age

When we attempt to determine at what age children are at most risk for child homicide, we find it is older teens. As you can see in Figure 10.3, those in the 17- to 19-year-old range far outnumber victims in other age categories. Very young children, age birth to 4 years, follow teens in the most likely risk for homicide. Elementary school age children (5 to 12 years) are least at risk. This is also the case in Australia, although the peak for those in the infant category is higher than that of the teenage category in Australia (Adler & Polk, 2001).

Sex

The data in Figure 10.4 for 2003 are typical of other research that finds the rate of homicide does not differ significantly for boys and girls at younger ages. However, as you can also see in Figure 10.4, there is a difference by sex in the teenage years. Boys make up 79% of the youngsters killed in the 13- to 16-year age category and 87% of those killed in the 17- to 19-year age group. Thus when Lord et al. (2002) report that juvenile homicide has been considered a public health emergency due to the high rates of homicide among adolescents in urban areas, they are largely talking about the homicides of adolescent *boys*.

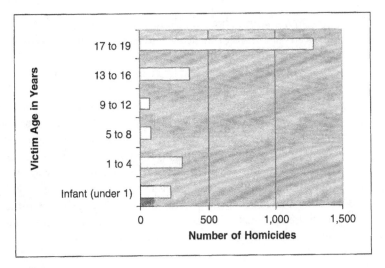

FIGURE 10.3
Ages of Child Homicide Victims in 2003
Source: Compiled from FBI, *Crime in the United States,* 2003 [*N* = 2,335].

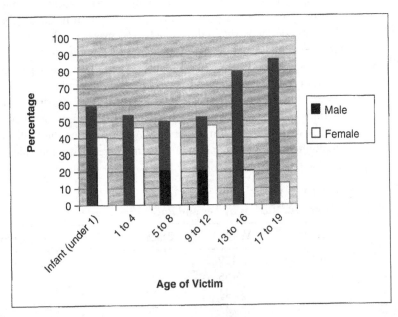

FIGURE 10.4
2003 Percentage of Male and Female Victims by Age Groupings When Sex Is Known
Source: Compiled from FBI, *Crime in the United States,* 2003 [*N* = 2,330].

Young women, however, do not escape the clutches of homicide offenders during the teen years. Instead, unlike male adolescent victims who are likely to be killed by other young male adolescents, young girls face another terror. School-age girls are more likely than boys of the same age to be victims in sexually motivated abduction homicides (Boudreaux & Lord, forthcoming, as cited in Lord et al., 2003). The types of homicide victimization experienced by adolescent boys and girls are reflected in my own analyses of 2002 National Center for Injury Prevention data. In 2002, 669 boys ages 13 to 17 were the victims of homicide, making the crime the third most common cause of death among boys in this age group. Furthermore, of those boys murdered, 86.1% were killed with firearms and 6.4% were stabbed. During this same year, 192 girls between the ages of 13 and 17 were victims of homicide in the United States, making homicide the fourth leading cause of death for teenage girls. Like teenage boys, most teenage girls were killed with firearms (63%); however, indicative of sexual victimization, many female teenage homicide victims were stabbed (9.4%) or suffocated (12%).

Race

When considering risk for child homicide in terms of race, the 2003 data reported in Table 10.1 reflect the 1997 rates reported by Lord et al. (2003): In 1997, the rate of homicide for African American children was 9.11 per 100,000, for Hispanic juveniles it was 5.0 per 100,000, and 1.8 per 100,000 was the rate for white children. The data for 2003 in Table 10.1 present the numbers of children killed in each age and race category. You can see that more white children are killed than children in other race groups in the three categories under the age of 12. However, remember that whites make up approximately 75% of the U.S. population (U.S. Census Bureau, 2000). The fact that whites are the numerical majority in the United States makes the data concerning the differences in race of child homicide victims even more astonishing for the last three age categories. Although approximately 15% of children in the United States are African American, African American child victims of homicide outnumber other race categories in the three oldest age group categories. In fact, in 2003, nearly half of 9- to 12-year-old victims and over half of the 13- to 19-year-old victims were African American.

A study of child homicide in Los Angeles during the 1980s suggests that similar to adult victims, child and infant victims were most often killed by offenders of the

TABLE 10.1
Homicide Victims by Age and Race Categories

Age	White	Black	Other	Unknown	Total
Under 1	139	73	7	6	225
1–4	165	131	6	5	307
5–8	44	34	3	1	82
9–12	33	34	1	1	69
13–16	150	202	14	3	369
17–19	549	689	34	11	1,283
Total	1,080	1,163	65	27	2,335

Source: Compiled from FBI, *Crime in the United States*, 2003 [$N = 2,335$].

same race. However, the victim/offender relationship varied for the different racial groups. Approximately two thirds (67.7%) of white child victims were believed to have been killed by family members, whereas family members were suspects in just under half (48.8%) of African American child homicides and just over a third (37.2%) of Hispanic child homicides (Sorenson & Richardson, 1993).

TRENDS: IS CHILD HOMICIDE INCREASING OR DECREASING?

As noted in Chapter 4, we cannot simply say that homicide is increasing or decreasing without being much more specific. What can be said about child homicide varies by the age of the children. Furthermore, when determining whether it is increasing or decreasing, the base rates must be clear. If infanticide is considered, the official data show that infanticide nearly doubled from 4.3 per 100,000 in 1970 to 9.2 per 100,000 in 2000 and then decreased to 7.8 per 100,000 in 2003 (Hoyert, Kung, & Smith, 2005). According to CDC data, there were 303 infanticides in 2002 and 318 in 2003. According to the U.S. Department of Justice, the 1,610 juveniles (younger than 18 years) murdered in the United States in 2000 reflected the lowest number of juveniles murdered since 1985. The peak was 2,880 in 1993 (Harms & Snyder, 2004). However, the data also show differences by sex, with the murder rate for girl children remaining approximately the same from 1980 to 1998 before it dropped to the lowest it had been in 21 years in 2000. At this same time, the murder rate among boy children increased 117% between 1984 and 1993 before dropping to 8% above its lowest level in the previous 21 years in 2000. The differences by race for those younger than 5 years are illuminated in Figure 10.5 where you can see that despite decreasing rates

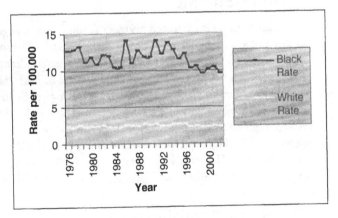

FIGURE 10.5
Rates of Homicide by Race for Victims Younger Than 5 Years

Note: Data from 9/11 terrorist attack not included.

Source: Compiled from FBI, *Supplementary Homicide Reports,* 1976–2002.

among black children, the rates have remained higher for black children as compared to their white counterparts. The murder rates among juveniles ages 12 to 17 show a similar pattern with an increase of 163% for blacks and an increase of 49% for whites between 1980 and 1993. The years between 1993 and 2000 saw a decrease of 64% for blacks 12- to 17 years old and a decrease of 51% for whites in this same age group (Harms & Snyder, 2004).

WHO KILLS CHILDREN?

When a child is killed, police know to investigate parents, family members, and the mother's paramour. These individuals who are known to the child are far more likely to be the perpetrators of child homicide than strangers (Lord et al., 2002). Furthermore, unlike other types of homicide, child homicide is frequently committed by women (Adler & Polk, 2001). However, as with other characteristics of child homicide, this pattern varies by age of the victims. As discussed earlier in this chapter, women are more often the offenders in neonaticide and infanticide cases (Lord et al., 2002). Lord et al. (2002) note that two thirds of children who are killed in the first 6 days of life are killed by their own mothers.

Because children are often killed by their parents or stepparents, it is not surprising that most child homicide victims are killed by adults. Of all child homicides with a known offender between 1980 and 2000, 75% were killed by adult offenders, 21% were killed by children (under 18 years of age), and 4% were killed by at least one child and at least one adult (Harms & Snyder, 2004). Child homicide victims who are killed by other children are most likely to be adolescents. In fact, 39% of all child murders with victims 12 to 17 years of age were committed by other children. Only 9% of those younger than 2 and 11% of those between ages 2 and 11 are killed by other children (Harms & Snyder, 2004).

Killed by Strangers

Even though the abduction and murder of a child by a stranger is a rare occurrence, it is greatly feared by parents (Browne & Lynch, 1995). Unfortunately, despite the rarity of strangers or even nonfamily members murdering children, it does happen. As illustrated in Figure 10.6, as the age of child victims of homicide increase, the likelihood that they were murdered by a stranger increases, especially for males (Harms & Snyder, 2004). However, remember that just because the homicide has been committed by a stranger or unknown perpetrator does not mean it was an abduction homicide. Especially as children age, the likelihood that they will be killed in the context of another crime increases. Unfortunately, juveniles may be the victims of gang violence or homicides, for instance, involving drug dealers or confrontational homicides (see Chapter 7).

Murder by Acquaintances

As also discussed in Chapter 10 on children who kill, children are sometimes killed by other children. When a child kills another child, it is most likely a teenage boy killing another teenage boy (Adler & Polk, 2001). In the United States in the early

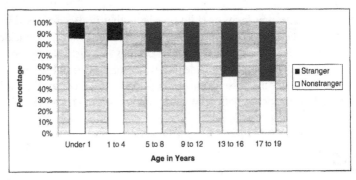

FIGURE 10.6
Percentages of Stranger and Nonstranger Homicides in the United States by Age Category

Note: Victims of the 9/11 terrorist attacks are not included in this data.

Source: Compiled from FBI, *Supplementary Homicide Reports,* 1976–2002 [*N* = 85,359].

1990s there were great increases in adolescent homicide. Male teenagers were killing other male teenagers at alarming rates. However, note that four cities— Chicago, Detroit, Los Angeles, and New York—accounted for nearly a third of the arrests of juveniles for homicide in 1994 (Lotke, 1997). Many of these killings fit the category of gang violence. Thus many of these homicides may be classified as either acquaintance or stranger homicides. In many cases, the offenders may have known one another as opposing gang members, although some of the victims could have simply been other youths from "enemy territory." Importantly, Adler and Polk (2001) report that the pattern of gang violence we saw among youth in the United States in the 1990s has not appeared in countries that are in many other ways similar to the United States, such as Canada, Australia, and the United Kingdom.

BOX 10.2

AMBER Alert

In 1996, the AMBER Alert System began in Texas when Dallas-Fort Worth broadcasters and police worked together to develop an early warning system to help find abducted children. AMBER stands for America's Missing: Broadcast Emergency Response, but the name also pays homage to 9-year-old Amber Hagerman, who was kidnapped in Texas while riding her bicycle and then brutally murdered. Other states and communities have initiated their own AMBER alert systems and plans to help provide quick response to child abductions (U.S. Department of Justice, http://www.amberalert.gov/).

Another form of child homicide that is also discussed in Chapter 11 in greater detail could also fall into the category of acquaintance homicide. Over the past decade, there have been several school shootings in which teenage boys have killed their classmates. Most of these incidents have occurred within the United States, although school shootings have also occurred in Canada and Germany and a few other countries. In these incidents, both schoolgirls and schoolboys have been killed by their classmates.

MOTIVES

Explanations for the homicide of children vary by discipline and are often included in more general explanations for homicide as discussed in Chapters 5 and 6 (Mann, 1993). However, within each discipline are explanations that are particularly important for explaining the homicide of children. Sociologists tend to see links among societal factors, social roles, and child homicide. For example, aggregate-level analyses of child homicide suggest that different structural factors are associated with infant and child homicide (Gartner, 1991). Homicides of children are highest in countries where it appears that women may have more responsibility for raising children without the assistance of the children's fathers. High rates of illegitimacy, higher numbers of births to teenage mothers, and high divorce rates are associated with child homicide but only in countries where the level of government spending on social programs is lower. Infant homicide is also more likely in countries lacking social welfare programs and where rates of births to teenage mothers are higher. Similarly, rates of child homicide are higher where there are larger percentages of racial minorities, greater poverty, and urbanization (Baron, 1993). We need to be careful, however, that we do not commit an ecological fallacy and assume that just because aggregate measures are related that they explain individual cases. For example, if divorce rates are associated with higher rates of child homicide, it is not necessarily the case that children whose parents are divorced are more likely to be victims of homicide.

However, in the case of child homicide, a study in Ohio demonstrates that some factors linked to child homicide at the aggregate level were also related to the killing of children—at the individual level at least in Ohio (Winpisinger, Hopkins, Indian, et al., 1991). Using information from death certificates of children under the age of 8 who were victims of homicide, some of the aggregate explanations for homicide of children were found to increase risks of homicide for children born in Ohio in the early 1980s. Children of younger, poorly educated mothers who were unmarried at the time of their birth and who lived in a metropolitan area were found to be at greater risk for homicide as were African American children and those children who were of low birthweight.

Psychologists and psychiatrists are likely to label those who kill children, especially mothers who kill their own children, as mentally ill (Silverman & Kennedy, 1988). Münchhausen by proxy and postpartum depression are examples of psychological explanations for the killing of children by mothers. Münchhausen syndrome by proxy, otherwise known as factitious disorder, is a controversial diagnosis. Caretakers suffering from Münchhausen syndrome by proxy report fictitious symptoms or, worse, cause symptoms in a person they are taking care of so they can gain attention (Ferak, 2005). Mothers are most often those diagnosed with Münchhausen syndrome by proxy, but I personally know of one case in which an aunt was found guilty of killing her niece in what some argued was a case of Münchhausen by proxy.

Münchhausen syndrome by proxy is rare, with an estimated 600 cases a year in the United States, and importantly, most individuals diagnosed with the syndrome do not kill their children. However, the syndrome has been linked to a few cases of homicide in which mothers have killed their own children. In November 2004, 17-month-old Andrea Yager died in Omaha, Nebraska, after numerous trips to a medical center where doctors could not determine what was wrong with the toddler. Noting that Jodi, her mother, was always the last one with Andrea before she began manifesting symptoms such as seizures and unresponsiveness, authorities now believe that

---

BOX 10.3

Postpartum Psychosis and Homicide

Much media attention focused on postpartum depression when Andrea Yates was first facing the death penalty for drowning her children in the family bathtub. Although there is no clear consensus among the experts, some type of postpartum depression is believed to affect as many as 80% of all women who give birth. Most of these women suffer from what is called the baby blues, which is relatively minor and last only a few weeks. Fewer women, around 15%, are believed to experience the more severe postpartum depression. Mothers suffering postpartum depression are often very anxious, depressed, exhausted, and they have feelings of hopelessness and worthlessness. Still fewer women suffer from a much more severe disorder called postpartum psychosis, believed to affect less than 1% of all new mothers. A woman who experiences postpartum psychosis loses her ability to determine what is real. She may have violent thoughts about her child or she may truly believe the baby is part of her. Although only about 4% of the very small numbers of women who experience postpartum psychosis kill their babies, it is a cause for concern.

Experts believe the postpartum disorders may be triggered by a rapid decline in progesterone and estrogen that result in a "break" with reality. However, social conditions, such as insufficient child care before and after birth, the romantic notions of motherhood, and the common belief that the maternal instinct is natural, are also believed to contribute to postpartum disorders. Women of all races, ethnic, and socioeconomic groups are believed to suffer from postpartum psychosis. Some argue, however, that the media is more likely to publicize cases like that of Andrea Yates because the religious middle-class white mother does not fit the stereotype of a woman who kills her child. In the United States, postpartum disorders remain controversial, especially in comparison to other countries as noted in this chapter.

Andrea's mother is responsible for her death. Importantly, though, Yager has not been found guilty of killing her daughter. However, she was committed indefinitely to a mental health facility until it is determined she is able to stand trial (Ferak, 2005).

Postpartum depression made the news in 2005 when actor Tom Cruise criticized fellow actor and author Brooke Shields for using antidepressants to treat her postpartum depression, a serious depression that occurs in approximately 10% of mothers following the birth of their child. In very severe cases, mothers suffering from postpartum depression have reported feeling they have wanted to kill their children. Andrea Yates, who drowned her five children early in 2001, is believed by some to have been suffering from postpartum depression.

Although not commonly accepted in the United States, postpartum depression is recognized as a legal defense in more than 25 countries, including Australia, Canada, Great Britain, and Italy. These countries have infanticide laws that state a woman who kills her infant child cannot be charged with any charge greater than manslaughter if she can prove the "balance of her mind is disturbed" by reasons relating to giving birth (Williams, 2002). In the United States, postpartum depression is not a defense for homicide. However, an attorney may introduce evidence of postpartum depression as part of an insanity defense, and then if the defendant is found guilty, postpartum depression may be introduced as a mitigating factor in the death.

ABUSE AND CHILD HOMICIDE

As cases in this chapter demonstrate, parents and others who care for children sometimes kill children in the process of abusing them. Without really considering it, most of us probably assume that abused children are at higher risk for homicide than children who are not abused. A 1994 California study examined whether abuse is a risk factor for homicide victimization among children. The researchers compared the backgrounds of children who were murdered and children who died of unintentional injuries (e.g., car wrecks) to determine whether murdered children were abused at higher rates than other children who died. Murdered children were 3.14 times more likely to have come to the attention of social service professionals because of abuse than those who died from unintentional injuries (Sorenson & Peterson, 1994). Still more than half of the murdered children (57.3%) in this study had no official history of abuse or maltreatment.

It is likely that many children who are abused never come to the attention of social service agencies, and thus their deaths may not be recorded as child abuse deaths. Additionally, some child fatalities caused by abuse may be incorrectly recorded as injuries or as sudden infant death syndrome (SIDS) (Creighton, 1995). The sudden death of a child younger than 1 year is labeled SIDS if an extensive investigation of the death finds no viable explanation. SIDS remains a mystery, although national campaigns encouraging parents to place babies face up in their cribs have reduced the number of SIDS deaths. However, because an autopsy cannot reveal whether a death is caused by SIDS or asphyxiation with a pillow or other soft object, some SIDS death may actually be homicides (American Academy of Pediatrics, 2001).

In other cases, there is little doubt that a parent or other caretaker has murdered a child, as was the case of 5-month-old Risha Lafferty described earlier in this chapter. Experts believe, however, that battered children are not necessarily killed deliberately. Rather, the murder of an abused child is frequently an impulsive act on the part of a parent or babysitter who just wishes to make a child behave or stop crying (Smith, 2006). Often, but not always, mothers who are stressed by unfavorable life conditions such as poor housing, marital stress, and financial problems easily lose their tempers and strike out against their children, accidentally killing them (Stanton, Simpson, & Wouldes, 2002).

Children also die from neglect. Such was the case of 7-month-old Raiden Robinson and his 17-month-old brother Justice. The two boys starved to death in November 2004, despite the fact that police found plenty of food in their house when they entered at the request of the boys' father, who could not get anyone to answer the phone or the apartment door. The police also found the boys' mother, Marie Robinson, passed out on the floor of the filthy apartment filled with empty beer cans. Prosecutors charged Robinson with two counts of murder, but the charges were dismissed in January 2007 when a judge determined that Robinson was not fit to stand trial. Robinson, who believes her sons were kidnapped by a secret police agency, was referred for civil commitment to a state mental hospital. If Robinson is later found mentally competent to stand trial, prosecutors can refile the murder charges against her (Johnson, 2007).

CRIMINAL JUSTICE PROCESSING: WHAT HAPPENS TO THOSE WHO KILL CHILDREN?

As you know from reading this chapter, there are a variety of types of child homicide. Likewise, the criminal justice system's responses to such homicide are varied. Moreover, there are not really any studies that focus on what happens to those who murder children. Nevertheless, a study by Coramae Richey Mann (1993) and an article by a North Carolina reporter give us some clues about what happens to those who kill children.

In her 1993 study of maternal filicide, Mann noted the outcome of cases in which women killed their preschool-age children in six cities in the years 1979 to 1983. She found that 84% were charged with murder and 16% were charged with manslaughter initially. In the end, manslaughter was the most common ruling, with 42.8% of the cases ending in a disposition of murder. Ten women were sentenced to prison, nine were sentenced to probation, three cases were dismissed or never processed, one woman committed suicide, and two cases of juvenile neonaticide were sealed by the court.

In 2005, Mandy Locke, a staff writer for *The News & Observer*, summarized the results of 44 cases of children who died from violent shaking in North Carolina from 1999 and 2003. She found that only two people were sentenced to prison for life after being found guilty of shaking a baby to death. Twenty-one others were sentenced to prison, but more than half of them received sentences of less than ten years. For the remaining 18 cases of shaken baby death, no prison sentences were ordered, and in ten cases, no one was charged in the death. As noted by Locke (2005), prosecutors note that these cases often lack much forensic evidence and rarely are there any witnesses, which make these cases difficult to prosecute (Locke, 2005).

SUMMARY

This chapter reviewed what criminologists know about the homicide of children. Starting with a brief history and the current data on child homicide, the chapter moved on to define and provide examples for the many different types of child homicide, including neonaticide, infanticide, filicide, filicide-suicide, and familicide. The weapons used by perpetrators to kill children was discussed next, including the fact that very young children are most likely to be killed with personal weapons, and as age increases, guns are more likely to be used. The curvilinear relationship between age and homicide for those under age 18 with peaks in homicide for the first year of life and the later teenage years was also discussed. Data also indicated that boys are more likely than girls to be victims of homicide, and the rates of homicide are highest for African American children, followed by Hispanic and then white children. Overall, it appears that child homicide is decreasing in the United States. Still, when children are killed, especially young children, it is most likely they were killed by an adult they know, and most often that adult is their own parent or stepparent. The chapter concluded by describing two studies that focused on what happens to those who kill children.

CHAPTER QUESTIONS

1. Is the murder of children more or less common than the murder of adults?
2. What is neonaticide, and who is most likely to do it?
3. How is infanticide defined differently in the United States and other parts of the world?
4. Define and give another word for the term *filicide*.
5. The perpetrators of child homicide in developed countries are most often parents. Research suggests that this may not be the case in less developed countries. What might account for this difference?
6. Does the data reported in this chapter about Fiji support the statement made in question 2? Discuss what might explain the Fiji data.
7. In this chapter, I noted that if we compared biological mothers and fathers only, the data may show that biological mothers edge out biological fathers among filicide offenders. Do you believe this may be true, and if so, what about how social life is organized may account for this?
8. What is it called when a parent kills him or herself after killing their own child(ren)?

9. Does your state have a law like Michigan's safe delivery of newborns law? If so, how many infants have been surrendered to authorities? Have there been fewer neonaticide cases since the law was introduced?

10. What weapon is used most to kill children? How does the weapon vary with the age of child victims?

11. Are there particular times of the day or year where child homicide is more common?

12. At what age are children most at risk for homicide?

13. Who is at greater risk of homicide in terms of sex and race?

14. If you were a homicide detective investigating the death of an infant, who might you suspect first and why?

15. What is Münchhausen syndrome by proxy?

REFERENCES

Adinkrah, Mensah. 2001. "Child Homicide Victimization in Contemporary Fiji." *International Journal of Comparative Criminology*, 1(1): 23–39.

Adler, Christine, and Ken Polk. 2001. *Child Victims of Homicide*. Cambridge: Cambridge University Press.

American Academy of Pediatrics. 2001. "Distinguishing Sudden Infant Death Syndrome from Child Abuse Fatalities." *Pediatrics*, 107(2): 437–441.

Baron, Larry 1993 "Gender Inequality and Child Homicide: A State-Level Analysis." In *Homicide: The Victim/Offender Connection* (pp. 207–226). Cincinnati, OH: Anderson Publishing Co.

Belt, Mike. 2007. "Father Gets Life for Infant Murder." Lawrence Journal World. Retrieved from http://www2.1jworld.com/news/2007/jan/04/father_gets_life_infant_murder/

Brown, Russel. 1999. *The Beaumont Children*. Accessed November 6, 2005, from http://www.beaumontchildren.com/

Browne, Kevin D., and Margaret A. Lynch. 1995. "The Nature and Extent of Child Homicide and Fatal Abuse." *Child Abuse Review*, 4: 309–316.

Bureau of Justice Statistics (BJS). 2003. *Homicide Trends in the U.S.* BJS website.

Centers for Disease Control and Prevention. 1997. "Rates of Homicide, Suicide, and Firearm-Related Death Among Children—26 Industrialized Countries." *Morbidity and Mortality Weekly Report*, 46(5): 101–105.

Chew, Kenneth S. Y., Richard McCleary, Maricres A. Lew, and Johnson C. Wang. 1999. "The Epidemiology of Child Homicide; California, 1981–90." *Homicide Studies*, 3: 151–169.

Correctional Services of Canada. 1995. *A Profile of Homicide Offenders in Canada*. Retrieved November 6, 2005, from http://www.csc-scc.gc.ca/text/rsrch/briefs/b12/b12e_e.shtml

Creighton, Susan, J. 1995. "Fatal child Abuse—How Preventable Is It?" *Child Abuse Review*, 4: 318–328.

deMause, Lloyd. 1988. *The History of Childhood: The Untold Story of Child Abuse*. New York: Peter Bedrick Books.

Downey, Dave. 2005, May 12. "Handwritten Lyrics Only Clue to Tragedy." *North County Times*. Retrieved November 11, 2005, at www.nctimes.com.

FBI. 2003. *Crime in the United States*. U.S. Department of Justice.

Ferak, John. 2005, November 18. "A Tragic Cry for Attention." *Omaha World-Herald*, Metro edition, p. 01A.

Gartner, Rosemary. 1991. "Family Structure, Welfare Spending, and Child Homicide in Developed Democracies." *Journal of Marriage and Family,* 53(1): 231–240.

Harms, Paul D., and Howard N. Snyder. 2004. *Trends in the Murder of Juveniles: 1980–2000.* Washington, DC: U.S. Department of Justice.

Hoyert, Donna L., Hsiang-Ching Kung, and Betty L. Smith. 2005. *Deaths: Preliminary Data for 2003.* National Vital Statistics Reports 53 (15), Hyattsville, Maryland: National Center for Health Statistics. Retrieved from http://origin.cdc.gov/nchs/data/nvsr/nvsr53/nvsr53_15.pdf.

INDYSTAR.com. 2005. "Excerpts from Father's E-mail." Retrieved November 9, 2005, from http://www.indystar.com/apps/pbcs.dll/article?AID=/20051103/NEWS01/511030512

Johnson, Carolyn Harris. 2005. *Come with Daddy: Child Murder-Suicide After Family Breakdown.* Crawley: University of Western Australia Press.

Johnson, Tracy. 2007. "No Trial for Mom Whose Babies Starved to Death." *Seattle Post Intelligencer,* February 1, 2007. Retrieved February 18, 2007, from http://seattlepi.nwsource.com/local/301986_mother01.html

Jubilee Action. 2005. "Brazilian Street Children," Jubilee Action website. Retrieved October 23, 2005, from http://www.jubileeaction.co.uk/

Lawrence Journal-World. 2005, October 21. "Dad Accused of Killing Infant Appears in Court." Retrieved November 6, 2005, from *http://mobile.ljworld.com*

Lazaruk, Susan. 2004. "Single Mom Murders Twins, Commits Suicide." *The Vancouver Province,* October 7. Accessed at http://www.ottawamenscentre.com/news/2004100_single_mom_murders_twins.htm.

Locke, Mandy. 2005, September 18. "A Moment of Violence, A Child's Life Destroyed; Shaken Babies Face Death, But Abusers' Punishment Often Light." *The News & Observer.* Accessed online at http://www.newsobserver.com/919/story/336264.html

Lord, Wayne D., Monique C. Boudreaux, John P. Jarvis, Jerry Waldvogel, and Hal Weeks. 2002. "Comparative Patterns in Life Course Victimization: Competition, Social Rivalry, and Predatory Tactics in Child Homicide in the United States." *Homicide Studies,* 6(4): 325–347.

Lotke, Eric. 1997. "Youth Homicide: Keeping Perspective on How Many Children Kill." *Valparaiso Law Review,* 31(2): 395–418.

Mann, Coramae Richey. 1993. "Maternal Filicide of Preschoolers." In Anna Victoria Wilson, ed., *Homicide: The Victim/Offender Connection* (pp. 227–246). Cincinnati: Anderson.

McCleary, Richard, and Kenneth S. Y. Chew. 2002. "Winter is the Infanticide Season." *Homicide Studies,* 6(3): 228–239.

McLean, Bruce. 2000. "Cultural Defense Will Play Big Part in Murder Trial." Scripps Howard News Service. Retrieved November 23, 2005, from http://www.sawnet.org/news/cultural_defense.html

Meyer, Cheryl L., and Michelle Oberman. 2001. *Mothers Who Kill Their Children.* New York: New York University Press.

Montgomery, Ben. 2005, July 15. "Jury Finds Father Guilty in Death of Little Boy." *Tampa Tribune.* Accessed online at http://news.tbo.com/news/MGBW7PUT5BE.html

Mouzos, Jenny. 2000. *Homicidal Encounters: A Study of Homicide in Australia, 1989–1999.* Canberra: Australian Institute of Criminology.

New Zealand Herald. 2005, June 22. "$108,000 Rewards to Solve Baffling Cases. Retrieved November 6, 2005. http://www.nzherald.co.nz/location/story.cfm?l_id=443&objectid=10331944

Oberman, Michelle. 2002. "Understanding Infanticide in Context: Mothers who Kill, 170–1930 and Today." *Journal of Criminal Law & Criminology,* 92(3/4): 707–738.

Overpeck, M.D., R. A. Brenner, A. C. Trumble, L. B. Trifilette, and H. W. Berendes. 1998. Risk factors for infant homicide in the United States. *New England Journal of Medicine,* 339(17): 1211–1216.

Paulozzi, Leonard, and M. Wells. 2002. "Variation in Homicide Risk During Infancy—United States, 1989–1998." *Morbidity and Mortality Weekly Report* 51;187–189.

Shackelford, Todd K., Viviana A. Weekes-Shackelford, and Shanna L. Beasley. 2005. "An Exploratory Analysis of the Contexts and Circumstances of Filicide-Suicide in Chicago, 1965–1994." *Aggressive Behavior*, 31: 399–406.

Silverman, Robert A. and Leslie W. Kennedy. 1988. "Women Who Kill Their Children." *Violence and Victims*, 3: 113–127.

Smith, Jaclyn. 2006. "Infanticide." In Doris L. Mackenzie, Lauren O'Neill, Wendy Povitsky and Summer Acevedo, eds., *Different Crimes, Different Criminals* (pp. 11–34). Cincinnati: Anderson.

Sorbet, Maureen, and Stepheni Schlinker. 2004, October 19. "Safe Delivery Act Provides Alternative to Abandoning Newborns," Accessed online at http://www.michigan.gov/som/0,1607,7-192-29941-102422—,00.html

Sorenson, Susan B., and Barbra A. Richardson. 1993. "Race/Ethnicity Patterns in the Homicide of Children in Los Angeles 1980 through 1989." *American Journal of Public Health*, 83(5): 725–727.

Sorenson, Susan B., and Julie G. Peterson. 1994. "Traumatic Child Death and Documented Maltreatment History, Los Angeles." *American Journal of Public Health*, 84(4): 623–627.

Stanton, Josephine, Alexander Simpson, and Trecia Wouldes. 2002. A Qualitative "Study of Filicide by Mentally Ill Mothers." *Child Abuse & Neglect*, 24(11): 1451–1460.

Takahashi, Yoshitomo, and Douglas Berger. 1996. "Cultural Dynamics and the Unconscious in Suicide in Japan." In Antoon Leenaars and David Lester, eds., *Suicide and the Unconscious* (pp. 248–258). Northvale: Jason Aronson.

Trounsen, Rebecca, and Nancy Wride. 2005, October 14. "USC Student Charged in Infant's Death." Accessed online at http://www.latimes.com/news/local/la-me-usc14oct14,1,7259432.story?ctrack=1&cset=true

U.S. Census Bureau. 2000. *USA State and County Quick Facts*. Retrieved October 23, 2005, from http://quickfacts.census.gov/qfd/states/00000.html

Vogt, Kimberly A., and Carolyn Rebecca Block. 2003. "Child Homicide Victims in Chicago, 1965–1995." In C. R. Block and R. L. Block, eds., *Public Health and Criminal Justice Approaches to Homicide Research. Proceedings of the 2003 Meeting of the Homicide Research Working Group*. Chicago: HRWG Publications.

Wallace, Anne. 1986. *Homicide: The Social Reality*. Sydney: New South Wales Bureau of Crime Statistics.

Williams, David. 2002, February 27. "Postpartum Depression: A Difficult Defense." CNN.Com 2002 Posted: 6:25 PM EST (2325 GMT) CNN.com Law Center. Retrieved November 23, 2005, from http://archives.cnn.com/2001/LAW/06/28/postpartum.defense/Daly, Margo, and Martin Wilson. 1988. *Homicide*. New York: Aldine.

Wilson, Margo, Martin Daly, and Antonietta Daniele. 1995. "Familicide: The Killing of Spouse and Children." *Aggressive Behavior*, 21: 275–291.

Winpisinger, Kim A., Richard S. Hopkins, Robert W. Indian, and Jeptha R. Hostetler. 1991. "Risk Factors for Childhood Homicides in Ohio: A Birth Certificate-Based Case-Control Study." *American Journal of Public Health*, 81(8): 1052–1054.

WRTV Indianapolis. 2005, November 3. "Murder-Suicide Shocks Community." WRTV Indianapolis Web page. Retrieved November 10, 2005, from http://www.theindychannel.com/news/5241565/detail.html

Chapter 11

MASS AND SPREE MURDER

Although some homicide may seem almost so ordinary that it may not even appear on our local newscasts or appear on the front page of our newspapers, mass and spree murders that occur in public are often deemed so newsworthy that the U.S. news media and even the world news media inform us about them almost immediately. Even if a public mass or spree murder does not happen in our own city or town, coverage of the event likely will be broadcast on national, local, and maybe even international news programs. Fox News Network, CNN, and other 24-hour news stations often give these cases extensive coverage. The immediate aftermath of such cases may be broadcast by all of the major networks. We only need to turn on the television or log on to the Internet to see victims being transported away and survivors being helped to safety minutes after these tragic events take place.

Unfortunately, when the news media cover these events, they may refer to such events incorrectly. Often the general public, including news personnel, confuse categorizations such as mass murder, serial murder, and spree murder. For those who study homicide and for criminal justice personnel, differences between the categorizations are important. The differences between mass and spree murder are emphasized in this chapter. Then, the scholarly research on these topics and examples from different parts of the world are presented. After reading this chapter, you will know how common multiple murders such as spree and mass murders are in the United States and in other countries. You will be able to make distinctions between both mass and spree killers. You will learn about the typologies that have been suggested for mass murder. Finally, you will learn about how the courts treat spree and mass murderers. Throughout the chapter, examples of both well-known and lesser known cases of both mass and spree murders are included, so that after reading this chapter you will be able to discuss the reality of mass and spree murder intelligently (or more intelligently than you do now).

OFFICIAL DATA ON MULTIPLE MURDER

Although definitions of mass murder and spree murder vary, they are both types of multiple murders and they are both relatively uncommon. Unfortunately, it is difficult to find out the exact number of spree and mass murder incidents that occur in the United States each year. Because of the way that homicide data is collected in the Uniform Crime Reports (UCR; see Chapter 3), the most reliable data we have is data on the number of victims in a homicide event. Although it is most likely that those incidents recorded in the UCR as having three or more victims should be classified as mass murders, there is also the possibility that some criminologists would count a few of these incidents as spree murders. As discussed in this chapter, the distinction between mass and spree murder is a matter of determining when a homicide incident or event began and when it ended.

As you can see in Figure 11.1, the number of U.S. homicide incidents with three or more victims has varied relatively little over the 27 years for which we have data. The fewest incidents (85) occurred in 1984, and the most (152) occurred in 1995. Although these numbers are, on one hand, disturbingly high, on the other hand, the number of homicide incidents with three or more victims has never reached even 1% of all homicide incidents during the years for which we have data. In 1991, when the number of homicide incidents in the United States peaked, 0.48% of the incidents had more than three victims—that is less than half of 1%. When homicide incidents with three or more victims peaked in 1995, they made up 0.74% of all homicide

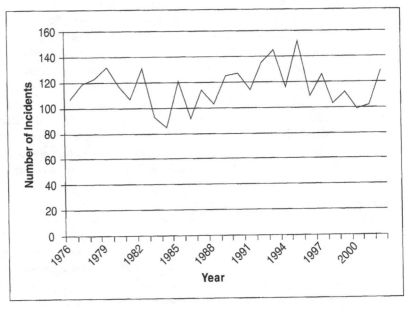

FIGURE 11.1
U.S. Multiple-Victim Homicide Incidents, 1976–2002

Source: FBI, *Uniform Crime Reports*, compiled by Fox and Zawitz, 2002.

incidents, and in 2002, the last year for which data are available for this chapter, they were at the highest percentage on record at 0.84%.

None of this is to say that we should be comfortable with the frequency of multiple-victim homicides (or single-victim homicides for that matter) in the United States each year. In comparison with the United States, Canada and Australia have far fewer incidents of multiple-victim murder. On average, Canada may have just over two per year and Australia averages approximately one multiple-murder incident per year (Mouzos, 2000). Mouzos (2000) reports that in the ten-year period she included in her study of mass murder in Australia, there were a total of 13 mass murder incidents. Each incident was committed by a male offender. In all, 94 individuals were killed in multiple-victim homicide incidents in Australia, including the 35 killed by Martin Bryant as described in Box 11.6. To put the U.S. data in perspective, in 1996, the same year that Bryant murdered 35 in Australia, there were 109 multiple-victim incidents with three or more victims in the United States resulting in a total of more than 357 U.S. victims.

Much is written about particular instances of mass murder, but because of the way official homicide data are collected, demographic data on mass murderers and their victims are sparse. Duwe (2005), who compared mass murder incidents examined by academics and media outlets to SHR data about multiple murders, provides some of the best demographic data on the phenomenon. Importantly, because of the way Duwe defines mass murder; his data most likely include both spree and mass murders. Duwe defined mass killings as those in which four or more victims were killed in a 24-hour period. Duwe reported that for the years 1976 to 1999, almost two thirds (61%) of mass murderers were white and 94% were male. They had an average age of 29 years. Most (69%) used firearms of which only 3% were assault weapons. Only 27% killed in a public setting. Under half (40%) killed family members, nearly as many (36%) killed acquaintances, and 24% killed strangers. The average victim age was 28 years, 72% of the victims were white, and 55% were male. The cases were fairly evenly distributed by region with approximately a quarter occurring in the Midwest (26%), the East (23%) the South (29%), and the West (22%).

Duwe's comparison of SHR data and cases used by academics to draw conclusions about mass murderers indicates that our knowledge about mass murder may be skewed toward cases that are more newsworthy. According to Duwe, the cases studied by academics and covered by the media were more likely than the SHR data cases to have high victim counts, public locations, and offenders who used assault weapons. They were also slightly more likely to have white offenders. Additionally, the typically reported cases were less likely to include familicides and felony-related mass murders (Duwe, 2005).

DEFINITION OF MASS MURDER

As noted earlier, in everyday conversations, many people confuse different types of multiple murders. Criminologists and criminal justice personnel make distinctions among serial killing, mass murder, and spree murder. Serial killing, the most well known of the three, is discussed in Chapter 12, and spree murder, the least well known, is discussed toward the end of this chapter. Here, then, we focus on mass murder. There is some disagreement as to how many victims there must be to define a homicide incident as a mass murder. Whereas Levin and Fox (1996) define mass murder as those with four or more victims, the more common definition is the killing of three or more victims as part of a single ongoing event (Holmes & Holmes, 2001).

Understanding this definition of mass murder might lead you to think about the Columbine school shooting or other recent school shootings. If you are a bit older or if you have completed Internet searches on mass murder, you might remember two infamous restaurant mass murders. The San Ysidro McDonald's massacre ended after James Oliver Huberty was shot by a SWAT sharpshooter but not before Huberty had killed 21 people and injured 19 others (see Box 11.1). George Hennard killed himself after shooting to death 22 people at Luby's Cafeteria in Killeen, Texas, in October 1991. Then again, many people probably think of workplace massacres such as that committed by postal worker Patrick Sherrill at the Edmond, Oklahoma, post office in August 1986 (see Box 11.2).

BOX 11.1

McDonald's Massacre

Shortly before 4 P.M. on Wednesday, July 18, 1984, in a small community directly above the Mexico border in San Diego, California, James Oliver Huberty entered a busy McDonald's restaurant. By 5:17 P.M. when SWAT sharp shooter Chuck Foster shot him to death with one shot, Huberty had killed 21 and injured 19 in what was, at the time, reported to be the worst massacre in U.S. history. Before he left for the restaurant, James Huberty reportedly told his wife Etna that he was going to "hunt humans." No one knows for sure why the recently fired security guard from Canton, Ohio, went on his rampage. In 1987, Huberty's widow Etna unsuccessfully sued the McDonald's Corporation, claiming that an additive in Chicken McNuggets interacted with lead and cadmium in Huberty's body from his years as a welder, which caused him to commit the deadly rampage (Gresko, 2004; Zúñiga, 2004).

A satellite campus of Southwestern College has been built on the site where the McDonald's once stood. A memorial to the victims, 21 hexagonal pillars ranging in height from 1 foot to 6 feet, has been erected in front of the campus. Not much has been written about the fact that most of those killed and wounded by Huberty were Mexican-American or Mexican, but the following list of victims makes this strikingly obvious:

- Elsa Herlinda Borboa-Firro
- Neva Denise Caine
- Michelle Deanne Carncross
- María Elena Colmenero Silva
- David Flores Delgado
- Gloria López González
- Omar Alonso Hernández
- Blythe Regan Herrera
- Matao Herrera
- Paulina Aquino López
- Margarita Padilla

continued

- Claudia Pérez
- Rubén Lozano Pérez
- Carlos Reyes
- Jackie Wright Reyes
- Victor Rivera
- Arisdelsi Vuelvas Vargas
- Hugo Luis Velazquez Vargas
- Aida Velazquez Vazquez
- Laurence "Gus" Versiluis
- Miguel Victoria Ulloa
- Alicia Victoria

*On May 18, 1927, Andrew Kehoe bombed a school in Bath, Michigan, killing more than 40 people, most of whom were children—this is a case that is infrequently included in discussions about mass murder.

BOX 11.2

Going Postal

Maybe someone has told you to "stop going postal," or you may have used this phrase on someone else. We use this phrase in everyday language to refer to someone who we believe is becoming overly angry or agitated or to refer to someone who has exploded into a violent rage. It is also used to refer to any mass murder in the workplace. You probably have some idea about the origination of the term *going postal*. Mass murders by postal employee Patrick Sherrill and former postal employee Thomas McIlvane led to the mistaken belief that postal employees were more likely to commit workplace homicides, making the phrase "going postal" synonymous with disgruntled workers taking out their anger by killing as many as they could at their workplace. There is no doubt that the killings by Sherrill and McIlvane were tragic, but studies have found that workplace violence is as uncommon in other workplaces as it is in U.S. postal service. More recently, in 2005, Jennifer Sanmarco, a former postal worker, killed five before killing herself in a mail-processing center in Goleta, California, in what is likely the deadliest workplace shooting by a woman in U.S. history.

Patrick Sherrill killed 14 employees at the Edmond, Oklahoma, post office on August 20, 1986. Sherrill, who was a postal carrier, shot himself after killing his 14 coworkers and seriously wounding 6 others.

Thomas McIlvane, who had been fired from the postal service, murdered four postal employees and then shot himself at a Royal Oaks, Michigan, post office on November 14, 1991.

Jennifer Sanmarco, a former postal worker who had been placed on medical leave for psychological problems in 2003, murdered six postal employees and possibly one of her neighbors before shooting herself on January 31, 2005, at a Goleta, California, U.S. postal processing center (CBS Worldwide, 2006).

Those who live near me have recently been reminded of the September 15, 1997, workplace murders by Arthur Hastings Wise. He was executed on November 4, 2005, for shooting to death four people at the R. E. Phelon Company in Aiken, South Carolina.

Even though we are likely to associate mass murder with workplace violence carried out by disgruntled employees or horrific massacres in schools or restaurants, mass murder is more likely to occur in the context of a domestic situation or a felony crime. It is not surprising that we often fail to think about mass murders that occur in these contexts; especially those that occur in the home, because they receive much less publicity than the mass murders that occur in public places (Petee, Padgett, & York, 1997).

WELL-KNOWN CASES OF MASS MURDER

Two infamous and widely covered cases of mass murder are often included in discussions about mass murder. These are the July 14, 1966, killing of eight student nurses by Richard Speck in Chicago and the killing of 16 and wounding of 30 by Charles Whitman from the clock tower at the University of Texas at Austin on August 1 of that same year. These cases are so well known, in fact, that Duwe (2005) has recently written about the coverage of these two cases for the general and academic understanding of mass murder. Duwe argues that these two mass murders have had a major impact on the view we have about such murders in our society and in the scholarly study of mass murder.

Ironically, however, there is some disagreement as to whether Whitman should be classified as a mass or spree murderer. Whitman killed his mother and wife. Then, the next day, August 1, 1966, he purchased a shotgun and ammunition to add to his stockpile of weapons and supplies and drove to the University of Texas tower where he killed 14 more people and wounded 30 others before being killed by police officers. Some argue he is not a mass murderer because the killing of his mother and wife in their separate households before moving on later in the day to kill and wound many from the tower makes his murderous rampage a spree event rather than a mass event. Others who categorize the event as a mass murder focus on the events that occurred during approximately two hours at the University of Texas tower (Barr, 2001).

TYPOLOGIES OF MASS MURDERS AND MURDERERS

Park Dietz (1986) categorized mass murderers into three categories that include family annihilators, pseudo-commandos, and set-and-run-killers. In their 2001 book on mass murder, Holmes and Holmes include the four additional categories of disciples, disgruntled employees, disgruntled citizens, and the psychotic mass murderers in their discussion of typologies. As noted by Petee et al. (1997), these categories are problematic for they are neither mutually exclusive nor exhaustive. In other words, some mass killers could fit in more than one category, making the categories not mutually exclusive. And other killers may not fit in any category, thus resulting in a nonexhaustive categorization. Nevertheless, these are categories that are known by any criminologist who studies mass murder and by many criminal justice personnel whose job it is to deal with such offenders. Consequently, definitions and examples of each type are included next in this chapter.

Family annihilators are those who kill their entire family and often themselves in one incident within the home. Often the killer is the patriarch of the family, who is depressed and frequently an alcoholic. The killing of the Belding family allegedly by the father/husband John Belding on November 16, 2005, may be considered a family annihilation homicide. According to newspaper reports, John Belding, a 42-year-old father of two who owned a termite inspection business, shot his wife and two children to death before committing suicide himself in his Fort Bend County, Texas, home (Dunn, 2005; Hanson, 2005).

Pseudo-commandos are mass murderers who are obsessed with weapons and often bring an ample supply to complete their massacre. Rather than acting impulsively, they carefully select a public place where many individuals may be killed quickly. Frequently pseudo-commando mass murderers commit suicide or force the police to kill them (suicide by cop) to end their rampage. James Huberty, who committed the McDonald's massacre, and Charles Whitman, who killed 14 people at the University of Texas tower, both fit the profile of a pseudo-commando mass murderer (Moore, Petrie, Braga, et al., 2003).

Set-and-run killers use methods such as bombing or poisoning to kill their victims to allow their own escape. Timothy McVeigh, the man who bombed the Oklahoma Federal Building on April 19, 1995, may fit best in this category. Despite his fascination with guns that might place him in the pseudo-commando category, he used a truck bomb to kill 169 people and injure hundreds more, making his escape possible (Clark, 1995). McVeigh reportedly told his biographers that although he was not afraid to die, he was intent on surviving the massacre to tell his side of the story (Handlin, 2001). (See Box 11.3 on the Tylenol cyanide killer for another possible example of a set-and-run mass murderer.)

The *disciple* mass murderer is a category that Holmes and Holmes added to Dietz's typology. Disciple mass murderers are those who kill because they are trying to attain acceptance from a charismatic leader like Charles Manson. This type of mass murderer usually does not know his or her victims. Instead, they are chosen by the charismatic leader, and they kill to please the leader. The quintessential disciple killers are those who killed for Charles Manson. Susan Atkins, Patricia Krenwinkel, and Charles Watson are three of Manson's followers who are believed to have murdered four people at the home of Roman Polanski and Sharon Tate on August 9, 1964, before killing Leno and Rosemary LaBianca two nights later on August 11. These killers were instructed by Manson to kill; he was the one to select the victims and the time and place of the murders, but the others are believed to have committed the murders to please Manson (Holmes & Holmes, 2001).

Disgruntled employee mass murderers may very well be the mass murderer category that we hear about most in the media, and Fox and Levin (2001) believe that in recent years, this may be the most common form of mass murder (see Box 11.2). Disgruntled employee killers are either current employees who are unhappy about something happening at their work or they are former employees who have been fired and return to their place of employment to retaliate against those who they believe have treated them wrongly. Although the focus of the killer's revenge is aimed

BOX 11.3

Tylenol Cyanide Killings and Changes in Food and Drug Packaging

In 1982, seven people died of cyanide poisoning from ingesting Extra-Strength Tylenol capsules laced with the deadly poison. The "Tylenol Killer," as he or she has been dubbed, is often categorized as a mass murderer. Indeed, if one killer poisoned all seven of the victims through Tylenol poisonings at the same place, he or she would be considered by many to be a set-and-run mass killer.

The cyanide-laced Tylenol capsules were from four different lots and shipped from two different plants and sold in several different stores in Chicago. Thus police believe that the poisoning was not done at the plant where Tylenol was manufactured. Instead, police believed the person who laced the Tylenol capsules with cyanide took the boxes of Tylenol from different stores over a period of months and then carefully distributed the deadly doses on the shelves of stores in the Chicago area (Kaplan, 1998).

Although the killer has never been arrested, he or she has greatly affected packaging in our society. The U.S. Food and Drug Administration introduced new regulations for tamper-resistant packaging. Johnson & Johnson, the parent company of Tylenol, was one of the first to comply. Tylenol capsules were reintroduced to the public in a triple-seal tamper-resistant package. The box had glued flaps that had to be ripped open. A tight plastic seal surrounding the cap had to be ripped off and an inner foil over the mouth of the bottle required the user to puncture it to get to the capsules. And the label warned the user not to use the product if the safety seal was broken (Kaplan, 1998).

For any reader born after the 1960s, this triple-resistant packaging probably seems quite normal. You probably do not realize how differently foods and drugs are packaged now. When I was a child, bottles of mustard and ketchup did not have plastic seals or metallic coverings that needed to be pulled off before using the product. You could simply twist up the lid on your mustard and squirt away. My Hershey bar was beautifully wrapped in foil with a paper sleeve over it. There were no sealed metallic wrappers that had to be ripped open. Instead, I could just pull on the paper sleeve and unfold the metal and my chocolate was ready to eat. It was so easy that I could pull off the sleeve, unfold the foil, remove my chocolate bar, and then refold the foil as if the chocolate were still in place. Then I could replace the sleeve and leave what looked like a delicious candy bar for my unsuspecting little brother.

Even if we have not personally experienced the loss of a friend or family member, the world around us has definitely been affected by the possibility of violent crime. Think about it the next time you unwrap your candy as you are going through the security check at the airport.

BOX 11.4

Disciple Killings in Japan

Shoko Asahara may not be a name you recognize. Asahara is the founder of Aum Shinrikyo, a religious organization in Japan that is a mixture of Buddhism, Christianity, Hinduism, Shamanism, and New Age beliefs. The organization, which is often referred to as a cult, is believed to be responsible for two mass murders. The first, on June 27, 1994, occurred in Matsumoto, Japan. Under the direction of Asahara, it is believed a group of disciple killers parked a converted refrigerator truck in a residential neighborhood. They then used a remote control to release a cloud of nerve gas from the truck. The gas blew through open windows and doorways, killing 7 people and injuring at least 500 more. You may remember hearing about the second mass murder directed by Asahara. On March 20, 1995, his disciples placed packages of poisonous chemicals on five different subway trains in Tokyo. Over 3,800 people were injured and 12 were killed. In 2004, Shoko Asahara was sentenced to death for masterminding the Tokyo attack (August, Bailey, Bland, et al., 2004; Olson, 1999).

---

at those who mistreated him or her, others are often killed in the rampage (Holmes & Holmes, 2001). Arthur Hastings Wise, who was executed on November 4, 2005, for killing four people at his former place of employment, serves as an example of a disgruntled employee mass murderer.

Executed mass murderer Arthur Hastings Wise (see Box 11.5) is typical of many workplace mass murderers in that he was a middle-age man (43 years) at the time of his crime. He was male, his chosen weapon was a firearm, and he was angry at how he was treated at his job. It is likely that he saw the loss of his job as the end of his life as he knew it (Fox & Levin, 2001). However, Wise is atypical in that he was an African American man. According to Fox and Levin's research, approximately 70% of workplace murderers are white.

Holmes and Holmes include the category of *disgruntled citizen* as a category in their 2001 book on mass murder. According to these authors, James Huberty, who killed 21 people in a San Ysidro McDonald's, is typical of the disgruntled citizen mass murderer. The disgruntled citizen, like the disgruntled employee, expresses his anger and rage by killing others. However, unlike the disgruntled employee, the disgruntled citizen tends to be angry at the world rather than particular individuals. As a result, the perpetrator kills strangers in an attempt to bring attention to the wrongs that he or she believes should be made public.

According to witnesses, 22-year-old Kenneth Junior French was angry about President Clinton's new "don't ask, don't tell" policy regarding homosexuals and lesbians in the military. French, who was an army sergeant stationed at Fort Bragg, expressed his anger by killing four people at Luigi's restaurant in North Carolina on August 6, 1992. Armed with two shotguns and a rifle, French entered the restaurant around 10 P.M. He shouted something about Clinton letting gays in the military before shooting restaurant owners Peter and Ethel Parrous. He continued to shout

---

BOX 11.5

Disgruntled Employee Arthur Hastings Wise

After working at R. E. Phelon for four years, Wise was fired from the
Aiken, South Carolina, plant in 1997. On September 17, 1997, approximately two months after Wise was fired from the plant, he returned to
seek revenge against those he thought caused him to lose his job and the
person who was hired to replace him. Arriving at the 3 P.M. shift change,
Wise shot a security guard (who survived), pulled the phone lines from the
guard shack, and continued on his way. Wise entered the plant and
headed for the personnel office. There, Wise found who he was looking
for: Charles Griffeth, the man who fired him. Wise shot the 56-year-old
human resources director twice in the back, killing him. Wise then moved
on to the tool and dye area where he had wanted to work. He fired his
semiautomatic pistol, killing Leonard Filyaw and David Moore before continuing on through the plant. Sheryl Wood was next to be shot in Wise's
rampage. Wise shot her in the back and leg before shooting her in the
head execution style. Wood was the unfortunate person who got the
quality control job that Wise had wanted. Wise continued to fire his gun,
but fortunately no one else was killed. As is typical of disgruntled employees who commit mass murder, Wise then attempted to commit suicide.
However, instead of killing himself by turning his own gun on himself or
forcing police to shoot him, Wise tried to commit suicide by drinking insec-
ticide. He was unsuccessful. At his trial, Wise refused to let his attorneys
make any arguments that might have spared him the death penalty. After
being sentenced to death for the four murders in February 2001, Wise
waived his appeals and asked to be executed. The sentence was carried
out in November 2005 (Collins, 2005a, 2005b).

---

at any person who talked or moved. Before being shot by police, French also killed
James Kidd and Wesley Cover and wounded several others (Reese, 1993). French is
one of several killers featured in *Licensed to Kill*, Arthur Dong's film about men who
have killed because of their contempt for gays. In the film, French makes the following
statement in which he admits to being an angry citizen:

> I'm not gonna apologize for the views that I hold towards gays or homosexuals
> but . . . I don't think that I went in with the intention of just singling out any
> certain group of people, be it black, white, male, female, gay, or straight. I was
> just angry at the world I guess at the time, I don't know. I was just taking out
> aggression and hatred on whoever was there.

French, as is typical of disgruntled citizen mass murderers, killed several
strangers to bring attention to a wrong he believed needed to be addressed. In his
case, he was angry about gays in the military and he killed to make his point
known.

BOX 11.6

Multiple Murder in Australia: The Port Arthur Massacre

On April 28, 1996, Australians witnessed one of the worst mass murders in their history in the town of Port Arthur in the southeastern corner of Tasmania. Twenty-nine-year-old Martin Bryant, a young tan man with long golden locks, was eating a meal at a café one moment and in the next he had shot and killed three people with a semiautomatic rifle that he had retrieved from his duffel bag. But Bryant did not stop at three dead; he continued to shoot at anyone in his sight. Crowds of people attempted to avoid his barrage of bullets, but he killed 20 people and wounded 15 others in the café before walking out to the parking lot where he continued to fire into a crowd of tourists gathered for a day out in Port Arthur. Bryant killed a tourist bus driver and three passengers as some tourists attempted to hide under the bus. Witnesses report that Bryant calmly squatted and shot those who sought refuge under the bus. He then got into his car and drove about 300 yards down a road before stopping to shoot at a woman and her two children; chasing one of the children who attempted to run from him. Bryant returned to his car; stopping to shoot three men and a woman sitting in separate cars. The carnage was still not over. Bryant continued on to the Seascape cottage, shooting at all who passed him along the way. Once at the Seascape, he barricaded himself inside. For the next six hours, the police attempted to negotiate with Bryant before his cordless phone went dead. Finally, the next morning around 8:30 A.M., Bryant ran from the cottage with his clothes on fire as smoke poured from the burning building. Police found three more bodies in the cottage after they arrested Bryant. In all, at the end of Bryant's rampage, 35 people were dead and another 18 were wounded. Some define Bryant as a spree killer because he killed at several places, but many others count him as a mass murderer because he killed in one string of events. Either way, Martin Bryant is likely the most infamous multiple murderer in Australian history. After recovering from his burns, despite a low IQ, he was determined to be sane enough to stand trial. He was found guilty and sentenced to life in prison without the possibility of parole (Bellamy, 2006; CNN, 1996).

Holmes and Holmes (2001) include a category in their typology of mass murderers that they call *psychotic mass murderers*. It is important to note that they are not sociopathic but psychotic. According to Holmes and Holmes, these individuals have had a break with reality and they are likely to hear voices or have visions. Just as with sociopaths, all psychopaths are not killers; however, Holmes and Holmes maintain that many of them have a history of trouble with the law. Although the category of psychotic mass killer is the smallest group in Holmes and Holmes (2001) typology, often these cases are focused on in more detail by the media rather than the more common family annihilator mass murderers. Sylvia Seegrist and Larry Gene Ashbrook serve as examples of the psychotic mass killer.

Dressed in green military fatigues and a knit cap, 25-year-old Sylvia Seegrist drove to the Springfield Mall in Philadelphia in 1985. As she exited her car, she began firing a Ruger semiautomatic rifle. She continued to fire the rifle as she ran through the mall. She killed three and injured at least six others. After the killing, Sylvia's mother, Ruth Seegrist, described her desperate attempts to find residential treatment for Sylvia who had been spiraling down further into a psychotic nightmare during the ten years previous to the mass murder. There were no doubts in her parents' minds that Sylvia was dangerous. Delusional with violent outbursts, she was diagnosed as schizophrenic at age 16. Sylvia had been institutionalized at least 12 times before her rampage but was released each time after psychiatrists reported that she was no longer a threat to herself or others. Seegrist is currently serving three consecutive life sentences in Muncy Correctional Institution after a jury found her mentally ill but guilty (Goodstein & Glaberson, 2000; Mengers, 2005).

In 1999 on September 15, more than 100 students were gathered at the Wedgewood Baptist Church in Fort Worth, Texas, for a youth prayer service. Larry Gene Ashbrook, a 47-year-old man, rolled a pipe bomb into the church and opened fire with his 9-mm semiautomatic handgun. Luckily, the pipe bomb did little damage. However, Ashbrook did manage to kill four teens and three adults before killing himself. Although Bob Garrity of the FBI believed the exact reason for the killing may never be known, Garrity also reported that Ashbrook "Has the appearance of being a very troubled man who for, whatever reason, in his own mind sought to quiet whatever demons were bothering him" (*PBS Online News Hour*, 1999).

Although not included in their discussion of mass murder typologies, Holmes and Holmes include a chapter on youthful school shooters in their 2001 book, *Mass Murder in the United States*. As with other categories, the school shooter category does not appear to be a mutually exclusive category. School shooters, for example, may also fit into the category of disgruntled citizen mass murderer or pseudo-commando mass murderer. Nevertheless, as Holmes and Holmes (2001) note and as discussed in Chapter 9 on children who kill, certain patterns emerge when we examine the recent school shooting incidents. The killers tend to be white males who strike out against their teachers or classmates. The boys who kill tend to be outcasts from middle-class families who, like many boys their age, spend much time playing elaborate video or computer games. Often, the school shooters, like pseudo-commando mass killers, have an interest in weaponry. In contrast to school shootings with a single victim, most mass murder school shootings occur in suburban or rural schools (Holmes & Holmes, 2001). There are exceptions, however, like Eric Houston, who killed four people and wounded ten at his former high school on May 1, 1992, in Olivehurst, California (*Indianapolis Star*, 2005). Unlike other school shooters, Houston was not enrolled at the school at the time of his shooting, and he did not kill his classmates. See Chapter 9 for detailed examples of youthful school shooters.

Dietz (1986) and Holmes and Holmes (2001) are not the only criminologists who have developed typologies of mass murderers. Fox and Levin (1998) developed a typology based on the offender's motivation. The motivations noted by Fox and Levin (1998) are revenge, power, loyalty, profit, and terror.

Mouzos (2000) is correct in noting that Fox and Levin's motivations overlap with the typologies presented by Dietz (1986) and Holmes and Holmes (2001). School shooters, disgruntled employees, disgruntled citizens, and even family annihilators and psychotic mass murderers could be motivated by revenge. Revenge mass murderers kill to get even with or retaliate against someone who they believe has hurt them. Power mass murderers may strike out to show they are powerful. Pseudo-commandos and some school shooters may be motivated by the need to seek power.

According to Fox and Levin, those who kill out of loyalty see themselves as saving their loved ones from a harsh or miserable life. The family annihilator who kills her three children so they will not have to live without her when she commits suicide is an example of a loyalty mass murderer. A disciple mass murderer who kills for his leader may also be motivated by loyalty.

Fox and Levin's final motivations of profit and terror appear less frequently in the criminological literature on mass murderers. A person who kills several people in the course of a robbery to eliminate the possibility that they could identify him could be said to be motivated by profit. Prosecutors in New Jersey claim that this is just what Edward McDonald, 25, and Hamilton Sanchez, 30, did in the slaying of Hossam Armanious, his wife Amal Garas, and their daughters Sylvia and Monica. The family was allegedly killed by McDonald and Sanchez in their own home on January 11, 2005, when Monica recognized McDonald as an upstairs neighbor as the pair was robbing the family (Fenner & Moritz, 2005; Troncone, 2005). Finally, the motive of terror probably brings the 9/11 terrorist attack on the World Trade Center to your mind. Indeed, the 9/11 mass murder of thousands and the July 7, 2005, bomb attacks in London appear to be acts of terrorism instituted to bring terror to the government and citizens of the United States and the UK.

BOX 11.7

Happy Land Social Club Fire

On March 25, 1990, Julio Gonzalez was angry at his girlfriend. She worked in the Bronx at the Happy Land Social Club, an illegal nightclub that was popular among Honduran Americans. The club had been ordered closed for numerous violations; including fire code violations. But it was open on the night of March 25 when Gonzalez purchased a dollar's worth of gasoline (three quarters of a gallon). He went to the club and doused the entryway of the club with the gasoline and then ignited it. Ironically, his girlfriend escaped, but 87 other victims did not. They perished in the fire, making it the largest mass murder in the United States at the time.

Gonzalez was convicted of killing each of the 87 victims and was sentenced to 25 years to life for each life he took. However, two others were prosecuted for these deaths. Because of the building violations, prosecutors also went after the owner of the building where the Happy Land Social Club was located and the man who had leased the building. Both men, Alexander DiLorenzo and Jay Weiss, pleaded guilty to building code violations to avoid more serious charges. DiLorenzo was sentenced to 50 hours of community service and to pay $150,000 that would be used for a community center for Hondurans living in the Bronx (Hevesi, 1992). Weiss also had to perform 50 hours of community service, and he had to pay $60,000 to help build the community center.

GOVERNMENT MASS MURDER

Throughout history, governments have committed mass murder in the act of *genocide*, which is the killing or annihilation of a group of people because they are part of a particular group. The systematic slaughter of Jews and Gypsies by the Nazis is often given as the quintessential example, but there are far too many more examples. Stalin's death camps, the Cambodia killing fields, the 1971 mass killing of Bengalis in Bangladesh, and the deaths of over 800,000 in Rwanda in the early 1990s are other examples of genocide that have included mass killings. In 1948, genocide was defined as a crime under international law by the United Nations (UN) General Assembly. The UN Convention defined genocide as follows:

> [A]ny of the following acts committed with intent to destroy, in whole or in part, a national, ethnical, racial or religious group, as such:
>
> (a) Killing members of the group;
> (b) Causing serious bodily or mental harm to members of the group;
> (c) Deliberately inflicting on the group conditions of life calculated to bring about its physical destruction in whole or in part;
> (d) Imposing measures intended to prevent births within the group;
> (e) Forcibly transferring children of the group to another group. (UN General Assembly, 1948)

Genocide has led to the largest mass murders in world history, and although it is defined by the UN as a crime, it is usually not studied by criminologists with other mass murder cases that we study in criminal justice. Nevertheless, on one level, mass murder in the context of genocide may be comparable to mass murders that are motivated by terror or power. Likewise, in cases of genocide, those who actually carry out the murders may be disciple killers who are killing to please their leaders. Finally, genocide, at the very basic level, appears to be mass hate crime.

DEFINITION OF SPREE KILLER

Like mass murder and unlike most murders, spree murder is a type of multiple murder. Spree killers are those who kill several victims at different locations within a short period of time. Like mass and serial killing, most definitions of spree killing set the minimum number of victims at three or four. Unlike mass murderers, the spree killer does not do his or her killing at one location. Instead, like the D.C. snipers, they kill at several different locations. Serial killers may also kill at several locations; however, the spree killer differs from the serial killer in that spree killers do not have long "cooling-off periods" between killings. The spree killer does not return to his or her regular behavior between slayings (Epps, 2002). Spree killers are also different from serial killers, in that there is usually no typical victim that the spree killer seeks out. Rather, anyone who comes across his path is likely to become his victim (Koerner, 2002).

BOX 11.8

Beltway Sniper

The Beltway sniper case helps illustrate the difficulty in determining whether particular incidents or killers fit into a particular category or type of homicide. As Koerner (2002) noted, before John Allen Muhammad and John Lee Malvo were arrested, the D.C. sniper did not quite fit in the serial or spree category. The fact that very little time elapsed between each homicide and the lack of pattern among the victims made it seem like the pair were spree killers. However, it also appeared that, more similar to a serial killer, the killer(s) may have employed more premeditation than that typically employed by a typical spree killer. Furthermore, the one geographic area was more similar to serial killer cases than spree killer cases that often cross greater distances.

Although it is difficult, if not impossible, to use available data sources to determine how many spree killings occur each year, spree killers are believed to be less common than mass murderers. Retired FBI profiler Gregg McCrary says his interviews with spree killers have led him to the conclusion that spree killers are motivated by both the thrill of killing and the excitement of evading law enforcement (Epps, 2002). Often the spree begins with a romantic breakup or other event that angers the killer. As with Mark Barton, the day trader who killed 13 in Atlanta, the spree killer frequently kills family members first and then continues killing people who cross his path. Typically, the shooting spree ends when the killer is arrested or when he or she commits suicide (Koerner, 2002).

WELL-KNOWN SPREE KILLERS

Two frequently cited cases of spree killing occurred nearly 40 years apart. The first is the 1958 case of Charles Starkweather and Caril Fugate, and the second is the 1997 case of Andrew Cunanan. You may have seen the 1973 film *Badlands*, starring Sissy Spacek and Martin Sheen, or *Natural Born Killers*, starring Woody Harrelson and Juliette Lewis. Or perhaps you have heard Springsteen's song *Nebraska*, released in 1989. Springsteen's song and both films were inspired by the 1958 killing spree involving Charles Starkweather and Caril Fugate.

Charles Starkweather and Caril Ann Fugate

In February 1958, 19-year-old Charles Starkweather and his 14-year-old girlfriend Caril Ann Fugate were arrested in Wyoming after a three-day killing spree that left ten people dead. Although it is not clear what led to the spree or the level of Fugate's involvement, the couple's killing spree began with the deaths of Fugate's stepfather,

Marion Bartlett, her mother, Velda Bartlett, and her 2½-year-old half-sister, Betty Jean, in their family home in Lincoln, Nebraska. Starkweather, a garbage collector with a ninth-grade education, had recently been kicked out of his home by his father. Having killed a gas station attendant in December 1957, Starkweather was probably not in the best of moods when he arrived at Fugate's family home with a .22 rifle on the afternoon of January 21, 1958 (Levin & Fox, 1985).

Starkweather may have argued with Fugate's parents about dating their daughter before he shot and stabbed them to death. He then slashed the throat of the infant, Betty Jean, and disposed of all three bodies on the Bartlett property. For the next six days, Starkweather and Fugate allegedly lived in Fugate's family home, telling inquiring neighbors that the Bartletts were sick with the flu. Worried that the neighbors would suspect something soon, Starkweather and Fugate took to the road. It was not long before a relative discovered that the Bartletts had been murdered. In an attempt to find out what had happened, the police immediately began looking for Starkweather and Fugate (Levin & Fox, 1985).

Meanwhile, Starkweather and Fugate were driving in Starkweather's black Ford to August Meyer's house in Bennet, Nebraska. There, Starkweather shot Meyer, whom he had known for years. The next evening with the Ford stuck in the snow, Starkweather and Fugate set out on foot. Two teenagers, Robert Jensen and Carol King, offered a ride to Starkweather and Fugate. For their kindness, the teens were brutally killed (Levin & Fox, 1985).

Starkweather and Fugate drove Jensen's car back to Lincoln where they drove around an upper-class neighborhood in search of a place to hide. Starkweather told Fugate to choose a house she liked. She selected the house of C. Lauer and Clara Ward. Before Starkweather and Fugate stole the couple's Packard, they killed the Wards and Lillian Fencl, their maid. The governor called in the Nebraska National Guard and offered a reward for Starkweather and Fugate. Announcers warned of the murderous couple over the radio and police set up roadblocks throughout Lincoln.

The roadblocks were useless because Starkweather and Fugate had already fled to Wyoming. An attempt to change vehicles, however, led to the couple's capture. Starkweather spotted Merle Collison parked on the side of the road. Starkweather shot Collison and tried to steal his vehicle. Unable to release the parking brake, Starkweather and Fugate were unable to flee before Joe Sprinkle stopped because he believed an accident had occurred. Sprinkle was quick to notice that Collison was slumped over and that Starkweather had a rifle. Sprinkle and Starkweather struggled for control of the rifle. Luckily, William Romer, a deputy sheriff, observed the two fighting. Fugate distracted Romer and Sprinkle by yelling that she needed help. Starkweather was able to take off in the Packard, but he was soon apprehended and the murderous spree ended (Horyn, 2004; Levin & Fox, 1985).

Fugate and Starkweather were both found guilty in separate trials. Starkweather was sentenced to death. He was executed on July 25, 1959. In contradiction to statements made while she was in custody, Fugate's attorneys claimed that she went along with Starkweather to protect her parents, who she believed were still alive. They argued that she was not responsible for the murders and had been terrified for her own life and her family's lives. The jury did not believe the version put forth by Fugate's lawyers and instead found her guilty. She was sentenced to life without the possibility of parole. In 1973, likely in response to a renewed interest in her story after

Badlands was released, Fugate's sentence was commuted to a term of 30 to 50 years. She continued to live in prison as a model prisoner until 1975 when she was paroled. Because she had studied nursing while in prison she was able to work in the health care industry once she was granted parole (Horyn, 2004; Levin & Fox, 1985).

Internet searchers, newspaper searches, and discussions with experts suggest that Caril Fugate is one of a very small category of female spree killers. Debra Brown is one of the few other female spree killers. Brown, who killed with Alton Coleman, appears to have taken a much more active role in even more horrendous crimes than those committed by Fugate and Starkweather. While physically she is serving a life term in Ohio for aggravated murder, she is also technically on death row in Indiana (Clark County Prosecuting Attorney, 2006). Notice that both of these examples of female spree killers killed with their male partners. Lone female spree killers who kill on their own may be so rare that they do not actually exist. Although I have failed to discover any through my exhaustive searches, I would guess that a woman spree killer would more than likely strike out against her family.

Andrew Cunanan

Media frenzy and much speculation surrounded Andrew Cunanan's 1997 killing spree. Cunanan's own mother described him as a gay prostitute. Although these facts were interesting to the media, that Cunanan killed fashion designer Gianni Versace appears to have mostly fed the media frenzy. Like Starkweather before him, Cunanan killed across state lines and stole cars in an attempt to allude arrest. Cunanan, however, was more successful than Starkwether at avoiding arrest. Cunanan is believed to have beaten Jeff Trail to death in Minneapolis on April 27 before he shot and killed David Madson on May 3. As is often the case with spree killers, it is clear that he knew these two men. However, it is unclear whether he knew any of his other victims.

Using Madson's car, Cunanan drove to Chicago where he killed his next victim. On May 4, evidence suggests that Cunanan used a screwdriver and gardening shears to kill real estate investor Lee Miglin. He abandoned Madson's car and took Miglin's Lexus. Cunanan then drove the Lexus to New Jersey where he then shot William Reese, a cemetery caretaker. In Reese's truck, it seems that Cunanan was able to allude police and lay low until July 15 when he killed Gianni Versace. A national manhunt for Cunanan ensued after police found Reese's truck and witnesses described a man fitting Cunanan's description. Finally, on July 23, 1997, police located Cunanan on a houseboat in Miami. After a siege that lasted hours, SWAT officers stormed the houseboat where they found Cunanan dead of a self-inflicted gunshot wound (CNN, 1997; Fox & Levin, 2001).

COURTS AND MULTIPLE MURDERS

Definitions or profiles of mass and spree murderers often refer to the fact that these types of killers often commit suicide. Thus it is often the case that there are no court proceedings in mass and spree murder cases. In Table 11.1, you can see the case outcomes for most of the cases mentioned in this chapter. Although this is in no way a representative or random sample of mass and spree murder cases, we may conclude

TABLE 11.1
Outcomes of Multiple Murder Cases Included in This Chapter

Killer(s)	Year(s) of Killing	Victims Died	Case Outcome
Charles Starkweather & Caril Fugate	1958	10	Executed (Starkweather) Life without parole (LWOP) but released in 1976
Richard Speck	1966	8	Sentenced to death*
Charles Whitman	1966	16	Killed by police
James Huberty	1984	21	Killed by police
Debra Brown & Alton Coleman	1984	8	Sentenced to death in Indiana & Ohio‡ Executed (Coleman)
Sylvia Seegrist	1985	3	Mentally ill but guilty Three life sentences
Thomas McIlvane	1991	4	Suicide
Eric Houston	1992	4	Sentenced to death
Timothy McVeigh	1995	169	Executed
Arthur Hastings Wise	1997	4	Executed
Larry Gene Ashbrook	1999	7	Suicide
Mark Barton	1999	13	Suicide
Kenneth French	1992	4	Four consecutive life sentences
Shoku Asahara	1994 & 1995	19	Sentenced to death (Japan)
Martin Bryant	1996	20	LWOP (Australia)
Andrew Cunanan	1997	5	Suicide
John Allen Muhammad & John Lee Malvo	2002	12	Sentenced to death (Muhammad)† LWOP (Malvo)†
Edward McDonald & Hamilton Sanchez	2005	4	Case outcome pending as of this writing
John Belding	2005	3	Suicide

*Sentenced commuted to eight consecutive terms of 50 to 150 years in 1972 when the death penalty was ruled unconstitutional in *Furman* v. *Georgia*. Speck became eligible for parole in 1976 but died in prison of a heart attack in 1991.

†May still face additional charges.

‡Sentenced commuted to life in Ohio by Governor Richard Celeste.

from this data that these types of murder are considered very serious by juries and judges. In a few cases such as that of David French and Sylvia Seegrist, questions of sanity appear to have led the juries to sentences of less than death. In the case of Lee Malvo, his youthful age may explain his sentence of less than death. Where the death sentence has been overturned by higher courts such as in the Manson case, there is no indication that parole boards will ever allow the offenders to be paroled. Only Caril Fugate has been released. She was released nearly 20 years after her crime and has had no difficulty with the law since that time. But she is atypical in that she was very young at the time of the spree, and some believe she would have never been involved in anything like the spree killing of 1958 without Starkweather.

SUMMARY

In this chapter, in addition to many brief case summaries, the frequency of multiple murders such as spree or mass murders was discussed. Although they are relatively rare in the United States as compared to other homicides, we saw that multiple murders are much more frequent in the United States than in other countries. The distinctions between mass and spree killers were made. Both kill at least three victims in a short period of time. However, spree killers usually take more time to commit several homicides, and their killings occur in more than one location. Mass killers are defined as those who kill three or more in one place and one location. Although little research has been done on how the courts treat mass and spree killers, we know that juries and courts take their crimes very seriously. It is common for mass and spree killers to kill themselves. However, when they do not kill themselves, the data presented in this chapter suggest they often are sentenced to death. Those whose lives are spared are often extremely young or undeniably insane.

CHAPTER QUESTIONS

1. How common are multiple murders in the United States?
2. How does the United States compare to other countries with regard to the frequency of multiple murders?
3. What do you think might explain the difference between the United States and other countries?
4. What is the challenge in determining how many spree and mass murders occur each year?
5. What is the distinction between mass and spree murder?
6. Would you classify Whitman as a spree or mass murderer? Why? Could he be both?
7. Are the categories of mass murder presented in this chapter mutually exclusive?
8. List and define at least four types of mass murderers.
9. How are disgruntled employee mass murderers and disgruntled citizen mass murderers different and how are they similar?
10. How is Wise typical and atypical of other mass murderers?
11. What type of mass murder may be most common? Two are noted as possibilities in this chapter. Which do you suspect are the most common?
12. How do the typologies of Dietz and of Holmes and Holmes compare with the typologies that Fox and Levin developed?
13. What type of murder is likely to be committed by governments?
14. Think about the description of Andrew Cunanan's crime spree in this chapter. Some criminologists may label him a serial killer; others categorize him as a spree killer. How would you categorize him and why?
15. Based on the data presented in this chapter, what patterns are found in the outcomes of multiple murder cases?

REFERENCES

August, Melissa, Peter Bailey, Elizabeth L. Bland, Barbara Burke, and Unmesh Kher. 2004. "Milestones." *Time*, 163(10): 22.

Barr, Alwin. 2001. "Whitman, Charles Joseph." *The Handbook of Texas Online.* The Texas State Historical Association. Retrieved January 1, 2006, from http://www.tsha.utexas.edu /handbook/online/articles/WW/fwh42.html

Bellamy, Patrick. 2006. "Martin Bryant." *CourtTV Crime Library online.* Retrieved January 20, 2006, from http://www.crimelibrary.com/serial/bryant/

CBS Worldwide. 2006, February 1. "Postal Worker May Have Killed Neighbor." CBS KCAL Website. Retrieved February 1, 2006, from http://cbs2.com/topstories/topstories_story _032121421.html

Clark County Prosecuting Attorney. 2006. *The Death Penalty.* Retrieved January 25, 2006, from http://www.clarkprosecutor.org/html/death/rownew.htm

Clark, Tony. 1995, December 30. "The Worst Terrorist Attack on U.S. Soil: April 19, 1995." CNN Interactive. Oklahoma City Tragedy. Retrieved January 1, 2006, from http://www.cnn .com/US/OKC/daily/9512/12–30/index.html

CNN. 1996, April 29. "Gunman Kills at Least 34 in Australia: Police Search for More Victims in Shooting Spree." Retrieved January 20, 2006, from http://www.cnn.com/WORLD /9604/29/australia.shooting/index.html

CNN. 1997, July 17. "Who Is Andrew Cunanan?" Retrieved January 28, 2006, from (http://www.cnn.com/WORLD/9707/17/cunanan/

Collins, Jeffrey. 2005a, October 30. "Man to be Executed Friday for Plant Shootings." *Myrtle Beach.com.* Retrieved January 18, 2006, from www.myrtlebeachonline.com/mld /myrtlebeachonline/news/local/13036813.htm

Collins, Jeffrey. 2005b, November 4. "Man Who Killed 4 in Aiken County Plant Put to Death." *The State.com.* Retrieved January 17, 2006, from http://www.thestate.com/mld/thestate /13085535.htm

Dietz, Park E. 1986. "Mass, Serial and Sensational Homicides." *Bulletin of the New York Academy of Medicine*, 62: 477–491.

Dunn, Bob. 2005, November 23. "Police Find Richmond Children, Parents Dead in Murder-Suicide." *Fort Bend Now Online Version.* Retrieved December 31,2005, from http://www.fortbendnow.com/news/406/police-find-richmond-family-of-4-dead-in-home

Duwe, Grant. 2005. "A Circle of Distortion: The Social Construction of Mass Murder in the United States." *Western Criminology Review*, 6(1): 59–78.

Epps, Keith. 2002, October 7. "Profiler: Killer Will Try Again Spree Killer Unlikely to Stop for Long, Veteran Profiler Says." *The Free Lance-Star.* Retrieved January 23, 2006, from http://www.fredericksburg.com/News/FLS/2002/102002/10072002 /7529431

Fenner, Austin, and Owen Moritz. 2005, March 5. "Coptic Family Killed in Robbery: Police." *Daily News Front Page.* Retrieved January 22, 2006, from http://www.nydailynews.com /front/story/287052p-245663c.html

Fox, James Alan, and Jack Levin. 1998. "Multiple Homicide: Patterns of Serial and Mass Murder." In Michael Tonry, ed., *Crime and Justice: A Review of Research* (Vol. 23, pp. 407–455). Chicago: University of Chicago Press.

Fox, James Alan, and Jack Levin. 2001. *The Will to Kill: Making Sense of Senseless Murder.* Boston: Allyn & Bacon.

Fox, James Alan, and Marianne W. Zawitz. 2002. *Homicide Trends in the United States: 2002 Update.* Washington, DC: U.S. Bureau of Justice Statistics.

Goodstein, Laurie, and William Glaberson. 2000, April 11. "The Well-Marked Roads to Homicidal Rage." *New York Times*. Retrieved January 21, 2006. http://www.nytimes.com/library /national/041000rampage-killers.html

Gresko, Jessica. 2004, July 18. "20 Years Later, San Ysidro McDonald's Massacre Remembered." *North County Times*. Retrieved December 30, 2005, from www.nctimes.com/articles/2004/07 /18/news/top_stories/16_42_237_17_04.txt

Handlin, Sam. 2001. "Profile of a Mass Murderer: Who Is Timothy McVeigh?" *CourtTV Online*. Retrieved January 1, 2006, from http://www.courttv.com/news/mcveigh_special /profile_ctv.html

Hanson, Eric. 2005. "Financial Worries May Have Led to Family's Slayings, Kin Say." *Houston Chronicle* online version. Retrieved December 21, 2005, from http://www.chron.com/disp /story.mpl/front/3481856.html

Hevesi, Dennis. 1992, May 9. "Guilty Plea by Landlord in Fire Case." *New York Times*. May 9, 1992, p. 1. Retrieved January 30, 2006, from http://proquest.umi.com/pqdweb?index=12&did =965154861&SrchMode=1&sid=1&Fmt=3&VInst=PROD&VType=PQD&RQT=309&VNa me=PQD&TS=1138565882&clientId=30209

Holmes, Ronald M., and Stephen T. Holmes. 2001. *Mass Murder in the United States*. Upper Saddle River, NJ: Prentice Hall.

Horyn, Cathy. 2004, August 29. "Secrets from the Badlands." *New York Times*, Sec. 9, p. 1.

Indianapolis Star. 2005. "School Violence Around the World." Indystar.com. Retrieved January 21, 2006, from http://www2.indystar.com/library/factfiles/crime/school_violence/school _shootings.html

Kaplan, Tamara. 1998. "The Tylenol Crisis: How Effective Public Relations Saved Johnson & Johnson." Retrieved January 28, 2006, from http://www.personal.psu.edu/users/w/x /wxk116/tylenol/crisis.html

Koerner, Brendan I. 2002, October 17. "Serial Killers and Spree Killers: What's the Difference?" *Slate.com*. Retrieved January 23, 2006, from http://www.slate.com/?id=2072666

Levin, Jack, and James Alan Fox. 1996. "A Psycho-Social Analysis of Mass Murder." In Thomas O'Reilly-Fleming, ed., *Serial and Mass Murder: Theory, Research, and Policy* (pp. 55–76). Toronto: Canadian Scholars' Press.

Levin, Jack, and James Alan Fox. 1985. *Mass Murder: American's Growing Menace*. New York: Plenum Press.

Mengers, Patti. 2005, November 15. "20 Years Later, Still Learning Lessons from Mall Shootings." *Delcotimes.com*. Retrieved January 21, 2006, from http://www.delcotimes .com/site/news.cfm?newsid=15581114&BRD=1675&PAG=461&dept_id=568338 &rfi=6

Moore, Mark H., Carol V. Petrie, Anthony A. Braga, and Brenda L. McLaughlin, eds. 2003. *Deadly Lessons: Understanding Lethal School Violence*. Washington, D.C.: The National Academies Press.

Mouzos, Jenny. 2000. *Homicidal Encounters: A Study of Homicide in Australia, 1989–1999*. Canberra: Australian Institute of Criminology.

Olson, Kyle B. 1999. "Aum Shinrikyo: Once and Future Threat?" *Emerging Infectious Diseases* [Special issue] 5(4): 513–516.

PBS Online News Hour. 1999, September 16. "Church Shooting." Retrieved January 21, 2006, from http://www.pbs.org/newshour/bb/law/july-dec99/shooting_9-16.html

Petee, Thomas A., Kathy G. Padgett, and Thomas S. York. 1997. "Debunking the Stereotype: An Examination of Mass Murder in Public Places." *Homicide Studies*, 1 (4): 317–337.

Reese, Pat. 1993, August 7. "Shot Kills 4 in Restaurant." *Fayetteville Observer*. Retrieved January 19, 2005. http://nl.newsbank.com/nl-search/we/Archives?p_action=list&p_topdoc=11

Troncone, Thomas. 2005, November 9. "Prosecutors Want Death Penalty; 2 to Stand Trial in Family Massacre." *The Record*, p. A06. Retrieved January 22, 2006, from http://web

.lexis-nexis.com.bindery.aug.edu:2048/universe/document?_m=52f2a5ce7366469df0351
ef29bfe8fb5&_docnum=2&wchp=dGLbVlz-zSkVb&_md5=994b2954692ca8ac2c1185e1
2e1cd54e

United Nations General Assembly. 1948. *Convention on the Prevention and Punishment of the
Crime of Genocide.* Retrieved January 28, 2006, from http://www.hrweb.org/legal
/genocide.html

Zúñiga, Janine. 2004, July 18. "Carnage Survivor Lives His Dream of Being Cop." *San Diego
Union Tribune.* Retrieved December 30, 2005, from www.signonsandiego.com/uniontrib
/20040718/news_1m18massacre.html

Chapter 12

SERIAL MURDER

The public holds a special fascination for serial murder and murderers. If you look around the United States or a number of other countries such as England or Australia, you could easily believe serial killing was an epidemic today because of the inordinate amount of attention paid to it relative to the actual number of serial murderers. In addition to the excessive coverage of serial killing in the news media, books, films, television shows, and Web pages are devoted to serial killers and serial killing. This chapter begins with a brief overview of this fascination with serial murder. Then the definitional issues with regard to serial killing are discussed. Once a definition is established, the chapter provides an overview of the extent of serial killing worldwide according to a variety of experts. Finally, within the chapter, femicide and contract killing, two topics sometimes left out of discussions of serial killing, are also discussed.

FASCINATION WITH SERIAL KILLERS

As noted, there is an immense public interest in serial killing and serial killers. It is easy to see the fascination with serial killing in several different venues. First, thousands of books are in print on serial killing. You only need to peruse the shelves of any major bookstore to find hundreds of true crime stories about the likes of Ted Bundy, Dennis Rader, Ian Brady, Myra Hindley, and many more. Pausing for just a minute among the fiction books, you can find an incredible amount of horror and murder mystery books that focus on serial killers and those who work to stop them. If you take the time to read many of these books, you will find determined protagonists matching wits with clever serial killers who are almost always captured in the end. Sometimes, of course, the serial killer is not caught until after he abducts the protagonist, especially if the protagonist is a woman. Typically, though, she triumphs sometimes with the help of her attractive and muscularly strong male counterpart. In addition to the true crime nonfiction books, there are other non-fiction books on serial killing, even textbooks that are not usually found on the shelves of noncampus bookstores. Think about it. When is the last time you saw a math textbook or biology textbook being sold at a noncampus bookstore? Probably not recently; but you will find textbooks relating to murder at noncampus bookstores.

Clearly, the interest in serial killing runs deep. Children do not even escape—stories of serial killers are to be found in the children's literature section. For the little ones, there are some classic fairy tales of serial murderers who are cannibals no less! There is the big bad wolf that kills and eats two of the little pigs before being thwarted by the third pig. Once we review the definition of a serial killer, you may argue that the big bad wolf is not a serial killer because he did not kill that third pig. But really, what do we know of his life before the three pigs? And then there is that horrid witch in the story of Hansel and Gretel. She built a house of candies and cookies to lure children to her house so she could eat them. Sounds like a serial killer to me. Taking a turn to the section for adolescents in your local bookstore, you can find some newer books that include serial killers. Elaine Alphin's *Counterfeit Son* published in 2000, for example, tells the story of a young man whose father is a serial killer. In 2005, Graham McNamee's *Accelerator* was published, an intriguing story of a young boy who discovers the diary of a serial murderer. It seems that wherever you turn in the bookstore, you can find books about serial killers.

Leaving the book section of the bookstore for the DVD section, you are likely to find documentaries about Aileen Wuornos, Jeffrey Dahmer, Henry Lee Lucas, William Heirens, and other serial killers. There are also those films that are more or less based on these real-life serial killers, including *Dahmer, Henry: Portrait of a Serial Killer*, and *Monster*, which won Charlize Theron an Oscar for her portrayal of Aileen Wuornos. You can also find slasher films with serial killers, like the *Nightmare on Elm Street* Series, action films like *Kill Bill*, and even comedies about serial killing like one of my favorites, *Eating Raoul*.

Turning on the television at nearly any time of the day in the United States, you can find entertaining programs that deal at times with serial murderers such as various *Law and Order* and *CSI* programs, *Numb3rs*, and *Medium*. In addition, some shows focus on real-life crimes such as Court TV's *Forensic Files*, and often entire newsmagazine shows like *48 Hours* are devoted to crime cases including serial murders. News coverage, at both the local and national level on television and in print, also includes extensive coverage of serial killer cases as when Dennis Rader's testimony was covered in detail on many stations. This is not all because there are made-for-television movies that overlap with the crime news coverage. In October 2005, for instance, a Sunday movie on CBS called *The Hunt for the BTK Killer* premiered. Even soap operas have had serial killer plots. Since 2000, *One Life to Live*, *Days of Our Lives*, and *As the World Turns* have all had at least one serial killer mystery plot.

Even if you manage to avoid television, books, and movies, you are still likely to discover the fascination with serial killing by surfing the Internet or observing adolescents across the globe play an RPG (role-playing game) on their computer or game system. In the game *Still Life*, players can act out the role of an investigator in a serial

---

BOX 12.1

BTK Pleads Guilty

One of the biggest crime stories, if not news stories, in 2005 was the capture of Dennis Rader, who terrorized citizens in and around Wichita, Kansas. Before being apprehended, Rader came to be known as the BTK Killer because his modus operandi was to bind, torture, and kill his victims. In 2005, Rader pleaded guilty to murdering ten victims between 1974 and 1991. Neighbors and friends were shocked to find that Rader was responsible for the horrific killings. At one time Rader was president of his church and a Boy Scout leader. Radio and television stations across the nation broadcast Rader's statements in court as he meticulously described how he stalked and killed his victims. He reported that he used a briefcase or bowling bag as a "hit kit" packed with rope and other supplies he used to carry out his crimes. At the time of his crimes, Rader wrote anonymous letters and made phone calls to the police. Until 2004, however, he had not been heard from since 1991 at the time of what is believed to be his last murder. Then in 2004, the *Wichita Eagle* newspaper published a story noting the 30th anniversary of the murder of the Otero family—Rader's first victims. In response to this article, Rader began taunting the authorities again by sending clues from the murders he committed to police and reporters. When Rader sent a computer disk, the police were able to trace it to his church. He was then arrested in February 2005, ending a mystery that had remained unsolved for more than 31 years (Wilgoren, 2005).

---

murder case, and in *Condemned: Criminal Origins*, game players are suspected serial murderers. There is also *Indigo Prophecy*, available for Xbox and Play Station 2 and in a Windows XP format. In *Indigo Prophecy*, you start the game standing over a dead body with a knife in your hand, and the game continues from there. The Internet also provides endless opportunities to learn about serial killers and their crimes. I recently typed "serial killer" into the Google search engine where I found more than 6.5 million hits. Sure some of the "hits" could reference the same page, but still 6 million is an amazing number. The sites vary from the professionally designed *Court TV* pages to those that amateurs post.

Finally, even if you are a bit more selective and stay away from such popular culture as daytime dramas and nighttime crime shows, so-called high culture is not serial killer free. James Griffin's comedy, *Serial Killers*, about a serial murder behind the scenes of a fictionalized Australian soap opera, premiered on stage in the United Kingdom the same month in 2005 that the BTK serial killer movie premiered on CBS in the United States. Over 64 years before the BTK movie premiered, *Arsenic and Old Lace*, a story of two seemingly sweet old ladies who are serial killers, first appeared on stage in New York City. There are even operas about serial killers. In 2001, for example, *Wuornos* written by Carla Lucero premiered in San Francisco. And although *Wuornos* may have been the "first opera to explore institutionalized abuse against women and children," it was not the first time that an opera featured a serial killer

(Lucero, 2004). Sondheim's opera *Sweeney Todd* tells the story of a barber who kills his customers and cuts them up so his wife can cook them in delicious meat pies. And even if you agreed with those who believe *Sweeney Todd* to be a musical and not opera, there is the opera *Duke Bluebeard's Castle* based on Charles Perrault's story of a woman who discovers that her husband has killed his former wives. Nearly everywhere you turn today—wherever you look—there are serial killers to be found.

Defining Serial Murder

Even though serial killing has existed as long as recorded history, the term *serial killer* was introduced only around 1980 (Fox & Levin, 1999). A serial killer is commonly defined as an individual who kills multiple victims at different times and often in different places with cooling-off periods in between the killings. Like mass murder and spree killing, discussed in Chapter 11, serial killing involves the killing of multiple victims. However, most definitions of serial murder distinguish it from mass murder by stipulating that serial murder involves killing multiple victims over time. And although spree killers may kill over time as well, serial killers are distinguished from spree murderers in that serial killers "cool down" between murders. Unlike spree killers, serial killers return to their normal lives or routines between killing episodes.

So how many murders does it take to become a serial killer? There is disagreement on this issue. Until recently the standard answer was that it takes three victims. The FBI, for example, defines serial killing as "a series of three or more killings, having common characteristics such as to suggest the reasonable possibility that the crimes were committed by the same offender or offenders" (Brantley & Kosky, 2005: 27). Among the many others who have used the three-victim standard are Egger (1998), Hickey (1991), and Holmes and Holmes (1998). Fox and Levin (1999) have straddled the fence a bit when they define serial killers as those who "kill repeatedly," and they define repeatedly as "at least three or four victims" (Fox & Levin, 1999: 165). In 1993, Jenkins used a more stringent level of five homicides in more than 72 hours (Jenkins, 1993).

Recently, however, the FBI has begun to operate under the premise that they may be investigating a serial killer when two separate killings over time are committed by the same offender (Egger, 2006; Jarvis, 2006). In an ongoing study on African American serial killers, Egger is also using this two-victim standard. The move to a two-victim definition likely reflects a belief that an individual who kills at least two individuals in two separate incidents is likely to keep killing unless someone or something stops him or her.

Experts make other distinctions between those who kill serially and those who do not. Fox and Levin (1999), for example, have explained that serial killers are murderers who kill "with increasing brutality, serial killers stalk their victims, one at a time, for weeks, months, or years, generally not stopping until they are caught" (Fox & Levin, 1999: 165). Others have included in their definitions of serial killing something about a serial killer's motivation, noting it is not something they do for profit and it involves a sexual component. Some definitions of serial killing indicate that the victim and offenders are strangers to one another. Later in this chapter, these ideas about serial killers' motives and modus operandi are discussed. For now, however, the definition to be used in this chapter for serial killing is the definition that appears to be the newest standard for criminal justice personnel and researchers, which stipulates that a serial killer is one who kills at least two victims over time with a cooling-off period in between killings.

BOX 12.2

The Derivation of Serial Murder

For many who read this book, the term *serial killer* may seem to have always existed. However, like the DVD and the Internet, it is a fairly recent invention in the history of humankind. Very few doubt that serial killing has been occurring for years—consider Jack the Ripper for one. However, *serial killer* as a term is relatively new. It was not until the 1980s that the term began to appear frequently in our lexicon.

The person responsible for introducing the term *serial killer*, however, is disputed. Most sources credit FBI agent Robert Ressler as the one who first introduced the term. However, others have credited retired investigator and author Dr. Robert Keppel or FBI agent John Douglas. And in *Green River, Running Red: The Real Story of the Green River Killer*–America's Deadliest Serial Murderer, renown true crime writer Ann Rule (2004) writes about Pierce Brooks as the individual who coined the term.

In his 2003 book on serial killers, Harold Schechter relates Robert Ressler's explanation for how he came up with the term. In his 1992 memoir, *Whoever Fights Monsters*, Ressler reports that he attended a British police academy conference in the early 1970s. Another conference attendee talked about crimes that had occurred in a series. Upon his return to the United States, Ressler reflected on his experiences as a boy waiting for the next installment in the weekend movie matinee stories that he anticipated so much. As a result of this matinee reflection and his experience at the British conference, Ressler began using the term *serial killer* when he talked about murderers who killed more than one victim over time in a similar way.

Although Ressler is likely to have popularized the term in the United States, Schechter (2003) cites European use of the term prior to the 1970s. For example, a citation in Merriam-Webster's 1961 *Third New International Dictionary* includes the following quote by German critic Siegfried Kracauer: "he is the pursued serial murderer." British writer John Brophy also uses the serial murderer in reference to Jack the Ripper in his 1966 book *The Meaning of Murder* (Schechter, 2003).

A search on the Internet also netted some interesting accounts of the term *serial killer*. On one site, the murders by David Berkowitz are said to have resulted in the term *serial killer* (Great Dreams, 2005). Yet other websites indicate that Ted Bundy's killings led to the institution of the term, and others credit the murders committed by Ed Gein. Still another credited the murders of dozens of young boys by John Wayne Gacy as the stimulus for the introduction of the term *serial murder*. Whatever the genesis or the inspiration for the terms *serial killing* and *serial murder*; they are now commonly used by criminologists, criminal justice workers, and the public at large.

SERIAL KILLERS THROUGHOUT HISTORY

As early as the 1400s, Gilles de Rais, a French aristocrat who battled alongside Joan of Arc, is believed to have kidnapped, tortured, raped, and killed as many as 200 young-sters between the ages of 6 and 20. Rais seemed to prefer boys but would kidnap young women if no boys were available. After ten years of sadistic killing, he was brought to trial, where under the threat of torture, he confessed to his heinous acts in detail including ejaculating on the bloodied and tortured bodies of his victims (Bataille, 1991; Gribben, 2005). Rais was sentenced to death, and on October 26, 1440, he was hanged and then burned (Vronsky, 2004).

It may be surprising to find that the next famous serial killer to appear in history is a woman. Countess Elizabeth Báthory was born to one of the most powerful and rich families in Transylvania in 1560. Although she was known to be extremely cruel in torturing her servants, it was not until 1600 that she began to kill. Supposedly, Báthory believed she found the secret to youthful beauty when blood from a servant girl splashed onto her hand. Báthory had the servant girl killed and her blood drained so Báthory could bathe in it. It is reported that with the assistance of her servants, Báthory murdered as many as 650 young women over ten years. Protected by her powerful position in Hungary at the time, it was not until the end of 1610 that Báthory stopped. After a trial early in 1611, Báthory's servants were executed for their role in the killing, and Báthory was only imprisoned because of her noble parentage. Interestingly, she was imprisoned in a small bricked-up room in her own castle, where she died four years later at age 54 in 1614 (Count, 2005; Vronsky, 2004).

BOX 12.3

A Case of Serial Murder in Atlanta

When you read the title of this box, there is a good chance that if you are familiar with well-known cases of serial murder, you thought of Wayne Williams, who is believed to have killed as many as 23 young African American male victims in what has been called the Atlanta child murders. Although the so-called Atlanta child murders took place during 1979 and 1980, more than 70 years before, in 1911 and 1912, another serial killer may have been prowling the city of Atlanta in search of victims. Twenty young African American women were killed in murders that were referred to as "Jack the Ripper" killings in the *Atlanta Journal Constitution*. Vance McLaughlin, a former police officer and professor, who has researched the case of the "Atlanta Ripper," reports that the killer was never captured. Further, McLaughlin reports that it is not clear whether one murderer was responsible for each of the homicides or if a copycat could have been operating as well (Fennessy, 2005).

THE EXTENT OF SERIAL KILLING

The evidence suggests serial killers have existed throughout history, but some believe the number greatly increased during the twentieth century. In the early 1980s after the FBI appeared before the U.S. Senate to acquire more funding to target violent crimes, different media outlets reported there were as many as 5,000 serial killer victims each year in the United States. Although the number of serial murder victims and the number of serial killers is actually unknown, the figure of 5,000 is now believed to be an extreme overexaggeration.

In 1992, the U.S. National Center for the Analysis of Violent Crime (NCAVC) determined that there had been 357 serial killers in the United States during the period from 1960 to 1991. Making it clear that the figure of 5,000 serial victims a year is greatly exaggerated, the NCAVC determined that these 357 killers had killed or were suspected to have killed 3,169 victims (Mitchell, 1997). In a 31-year period, this would work out to an average of 102 victims a year; a number far below the 5,000 victim average per year bandied about in the 1980s. The number of serial killers currently practicing in the United States, so to speak, is a matter of contention. The figure for the United States ranges from a reasonable 35 (Levin & Fox, 1985) to an incredible 500 (Norris, 1988).

Within the United States, California stands out as having several serial killers. Other states known for an abundance of serial killers include Florida, New York, Texas, Illinois, Georgia, and Ohio (Hickey, 2006). Thus region does not appear to be a factor in serial killing as it may in homicide (see Chapters 4 and 7). As always with any data on crime or homicide, it is important to compare not just numbers (known as frequencies) but also to compare rates. When we look at rates of serial murder, Alaska, Delaware, Idaho, Kansas, North Dakota, Rhode Island, South Dakota, Utah, Vermont, and Wyoming lead the nation (Hickey, 2006).

As with other types of homicide, serial killing is not limited to the United States. In fact, research indicates that serial killers have existed in many different countries. Between 1982 and 1991, 58 serial killers are believed to have killed 196 victims in England and Wales (Gresswell & Hollin, 1994). Gresswell and Hollin suggest there may be two serial killers murdering at any one time in England and Wales. In Australia, officials believe there were three serial killer "clusters" between 1989 and 1999 (Mouzos, 2000). These three groups of serial murders are believed to have been committed by Paul Denyar, Ivan Milat, and the Snowtown serial killers, who are a group of four killers who "acted in concert" (Mouzos, 2000: 94). Interestingly, however, these three clusters do not include the case of Kathleen Folbigg, who killed four of her children in Australia between 1989 and 1999. It is likely that the authorities did not know yet of Folbigg's killing when they reported the three clusters between 1989 and 1999. Folbigg, who is now thought to be Australia's worst female serial killer, brings the number to four clusters in Australia during the 1990s (Mandel, 2003).

In 2000, two men were arrested in South Africa where they were to be charged with killing 51 individuals over a three-year period. Most of the 51 victims were women, although some were children and fewer were grown men (BBC News, 2000). These were by no means the first serial killers to be arrested in South Africa. In 1997, Moses Sithole was sentenced to more than 2,400 years of incarceration for 38 murders in South Africa (BBC News, 2000). Research by Brin Hodgkiss (2004) indicates there

---

BOX 12.4

More Deadly Than Jack the Ripper: Dr. Harold Shipman

Jack the Ripper may be better known than Dr. Harold Shipman, but Shipman killed many more people in England than Jack the Ripper. Although convicted of killing 15 of his patients, Dr. Shipman is believed to have killed at least 215 and as many as 260 people during a 23-year period ending in 1998. Shipman used lethal doses of heroin to kill his victims; most of whom were elderly women. At least 171 of those killed by Shipman were women, and it is estimated that he killed 44 men. Although many were elderly, he is believed to have killed patients as young as 41 years old and as old as 97 years. Shipman's crimes were not discovered until he attempted to forge one of his victim's wills. Shipman was sentenced to 15 concurrent life sentences for the 15 murders he was found guilty of committing. In January 2004, Shipman apparently killed himself by hanging in his prison cell (BBC, 2004).

---

have been almost 50 serial killers in South Africa in the past two decades, making South Africa one of the top five countries with the most serial killers.

DEMOGRAPHIC PROFILE OF SERIAL KILLERS

Certainly, there are characteristics shared by most serial killers and factors that are typical of many serial killings. However, if one true statement can be made about serial killers as a group; it is that there are exceptions to the frequently reported facts about serial killers (see Box 12.7). For example, studies of known serial killers indicate that most serial killers are lower-class white males in their late 20s or 30s (Fox & Levin, 2001; Hickey, 2006). For the most part, this is true. However, there are serial killers who are known as outliers. Statistically, they do not fit the typical demographic profile because they are female or nonwhite, or middle or upper class, or they are older than 30 years. And perhaps, most surprisingly, some evidence suggests there have been a few serial killers who were younger than 20 years. Later in this chapter, we discuss serial killers who do not fit the prototypical serial killer, including women serial killers, serial killers who are not white, and serial killers who are outside of the typical age range. In the next sections, we look at the typical victims of serial killers and the methods that serial killers use to kill with the same caveat: There are exceptions to almost every rule.

WHO SERIAL KILLERS KILL

In contrast to the average or typical murder between acquaintances, family members, or friends; serial killers tend to kill victims who are strangers to them (Fox & Levin, 2001). In his study of U.S. serial killers from 1975 to 2004, 91.5% of male serial killers killed at least one stranger (Hickey, 2005). Male serial killers also tend to seek out victims who are not likely to be reported missing or those who are otherwise vulnerable. As a result, serial killers often select people who are treated as throwaways in our society, such as the homeless, runaways, migrants, or prostitutes. Egger (2002) refers to these victims as "less dead" because he says they were "less alive" before they were killed. It may take a while, if ever, for such victims to be reported as missing or for police to find a link between their deaths (Egger, 1984; Jenkins, 1993). Gary Ridgeway, the "Green River Killer," for example, said he killed prostitutes because he thought he could kill them without getting caught (Hickey, 2006). Sadly, Ridgeway was right; it was not until early in the twenty-first century that he was arrested and convicted for the homicides he first began committing in the early 1980s. Children, women, and gay men may also be sought out by male serial killers to feed their sexual fantasies or simply because the serial killers believe they will be easy to overpower and control (Jenkins, 1993; Mitchell, 1997).

A comparison between serial murderers and murderers who killed only one victim found that serial murders were more likely to kill women than men. In comparison to other murderers, serial murders were also more likely to kill strangers and less likely to kill family members and acquaintances. Hickey (2006) reported that young women

---

BOX 12.5

Femicide and Violence Against Prostitutes

Serial killers are definitely very rare. However, they are not necessarily unusual among violent men in terms of victim selection. Official statistics indicate that males are more likely to be the victims of violence (see Chapter 7 on confrontational homicide). However, much research suggests there are a significant number of men who victimize women in a variety of ways. In fact, the originators of the term *femicide*, Caputi and Russel (1992), defined the term as being "on the extreme end of a continuum of antifemale terror that includes a wide variety of verbal and physical abuse, such as rape, torture, sexual slavery (particularly in prostitution), incestuous and extrafamilial child sexual abuse, physical and emotional battery, sexual harassment" (p.1 on website), and their list continues. *Femicide*, in more common usage, has come to be known as the killing of women because they are women. Often, but not always, men who set out to harm women prey on women who work as prostitutes. It is likely that you know of examples among serial killers, such as the Green River killer Gary Ridgway, pig farmer Robert Pickton, or Maury Travis. These serial killers are not the only men to prey on prostitutes. Research about violence against prostitutes including my own research about British prostitutes who work indoors indicates that women who work in the sex industry are often attacked by men who appear to seek them out as victims (Davies & Evans, 2004). Sex workers, however, are not the only victims of femicide and other misogynist violence, as should be clear from Caputi and Russel's definition of femicide.

who were alone and children account for most of the strangers sought out by serial killers. Friends and neighbors were the most common acquaintance victims, although waitresses and prostitutes were also commonly reported acquaintance victims. Finally, in the family category, serial murderers were most likely to kill their own children and their spouses. Hickey (2006) also reported that young and middle-age adults were most often targeted by serial murderers, although he found that serial offenders are increasingly seeking out the elderly as victims. Of course, the number of elderly in the United States and other countries is also increasing as the population ages.

Female serial killers, in contrast to male killers, commonly kill people they know, such as their own children, their spouses, and elderly or young people in their care (Kelleher & Kelleher, 1998). Blanche Moore of North Carolina, for example, poisoned two of her husbands, a lover, her mother-in-law, and her father between 1966 and 1989 (Kelleher & Kelleher, 1998). Still, as noted earlier, there are exceptions to every so-called rule about serial killers. Of 64 serial killers studied by Hickey (2006), 25% killed only strangers and 31% reportedly killed at least one stranger. Just over half (53%) of the female serial killers studied by Hickey killed only family members or acquaintances; 69% or just over two thirds killed only those known to them.

Serial killers kill between 2 or 3 to as many as 44 or more victims depending on how we define serial killing. However, the average number of victims killed by each serial killer—whether female or male—falls in the 7 to 12 range, according to Hickey (2005). Sometimes, especially with historical cases, it is difficult to determine just how many victims have fallen to any one serial killer.

HOW SERIAL KILLERS KILL

Whereas the majority of murder victims in the United States die of gunshot wounds, those who are killed by serial killers are more likely to be killed in other ways. Male serial killers tend to strangle their victims; however, male serial killers also have beaten, shot, or injected their victims to kill them. Fox and Levin (2001) argue that many male serial killers do not use a gun because it would take away part of the pleasure for the killer. Many serial killers kill for the feeling of power or sadistic pleasure they get from torturing another and taking his or, more often, her life. Torturing one's victims before killing them appears to be common among male serial killers and more common among serial killers who kill with another in what has come to be known as serial killing teams (Fox & Levin, 2001). These serial killing teams, such as Kenneth Bianchi and Angelo Buono (the Hillside stranglers), are believed to make up as many as 20% of all serial killers (Fox & Levin, 2001).

Female serial killers may also commonly kill for the feelings of power it gives them. However, their methods are often different than those employed by their male counterparts. Like the ladies in Joseph Kesselring's *Arsenic and Old Lace* and Blanche Moore mentioned earlier, female serial killers often use poison to end their victims' lives. Like male serial killers, however, female serial killers have used a variety of methods to complete their murders. Women who kill alone have shot, suffocated, and used lethal injections to kill their victims (Kelleher & Kelleher, 1998). When women

---

BOX 12.6

Aileen Wuornos: The First Real Female Serial Killer?

Because it is a common belief among law enforcement personnel that serial killers stalk and then sexually attack and murder their victims, many individuals are under the mistaken belief that there are no female serial killers. In a lecture in 2004, for example, former FBI agent Robert Ressler told the audience that female serial killers do not exist. If we define serial killers as those who kill for some type of sexual gratification, Ressler is likely correct. But if we use a definition that focuses on more than one victim being killed over time, then clearly there have been female serial killers even before Aileen Wuornos was discovered in 1991.

When Wuornos first made the news, however, it was not uncommon to hear her referred to as the first female serial killer. Because she is believed to have killed seven victims who were believed to be strangers to her before she killed them and perhaps because her victims were often left partially clothed in the woods, she was touted as the first female serial killer. Before Wuornos, there does not appear to have been a woman who killed several strangers by herself, in the open by shooting them, with a cooling-off period in between each killing. For the first time in history, it seemed that we had a woman in the United States who was killing strangers in cold blood in much the same way as the Son of Sam had in the 1970s.

---

and men kill together in a serial killing team, they tend to operate more like male serial killers than like female serial killers. In these teams, torture is again more likely than when women kill by themselves. Paul Bernardo and Karla Homolka, a husband-and-wife serial killing team in Canada, for example, raped and murdered three young women together including Karla Homolka's sister.

RACE AND SERIAL KILLERS

The research on serial killers indicates that despite the myth that African Americans are not serial killers, there are definitely African Americans who kill serially. Furthermore, Egger's (2006) research suggests that at least since the 1980s, African Americans are slightly overrepresented among serial killers. Egger found that despite making up about 17% of the U.S. population, 25% of his sample of serial killers who killed between 1980 and 2005 are African American. Although underrepresented as related to the overall U.S. population, there are also Asian and Latino serial killers. Egger (2006), for example, reports that eight tenths of his sample of serial killers are Asian and just over 7% are Latino. Among female serial killers, however, according to Hickey (2006), whites appear to be overrepresented and African Americans, Latinas, Native Americans, and Asians are underrepresented. In Hickey's study of 64 female serial killers, nearly all (93%) were white, and none were Asian or Latina. Only 7% were African American.

It is more recently that criminologists have noted that African Americans are not underrepresented among serial killers. Jenkins (1993) suggested that serial murder by African Americans may be underreported because of law enforcement practices. Historically, Jenkins argues that racism may explain the underreporting of serial murder. Because victimization is often intraracial, it is likely that African American serial killers kill other African Americans. Institutionalized and individual racism has led police to take cases involving African American victims less seriously, and thus serial patterns may go unnoticed and serial killers may roam free. Additionally, because law enforcers are aware that crimes are often intraracial, they may fail to consider an African American when attempting to find a killer who appears to be targeting victims who are not African American (and vice versa). Police in Louisiana, for example, were seeking a white man for several murders in the Baton Rouge area before a DNA test revealed that the offender was African American. Eventually Derrick Todd Lee was arrested and found guilty (*USA Today*, 2003).

CHILD SERIAL KILLERS

It is extremely rare for a serial killer to be under the age of 20. Jeffrey Dahmer, however, was 18 years old when he killed his first victim in Ohio. As noted throughout this chapter, there is an exception to almost every so-called fact known about serial killers. Although it is often reported that serial killers are most often in their 30s, there are two well-known examples of youngsters who have killed serially. However, it may be surprising that these are not recent cases. First, in 1870s Boston, Jesse Pomeroy was arrested at the young age of 14 for torturing and murdering children. Treated with leniency (he was not sentenced to death), Pomeroy spent years locked in solitary confinement before being released to the general population of inmates (Schechter, 2000). During the twentieth century, 10-year-old Mary Flora Bell of England killed two young boys in two separate incidents spaced months apart in 1968. She was sentenced to life detention but was eventually released once she reached adulthood (Harding, 1998).

BOX 12.7
Serial Killer Myths

Many myths exist about serial killers and serial murders. In his 2006 book *Serial Murderers and Their Victims*, Eric Hickey lists several myths about serial killers. Although he notes some of these myths are true for some serial killers, they are certainly not true of all serial killers. The myths he lists are as follows:

1. Serial killers are all male.
2. Serial killers are white.
3. Serial killers kill for sexual thrills.

continued

> 4. Serial killers are very intelligent.
> 5. Serial killers are insane.
> 6. Serial killers are highly mobile.
> 7. Serial killers operate alone.
> 8. Serial killers kill dozens of victims.
> 9. Serial killers were abused as children.
> 10. Serial killers beat, stab, strangle, or torture their victims.
>
> As Hickey argues, these are myths. They apply to some serial killers but not to others. For each one of these myths, there are dozens of exceptions. If you try, you can probably think of an exception to each of these myths yourself. For example, Aileen Wuornos was female; Coral Eugene Watts is African American, and Diana Lumbrera appears to have killed for insurance money. See if you can find an exception or two to the other myths that Hickey discussed.

TYPES OF SERIAL MURDERERS

Since the 1980s, criminologists have made several attempts to classify serial killers. Some of these classifications were developed to help law enforcement authorities detect and apprehend serial killers; others are more academic in providing descriptions of typical categories of such killers. The most common classification for serial killers is one based on the crime scene evidence developed by two FBI agents.

Roy Hazelwood and John Douglas, members of the FBI Behavioral Science unit, first made the distinction between *organized* and *disorganized* criminal behavior in 1980 in an FBI publication. Organized crime scenes suggest that the killer carefully planned and executed the murder in contrast to the disorganized scene where the killing appears to have been a spontaneous and chaotic act. Whereas the organized killer is likely to exercise power over the victim by using restraints and raping or torturing their victim while he or she is alive, the disorganized killer is more likely to perform sexual acts on the victim after death and leave evidence of weapons at the scene. Mitchell (1997) notes that this organized/disorganized distinction may better fit along a continuum with serial killers becoming more disorganized as their criminal career advances.

Holmes and DeBurger (1988) developed a typology that relies on factors other than crime scene evidence. They base their four-category typology, the visionary, the missionary, the hedonistic, and the power and control serial killer, on the killer's motives and on characteristics of the victims:

1. Visionary: Like the Son of Sam killer David Berkowitz who killed because barking dogs told him to, these killers kill because of visions that are believed to be the result of some type of psychosis.
2. Missionary: These offenders, who are not believed to be suffering from any type of psychosis, kill to do away with certain types of people in the world

such as prostitutes or homosexuals. Robert "Willie" Pickton, a pig farmer who is suspected of killing dozens of prostitutes and feeding them to his pigs, may be a missionary killer.

3. Hedonistic: This type of serial killer murders for the satisfaction obtained from the process of killing. Holmes and DeBurger (1988) describe three sub-types of hedonistic serial killers. First, there are lust murderers who kill for sexual pleasure. Otherwise known as erotophonophilia, sexual murder often involves the brutal torture for the sadistic pleasure of the offender (Hickey, 2006). Second are the thrill-oriented killers, who murder for excitement and may also torture or mutilate their victims. Third, comfort-oriented killers kill for the benefits they receive from killing, such as financial gain or psychological pleasure (Holmes & DeBurger, 1988; Mitchell, 1997).

4. Power and control: This type of killer gains great pleasure from the absolute power and control he has over his victims. Satisfaction may come from making his victims squirm. As such, he may torture or sexually mutilate his victims, not for his sexual pleasure but as a way to dominate his victim (Hickey, 2006; Holmes & DeBurger, 1988; Mitchell, 1997).

Hickey (2006) categorized serial killers in terms of their geographic mobility. Traveling serial killers, such as Theodore Bundy who killed in both Washington and Florida, commit murders in several states as they travel or move from location to location. Local serial killers stay in one geographic region as they commit their murders; however, they may cross jurisdictional boundaries, which may make it more difficult for authorities to realize a serial killer is in their midst. For example, Reynaldo Rivera killed in one geographic area close to his home but because he lived on the border of South Carolina and Georgia, he killed women in both states. Place-specific serial killers kill in one specific site such as at their home or in their workplace. Nurse Charles Cullen, who killed victims in the nursing homes and hospitals where he worked, would fit the definition of a place-specific serial killer (Usborne, 2003).

Whereas some experts on serial killers only consider those who have a sexual motive to be true serial killers, Mitchell (1997) presents a typology that recognizes what he calls a "criminality dimension" among serial killers (p. 7). According to Mitchell, there are the *strictly amateur* killers for which serial murder is their only crime. There are *killer-amateurs* who commit other crimes more often than murder, and they keep their other crimes separate from the murders. *Career criminals who kill* are those that kill but only as part of their other criminal activity, such as within a robbery or to make a point in the world of illegal drugs. Finally, *professional killers* are those who kill for pay (Mitchell, 1997).

Mitchell's typology is valuable because of the addition of what he calls a "criminal dimension" (Mitchell, 1997). However, like the other typologies in this chapter, the categories are not mutually exclusive. An individual serial killer could fit in more than one category. Richard Kuklinski, for example, who admitted in a 1992 HBO film to murdering over 100 persons, appears to be both a professional killer and a career criminal who kills. He was known as a Gambino mob enforcer who killed for pay. But he also killed in the commission of robberies. Kuklinski used a variety of methods to kill his victims, including strangling, poisoning, shooting, and even blowing up one man with a grenade. He was known as the "iceman" because he froze the body of a Pennsylvania businessman he killed to make the time of death confusing for the police. Kuklinski, who died at age 70 early in March 2006, was serving consecutive life sentences for killing two men who worked with him in a robbery ring (Markos & Tronconce, 2006).

Finally, Keppel and Walter (1999) focused on sexual serial homicide in suggesting a four-part typology that included power-assertive, power-reassurance, anger-retaliatory, and anger-excitation. In power-assertive, the rape is planned but the murder is not. The offender, motivated by holding power over the victim, becomes increasingly aggressive to control the victim. The power-reassurance rapist murderer is also motivated by power and plans the rape but not the murder. However, during the rape, the offender is acting out a fantasy and wants reassurance from his victims. When he does not receive reassurance, he kills his victim. An anger-retaliatory rape-murderer, acting out of anger, plans both the rape and murder. He attacks a symbolic victim to seek revenge. Finally, murderers in the anger-excitation category plan both the murder and rape. They, too, are driven by anger. However, they often torture their victim and perhaps mutilate the victim to feed their fantasies (Keppel & Walter, 1999).

BOX 12.8

Serial Sexual Homicide in Juárez, Mexico

Since 1993, an offender or a group of offenders have raped, mutilated, and murdered approximately 400 women in the Mexican city of Juárez. Another 70 women from the U.S. town across the Rio Grande from Juárez are missing as well. Family members and others who know of the missing and dead women are frustrated and angry. Many suspect that the murders remain unsolved because of police complicity. Others point fingers at multinational corporations along the border, not for committing the murders but for doing nothing to prevent them. Since the North American Free Trade Agreement (NAFTA) permitted the multinationals to move into Mexico to take advantage of cheap labor in 1993, sweatshops known as *maquiladoras* have helped quadruple the population of Juárez to more than 1 million. Over 80% of the maquiladoras employ women, and many of these women live alone. The wages are low and the women work long hours. Many of the murdered women have been abducted as they walked the unlit streets in the dark on their way to or from work. The well-known companies who run the maquiladoras have done little to make the streets to their sweatshops safer. Some have suggested that the companies should provide better transportation, but so far little has been done to try to prevent the murders. Various suspects have been arrested, but the killings have continued. The victims have much in common: Most are poor, young, and they have long hair, and most importantly, their murders remain an unsolved mystery (Graham, 2005).

TYPES OF FEMALE SERIAL KILLERS

Kelleher and Kelleher (1998) argue that female serial killers are so different from male serial killers that the standard serial killer typologies fail to categorize female serial killers adequately. As a result, Kelleher and Kelleher (1998) provide a nine-category typology particular to female serial killers, as follows:

1. *Black widows* are named after the arachnids that devour their own mates following coitus. This female killer, who is often intelligent and manipulative, methodically plans and kills one individual after another, often with many years in between murders. They may kill their spouses, other family members, or others whose trust they have gained. Poison is often their weapon of choice because it is likely to go undetected. This category is quite broad and may overlap with other categories such as profit for crime and revenge. There are many examples of women who fit in this category, including Diana Lumbrera who murdered six of her own children between 1977 and 1990. She earned as much as $5,000 from insurance policies she had on each child. Finally in 1986, after killing her 4-year-old son José, medical authorities encouraged the police to investigate José's death. In 1990, Lumbrera was convicted for the murders of her first three children. She then pleaded guilty to the death of her other children, which had occurred in other jurisdictions. She was sentenced to several life sentences (Kelleher & Kelleher, 1998). According to the Texas Department of Criminal Justice website, Lumbrera is eligible for parole in 2013. But there is no indication that she will be released at this time (TDCJ, 2001).

2. *Angels of death* are those women (and several men could fit in this category as well) who kill individuals in their care or those who rely on them for medical attention. Often these killers work in the medical profession as nurses or nurse assistants. According to Kelleher and Kelleher, these women kill for a variety of reasons. Like the power and control serial killer, angels of death may kill out of a compulsion to control those under their care. Others may kill because of psychological issues such as Münchhausen syndrome by proxy (see Chapter 10). Often angels of death commit their crime by giving their victims a lethal injection of insulin, potassium, or potassium chloride. Genene Jones killed at two different Texas hospitals in the early 1980s. She was subpoenaed for grand jury hearings for nearly 50 mysterious death cases involving children before being indicted and convicted of several murders. Jones was sentenced to 99 years in prison (Kelleher & Kelleher, 1998). She has been eligible for parole since 1990, although according to the Texas Department of Criminal Justice website, she is likely to be incarcerated until at least 2017 (TDCJ, 2006).

3. The third category of female serial killer, the *sexual predator*, is the most controversial in the Kelleher typology. They define the sexual predator as "a woman who systematically murders others in what are known to be clear acts of sexual homicide. The motive for these murders must be sexual in nature" (Kelleher & Kelleher, 1998: 11). Although women like Karla Homolka, who

killed with her husband Paul Bernardo, may fit this category, Kelleher and Kelleher explain that this category is so rare that only one woman in the United States fits this category without being part of a killing team: Aileen Wuornos. However, Kelleher and Kelleher provide no evidence to suggest that Wuornos's crimes were sexual. At the time of the crimes, she was working as a prostitute, and most of her victims were her customers. However, no evidence suggests the murders were sexual. Kelleher and Kelleher (1998: 75–76) say the following about the murders Wuornos committed:

> [T]he murders were not motivated by a drive for bizarre sexual satisfaction as is often the case with male serial killers. Rather, Wuornos lashed out against her victims in a rage that originated in decades of abusive and debilitating encounters with men that began in her early childhood.

Thus even Kelleher and Kelleher (1998) fail to prove or really even suggest that Wuornos was a sexual predator. Instead, she appears to fit in the category of *profit for crime*. Further, if we were to believe Wuornos's account of what happened, she was defending herself.

4. The *revenge serial killer* kills for revenge. This motive is much more typical in a crime of passion as compared to a serial killing because serial killers, by definition, have downtime between killings. However, Georgia native Martha Ann Johnson, who killed four of her children over five years, appears to have killed for revenge. She killed at least two of her children by smothering them as a way to punish her husband after arguments with him (Kelleher & Kelleher, 1998). As a result, she is a quintessential example of revenge serial killer.

5. To be placed into the Kelleher category of *profit for crime*, Kelleher and Kelleher (1998) stipulated that a female serial killer must clearly murder to profit, and they must act alone and seek out nonfamily members. Police dug up seven bodies in Dorothea Puente's backyard. She was eventually sentenced to life in prison for the death of three of her victims. Prosecutors argued that she killed elderly boarders for their social security funds.

6. *Team killers* are women who kill with a partner. It is unlikely that they would have killed alone. It is only in this category where there are examples of women killing as sexual predators. For any British person, the infamous Moors murders are likely to come to mind when one thinks of horrendous serial killers. Myra Hindley and Ian Brady murdered at least five children younger than 17 years old as part of their sexual life together.

7. Women who belong in the *question of sanity* category are those for whom the killing seems to be random, or they are found to be legitimately insane. Nora Kelly, also known as Jane Toppan, is an example of a question of sanity serial killer. She was arrested in Massachusetts in 1901 for killing 31 patients. Found insane, she spent the remainder of her life in a Massachusetts state asylum (Olmstead, 2000).

8. *Unexplained* is a somewhat of a leftover or catch-all category for women who kill for no clear reason. With the arrest of Juana Barraza, a onetime professional wrestler, the police in Mexico City believe they have finally caught

> ## BOX 12.9
> ### Russia's Hannibal Lecter
>
> On October 14, 1992, Andrei Chikatilo was convicted of murdering 52 peo-
> ple. Chikatilo, who was known as the "Forest Strip Killer," appeared to be
> a real-life Hannibal Lecter. Chikatilo lured women and children to a
> wooded area where he killed them. He then dismembered their bodies
> and ate some of their remains. In all, he killed 21 boys, 14 girls, and 17
> women between 1978 and 1990 in Rostov-on-Don and other cities in
> Russia. Although convicted of 52 murders, Chikatilo confessed to more
> during his trial. Chikatilo was sentenced to death for these crimes and exe-
> cuted in 1994. Chikatilo was the second man sentenced to death for his
> crimes. Another man who was not responsible for the killings was exe-
> cuted by Russian authorities who tried to stop the horrible killings quickly
> and quietly (*Columbus Dispatch*, 1992a, 1992b).

mataviejitas, the "little old lady killer." As I write this chapter, Barraza, who is believed to have killed as many as 24 elderly women since 2003, belongs in the category of unexplained. Barraza apparently posed as a social worker to gain entry into the women's houses where she strangled them and took an item as a trophy of her killing. Barraza's motive, however, is not apparent. The police were slow to find Barraza partly because they believed the killer to be a man dressed as a woman. Witnesses had described a person in a skirt, but the crime scene evidence suggested the killer was very strong (Tuckman, 2005; *U.S. Today*, 2006).

9. The *unsolved category* exists for the cases of serial killing that might possibly be committed by a woman but the case is yet unsolved.

THEORIES ABOUT SERIAL KILLERS

In addition to the theories about homicide included in Chapters 5 and 6, some criminologists have focused on explaining serial killers in particular. Many scholars who have attempted to explain why serial killers kill have explored the backgrounds of serial killers. As a result, we know that many serial killers did not grow up in nuclear families. Many grew up in homes with only one parent because of divorce, death, or simply because their parents never married. In addition, it has been noted that many serial killers have been adopted (Keeney & Heide, 1994). Additionally, criminologists who have studied the childhoods of serial killers have found that many of them were victims of abuse or neglect and several had severe head injuries while growing up. Furthermore, several of those known to have killed serially had parents who were addicted to drugs including alcohol (Hickey, 2006; Keeney & Heide, 1994; Mitchell, 1997).

Anyone who studies serial killers is also aware that the MacDonald triad appears to have been quite common in the childhood histories of serial killers. The MacDonald triad is named after J. M. MacDonald, who first "discovered" that many sadistic killers had three behaviors in common as children: fire setting, torturing animals, and bedwetting (otherwise known as enuresis) (Keeney & Heide, 1994; Mitchell, 1997).

Although all of this information about the childhoods of serial killers is interesting to many of us, it fails to explain why serial killers kill. Sadly, hundreds of thousands of individuals were abused and neglected while they were growing up. Even more of us were raised by single parents for one reason or another or had to deal with a parent's alcohol or drug abuse while growing up. Yet most of us have not become serial killers. In fact, the vast majority of adults who suffered from imperfect childhoods have not become serial killers. If we did, far more serial killers would be roaming the streets throughout the world. Furthermore, scientists have no idea how many individuals have had the symptoms of the MacDonald triad during childhood or how many of us have suffered severe head injuries. Even if these are common among serial killers, they are not present in the histories of all serial killers, and they are not unheard of among kind caring adults who have never killed or injured anyone. Thus we have to be very careful in reaching any conclusions about what causes serial killing—even when we do good research.

As noted by Mitchell (1997) and Robinson (2004), a theory that explains any human behavior by incorporating only a psychological or biological or sociological explanation is very likely to come up short. As a result, in all likelihood, the best theories for explaining serial killings are likely to be integrated theories that employ the collective wisdom of many scientific disciplines. This is a challenge, however, for scientists in different disciplines are often weary of one another. Cooperation across disciplines—especially social and natural sciences—is rare (Mitchell, 1997).

Nevertheless, in his thesis, Mitchell (1997) proposed an integrated model to explain serial killing. In his model he posits that the sociocultural environment and one's home situation interact with biological factors such as a predisposition to violence to cause what he calls "diathesis-stress syndrome" (Mitchell, 1997: 34). This syndrome leads to psychological problems, possibly including cognitive difficulties or even psychiatric illnesses. Life stressors that many of us manage to deal with, such as the death of a family member or rejection by someone we love or are attracted to, may lead to the commission of a homicide by the individual with diathesis-stress syndrome. The killing brings on feelings of relief in the face of the life stressors for the would-be serial killer. He or she may be able to continue to relive the killing in his or her mind to manage any new buildup of stress. But eventually, stressors are likely to lead him or her to kill again and again as the cycle continues until something stops it (Mitchell, 1997).

Mitchell's 1997 theory is valuable because it provides an example of an integrated model that employs valuable insights from various academic disciplines. For now, however, it is untested. Perhaps, you or your professor will develop a way to test Mitchell's model and your research will appear in future editions of this text. More importantly, however, maybe this research will help us make progress in finding ways to deal with and perhaps prevent serial killers in the United States and other countries around the world.

CRIMINAL JUSTICE PROCESSING: WHAT HAPPENS TO SERIAL KILLERS IN COURT?

For now, we mostly deal with convicted serial killers by locking them up and/or sentencing them to death. Although serial killers such as Charles Manson and his followers come before the parole board every few years, most serial killers are sentenced to death or to life in prison without the opportunity for parole. Hickey (2005) found that 29% of the 366 male serial killers in his study were sentenced to death and 43% were sentenced to prison. Despite what we may expect, only 3% of those in Hickey's study were confined to a mental institution. Others had committed suicide or their cases were pending. Once sentenced, some, like Jeffrey Dahmer, were killed in prison by other prisoners; others died of natural causes. Most convicted male serial killers, according to Hickey, will in all likelihood spend the rest of their lives in prison or in a psychiatric institution.

In contrast to male serial killers, only 19% of convicted female serial killers were sentenced to death, and very few have actually been put to death. Nearly two thirds (66%) were sentenced to prison, and 5% were confined to a psychiatric hospital. It appears that males who kill serially are treated more harshly than females who kill serially. However, note that to be able to make any sound conclusions on this issue, one would have to control for factors such as numbers of victims killed and how the killing was done. As noted in this chapter, male serial killers are more likely than are female serial killers to torture their victims. Apparent differences between the dispositions of male and female serial killers may be explained by factors other than biases of the courts and juries to either men or women.

SUMMARY

This chapter began by discussing the intense interest serial killers foment in U.S. society. After a discussion of the various definitions of serial killing, it was noted that the definition used that appears to be the most recent standard among criminologists in defining a serial killer is one who kills at least two victims over time with a cooling-off period in between killings. A brief review of historical cases of serial murder was presented to make the point that although the concept may be a twentieth-century invention, the actuality of serial killing has existed throughout history. Even though serial killing has existed for years, the extent of serial killing remains unknown. However, the different figures noted by experts on the extent of serial killing are discussed before moving on to a section about what else is apparently "known" about serial killers and serial murder. With the caveat that there is an exception to nearly every so-called fact about serial killers, demographic profiles of serial killers, their victims, their methods, the debunking of the myth of the white serial killer, and the existence of children who have killed serially are discussed. Many criminologists have posited typologies of serial killers, and some of the more common typologies, including Kelleher and Kelleher's typology of female serial killers, were presented. Finally, the chapter ended with ideas about what may cause serial killers to kill and a section on what happens to those convicted of serial killing.

CHAPTER QUESTIONS

1. What evidence does this chapter provide to demonstrate the great fascination with serial killers? What, if anything, was left out?
2. How is serial murder different from spree murder and mass murder?
3. What definition of serial killing is used in this text and why?
4. The two historical serial killers discussed appear to be much wealthier than many of the serial killers we hear about today. What might explain this difference? Does it have to do with who is apprehended or who is included in history or something else?
5. What might be the disadvantages and advantages of exaggerated numbers of serial killers for law enforcement?
6. How might we best determine how many serial killers exist at any one time?
7. Discuss whether there is an accurate "serial killer profile."
8. What do we know about the demographics of serial killers?
9. Who do serial killers kill and why?
10. How do serial killers kill?
11. Why is there a common belief that serial killers are white males?
12. Can children be serial killers?
13. What is meant by organized and disorganized criminal behavior?
14. List and explain Holmes and DeBurger's four categories of serial killers.
15. How has Hickey categorized serial killers?
16. Mitchell goes beyond the assumption of sexual serial murder in his typology. What are the four types of serial killers included in his typology?
17. Kelleher and Kelleher have nine types of female serial killers in their typology. List each type.
18. Discuss whether you agree with the author's discussion about Kelleher and Kelleher's third category of *sexual predator* as relevant for female serial killers.
19. Discuss the factors found to be common in the childhood of serial killers, and explain whether you believe they are good predictors of serial murder.
20. What happens to serial killers who are convicted?

REFERENCES

Bataille, George. 1991. *Trial of Gilles De Rais*. Richard Robinson (Trans.). Los Angeles: Amok Books.

BBC News. 2000, July 5. "SA 'Serial Killers' Face 51 Charges." Retrieved March 16, 2006, from http://news.bbc.co.uk/1/hi/world/africa/820680.stm

BBC News. 2004, January 13. "Harold Shipman Found Dead in Cell." Retrieved March 28, 2006, from http://news.bbc.co.uk/1/hi/uk/3391871.stm

Brantley, Alan C., and Robert H. Kosky Jr. 2005. "Serial Murder in the Netherlands A Look at Motivation, Behavior, and Characteristics." *FBI Law Enforcement Bulletin*, 74(1): 26–32.

Caputi, Jane, and Diana E. H. Russell. 1992. "Femicide: Speaking the Unspeakable." In Jill Radford and Diana E. H. Russell, eds., *Femicide: The Politics of Woman Killing*. New York: Twayne Publishers. Accessed online at http://www.dianarussell.com/femicide.html

Columbus Dispatch. 1992a. October 15. "World's Worst Serial Killer Convicted," p. 2A.

Columbus Dispatch. 1992b, October 16. "Serial Killer to Be Executed," p. 2A.

Count, Carpathian Dark. 2005. Elizabeth Báthory Website. Retrieved October 16, 2005, from http://bloodbath.host.sk/elizabethbathory

Davies, Kim, and Lorraine Evans. 2004. "Skirting Danger and Sharing Connections: Internet Postings by British Escorts." Paper presented at the 2004 American Sociological Association meeting, August, San Francisco, CA.

Egger, Steven A. 1984. "A Working Definition of Serial Murder and the Reduction of Linkage Blindness." *Journal of Police Science and Administration,* 12: 348–57.

Egger, Steven A. 1998. *The Killers Among Us.* Upper Saddle River, NJ: Prentice Hall.

Egger, Steven. 2002. *The Killers Among Us.* Upper Saddle River, NJ: Prentice Hall.

Egger, Steven. 2006, March 2. "The Myth of the White Serial Killer." Presented at the 43rd Annual Meeting of the Academy of Criminal Justice Sciences.

Fennessy, Steve. 2005, October 27. "Atlanta's Jack the Ripper." *Atlanta Creative Loafing, pp. 34–43.*

Fox, James Alan, and Jack Levin. 1999. "Serial Murder: Popular Myths and Empirical Realities." In M. Dwayne Smith and Margaret A. Zahn, eds., *Homicide: A Sourcebook of Social Research.* Thousand Oaks, CA: Sage.

Fox, James Alan, and Jack Levin. 2001. *The Will to Kill: Making Sense of Senseless Murder.* Boston: Allyn & Bacon.

Graham, Caroline. 2005, November 12. *Mail on Sunday.* "In Most Cases a Family Member Is Responsible for the Death of a Woman. No More Questions. Goodbye." Retrieved March 25, 2006, using LexisNexis.

Great Dreams. 2005. Serial killers website. Retrieved November 28, 2005, from http://www.greatdreams.com/serial-killer.htm

Gresswell, David M., and Clive R. Hollin. 1994. "Multiple Murder: A Review." *British Journal of Criminology,* 34(1): 1–14.

Gribben, Mark. 2005. *Gilles de Rais.* Retrieved October 9, 2005, from www.crimelibrary.com

Harding, Luke. 1998, April 30. "Hounding of Mary Bell: Child Killer Forced into Hiding After Tabloids Track Her Down." *Guarding Unlimited Online.* Retrieved March 27, 2006, from http://www.guardian.co.uk/child/story/0,7369,960690,00.html

Hickey, Eric W. 1991. *Serial Murderers and Their Victims.* Belmont, California: Brooks/Cole Publishing Company.

Hickey, Eric W. 2005. *Serial Murderers and Their Victims,* 3rd Edition. Belmont, California: Wadsworth Publishing.

Hickey, Eric W. 2006. *Serial Murderers and Their Victims.* Belmont, CA: Thomson.

Holmes, Ronald M., and James DeBurger. 1988. *Serial murder: Studies in crime, law and justice, Vol. 2.* Newbury Park, CA: Sage.

Holmes, Ronald M., and Stephen T. Holmes, eds. 1998. *Contemporary Perspectives on Serial Murder.* Thousand Oaks, CA: Sage Publications.

Hodgkiss, Brin. 2004. "Lessons from Serial Murder in South Africa." *Journal of Investigative Psychology and Offender Profiling,* 1: 67–94.

Jarvis, John. 2006, March 2. Discussion session at the Academy of Criminal Justice Sciences meeting, Baltimore, MD.

Jenkins, Philip. 1993. "Chance or Choice? The Selection of Serial Murder Victims." In Anna Victoria Wilson, ed., *Homicide: The Victim/Offender Connection.* Cincinnati: Anderson.

Keeney, Belea T., and Kathleen M. Heide. 1994. "Gender Differences in Serial Murderers: A Preliminary Analysis." *Journal of Interpersonal Violence,* 9(3): 383–398.

Kelleher, Michael D., and C. L. Kelleher. 1998. *Murder Most Rare: The Female Serial Killer,* Westport, CT: Praeger.

Keppel, Robert D., and Richard Walter. 1999. "Profiling Killers: A Revised Classification Model for Understanding Sexual Murder." *International Journal of Offender Therapy and Comparative Criminology,* 43(4): 417–437.

Levin, Jack & James A. Fox. 1985. *Mass Murder: America's Growing Menace.* New York, NY: Plenum Press.

Lucero, Carla. 2004. "*Wuornos*, a Tragic Love Story of Operatic Proportions." Retrieved October 10, 2005, on www.wuornos.org

Mandel, Michele. 2003, May 23. "Murder in the Nursery: Australian Mom Killed Her 4 Babies." *Toronto Sun.* Retrieved March 17, 2006, from http://www.canadiancrc.com/articles /Toronto_Sun_Murder_in_the_nursery_23MAY03.htm

Markos, Kibret, and Tom Tronconce. 2006, March 7. "Iceman Dead; Hit Man Richard Kuklinski, 70, Claimed 100 Victims; Officials Now Dropping Charges Against Gravano in Cop's Killing." *The Record.* Retrieved March 25, 2006, on LexisNexis (2006–03–07).

Mitchell, Edward W. 1997. *The Aetiology of Serial Murder: Towards an Integrated Model.* Master's thesis, University of Cambridge, UK.

Mouzos, Jenny. 2000. *Homicidal Encounters: A Study of Homicide in Australia, 1989–1999.* Canberra: Australian Institute of Criminology.

Norris, Joel. 1988. *Serial Killers: The Growing. Menace,* New York: Doubleday.

Olmstead, J. Papi. 2000. *Chemical Balance Website E-Book for May 2000.* Retrieved March 25, 2006, from www.chemicalbalance.com/website_e_book.htm

Robinson, Matthew. 2004. *Why Crime? An Integrated Systems Theory of Antisocial Behavior.* Upper Saddle River, NJ: Prentice Hall.

Rule, Ann. 2004. *Green River, Running Red: The Real Story of the Green River Killer—America's Deadliest Serial Murderer.* New York: Free Press.

Schechter, Harold. 2000. *Fiend: The Shocking True Story of America's Youngest Serial Killer.* New York: Pocket Books.

Schechter, Harold. 2003. *The Serial Killer Files.* New York: Ballantine Books.

Texas Department of Criminal Justice (TDCJ). 2006. TDCJ Website. Accessed March 26, 2006, from http://168.51.178.33/webapp/TDCJ/index2.htm

Tuckman, Jo. 2005, November 21. "'Old Lady Killer' Set to Strike Again." *The Guardian.* Retrieved March 25, 2006, from http://www.guardian.co.uk/international/story /0,,1647163,00.html

USA Today. 2003, June 5. "DNA Test Showing Ancestry May Have Helped La. Search." Retrieved March 26, 2006, from http://www.usatoday.com/tech/news/techinnovations /2003–06–05-dna-ancestry_x.htm

USA Today. 2006, January 26. "Police Nab Two in Serial Killings Case." USA Today.com. Retrieved March 25, 2006, from http://www.usatoday.com/news/world/2006–01–26-mexico-serial-killer_x.htm.

Usborne, David. 2003. "Former US Nurse Admits Hospital Serial Killings," *The Independent* Dec 16, 2003. Retrieved June 27, 2007 from http://findarticles.com/p/articles /mi_qn4158/is_20031216/ai_n12716957.

Vronsky, Peter. 2004. *Serial Killers: The Method and Madness of Monsters.* New York: Berkley.

Wilgoren, Jodi. 2005, June 28. "Kansas Suspect Pleads Guilty in 10 Murders." *New York Times.* Retrieved July 3, 2005, from www.nytimes.com.

Chapter 13

MURDER AS HATE CRIME

Those who study murder, and even those who read many murder mysteries or watch a lot of media portrayals of homicide detectives, will tell you that particularly brutal homicides usually reflect a familiarity between the victim and offender. It seems there may be something to the saying that familiarity breeds hate. However, the reality of many hate crime murders makes it clear that hate also breeds brutality.

Approximately ten years ago, on the morning of June 7, 1998, the brutality of hatred became all too clear for the town of Jasper, Texas. Police officers were dispatched to Huff Creek Road to investigate reports of a dead body. They did not exactly find a body—at least not in one piece. The police found a torso and a mile-long trail of blood that led to James Byrd Jr.'s head. The officers continued to follow blood splattering that led to Byrd's wallet, his tennis shoes, and his dentures. A lighter with a Ku Klux Klan (KKK) insignia at the end of the bloody trail helped validate what the police may have already begun to suspect: The killing of James Byrd Jr., a 49-year-old African American, was likely racially motivated (Van Boven & Gesalman, 1998).

The officers quickly located a witness who reported he had seen Byrd in the back of a gray pickup. Based on the report about the truck and the discovery of a wrench set at the scene that had the name "Berry" scrawled on it, a police investigator came to the conclusion that Shawn Berry might know something about the brutal slaying. The police brought Berry in for questioning (Van Boven & Gesalman, 1998). Before long, the police were able to piece together the horrible details of Byrd's murder by three white supremacists. Twenty-three-year-old Shawn Berry, James King, also 23, and 31-year-old Lawrence Brewer offered Byrd a ride in the back of Berry's pickup truck. Although stories differed as to who did what, there is no doubt that Byrd was severely beaten, chained to the bumper of Berry's truck by his ankles, and dragged three miles, causing Byrd's death and dismemberment (Rushdy, 2000; Van Boven & Gesalman, 1998).

The appalling murder of Byrd at the hands of white supremacists may be the quintessential hate crime murder incident. Nevertheless, Texas did not have a hate crime statute, and none of the men were actually charged with a hate crime. All three were found guilty of capital murder; King and Brewer were sentenced to death, and Berry was sentenced to life in prison (Texas Department of Criminal Justice, 2006).

It is likely that most anyone would identify the murder of James Byrd Jr. as a hate crime. However, not everyone agrees about what should be counted as a hate crime or even whether hate crimes should be counted. Many also disagree about whether there should be sentencing enhancements for hate crimes. In this chapter, you will learn about these controversies. You will also learn about laws regarding hate crimes in the United States and other countries, as well as motivations or explanations for hate crimes. First, however, a definition of hate crime is provided, followed by information on the extent of hate crime and hate crime homicide in the United States. As in previous chapters, specific cases of homicide are described throughout the chapter as examples.

DEFINITION

When the motivation to do a crime is "hatred, bias, or prejudice, based on the actual or perceived race, color, religion, national origin, ethnicity, gender, or sexual orientation of another individual or group of individuals," the crime fits the definition of a hate crime according to the U.S. Congress (Schmallenger, 2007). The key is not so much the hatred of the victim but that the crime against him or her is committed out of prejudice toward the group the offender represents (Lawrence, 1999). Although most hate crimes involve intimidation or assault, some particularly horrific homicides have been motivated by bias, as was the case with the murder of James Byrd Jr. just described.

DATA ON HATE CRIMES

In 1990, President George H. Bush signed the Hate Crime Statistics Act, which mandated that data be collected on hate crimes across the United States. As a result, the FBI has been collecting data on hate crimes motivated by a race, religion, ethnicity/national origin, or sexual orientation bias since 1992. In 1994, the FBI added crimes based on disability bias to those they count as hate crimes (FBI, 2004).

A total of 8,715 hate crime offenses were reported to the FBI for 2003. In all, 6,934 offenders committed 8,715 offenses against 9,100 victims. Over a third (3,150) of the victims were African Americans, targeted because of their race in 2,548 incidents. Jews were singled out 927 times in 2003 for religious-based hate crimes because of their religion; more often than those of other faiths according to official statistics. More than 1,200 hate crimes were committed against individuals because of their perceived sexual orientation with over 60% against male homosexuals (Associated Press, 2004).

In some ways hate crime incidents are similar across different bias types. An analysis of National Incident Based Reporting System (NIBRS) data for 1997 to 1999 revealed that hate crimes are most likely to occur at the victims' residence or in open spaces regardless of bias motivation. When a weapon was used by the offender, personal weapons such as the offenders' hands and feet were most common. A comparison of crime type by bias motivation revealed that the majority of offenses motivated by race, ethnicity, sexual orientation, and disability bias are violent offenses and in particular assault. The majority (68.9%) of religiously biased hate crimes, however, are property offenses, with vandalism making up 52.7% of all religiously motivated hate crimes (Strom, 2001). Data also reveal that a larger percentage of victims of religious, biased, and disability hate crimes as compared to other hate biases are older than 40 years. The largest percentage of victims of race and ethnicity crimes are younger than 18 years, and sexual-oriented biased crime victims are more likely to be over 18 years with the largest percentage (37%) falling in the 25- to 29-year-old category (Nolan, Mencken, & McDevitt, n.d.).

If we focus on hate crime murders in particular, we find another way that hate crime incidents are similar: Most of them are not murders. Less than 1% of the 8,715 hate crimes reported to the FBI by police agencies were murders or nonnegligent manslaughter. In all, 14 victims were killed in cases classified as hate crime murders in 2003. Eleven of the 14 victims were killed by white offenders, two were killed by black offenders, and the remaining offenders' race was unknown. However, racial hatred was not the motive for all 14 murders. Five, or approximately 36%, were racial, with 4 antiblack and 1 antiwhite. Two (14%) of the homicides were categorized as antiethnicity/national origin bias (one Hispanic and one other). Six (42%) were antimale homosexual murders, and one was categorized as an antimental disability murder. With only 14 hate crime murders, not every state reported an antibias murder. Three were reported in Washington; two were reported in Arkansas; California had four, and one was reported in each of the following states: Louisiana, Tennessee, and Texas.

It is possible, however, that hate crime murders are underreported in some jurisdictions. In other jurisdictions, law enforcement agencies may be more politically aware and trained in the detection of bias-motivated homicide, making it more likely for a murder to be defined as a hate crime. For the FBI to record a crime as a hate crime, the investigation of the crime must lead to evidence that supports that the crime was biased motivated. Comments made by the offender, his or her written statements, or the gestures used at the time of the crime may all be used as evidence that a crime was a hate crime.

When Richard Baumhammer went on a rampage in which he killed five people and injured more, the evidence clearly suggested a hate crime. On April 28, 2000, Baumhammer, who had formerly worked as an attorney, appeared systematically to seek out nonwhites. Baumhammer began his rampage by visiting his Jewish neighbor. He shot her six times and set her house on fire. He then drove to India Grocers where he shot two employees. Baumhammer next stopped to shoot at two synagogues and painted swastikas and the word "Jew" on one of the synagogues. He continued his shooting rampage at a Chinese restaurant where he shot two more people. Baumhammer ended his spree at a karate school where he spared a white student and instead shot a young black karate student. The police apprehended Baumhammer a few minutes after the last killing (Randall, 2000). In 2001, a jury found Baumhammer guilty and he was sentenced to death.

HATE CRIME LEGISLATION JUSTIFICATION AND CONTROVERSY

Most hate crime statutes mandate the counting of hate crimes or the addition of sentencing enhancements for hate crimes or both. What is the reasoning behind counting particular crimes as hate crimes or for adding additional penalties to those convicted of hate crimes versus other crimes? The justification for hate crime legislation centers on the belief that although only a small fraction of crimes in the United States are categorized as hate crimes, crimes motivated by bigotry are "particularly dangerous and socially disruptive" (Grattet, Jenness, & Curry, 1998). Hate crimes are believed to have a far-reaching impact beyond the particular individual who has been victimized. It is believed that hate crimes affect not just the individual victim but the group to which the individual belongs. Hate crimes serve as a means to terrorize entire groups of people; they send the message that violence against certain categories of people is condoned (Gelber, 2000).

BOX 13.1

Wisconsin v. *Mitchell* (1993)

On October 7, 1989, after watching the film *Mississippi Burning*, 20-year-old Todd Mitchell and several of his friends, all of whom were African American, were walking outside when they saw 14-year-old Gregory Redding. Mitchell, incensed over what he viewed in the film, allegedly pointed out Redding and said, "Do you all feel hyped up to move on some white people? There goes a white boy! Go get him!" Nine young men ran across the street under Mitchell's direction and attacked Redding. They beat Redding so severely that he remained in a coma for four days. Mitchell was convicted for his part in the crime and sentenced to two years in prison, which the judge then doubled to four years. The judge was enacting a 1987 Wisconsin hate law statute that allows judges to increase penalties for crimes that are racially motivated (Margolick, 1993).

   Mitchell appealed his sentence on the basis that the penalty enhancement was a violation of his First Amendment right to free speech. In other words, Mitchell's attorneys argued the sentencing enhancement meant that Mitchell was being punished for his bigoted words instead of for his actions and the Wisconsin hate crime statute was unconstitutionally overbroad and had a "chilling effect" on free speech (*Wisconsin* v. *Mitchell*, 1993). The Court unanimously ruled that Wisconsin's law was not overly broad. Further, they explained that the First Amendment did not "prohibit the evidentiary use of speech to establish the elements of a crime or to prove motive or intent" (*Wisconsin* v. *Mitchell*, 1993). In other words, the sentencing enhancement did not violate Mitchell's First Amendment rights because he was not being punished for what he said. Rather, what he said was used to prove that his crime was racially motivated. He was sentenced for the crime and not for what he said (*Wisconsin* v. *Mitchell*, 1993).

Although there has been enough support for hate crime legislation that 45 states and the District of Columbia had some type of hate crime law by March 2006, hate crime legislation, especially when it includes sentencing enhancements, remains controversial. Those who argue against the enactment of hate crime legislation and especially legislation that includes sentencing enhancements, make several arguments against hate crime legislation. First, they argue that hate crimes are not necessarily any more harmful than other crimes. They believe there is no support to the contention that hate crimes affect nonvictims any more than regular crimes. Second, they argue that it is both costly and difficult to prove that hatred or bias is the motivation for a particular crime. Third, those against hate crimes have argued it is the first step to punishing individuals for their speech, which would be an egregious violation of First Amendment rights in the United States (Religious Action Center, 2006; Rozeff, 2006).

HISTORICAL CASES OF HATE CRIME MURDERS

It was not until the late 1970s that U.S. lawmakers began to make laws against hate crimes, and it was not until 1992 that the FBI began to collect data on hate crimes (Grattet et al., 1998). It is clear, however, that crimes motivated by bias against particular groups of people have a long history. Dozens of examples of genocide throughout history, as discussed in Chapter 11, are easily categorized as hate crimes. But there are also homicides in U.S. history that could be categorized as hate crimes. The 1955 murder of 14-year-old Emmett Till in Money, Mississippi, is an example of a well-publicized hate crime that occurred during a time and in a place where hate crimes were commonly committed against African Americans by white racists in the United States.

Young Till, who had traveled from Chicago to visit family in Mississippi, allegedly broke a social taboo when he said "Bye, baby" to a white woman and whistled at her. His life would end that same day when Roy Bryant and J. W. Milam abducted Till at gunpoint from his relative's home. The two men forced Emmett to take off his clothes. They beat him mercilessly, gouged out his eye, shot him in the head, and disposed of his body in the Tallahatchie River. Till's horribly mutilated body was found three days later floating in the river. The men who abducted and murdered Till were acquitted of the murder in a bogus trial in 1955. More recently, in 2004, the case was reopened by the U.S. Department of Justice, however, and the Mississippi's district attorney's office. A press release by the U.S. Department of Justice suggested that Bryant and Milam may have had other accomplices in murdering Till who could still be prosecuted (U.S. Department of Justice, 2004). The case was still open at the time this chapter was written.

Similarly, early in 2007, former sheriff deputy James Ford Seale was arrested for the 1964 kidnapping and murders of two young African American men named Charles Eddie Moore and Henry Hezekiah Dee in Mississippi. Seale, believed to be a KKK member, was arrested in 1964 but never charged. In January 2007, Seale was charged with two counts of kidnapping and a count of conspiracy. Seale, who was believed to have died, was found alive and living close to the scene of the original kidnappings by Charles Moore's brother and a Canadian filmmaker. Time will tell whether the federal authorities will be successful in their prosecution of Seale, who is now 71 years old (Associated Press, 2007).

RACE, HATE CRIME, AND MURDER

Tragically, despite the successes of the civil rights movement in the United States, five decades after the murder of Emmett Till, racists like Roy Bryant and J. W. Milam still brutally murder individuals because of their race in the United States today. FBI data indicate that racial hate crime is the most common type of hate crime. Vandalism of black churches, cross burnings, bombings, and murder are still common hate crimes perpetrated against African Americans in the United States. They are the most targeted racial group, followed by whites, Asian Pacific Americans, multiracial groups, and Native Americans and Alaskan Natives (American Psychological Association, 2006).

BOX 13.2

Hate Crimes Against the Majority Group

Some of those vehemently opposed to hate crime legislation have argued that it makes crimes against minorities more important than crimes against those who are not members of a minority group. However, hate crime legislation has been written in such a way that a crime can be considered a hate crime if it is committed because of a bias against a person related to his or her race, ethnicity, religion, or sexual orientation. As such, if someone seeks out a white person or a Christian or a heterosexual because of their race, religion, or sexual orientation and commits a crime against the person, it could be considered a hate crime. In March 2000, Ronald Taylor, an African American, went on a rampage against white people in Wilkinsburg, Pennsylvania. Taylor killed a white maintenance worker in his building and then allegedly set the apartment on fire before he walked to a Burger King where he shot and killed another white man who was drinking coffee. Taylor then crossed the street and shot at two white men outside a McDonald's before going into the fast-food establishment where he shot and killed the assistant manager. According to witnesses, Taylor told an African American woman, "Not you, sister," indicating he was seeking out white people only. Additionally, investigators reported that they found a notebook in which Taylor had written antiwhite and anti-Jewish comments. Taylor was charged for committing a hate crime in addition to other crimes. CNN reported that in a letter to then Attorney General Janet Reno, Kweisi Mfume, the president of the National Association for the Advancement of Colored People, urged Reno to prosecute Taylor as she would any person of any race who had allegedly committed a hate crime (CNN, 2000).

This chapter opened with the brutal murder of James Byrd Jr. Unfortunately there are additional recent examples of murderers who seek out victims based on their race. In December 2006, eighth grader Cheryl Brown was outside with her friends when Latino gang members began firing on Cheryl and her friends. Cheryl was killed and her friends were injured. The police believed that Cheryl's murder was the result of ongoing racial tensions in Los Angeles. News reports indicated that the Latino gang members were seeking out African American individuals to kill when they found Cheryl and her friends. Two of the gang members have been arrested and charged with murder, and the prosecutor is alleging that the accused were motivated by hate. If determined to be guilty, the accused may be sentenced to death or to life in prison without parole (Archibold, 2007).

ETHNICITY/NATIONAL ORIGIN, HATE CRIME, AND MURDER

Hate crime offenders may be *nativists* who seek out ethnic minorities to victimize because they believe them to be immigrants who are taking away opportunities from Americans. Sometimes these nativist offenders attack ethnic minorities whose families have lived in the United States for several generations. Hate crime offenders may also strike out against ethnic minorities because they view them as different, and negative stereotypes in the society at large often fuel these antiethnic hate crimes (APA, 2006). As the Latino population in the United States increases, so too do anti-Latino hate crimes. Asian Americans are also attacked based on their ethnicity, and, more recently, those of Middle Eastern heritage have been targeted. California, for example, showed an increase from 99 hate crimes against those believed by the offenders to be Middle Eastern in 2000 to 501 incidents in 2001 (Squatriglia, 2002).

On September 15, 2001, Balbir Singh Sodhi was murdered by Francisco Roque, who believed Sodhi was a Middle Easterner because of his turban and long beard. Sodhi, who was born in India, was a Sikh, who wore a turban and kept his beard long because of his religion. Although not charged with a hate crime, Roque was convicted of first-degree murder in September 2003. In 1982, Vincent Chin was killed in similar circumstances in Detroit, Michigan. Ronald Ebens and Michael Nitz mistook Chin, who was Chinese American, for Japanese. Nitz held Chin while Ebens hit him repeatedly with a baseball bat in an attack fueled by their anger over the loss of American auto industry jobs, which they blamed on the Japanese. Nitz and Ebens made a plea deal which resulted in both of them being convicted of manslaughter. However, they did not receive a prison sentence but were instead given three years of probation, fined $3,000, and ordered to pay $780 in court costs. Responding to outcries for justice, the federal government charged Ebens and Nitz with violating Chin's civil rights. Ebens, the one who wielded the bat, was convicted in federal court and sentenced to 25 years in prison. The conviction was overturned due to a technicality and retried in Cincinnati, Ohio, after a change of venue. The jury, consisting mostly of white

---

BOX 13.3

Hate Crime in Civil Court

For a variety of reasons, hate crime offenders may not be charged with a hate crime or be found guilty, as was the case in the murder of Vincent Chin discussed in this chapter. In other cases, offenders may be found guilty. In either case, victims, or their survivors in the case of homicide, may decide to sue offenders in civil court for violations of their civil rights. As discussed in Chapter 2, because of two major differences between criminal and civil court rules, it is easier to find someone responsible in civil court than it is to find them guilty in criminal court. In civil cases the burden of proof is lower, making it easier to convince the jury that the plaintiff is responsible. Additionally, in civil cases where the plaintiff faces the possibility of paying damages, he or she must take the stand and testify. Thus it is easier to demonstrate that an individual has committed a hate crime in a civil court.

---

blue-collar men, acquitted Ebens and Nitz of all charges. Chin's mother then pursued the defendants in a civil suit. The court awarded her $1.5 million. To date, Mrs. Chin has received only a small amount of the settlement, and Ebens stopped making payments in 1989 (Le, 2006).

RELIGION, HATE CRIME, AND MURDER

In July 2006, American Naveed Afzal Haq sought out Jewish people to kill at the Seattle Jewish Federation Office. Haq held a pistol to the back of a 14-year-old girl and demanded the Federation Office staff let him in. Reports indicate that after he entered he said, "I am only doing this for a statement." He then aimed one of his two guns and began shooting. Walking through the office as he continued shooting, he killed Christina Rexroad and injured five others. Prosecutors charged him with nine felonies including malicious harassment, which is Washington State's hate crime law. According to witnesses, Haq made several anti-Semitic statements, and 911 recordings indicate that he said, "These are Jews; I want these Jews to get out" (Carter, Singer, & Sullivan, 2006).

Religious bias hate crimes such as those committed by Haq are aimed at people of many different faiths. Much of the hate crime involves property damage including vandalism, such as the defacing of property with swastikas. Violent crimes, however, continue to be committed against people of all faiths. Although official data indicate that Haq's attack and most religious bias hate crimes in the United States are aimed at Jews, crimes against Muslims have increased in the United States since the 9/11 terrorist attacks. For example, the FBI reported that hate crimes against Muslims or those believed to be Muslim were 17 times higher in 2001 after the 9/11 terrorist attacks than in preceding years (APA, 2006).

SEXUAL ORIENTATION, HATE CRIME, AND MURDER

Those who have argued for the inclusion of sexual orientation in hate crime legislation have faced organized opposition. In addition to the general arguments against hate crimes, some opponents have argued that including sexual orientation as a category in hate crime legislation would give gay men and lesbians special rights. Furthermore, some have argued that legislation that makes violence against lesbians and gay men a hate crime will help legitimize homosexual behavior, which they believe is wrong.

Nevertheless, 29 states and the District of Columbia have enacted hate crime statutes that include crimes based on the sexual orientation of the victim. The FBI began collecting data on hate crimes motivated by sexual orientation bias in 1992. According to the National Gay and Lesbian Task Force (NGLTF, 2006), antigay violence has consistently been ranked as the third most frequent form of hate crime. Yet the data from 2003 indicate that 6 of the 14 victims of hate crime murder cataloged by the FBI were gay males. Furthermore, a 1994 study by the National Coalition of Anti-Violence Programs found that those who kill gay victims are far more likely to use the utmost brutality in comparison to those who kill heterosexual victims. Gay murder victims were more likely to be dismembered and suffer multiple stabbings and severe bludgeoning. Almost 60% of 152 antigay murders between 1992 and 1994 involved "overkill" (NGLTF, 2006).

Hate crime homicides are often very brutal, and they often involve more than one offender. A study in Australia compared hate crime murders in which the victim was a gay male (or believed to have been gay) to the murders of other males in New South Wales, Australia. The findings revealed differences between the homicides committed against gay men that were motivated by bias and other murders of males. The hate crime incidents were more likely to involve multiple offenders, and the offenders were more likely to beat the victims brutally with their hands, feet, or a blunt object than in other homicides against males. More often than in other cases in which men were killed, and unlike the confrontational homicides discussed in Chapter 7, the gay bias killings were likely to occur in the victim's home and the victims and offenders were more likely to be strangers to one another (Mouzos & Thompson, 2000). In other words, offenders in gay male hate crimes specifically sought out gay men to harm because of their biases against gay men, and the anger is reflected in the damage done to the gay male victims.

The fatal 1998 beating of 21-year-old University of Wyoming student Matthew Shepard by 21-year-old Aaron McKinney and 21-year-old Russell Henderson serves as an example of the brutality used against gay males in antigay homicides. On October 7, 1998, a cyclist found Shepard unconscious, nearly frozen, and tied to a split-rail fence east of Laramie, Wyoming. Shepard's skull was crushed and he had several wounds on his face and head. He also had bruises on the back of his hands and in his groin area. Shepard was taken to the hospital, but his injuries were so severe that the doctors could not operate. Shepard died five days later.

McKinney admitted that he beat Shepard with a foot-long .357 magnum handgun. Although there were suggestions that McKinney was going to claim Shepard made a sexual advance toward him that led to his murderous rage, McKinney's girlfriend reported that McKinney and Henderson lured Shepard into his truck by pretending they were gay. Henderson and McKinney now argue from their prison cells that the crime was not motivated by hate but they had only intended to rob Shepard for drug money; other evidence suggested that the crime was a hate crime. Both McKinney and Henderson made plea deals to avoid the death penalty, and they are both serving two life sentences in prison. However, note that McKinney and Henderson were not prosecuted for a hate crime. The state of Wyoming did not have a hate crime law in 1998 when Shepard was murdered; nor did Wyoming have one as of March 2006 (Ramsland, 2005; Religious Action Center, 2006).

Gender, Hate Crime, and Murder

On October 2, 2006, Charles Carl Roberts IV entered a one-room Amish schoolhouse and ordered the boys and adults out of the room. Roberts, a milk truck driver, brought various items, including tape and lubricant, which indicated he may have been planning to assault his victims sexually. Although news reporters reported that Roberts did not sexually assault the girls, he shot ten of the young girls; killing five of them. Just five days before Roberts's terrible attack, Duane Morrison sexually molested six high school girls he held hostage inside a Colorado high school before shooting Emily Keyes to death and killing himself. These two attacks reminded criminologists and others of the December 1989 mass murder by Marc Lepine at the University of Montreal's Ecole Polytechnique. Like the two murderous attacks in the fall of 2006, Lepine also ordered men out of a classroom so he could focus his violence on women students. Lepine shot and killed 14 women and injured 13 others before he killed himself. Notes left behind by Lepine indicated that he was angry at feminists (Gendercide.org, 2002). It would seem as if these incidents fit the definition of a hate crime. Each of these men sought out women or girls to victimize because of the category they belonged to. These men displayed a deadly bias against women.

Philosopher Mary Anne Warren coined the term *gendercide* as analogous to genocide. She defined it as the "deliberate extermination of persons of a particular sex (or gender)" (Warren, 1985: 1). Warren was careful to note that *gendercide* is a sex-neutral term. The victims of gendercide could be sought out for being male or for being female. Gendercide, as defined by Warren, fits the murders by Roberts, Morrison, and Lepine. Seeking out a person to kill or harm because of a prejudice against the group to which they belong is a hate crime. However, gendercide and the three killing incidents just described in which females were selected as victims because they were females are not usually defined as or treated as hate crimes.

The Hate Crime Sentencing Enhancement Act of 1992 did not become a law, but the definition of hate crime that appears in the bill, frequently quoted as the quintessential definition, includes criminal acts that are motivated by "hatred, bias, or prejudice" based on *gender*, among other categories (H.R. 4797, 1992). However, the FBI does not collect data on gender-motivated hate crimes; nor was gender included in most early hate crime legislation. Gender was not originally included in hate crime legislation for fear that its inclusion would slow the passage of hate crime bills and including gender would open the door to including a whole host of additional categories such as age and disability. Also, as discussed next, there is also widespread belief that crimes against women are not the same as hate crimes against other minorities such as African Americans or gay men (McPhail & DiNitto, 2005).

Those who argue that gender should not be a status included in hate crime legislation often make the assumption in their arguments that "gender" means "women." In actuality, if gender were to be included as a category, crimes in which men were sought out to victimize because they were men or because of the offender's bias against men, the crimes could be counted as a hate crime. That being said, those who are against the inclusion of a gender category argue that crimes against women are not the same as hate crimes against members of other minority status categories. First, they note that crimes against women are most often committed by offenders who are known to the women, whereas hate crimes are most often committed by strangers. Second, violence against women is commonplace; hate crimes are less frequent, making the special prosecution or counting of hate crimes against women a logistical nightmare. Third, special laws are already in place to deal with crimes against women, such as domestic violence and sexual assault laws. Finally, an often stated argument against the inclusion of gender in hate crime legislation is one about motivation. Men who seek out women as victims do not necessarily hate them nor are they biased against them; the choice of a female victim is often more about power and control and less about hate. Others have noted that offenders who perpetrate against women do so as recreation or for fantasy fulfillment and not for hate (McPhail, 2002; McPhail & DiNitto, 2005).

Those on the other side of the argument believe that violence against women is rampant and it is often a hate crime. They argue that crimes against women often have the same features as hate crimes against other minorities. It is not uncommon, for instance, for those who attack women to use derogatory terms against the women they attack parallel to the derogatory terms used against racial or religious minorities. Second, those who argue that gender should be a category included in hate crime legislation say that often women are targeted because they are women. They argue that misogyny, the hatred of women, may be at the root of attacks against women. As such, some offenders seek out women to rape and assault, and these same offenders would not consider offending against a man in the same way. Finally, as with hate crimes overall, the crime committed against one member of the group often affects the larger group. The fact that a serial rapist is attacking women makes all women fearful and thus affects the way they live their lives (McPhail, 2002; McPhail & DiNitto, 2005).

More recently in the United States, there has been a trend toward the inclusion of gender as a status in hate crime policies, with at least 20 states including gender as a hate crime category. Still, the gender category remains essentially unused by prosecutors. In a Texas study, prosecutors were questioned about the inclusion of gender as a hate crime category in the newly enacted James Byrd, Jr. Hate Crime Act. Out of 17 prosecutors interviewed in 2002, only 2 were aware that the act enacted on September 1, 2001, included the status category of gender. Most also found the inclusion of gender problematic. They were uncertain that it could be used and in what cases they might use it. Not surprising, then, although at least 20 states have gender as a status category in their hate crime statutes, researchers have noted only two successful prosecutions in which hatred based on gender was employed (McPhail & DiNitto, 2005).

DISABILITY, HATE CRIME, AND MURDER

In 1994, the U.S. Congress amended the Hate Crime Statistics Act by adding disabilities to the list of categories for which data are collected by the FBI. Very few disability hate crimes have been reported since the collection of this type of hate crime began. Between 1997 and 2001, only 133 disability-bias hate crimes were reported to the FBI. Some researchers have argued that the number is so low because disability hate crimes are often, if not always, unreported due to a lack of awareness and understanding of such crimes by law enforcement personnel (Maclay, 2002). Nevertheless, in 2003, one of the 14 hate crime murders reported to the FBI was categorized as an antimental disability hate crime.

The one disability murder listed in the 2003 data may indicate a greater willingness to view crimes as disability hate crimes. Until recently, the category of disability crime received little attention. As such, it is difficult to find an example of a disability hate crime murder, even though there are likely to be such cases that were not categorized as hate crimes. Floyd "Todd" Tapson, however, was convicted of the attempted murder of a woman with a mental disability in Billings, Montana, in 1998. After his original conviction was overturned, he pleaded guilty to the attempted murder. Tapson, who worked in various group homes, is also suspected in the disappearance and murders of at least three other women with a disability, making it possible that he sought out these women because of their disability and thus committed hate crime murders. Some people, however, may argue that he killed them because they were easy to victimize rather than because he had a bias against them (Associated Press, 2006).

HATE CRIMES AROUND THE WORLD

Most Western countries have laws against hate crimes. However, hate crime is defined differently in different countries. In many European countries such as England and Germany, hate crimes are most likely to refer to crimes aimed at racial minorities. Such crimes may not be referred to as "hate crimes" but as "xenophobic criminality" or "politically motivated violence." In Canada and the United States, hate crimes are more widely defined as including crimes motivated by sexual orientation, age, and disability biases (Shaw, 2002). Despite objections by civil libertarians, homophobic and sexist speech is illegal in France. In contrast, Australia is one of the few Western countries that has not enacted hate crime legislation. However, if it is proven that a convicted offender was motivated by the race, ethnicity, religion, disability, age, sexuality, or language of his or her victim, the judge may take this into consideration as an aggravating factor when sentencing the offender (Walters, 2006).

EXPLANATIONS AND MOTIVATIONS

Research on hate crime offenders suggests three major motivations for hate crime offenders. First, a very small number of hate crime offenders are part of larger organized hate groups that are attempting to make changes to society that would support their biased ideology. Second, and more prominent than the first motivation, hate crime offenders can be seen as individuals who are fighting to keep others off their turf. Finally, many hate crime offenders commit hate crimes for the fun of it. They find it exciting or thrilling (McDevitt, Levin, & Bennet, 2002).

Although some hate crime murderers are part of organized hate groups, research about hate crime offenders in Los Angeles revealed that fewer than 5% of those who committed 1,459 hate crimes in the Los Angeles area in 1994 and 1995 were members of organized hate groups. According to the American Psychological Association (APA, 2006), most hate crimes are committed by young people who mostly follow the law and see little wrong with their actions. Although drugs and

BOX 13.4

9/11 Attack on the United States: A Hate Crime?

Approximately 3,000 individuals died as a result of four planes crashing into the World Trade Center, the Pentagon, and a field in southern Pennsylvania. Were these individuals murdered? Should the attacks that led to these murders be considered acts of war or crimes? How they are counted has psychological and other implications. For example, the psyche of the nation, so to speak, can be differently affected by whether we view the 9/11 attacks as crimes or war. And practically, insurance companies may follow different rules based on how the deaths are categorized. Likewise, the crime rates in the nation and in the jurisdictions where the individuals perished would be greatly increased if the homicides are counted as crimes. The 2001 U.S. homicide rate is about 20% higher when the 9/11 deaths are classified as murders. In a *Homicide Studies* article, Weaver and Wittekind (2002) considered the question of how to count the September 11 fatalities as an extension of a discussion that began at the Homicide Research Working Group's 2001 midyear meeting. Weaver and Wittekind considered the possibility that the killings could be considered hate crimes. In 1999, the FBI expanded the definition of hate crimes to include crimes based on prejudice against a national origin. All the victims of the attack were not U.S. citizens, but the intended victims, according to Weaver and Wittekind, were identified as being Americans. As such, the attack could be considered a hate crime because the crime was motivated by a bias against Americans (Weaver & Wittekind, 2002). What do you think? How should these fatalities be counted? What do you think the implications are for counting them as murders or as something else?

alcohol are sometimes used by hate crime offenders, the main motivation for hate crimes is prejudice. According to the APA, such prejudice is often supported by the social environments in which the offender lives (APA, 2006). In fact, some academics have argued that "Hate crimes are as much a product of the society as they are of the individual" (Golden et al., 1999). Thus, in the United States and many other countries, prejudice against those who are viewed as different is common (APA, 2006).

One sociological theory that contributes much to our understanding of who is victimized in hate crime offenses is the lifestyle or routine activities theory. As noted in Chapter 6, the odds of being a murder victim are higher for some people and lower for others because the habits of both victims and offenders affect whether they will be involved in crime (Barkan, 1997). Lifestyle and routine activities theories focus on how the lifestyle or routine behavior of an individual may place him or her more at risk for victimization (Cohen & Felson, 1979). As noted earlier in this chapter, vandalism is a common religiously biased hate crime. This is easily explained by the fact that someone who is motivated to commit a religious bias crime may be able to identify a building as belonging to those of a particular religion more easily than finding a person of a particular religion. Because there are so few hate crime murders, it is more difficult to determine statistically whether routine activities theories explain hate crime murder. Nevertheless, infamous cases such as the murder of Matthew Shepard and the murders at the Seattle Jewish Federation, suggest that motivated hate crime murderers plan their murders and seek particular types of victims at places where they believe they will find such victims. The murder of James Byrd Jr., in contrast, suggests that hate crimes may sometimes occur on the spur of the moment and are more opportunistic than planned.

SUMMARY

This chapter focused on homicides motivated by bias or prejudice against the category to which the victim belonged. The chapter included data about hate crimes generally and about hate crime homicides in particular. The specification of some crimes as hate crimes is controversial, and the many controversies about hate crimes were discussed throughout the chapter. In this chapter, you read about the concern about the potential violation of an individual person's right to free speech in the United States as well as arguments for and against including gender and sexual orientation in hate crime legislation. Many well-known cases of crime that fit the definition of a hate crime were presented, including the murders of Emmett Till, James Byrd Jr., and Matthew Shepard, along with lesser known incidents of hate crime homicide. Hate crime murders motivated by race, ethnicity/national origin, religion, sexual orientation, gender, and disability were discussed. You also read about how hate crimes are defined in many other countries before learning about explanations for hate crimes and hate crime murder that conclude the chapter.

CHAPTER QUESTIONS

1. Define hate crime.
2. According to the FBI, what evidence supports the contention that a particular crime was a hate crime?
3. Discuss the arguments for and against hate crime penalty enhancements.
4. What would you say to someone who asks you if hate crimes are new?
5. What group is most targeted for hate crimes?
6. True or false: Only members of minority groups can be victims of hate crimes.
7. Discuss explanations for ethnic/national origin hate crimes.
8. What was at issue in *Wisconsin* v. *Mitchell*, and what did the Supreme Court decide?
9. True or false: Most religious-based hate crime in the United States is aimed at Muslims.
10. How are hate crime murders of gay men different from other murders of men?
11. Do you think the murders of women described in this chapter should be defined as hate crimes? Why or why not?
12. Discuss arguments for and against including "gender" in hate crime legislation.
13. Do countries outside of the United States have hate crimes and hate crime laws?
14. Discuss likely motivations for hate crimes.
15. Discuss whether the 9/11 attack on the United States was a hate crime.

REFERENCES

American Psychological Association. 2006. "Hate Crimes Today: An Age-Old Foe in Modern Dress Position Paper." Accessed online at http://www.apa.org/releases/hate.html

Archibold, Randal C. 2007, January 17. "Racial Hate Feeds a Gang War's Senseless Killing." *New York Times.* Accessed online at http://www.nytimes.com/2007/01/17/us/17race.html?ei=5090&en=a34ac77e3d9a409f&ex=1326690000&partner=r

Associated Press. 2004, November 22. "FBI: Race Inspires Majority of Hate Crimes; Number of Crimes Rose Slightly to 7,489 in 2003, Agency Reports." Accessed online at http://www.msnbc.msn.com/id/6557708/

Associated Press. 2006, November 3. "Grand Forks Police Checking Out Human Remains Found in Montana." KX Net.com. Accessed online at http://www.kxmd.com/t/montana/61603.asp

Associated Press. 2007, January 24. "Ex-Miss. Sheriff's Deputy Charged in '64 Deaths; James Seale Suspected of Killing Black Teenagers; Indictment on Thursday." Accessed online at http://www.msnbc.msn.com/id16792385/?GT1=8921

Barkan, Steven. 1997. *Criminology: A Sociological Understanding.* Upper Saddle River, NJ: Prentice Hall.

Carter, Mike, Natalie Singer, and Jennifer Sullivan. 2006, August 3. "Haq allegedly Shot Woman, Then Chased Her Upstairs, Killed Her." *Seattle Times,* p. A1.

Cohen, Larry, and Marcus Felson. 1979. "Social Change and Crime Rates." *American Sociological Review,* 44: 588–608.

CNN. 2000, March 11. "NAACP Leader: Prosecute African-American Suspect 'Like Any Other Hate Crime.'" *CNN.com.*

FBI. 2004. *Hate Crime Statistics 2003.* Washington, DC: U.S. Department of Justice.

Gelber, Katharine. 2000. "Hate Crimes: Public Policy Implications of the Inclusion of Gender." *Australian Journal of Political Science,* 35(2): 275–289.

Gendercide.org. 2002. "Case Study: The Montréal Massacre." Accessed online at http://www.gendercide.org/case_montreal.html

Golden, C. J., M. L. Jackson, and T. A. Crum. 1999. "Hate Crimes: Etiology and Intervention." In Harold V. Hall and Leighton C. Whitaker, eds., *Collective Violence—Effective Strategies for Assessing and Interviewing in Fatal Group and Institutional Aggression.* Boca Raton, FL: CRC Press.

Grattet, Ryken, Valerie Jenness, and Theodore R. Curry. 1998. "The Homogenization and Differentiation of Hate Crime Law in the United States, 1978 to 1995: Innovation and Diffusion in the Criminalization of Bigotry." *American Sociological Review,* 63: 286–307.

H.R. 4797. 1992. 192d Cong. 2nd Session.

Lawrence, Frederick M. 1999. *Punishing Hate: Bias Crimes Under American Law.* Cambridge, MA: Harvard University Press.

Le, C. N. 2006. "Anti-Asian Racism & Violence." *Asian-Nation: The Landscape of Asian America.* Accessed online at http://www.asian-nation.org/racism.shtml

Maclay, Kathleen. 2002, December 18. "Flawed FBI Reporting System Undercounts Disability Hate Crimes." University of California at Berkeley press release. Accessed online at http://www.berkeley.edu/news/media/releases/2002/12/18_crimes.html

Margolick, David. 1993, April 20. "Test of a 'Hate Crime' Law Reaches Center Stage." *New York Times on the Web.* Accessed online at http://partners.nytimes.com/library/national/race/042093race-ra.html

McDevitt, Jack, Jack Levin, and Susan Bennet. 2002. "Hate Crime Offenders: An Expanded Typology." *Journal of Social Issues,* 58: 207–410.

McPhail, Beverly A. 2002. "Gender-Bias Hate Crimes: A Review." *Trauma, Violence, & Abuse,* 3(2): 125–143.

McPhail, Beverly A., and Diana M. DiNitto. 2005. "Prosecutorial Perspectives on Gender-Bias Hate Crimes," *Violence Against Women,* 11(9): 1162–1185.

Mouzos, Jenny, and Sue Thompson. 2000. *Gay-Hate Related Homicides: An Overview of Major Findings in New South Wales.* Canberra: Australian Institute of Criminology.

National Gay and Lesbian Task Force. 2006. "Hate Crimes." Accessed online at www.ngltf.org

Nolan, James, J. F. Carson Mencken, and Jack McDevitt. No date. *NIBRS Hate Crimes 1995–2000: Juvenile Victims and Offenders.* Accessed online at http://www.as.wvu.edu/∼jnolan/nibrshatecrime.html

Ramsland, Katherine. 2005. "Forensic Psychiatry." *Court TV Crime Library.* Retrieved November 18, 2006, from http://www.crimelibrary.com.

Randall, Kate. 2000, May 2. "Five Killed In Racist Shooting Rampage In Pittsburgh." *World Socialist Web Page.* http://www.wsws.org/articles/2000/may2000/pitt-m02.shtml

Religious Action Center. 2006. "Hate Crimes." Accessed online at http://rac.org/advocacy/issues/issuehcp/

Rozeff, Michael S. 2006, August 18. "The Case Against Hate-Crime Laws." Accessed online at LewRockwell.com

Rushdy, Ashraf H. A. 2000. "Reflections on Jasper: Resisting History." *The Humanist,* 60(2): 24–28.

Schmallenger, Frank. 2007. *Criminal Justice Today: An Introductory Text for the 21st Century.* Upper Saddle River, NJ: Pearson.

Shaw, Margaret. 2002. *Preventing Hate Crimes: International Strategies and Practices.* International Centre for the Prevention of Crime.

Squatriglia, Chuck. 2002, September 19. "Middle Eastern Backlash Blamed for Leap in Hate Crimes; Otherwise, Says State Report, Tally Would Have Dropped." *San Francisco Chronicle*, p. A21.

Strom, Kevin. J. 2001. *Hate Crimes Reported in NIBRS, 1997–99*, Washington, DC: Bureau of Justice Statistics.

Texas Department of Criminal Justice. 2006. *Offender Information Search Web page*. Accessed online at http://168.51.178.33/webapp/TDCJ/index2.htm

U.S. Department of Justice. 2004, May 10. "Justice Department to Investigate 1955 Emmett Till Murder." Press release.

Van Boven, Sarah, and Anne Bell Gesalman. 1998. "A Fatal Ride in the Night." *Newsweek*, 131(33): 2–3.

Walters, Mark. 2006. "Why ACT Government Has an Obligation to Legislate Against Hate Crimes." *Canberra Times, April 12*. Accessed online at http://canberra.yourguide.com.au/detail.asp?story_id=472753.

Warren, Mary Anne. 1985. *Gendercide: The Implications of Sex Selection*. Totowa, NJ: Rowman & Allanheld.

Weaver, Greg S., and Janice E. Clifford Wittekind. 2002. "Categorizing September 11: Casualties as Acts of Terrorism." *Homicide Studies*, 6(4): 327–376.

Wisconsin v. Mitchell. 1993. (92–515), 508 U.S. 47. Accessed online at http://www.law.cornell.edu/supct/html/92–515.ZO.html

Chapter 14

SOLVING HOMICIDES

Approximately ten minutes into *CSI New York*, the medical examiner is telling the crime scene investigator that the bullet entry wound in the victim's shoulder is jagged. The crime scene investigator notes that this indicates the bullet had hit something prior to hitting the victim, causing it to ricochet into the victim's shoulder. "Usually," says the medical examiner, but this time the hole in the clothing is not jagged, suggesting that the bullet directly entered the body. So what does that mean? According to the medical examiner, it means the offender pulled the bullet out of the victim's shoulder. This tells the medical examiner and the crime scene investigator that the ballistics information on the gun is in NIBIN (National Integrated Ballistics Information Network). They say aloud that this means the gun has either been used in another crime or is a police-issued weapon. The crime scene investigator is on the way to solving the mystery, and we only have about 45 minutes to go before the show is over. What is great entertainment for many of us, according to any honest police investigator, is fiction. Although some cases shown on television and in the movies are based on real cases and details are sometimes accurate, solving homicides is not like a television show. In reality, homicide investigations are more mundane. The work is a lot less flashy, and cases take more of the investigator's time than shown on television. Moreover, for investigators in bigger cities, it would be a luxury to work on one case at a time, and for those in most smaller jurisdictions, a case a week would be extraordinary.

There are 900-page books and multiweek training courses dedicated to teaching homicide investigation to officers who already know much about law enforcement practices. This chapter touches on some of the information taught to those who are being trained to work in law enforcement. The basic steps of the investigative process are covered with special attention paid to Supreme Court rulings that affect how law enforcers must carry out their investigations. This chapter also presents an overview of evidence that may be available to help solve homicide cases, including an introduction to some newer technological advances that have made the recovery of evidence more likely. To begin, however, the important concept of homicide clearance is explained before a look at the data on clearance in the United States and other countries. Less academic research is available on solving homicide than on other topics covered in this book. Nevertheless, when possible, this chapter includes academic research on homicide investigation.

HOMICIDE CLEARANCE

A crime is considered "cleared" by the police when it is solved. Crimes, including murder, are usually deemed to be cleared when the police make an arrest. However, crimes can be cleared in other ways. When a crime is solved by a means other than an arrest, it is said to be "cleared exceptionally." In the National Incident Based Reporting System (NIBRS), a crime must meet four criteria to be counted as cleared by exceptional means. First, the identity of at least one offender has to be certain. Second, sufficient probable cause must exist that would justify prosecution for the crime. Third, the location of the offender must be known. Fourth, and most importantly, there must be something that prevents law enforcement from making an arrest (FBI, 2005). When a murderer kills himself or is killed by the police, the murder is cleared exceptionally.

In the last several years, homicide researchers have turned their attention to homicide clearance trends. In the United States, the highest rates of homicide clearance are for cases involving African Americans and the lowest are for homicides involving Latinos. When victims are older than 65 years, the homicide is less likely to be solved, and when the homicide is part of another felony crime, clearance is less likely (Regoeczi, Kennedy, & Silverman, 2000). Additionally, it is not surprising that when the offender is a family member, a homicide is more likely to be solved (Regoeczi et al., 2000). Also, logically, homicides with more physical evidence are more likely to be cleared, and when detective have lower caseloads; they have higher clearance percentages (Puckett & Lundman, 2003).

Unfortunately, as seen in Figure 14.1, the percentage of homicides that are cleared has continued to drop in the United States since 1976. In the United States, the percentage cleared decreased from 79% in 1976 to 63% in 2004. Australia, which has far fewer homicides than the United States, maintains a stable clearance rate of approximately 88%, suggesting that having fewer homicides to solve may make it easier to clear the cases (Mouzos & Muller, 2001). Canada also has far fewer homicides than the United States however, it has also been experiencing a decrease in solved homicide cases (Regoeczi et al., 2000). What accounts for this increase in unsolved homicide cases in Canada and the United States; especially when crime-solving technology has improved? By studying the circumstances and relationships among solved and unsolved cases, homicide scholars have suggested that the decrease in homicide clearances reflects changes in the types of homicide committed. Most research suggests that homicide committed during the commission of another felony

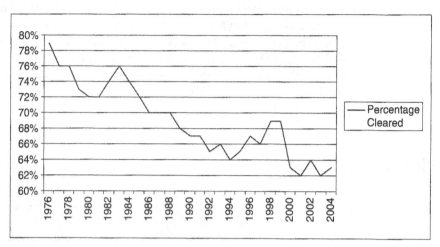

FIGURE 14.1

U.S. Homicide Clearance Rate Over Time, 1976–2004

Source: Compiled from Bureau of Justice Statistics, 2006.

and homicides committed by strangers are less likely to be solved. It may be, then, that an increase in the killings of strangers and killings in the commission of another crime without increases in other types of crimes could explain the increase in unsolved homicide. Likewise, a decrease in the type of homicide that is more likely to be solved, such as intimate partner homicide, could result in a relative increase in unsolved homicide.

HOMICIDE INVESTIGATION

Sometimes cases are "dunkers"; that is, they are amazingly easy to solve because the offender kills himself or the offender is obvious for another reason (Puckett & Lundman, 2003). Such was the case of a triple homicide in Altoona, Pennsylvania. Miguel Padilla called the police after three men were shot outside of a bar. Padilla told the police that he "believed he had hurt somebody but had been having blackouts" (Hamill, 2005). Within slightly more than a year after he first called the police, Padilla was arrested, charged, brought to trial, convicted of three counts of first-degree murder, and sentenced to death (Altoona.com). Other cases are more challenging, like the murder of Martha Moxley who was beaten to death with a golf club in 1975. It was not until 2000 that Michael Skakel (a Kennedy family member) surrendered to police after being indicted in Moxley's murder (CNN.com, 2000). Other murders are so challenging that they are never solved, which seems to be the fate of the JonBenet Ramsey case.

What happens early in a homicide investigation may make or break a case. In fact, the likelihood that a homicide will be solved decreases with time. Early in an investigation, witness memories are most accurate and witnesses are easier to locate. With time, however, the trail goes cold; witnesses' memories fade, and witnesses may be more difficult to locate (Keppel & Weiss, 1994; Regini, 1997). Similarly, a mistake made by detectives early in an investigation can lead to nightmares for prosecutors who prosecute a suspect. Thus it is critical that the responding officers and homicide investigators are careful to work fast and follow proper procedure whenever a possible homicide is discovered or reported.

Homicide investigation has evolved with technological advances in the analysis of physical evidence (National Institute of Justice, 2004), but the process involved in a good homicide investigation remains the same. Attention to detail and proper procedure is necessary at every step of an investigation, beginning with the arrival of the responding officer and following through from the collection of evidence to cooperation with the district attorneys in prosecuting the case. This section provides an overview of important steps in the investigative process beginning with the most important: the initial response.

Initial Response by Responding Officer

The initial response by officers to a potential murder scene is vastly important. Vital information and lives may be lost if the responding officers fail to arrive quickly and perform their duties well. It is important that the officers are well trained because there is much for them to do. They have three major responsibilities. They must first determine if the victim is alive or dead and proceed as appropriate. Second, they need to arrest an offender if one is present and notify appropriate chains of command to apprehend an offender if an immediate arrest is not made. Finally, the arriving officers must take the steps necessary to preserve the crime scene evidence and detain any witnesses or possible suspects (Geberth, 1996). Each of these three major responsibilities includes many aspects, presented in more detail here.

As the responding officers arrive at the primary crime scene (where the body is found, according to Geberth, 1996), they should be particularly aware of any vehicles or persons leaving the scene and should take care to note descriptive information of such vehicles and persons and the direction they head. It is also important that the

---

ADAPT

Retired lieutenant commander of the New York Police Department's Bronx Homicide Task Force, Vernon Geberth (1996), suggests the acronym ADAPT to coincide with the five steps that an officer should take when arriving at a crime scene:

A—Arrest the offender when possible

D—Detain and identify witnesses and suspects

A—Assess the crime scene

P—Protect the crime scene

T—Take notes on everything

arriving officers take care in approaching the scene, carefully noting any possible secondary crime scenes that will need to be secured for evidence collection. They should also be aware of anyone in the vicinity that may be linked to the crime as an offender or witness. At the same time, officer safety is important. Officers should use all their senses to assess possible danger and to continue to take in information (National Institute of Justice, 2004).

After initially assessing the scene for safety and security, it is the responding officer's duty to follow departmental guidelines in calling for backup or supervisors and notifying any other agencies that may be necessary, such as the fire department or emergency medical personnel. Upon the arrival of any medical personnel, the integrity of the crime scene must be maintained. Officers need to indicate potential evidence to medical personnel and instruct them not to destroy any evidence. If there are victims who are alive but suffering from a life-threatening injury, the officer should be certain to obtain any "dying declarations" if appropriate. The officer should also take notes on the name and agencies of any medical personnel and note the location where they will transport victims. As soon as possible, the officer must document the steps taken at each stage and the movement of any persons or items from the scene. All investigative and medical personnel at the scene should log in, and they must be willing to provide fingerprints, DNA, or other evidence to ensure that the evidence collected at the scene is linked to the crime. If possible, an officer should ride with and record any statements made by injured persons as they are transferred to a medical facility. If an officer is not available, the medical personnel should be asked to write down any comments and statements made (Geberth, 1996; National Institute of Justice, 2004).

To protect the integrity of the scene and ensure safety, the officer who arrives on the scene is also expected to preserve the boundaries of the scene while securing and controlling individuals at the scene. Establishing the boundaries of the scene requires the officer to secure any areas relevant to the crime scene, including where the crime occurred, where the victim was discovered, as well as possible entry and exit paths of suspects. The area should be secured physically with boundaries such as walls and gated areas when possible and with crime scene tape, vehicles, and personnel in such a way that unauthorized people and animals are prevented from entering the scene. It is best to secure a wider area than necessary because it is easier to shrink the boundaries than to expand them. Officers also must be careful to consider any possible contaminators and take reasonable precautions to prevent them from destroying the scene's integrity. Rain, snow, wind, sprinklers, helicopters, and animals are all listed by the National Institute of Justice as possible contaminators. Finally, officers must follow search and seizure laws and obtain consent and search warrants as necessary (National Institute of Justice, 2004).

Unless the case starts in the hands of a homicide investigator, at some point, the control of the scene must be turned over to the homicide investigator. The initial officer needs to communicate all important information to the investigator. The homicide investigator needs to be informed of the scene boundaries, potential witnesses, and any surviving victims, items possibly related to the homicide, statements heard, and any other relevant information. Transfer of scene control and scene boundaries must be clearly communicated so the scene remains secure. Finally, the responding officer needs to document all possibly important information as soon as possible about the crime scene, witnesses, victims, and all actions performed by the responding officer and anyone else on the scene including medical personnel and other officers (National Institute of Justice, 2004).

Preliminary Scene Assessment by Homicide Investigator

Once investigators have the information from the first responder, they should be sure proper procedures are being used. Investigators need to evaluate and determine if safety practices are adequate and initiate their use if necessary. Pathways and scene boundaries should be assessed and changed if necessary, and all personnel should be made aware of any changes (National Institute of Justice, 2004).

Investigators should prioritize the investigative steps to be undertaken and to ensure the integrity and security of the scene. Staging areas for consultation, equipment, and temporary evidence storage should be set and secured. It is important to consider environmental factors when establishing evidence storage. When there are more than one related crime scene, investigators should establish communication between each scene. It is important that search and seizure rules are followed and necessary legal and or prosecutorial resources are brought in. The lead investigator must also determine any additional needs, such as specialized equipment, units, and additional investigative resources (National Institute of Justice, 2004). It is also of utmost importance that homicide investigators ensure that search warrants are obtained so any evidence collected will be available to the prosecutors.

Officers who first arrive on the scene and investigators must observe the rules of search and seizure because valuable evidence that can help convict an offender may be lost if the police do not follow search and seizure rules. In *Katz* v. *United States* (1967), the Supreme Court ruled that citizens have a reasonable expectation of privacy. The police cannot search where a reasonable person would expect to have privacy. As a result, law enforcement officers must take care not to conduct warrantless searches unless certain conditions are met. Moreover, law enforcement officers must take care to follow proper procedures in obtaining warrants and conducting searches with warrants.

Although every situation in which the police can or cannot conduct searches has not been determined, several Supreme Court Cases are used as guidelines in establishing rules and regulations for police searches in different jurisdictions. Police investigators may request that a judge or magistrate issue a search warrant that will allow the officers to conduct a search legally. To obtain a search warrant that will allow an individual's right to privacy to be breached, law enforcement officers must show probable cause (reasonable belief) that specific illegal activities will or have been committed and detailed information about where the police will search, what they will be searching for, and what they hope to seize. Law enforcement officers must take great care in specifying the details in requesting a warrant. To avoid the possibility that evidence will be thrown out, officers must be sure to record correct addresses and to be broad enough in their descriptions to cover what they may find but specific enough to convince a judge they are looking for evidence that is likely to exist.

In certain situations, the Supreme Court has determined that police can conduct searches without a warrant. For their own safety and to preserve evidence, officers may conduct warrantless searches that are incidental to an arrest. An officer may search a suspect and the immediate area within the control of the suspect to be certain no weapons are present and the accused cannot destroy any evidence. Interestingly, in *New York* v. *Belton* (1981), the Supreme Court ruled that an entire car would be considered in the "immediate area of a suspect." In other words, the police can search the trunk and other areas of a car when they arrest a suspect who is driving a car. Without an arrest, however, citizens are not required to allow police to search their vehicles. The police can only search a car if they have probable cause to believe the vehicle has evidence of criminal activity (Gaines & Miller, 2004).

Police may also conduct consensual searches—those in which the person who has the privacy right to the area being searched voluntarily agrees to the search. Officers may also enter a building and search for a suspect if they are in "hot pursuit" of a suspect and the suspect enters the building. In *Flippo* v. *West Virginia* (1999) (see Box 14.1), the Supreme Court cited their 1977 ruling in *Mincey* v. *Arizona* when they ruled that a homicide crime scene did not in itself constitute an emergency situation that would allow officers to search without a search warrant. Because in *Katz* v. *U.S.* (1967) the Supreme Court ruled that it is the responsibility of the police to make the case that the situation was an emergency and they could not have waited to get a search warrant, officers must be certain to take care in moving forward in a murder investigation. Although much of what you see about police on television is not accurate or is, at the very least, misleading, it is true that prosecutors will not be able to use evidence that the police obtain illegally.

Witnesses' memories may be affected by their interaction with others, so it is vital to separate them from each other and from any other people. It is also important to attain and record valid witness identification. The lead investigator must also assign officers to canvass the surrounding areas to ascertain who else may be a witness. These officers must understand that they should document what they learn, who they have talked to, and who may have been unavailable to them (National Institute of Justice, 2004).

The lead homicide investigator must also be sure the scene is fully documented. The scene should be documented as first observed through photography, rough sketches, and notes. The photographing of evidence has been an important investigative process for years, and its value has grown as the ease of digital photography has increased (National Institute of Justice, 2004).

It is the lead homicide detective's responsibility to oversee the collection of evidence and ensure that the proper chain of custody is followed and documented. If a proper chain of custody is not employed, an important piece of evidence can be excluded from trial. Geberth (1996) gives these seven guidelines for collecting evidence properly in a homicide investigation:

1. Each piece of evidence should be properly labeled so its original location and position is known. The investigator should also note this information in his or her notebook.

BOX 14.1
Flippo v. *West Virginia* (1999)

In the early morning hours of April 30, 1996, James Flippo called 911 and reported that he and his wife, Cheryl, had been attacked at a West Virginia state park. The police responded quickly and found Flippo standing outside the cabin he had rented. The police found Flippo's dead wife in the cabin. It appeared she had died of fatal head wounds. The police took Flippo to the hospital because he was suffering from head injuries. The officers secured the area and searched inside and outside of the cabin for footprints and any signs there had been a break-in. After a period of time when a police photographer arrived at the scene, the investigators began to search the crime scene more thoroughly. They carefully searched the scene for over 16 hours, at which time they collected evidence and took photographs. During this search, the investigators found an envelope with negatives and photographs in a briefcase, which they seized. The pictures showed a male friend of Flippo's taking off his pants. The prosecutor used the pictures at trial to argue that Flippo killed his wife after they argued about Flippo having an affair with the man. On appeal, Flippo's attorneys argued that because the police had not obtained a warrant to search the premises, the photographs and negatives were illegally seized during an illegal search and should be suppressed. In other words, the prosecutor should not be allowed to use the photographs and negatives as evidence against Flippo. Flippo's attorneys argued that no exception to the need for a warrant existed. The Supreme Court agreed based on the 1978 case *Mincey* v. *Arizona* in which they stated there is not a "murder scene exception" to the Warrant Clause of the Fourth Amendment. The Court stated that the police may enter premises to be sure no victims or killers are on the premises. The negatives and photographs, however, were found in a briefcase, not in plain view or where the police would reasonably expect to find a victim or offender (Biskupic, 1999).

2. The label should also note who discovered the item.
3. Proper case numbers, date, and time of collection should also be indicated on the evidence.
4. Each piece of evidence should be packaged in a separate, properly sized, clean container that will protect the item and prevent cross-contamination.
5. The evidence packaging should be sealed to protect the evidence and prevent unauthorized individuals from handling it.
6. Items of evidence should be marked to indicate where they should be delivered for analysis (FBI or police laboratory) or whether it should be sent to evidence lockup.
7. Careful records detailing chain of custody (where the evidence is moved to and from and by whom) must be maintained.

> ## BOX 14.2
> ### The Body Farm
>
> "The Body Farm" is a nickname for the University of Tennessee's Anthropology Research Facility. It is the only facility in the world established for the study of decaying corpses. Dr. William Bass started the research facility in 1980. Since that time, Bass and his research students have completed dozens of studies to determine how different factors affect body decomposition. They have left bodies exposed to the weather, they have buried them in various types of graves, and they have locked them away in car trunks. They have carefully analyzed the decomposition, noting everything from the gases and smells given off to the different insects that feast on the corpses throughout the decomposition process. These odorous and grotesque studies are all done in the name of science— science that has helped solve thousands of crimes (Bass & Jefferson, 2003; Montgomery, 1999).

EVIDENCE

Experienced homicide detectives know that anything and everything has the potential to be evidence. Physical evidence may include any concrete object, no matter how small or large, that could possibly be used by a prosecutor or defense attorney during the course of a trial (Geberth, 1996). The details of the various classifications of physical evidence are beyond the scope of this chapter, but examples of physical evidence often collected in homicide investigations are discussed in the next sections of the chapter.

THE BODY

Although there have been successful homicide prosecutions without the discovery of a victim's body, most often a homicide investigation begins with the body, and the body often provides important evidence for further investigation and ultimately for the prosecution of a case. According to Snow (2005), when homicide detectives first come upon a dead body, they attempt to determine cause of death and the manner of death. Cause of death may have two components: proximate cause, which is the initial event that led to the death, and the immediate cause, which is what actually caused the person to expire. In other words, the proximate cause could be a gunshot wound and the immediate cause could be loss of blood (Snow, 2005). Manner of death is usually classified as one of the following: natural, suicide, accidental, undetermined, and the one we are most interested in: homicide.

The victim's body is often an important clue for determining time of death, which can be important for narrowing in on particular suspects. Determining time of death from the examination of a body often appears easy when Briscoe and Green arrive at a murder scene on *Law & Order*. In real-life homicide detection, however, it is often difficult to determine the time of death because so many factors may affect the variables investigators consider. Nevertheless, time of death can be an important factor in solving a case, so medical examiners usually use several methods to determine a time range within which the death was likely to have occurred (Snow, 2005). In his very interesting book on homicide investigation, former homicide investigator Robert Snow discusses what examiners use to determine time of death with the caveat that different conditions, including air conditioning, body size, humidity, and more, may affect the time periods noted. The factors are listed in Box 14.3.

Blood Splatter Evidence

Blood splatter evidence is where physics and criminal investigation meets. As blood drops splatter or drop from the human body, they are affected by gravity and velocity. By studying the patterns of blood, we can learn much. The shape of a blood droplet, for instance, can tell us the direction from which the blood traveled. A round drop tells us it dropped directly down to rest on the surface where it is discovered. Any other shape indicates the blood has not simply dropped. If there is a long oblong-shaped drop with what may look like a tail, the tail points to the direction from which the blood came. Because of computers today, it is easier than ever to use mathematical formulas and details about blood splatter to determine where offenders and victims were as a murder happened. Blood splatter may also tell us whether an offender used the right or left hand to beat or bludgeon a victim. Snow (2005), for example, notes that when facing a victim, if the blood track is to the victim's right and going away from the victim, the offender used the right hand to beat the victim. Several lines of blood indicates more than one strike, and a wider blood track tells the investigator that a knife was an unlikely weapon because knives leave thinner tracks whereas objects like pipes leave wider tracks (Snow, 2005: 82).

Fingerprints

Fingerprints are unique to each individual; however, they do not prove an individual is guilty. If an offender admits they have been at a crime scene, finding their fingerprints at the scene does not solve a case. Often, however, fingerprint evidence can be quite valuable. If a suspect denies being at the crime scene, finding his or her fingerprints there can be damning, and the same might be true for fingerprints on a murder weapon as it was in October 2006 in St. Paul, Minnesota. April Salinas called 911 and reported she had been stabbed. She was rushed to the hospital where she died without naming her attacker. The police soon discovered a bloody fingerprint on a kitchen knife found less than a mile from where Salinas had been stabbed. Armstrong

BOX 14.3
Indicators of Time of Death

Indicator	Time
Temperature of body	Body loses 1.5°F every hour until it reaches the surrounding air temperature.
Thin film formed over eyes and appears cloudy	Film appears cloudy approximately 3 hours after death.
Skin has greenish hue; body bloated	This is caused by a bacterial reaction in the body that usually occurs with 48 hours after death.
Dried blood	Blood takes approximately 1/2 to 4 hours to dry.
Discoloration on the skin due to lividity (livor mortis) or settling of blood after death due to gravity	Discoloration is perceptible after 1 hour and becomes set within approximately 8 hours.
Rigor mortis (stiffening of body)	Full rigor usually takes between 10 and 12 hours to set and lasts 24 to 36 hours.
Undigested food in the stomach	Indicates the person died not long after he or she ate the food in the stomach.
State of insect larvae found in or around the remains	Indicates victim has been dead for at least several days and the determination of how long may be loosely determined by careful examination of the larvae including the type and condition.
Factors unrelated to the body: when mail last picked up, when most recent phone calls or e-mails recorded, when last seen by family, coworkers, and neighbors, and even factors such as a half-eaten or prepared meal being present	Varies by what investigators find.

Weston was arrested when it was determined that his fingerprints matched those found on the weapon (Associated Press, 2006).

Investigators seek out three types of fingerprints at a crime scene. First and most common are *latent* prints. Naturally, we have oil and perspiration on our

BOX 14.4
Locard's Exchange Principle

Dr. Edmond Locard (1877–1966), the director of the first crime laboratory in Lyon, France, is credited with establishing the foundation of forensic science. Locard's exchange principle states that whenever two items come into contact with one another, some kind of an exchange takes place between the two items. As such, careful collection of evidence can help prove a specific offender has been in contact with a specific victim or at a particular location (Chisum & Turvey, 2000).

skin, and when we touch surfaces, the natural substances on our fingers transfer to the surface. If you touch a glass and hold it front of a light source at the right angle, you will be able to see the fingerprints you left on the glass. The second type of prints are called *patent* prints, those that are left when an individual touches a foreign substance like ink or blood and then transfers the finger imprint in that substance to another object. The third type is called a *molded* fingerprint, those prints that individuals leave in a soft substance that they touch, such as might be found in wet paint (Snow, 2005).

Although fingerprints have been used at least since the late 1800s in homicide cases, recent innovations have made it possible to obtain fingerprint evidence from surfaces such as human skin that do not usually show finger imprints (Moore, 2006; Snow, 2005). Some of the innovations involve the use of different types of light that make the fingerprints visible, so the fingerprint technicians can use the regular means of fingerprint powder to make the prints visible for photographing. Then they can be collected with the use of tape and a fingerprint card.

You may have seen the dramatization of another innovation in the collection of fingerprints on *CSI Miami* or another fictional crime show. Crime lab technicians use cyanoacrylate, a chemical found in Super Glue, to make fingerprints seemingly appear out of thin air on many surfaces. The technician places the object that may have fingerprints on it in a closed container along with a heat source that allows him or her to heat the cyanoacrylate slowly. The cyanoacrylate sticks to the fingerprint residue, and suddenly, almost like magic, the crime investigator has a usable fingerprint.

Of course fingerprints help identify suspects, but the police must already have fingerprints to compare with those found at the scene of a crime. If the police have a suspect already in mind, a match between the suspect's fingerprints and those found at the scene may help tie a case together. However, if there is no suspect, the fingerprints lifted at a scene are only going to be helpful if the prints are on file and accessible to the police. Today, in addition to their own fingerprint files, law enforcement personnel can use the Automated Fingerprint Identification Systems (AFIS) to compare the prints found at the scene with millions of prints stored digitally. If the fingerprints are on file, the investigator's job has been made much easier. In the Night

BOX 14.5

Sticky Fingerprint Leads to the Night Stalker

In the summer of 1985, journalists gave the name "Night Stalker" to a killer who was terrorizing Los Angeles. The killer struck at night, breaking into houses and robbing, raping, and murdering those he found. Unlike many other serial killers, he used various methods to kill his victims. Some victims were shot, some stabbed, and others were beaten with hammers and crowbars; and often female victims were sexually assaulted. It was also not unusual for him to attack more than one person in a night. The police in Los Angeles were able to get a description of the "Night Stalker" from a surviving witness. When they aggressively distributed police sketches made from the survivor's description, the "Night Stalker" fled to San Francisco.

The "Night Stalker" continued his killing in San Francisco. Unfortunately, for the stalker and fortunately for the citizens of San Francisco, an astute teenager, James Romero III, wrote down a license plate number of a Toyota station wagon that passed by his house several times one evening. The same night, a woman who had survived a sexual assault reported the offender left in a Toyota station wagon. After locating the car, the police did not originally find any fingerprints. However, using the cyanoacrylate warming process in an attempt to find any fingerprints, a single print was located. Using AFIS, the police were able to match the print to 25-year-old Richard Ramirez, who was soon arrested. After numerous delays in the court system, he was eventually found guilty and sentenced to death (Summers, 2006).

Stalker Case (see Box 14.5), had Ramirez's print not been in the AFIS system, he may not have been apprehended so quickly after the one print was located in his abandoned car (Wilson & Woodard, 1987).

DNA

Deoxyribonucleic acid analysis, more commonly known as DNA analysis, has become an important tool for solving homicides. With the exception of identical twins, each person's DNA is unique, and importantly for crime investigations, it may be recovered from almost any part of the human body. A drop of blood, a piece of broken fingernail, hair, and saliva and other bodily fluids contain DNA. Thus even the smallest piece of evidence at a crime scene can be traced to the offender. Likewise, just a hair left by a victim can help place the victim in an offender's automobile or house. Although DNA analysis is not as quick as one might believe after watching an episode of *CSI*, it is a valuable tool for solving homicides and prosecuting homicide offenders.

Importantly, however, like with fingerprints, recovering DNA at a crime scene does not guarantee that a suspect will be apprehended. In some cases, law enforcement has a suspect in mind and a comparison of DNA found at the scene to the suspect's DNA can tie up the case, or in some cases, the DNA may rule out a suspect. Either way, the DNA of a suspect is necessary for comparison.

When the police do not have a suspect in mind, DNA can still be helpful but only with the creation of DNA banks where DNA samples of convicted criminals are stored for comparisons in crime cases. Many states established their own DNA banks in the 1990s, and in 1994, the DNA Identification Act allowed the FBI officially to establish a national DNA file system that would allow jurisdictions across the United States to share DNA profiles. By the end of 1998, the FBI launched the Combined DNA Index System (CODIS). By December 2006, CODIS already contained over 4 million DNA profiles (FBI, 2000; 2007).

CODIS has also become a valuable tool for solving so-called cold cases. The 1977 murder of Henry Long at a Richmond, Virginia, pizzeria was cleared in 2005 when a Virginia state lab found a DNA match for blood left at the scene of the 1977 crime. When Benjamin Johnson was arrested on a felony gun charge in 2004, he was required to submit a DNA sample. The sample matched the blood left at the 1977 homicide (Bowes, 2006). Police were then able to arrest Johnson for Long's murder.

Ballistics

In 1889, Alexandre Lacassagne, a professor of forensic medicine at the University of Lyons in France, discovered that firearms leave unique markings on bullets, and thus the field of ballistics was born (Forensic Technology Inc., 2006). Today, ballistics experts can help identify potential suspects by comparing bullet and bullet casings with firearms. Like AFIS and CODIS, a national system maintained by the Bureau of Alcohol, Tobacco, Firearms and Explosives (ATF) links information about firearms across the nation. This database system is called the National Integrated Ballistics Information Network (NIBIN). ATF reported that as of December 2005, over 9 million pieces of crime scene evidence had been entered into NIBIN and over 12,500 hits had been made with the system (ATF, 2005).

Ballistics, however, involves more than determining whether a bullet was fired from a particular firearm. Ballistics is another area in murder investigations where physics is used. Ballistics is the science of all types of projectiles, but most often we hear it used to refer to the study of bullets. Interior ballistics involves the movement of the bullet within the firearm; exterior ballistics is the study of the bullet (or other projectile) in flight. Ballistics also includes the study of the impact of bullets and what happens to bullets on impact. Forensically, ballistics experts may be used to help determine what firearms were used, where they were fired from, and where the offender and victim were and what they were doing at the time of the shooting (*World Encyclopedia*, 1980).

Other Evidence

In addition to DNA, ballistic, fingerprint, and blood evidence, investigators use other evidence to help make their cases. Cloth and carpet fibers, tires and shoe prints, and even the methods used by a killer to commit a murder or to access the

---

BOX 14.6

Preparing to Be a Crime Scene Investigator

If you are majoring in criminal justice because you want to be a crime scene investigator, you may want to do a little investigation of your own to learn whether a criminal justice degree is the best degree for you. If you want to work as a CSI at the federal level, switching your major to a natural science such as biology, chemistry, or physics may serve you better. Other possibilities include degrees in toxicology and forensic science. You do not have to abandon criminal justice altogether. A double major with criminal justice or perhaps a minor in criminal justice will in most cases serve you well.

Before you head off to the science building, you might want to contact your local police departments and find out if your local police are as strict about who they hire as the federal government. It is quite likely, depending on where you want to work, that a criminal justice degree and several years of experience will open the door to crime scene investigation. What is most important is that you find out early in your career and do all you can to make your dreams come true. You may want to start your career investigation online or with Prentice Hall's book, *Work in Criminal Justice: An A–Z Guide to Careers in Criminal Justice* by Debbie Goodman and Ron Grimming.

---

victim may help an investigator solve a murder. Sometimes finding similarities between cases may help the investigators. VICAP, the Violent Criminal Apprehension Program, is a national database that the FBI established to help investigators share information across jurisdictions in the case of a serial offender. Law enforcement agencies across the nation voluntarily submit information about unsolved cases to VICAP, which can then be used to find similarities across cases. With VICAP, the FBI can determine whether there are similarities in the way violent crimes are committed or witness descriptions of possible offenders that may suggest the existence of a serial offender. The FBI can then help link investigators in various jurisdictions who are seeking out the same offender. With cooperation and the sharing of information, the suspect may be located and apprehended.

It is the duty of the police to solve murders and arrest the offenders, but their job does not end with the arrest. The police must also help the district attorney who prosecutes the accused. As the general public may be more aware of than ever before, the police officer or detective is not the only one involved in solving crimes these days. Depending on the complexity of the crime, a whole host of other professionals may play a role in identifying the offender and ensuring that the prosecutor can convince the judge or jury of the offender's guilt. Others involved in solving crimes include crime scene investigators, fingerprint analysts, crime lab technicians, and sometimes forensic anthropologists, psychological profilers, and even entomologists (Snow, 2005).

> ## BOX 14.7
> ### Lighting up the Crime with CLU
>
> In 2003, the U.S. Department of Justice announced the development of a Criminalistics Light-Imaging Unit (CLU) that allowed investigators to detect minuscule evidence not visible with the naked eye or even with the blue light used widely by crime scene investigators. The CLU is helpful in detecting fingerprints, blood, semen, and other fluids (Snow, 2005). Unlike regular fluorescence detection that requires nearly complete darkness to work, CLU can be used in regular lighting, making it work better in crime scenes outside than the blue lights used by most departments (National Institute of Justice, 2003).

DO THE RACE AND CLASS OF THE VICTIM MATTER IN HOMICIDE CLEARANCE?

Janice Puckett and Richard Lundman (2003) studied all 802 murders that occurred in Columbus, Ohio, between 1984 and 1992 to determine whether extralegal factors such as a victim's race and social class status affect homicide clearance. Although the victim's social class, race, and sex did not appear to make a difference, homicides that occurred in African American communities were less likely to be solved. Puckett and Lundman argued that this had more to do with the lack of cooperation from citizens in African American communities than with homicide detectives treating homicides differently. Citizens in African American communities are suspicious of the police because of previous interactions, according to the researchers, and as a result they are less cooperative with the police. Puckett and Lundman (2003) conclude that homicide detectives work diligently on every case. Ken Litwin (2004) found similar results using Chicago homicide cases. However, in Litwin's study, cases with Latino victims were less likely than those with white victims to be cleared by arrest. Still, it may be the case that the differences in clearance have less to do with police discretion and more to do with the availability of useful witness information (Litwin, 2004).

> ## BOX 14.8
> ### Attention to Detail and Experience Are Invaluable
>
> In his book on crime scene investigation, Snow (2005) tells the story of Ten Binion's death. Las Vegas investigators believed Binion had died accidentally. However, his family asked Dr. Michael Baden to take a look at Binion's body. Baden, who had conducted over 20,000 autopsies as a
>
> continued

medical examiner in New York City, found evidence to suggest Binion had been "burked" to death. *Burked* is a slang term that refers to suffocating someone by covering their nose and mouth and applying pressure to the chest until the victim suffocates. Killers may use this method in an attempt to make a murder look like an accidental death. What did Baden see that led him to believe Binion had been murdered? First, he noted scrapes on Binion's wrists that suggested to Bader that Binion had been handcuffed. Baden also reported a red mark on Binion's mouth and several small round red marks found on his chest. Bader believed the red mark on the mouth suggested Binion's mouth had been covered forcefully and that the red marks on his chest were imprints from his buttons that were made when Binion's killer applied pressure to his chest to suffocate him. This information and other details about some of Binion's supposed friends led prosecutors eventually to prosecute Binion's former girlfriend and her boyfriend for Binion's murder. A jury found them guilty largely based on Baden's testimony and the evidence he had discovered (Snow, 2005).

INTERVIEWING WITNESSES

There is no doubt that physical evidence is often important for solving murders. As discussed in Chapter 15, the testimony of an individual who witnesses a murder has served as very powerful direct evidence for a prosecutor's case. As with good journalism, the murder detective needs to inquire about who, what, where, when, why, and how when questioning witnesses. However, unlike the basics of journalism, a good detective needs to move beyond these basic questions to pay attention to everything that a witness reports and to probe him or her for details that the witness may not consider important. To ensure that the basic information if acquired and to help probe for all important details, some homicide detectives are required, encouraged, or volunteer to use standardized interview guides. These guides include questions about the basics, such as all the details needed about the witnesses, so the detective can contact them again. A whole host of other questions are included on detective interview guides about any incidents the eyewitness witnessed and usually specific questions to help stimulate the witnesses' memory, especially with regard to a description of the suspect (Osterburg & Ward, 2004).

To help witnesses identify a suspect—especially those for which the police have no leads, three main methods are used to create a picture of the suspect. It is likely that you have seen fictional depictions of all three methods. First, an artist may listen to descriptions provided by witnesses and ask them questions as they make a sketch of the suspect. Second, in some jurisdictions, kits such as *Identi-Kit* are used to generate a composite of the suspect. Identi-Kits include several versions of facial features, including eyes, ears, noses, mouths, and facial hair, that can be put together to construct a likeness of a suspect. Third and the most technological, computer graphic Identi-Kit–type software programs are now available. This cutting-edge software allows detectives to use witness information to create three-dimensional lifelike composites of suspects.

INTERROGATING SUSPECTS

In contrast to the interviewing of witness, detectives are said to interrogate suspects (and often their loved ones) to help solve cases. Interrogations are necessarily different than interviews because those being interrogated are believed to have reasons to be deceptive. Moreover, to meet Supreme Court requirements that a suspect must be made aware of his or her rights, the police are obliged to give what is known as the Miranda warnings to any suspect who they arrest (see Box 14.9). The Miranda warnings specify that the suspect has the right to remain silent and the right to have an attorney present during questioning. Furthermore, the police must tell a custodial suspect that any statements he or she makes may be used against the suspect in court. Finally, the Miranda warnings indicate that an attorney will be provided for him or her if the suspect cannot afford an attorney. Although there are exceptions, generally if the police do not inform a suspect who is in custody of his or her rights, any statements made by the suspect will not be able to be used by the prosecutor in prosecuting the case. Additionally, any evidence that the police may obtain from information given by a suspect in custody who has not been given the Miranda warning may also be inadmissible in court. Thus it is extremely important that homicide investigators and other law enforcement officers read suspects their Miranda rights when they take them into custody.

BOX 14.9

Miranda Warnings

Before the U.S. Supreme Court Ruling in *Miranda* v. *Arizona*, most U.S. citizens were not aware that the U.S. Constitution and Bill of Rights guaranteed citizens rights that were established to protect citizens from an overbearing government. Prior to the 1966 Supreme Court decision, police could take advantage of suspects' ignorance about their rights. In 1963, police in Arizona believed that Ernesto Miranda had kidnapped and raped an 18-year-old woman with mild retardation. During questioning by the police, Miranda confessed to the crime. The judge in Miranda's original trial allowed the confession to be used by the prosecutors despite the fact that Miranda's attorney argued the confession should be thrown out because Miranda was not advised of his rights (Mount, 2006).

In 1966, however, the Supreme Court heard Miranda's appeal. The Court ruled that Miranda's confession could not be used as evidence because Miranda had not been advised of his rights. Now police must "Mirandize" suspects when they are arrested. What happened to Ernesto Miranda, who confessed to a rape? His first conviction was thrown out because the Supreme Court ruled his confession could not be used. However, when he was retried a second time without the confession used as evidence, he was convicted of the crime and sentenced to prison. After serving time for the rape, Miranda was released from prison. In 1976, Miranda was killed in a bar fight (Mount, 2006).

Although it is not admissible in court, homicide investigators sometimes ask suspects to take a lie detector test. The most common lie detection devices used in the United States are the polygraph and the voice stress analyzer. The older of the two methods, the polygraph, measures any change in several physiological functions, including breathing, blood pressure, heart rate, and perspiration. Many studies have attempted to test the validity of polygraph testing. According to one review done for Congress, these studies reported an accuracy rating for polygraph as low as 64% to as high as 98%. Importantly, in at least one study, 75% of persons who were innocent were found to be deceptive (Office of Technology Assessment, 1983). In addition, there are cases where those later found to be guilty had previously passed polygraphs. Such was the case of Gary Ridgway who was a suspect in the Green River murders. In the early 1980s, Ridgway passed a polygraph test. Nearly 20 years later in 2001, Ridgway was arrested when police matched his DNA and other trace evidence to the Green River Murder cases (Snow, 2005). With results like this, it is no surprise that polygraph results are not admissible in court. Still, many homicide investigators find polygraphs to be a valuable tool for gaining confessions and in ruling out some suspects (Snow, 2005).

The use of voice stress analyzers is at least as controversial as polygraph tests. Voice stress analyzers are said to measure tiny differences in a person's voice that are believed to indicate stress and thus deception. Those who believe it is a valuable tool argue that the cost of a voice stress analyzer is about half the cost of a polygraph machine (Snow, 2005). However, many like Steven Drizin, the legal director for the Center for Wrongful Convictions at Northwestern University's School of Law, believe the voice stress analyzer fails to produce accurate results (Lowe, 2006). Some still argue that the point is not that the voice analyzer can accurately tell whether someone is lying but that it can be used as a tool to get a confession out of a guilty suspect (Lowe, 2006).

INVESTIGATIVE PROFILING

Investigative profiling is a method used by law enforcement personnel to attempt to learn what they can about a suspect when little is known. A behavioral and sometimes physical description of the offender is generated from what is known about the crimes the killer has committed. Using psychological and sociological knowledge gleaned from the crime scenes, the types of victims chosen, where and how the victims are discovered, and where the victims are believed to have met up with the offender, a profiler provides a description, so to speak, of the offender. The profiler may tell law enforcement that they are looking for a man or a person of a certain race; it may be the person is outgoing or a loner or that he or she works the night shift or travels for business. Any of these pieces of information may help the investigator narrow the focus. There is the possibility for error in investigative profiling, however, that the investigator would need to remember as well (see Box 14.10).

Although not directly assessing the validity of profiling, Salfati (2000) examined whether there were differentiations in the background characteristics of homicide offenders based on the scene of the homicide. In theory, if homicide scenes are a

BOX 14.10

Is Profiling Reliable and Valid?

Academic reviews of profiling have noted that empirical evidence for the claims made by FBI agents in their early descriptions of how they practiced profiling is lacking (Coleman & Norris, 2000; Hazelwood, Ressler, Depue, & Douglas, 1987; Muller, 2000; Alison & Canter, 1999). Some academics have pointed out that what has been defined as psychological profiling by the FBI is not scientific but actually guesswork by experienced investigators based on little more than their own experiences and perceptions. As a result, it is not surprising that no evidence supports or goes against claims that profiling conducted in this way works (Salfati, 2000).

Damon Muller (2000) critically examined two main approaches to profiling. First, crime scene analysis (CSA) is the approach used by the FBI. In CSA profiling, offenders are divided into those who are disorganized asocial offenders and those who are organized nonsocial offenders. Disorganized offenders are believed to have low IQs, and they are often suffering from some mental disorder. The disorganized offender attacks with less thinking and may select victims at random. The crime scene left by the disorganized offender reflects brutality. The organized offender is more intelligent and more likely to be married and appear normal, although he may be a sociopath. The organized offender is more likely to plan the attack and bring weapons and restraints so he can control the victim. Knowing these two broad types of offenders, a profiler using the CSA approach uses information from the crime scene to construct a general profile of the offender.

Investigative psychology (IP) is a popular method of profiling used in the United Kingdom. David Canter has been instrumental in popularizing the IP method, which uses psychological knowledge to hypothesize information about the offender. This method takes into account factors such as the race of the offender because we know offenders usually attack those of the same race. More importantly, however, the person attacked is believed to have some type of significance for the offender. The time and place of the crime is also relevant in IP profiling. Muller's review of the literature leads him to the conclusion that offender profiling has yet to be proved effective. He also concludes that IP is more scientific than CSA because IP has testable hypotheses and empirical studies that demonstrate the effectiveness of IP as a method. CSA, in contrast, appears to be largely based on experience and intuition, which is difficult if not impossible to test. Thus Muller does not state which is more effective but notes that IP is testable and some evidence exists to support it (Muller, 2000).

reflection of an offender's background characteristics, the scenes could be used to profile offenders. Salfati (2000) found that those who committed expressive homicides had different criminal backgrounds than those who committed instrumental homicides. In expressive homicides, the offender expresses aggression, and signs, such as multiple wounds to the victim's face, indicate the offender's goal was to punish the

---

BOX 14.11

Initiating a Serial Murder Investigation

Egger (2002) lists four ways investigators determine that they need to initiate a serial murder investigation. First, investigators may discover links between the murder they are investigating and other unsolved cases. Factors believed to be relevant in linking cases include similarities in at least one of the following: the methods used to kill, the type of victim, the crime scenes, or the area in which the bodies are being discovered or where the victims are last seen. Second, sometimes law enforcers are encouraged to consider the possibility of a serial killer by victim's families who demand the possibility be considered or sometimes by reporters who through their own investigations make a case that the possibility of a serial killer exists. Third, law enforcement may accidentally stumble on a serial killer as they did with Jeffery Dahmer when officers responding to an assault call discovered the gruesome remains of many of Dahmer's victims. The fourth way a serial killer investigation is initiated is also somewhat happenstance. A suspect who is under investigation for a single crime confesses to killing several victims (Egger, 2002).

BOX 14.12

HITS: Homicide Investigation Tracking System

The failure of investigators to connect related crimes is called *linkage blindness* (Egger, 1984). It is a well-known problem faced by law enforcement officers when offenders commit crimes in different jurisdictions. The investigations of serial killings by the Green River Killer and Ted Bundy led Washington State officials to develop a database that would help prevent linkage blindness. The Homicide Investigation Tracking System (HITS) allows different law enforcement agencies in the Pacific Northwest to share information about violent crimes occurring in their jurisdictions. Each agency can use HITS to find patterns among cases within their own jurisdictions, but it also allows officers to compare details about crimes occurring in their jurisdictions with crimes in Washington and Oregon. HITS contains data on over 6,000 homicides and more than 7,000 sexual assaults. Other states have followed Washington's example and created their own homicide investigation tracking systems, including New York's Homicide Assessment and Lead Tracking (HALT) and New Jersey's Homicide Evaluation and Assessment Tracking (HEAT).

Source: Washington State Attorney General, 2004.

victim. These crimes, according to Salfati's findings, were often committed by an offender who had a current or previous intimate relationship with the victim. Instrumental offenders often were known to have previous psychological or psychiatric problems. In contrast, the offender's goal in an instrumental attack is not to hurt the victim; instead the killing was necessary to gain something, whether territory, money, or other valuables, from the killing. An instrumental offender was likely to be unemployed and have a previous criminal record for theft or burglary. Further, when compared with expressive homicide offenders, instrumental homicide offenders were more likely to have previous convictions for violent offenses and to have spent time in prison. Although some offenders did not fit these findings, overall offender characteristics appeared to distinguish between the instrumental and expressive homicides. As a result, an investigator or profiler could use the information generated by scientific studies to gain insight about the offender based on the scene. However, it is not a perfect science; there will be offenders who do not fit the model.

COLD CASE SQUADS

In 1979, the Metro-Dade Police Department in Miami, Florida, created what they called the "Pending Case Squad." This squad was established to work on uncleared cases. Although the uncleared cases were still important to the department; they were not actively being investigated because leads appeared exhausted and more recent cases had taken precedent. The Miami squad temporarily disbanded and was brought together again in 1983 as "the cold case squad," at which time they solved the 1982 murder of a young girl (Horn, 2005). With advances in criminalistics and well-publicized cold case squad successes, cold case squads have become increasingly common.

The success of cold case squads depend on the selection of effective supervisors and investigators who are experienced, persistent, and innovative (Regini, 1997). The cases handled by cold case squads are some of the most challenging cases faced by homicide detectives. Other competent investigators were unable to solve these cases when they were fresh, and now that the cases are older, the challenge can be even greater (Regini, 1997). But the successes come as a relief to victim's family members who have lived with the murders unsolved.

The San Antonio Police Department's cold case squad has solved over 20 cold cases since 1998 including the murder of Jayne Hays. The bludgeoned body of Jayne Hays, an elderly woman who lived alone, was found by her neighbor in 1989. In 2003, the cold case squad began working the case by reinterviewing all the witnesses they could locate. They found that Hays had fired Marie Reilly, who had been working as her maid for stealing. Reilly, who was 61 years old at the time of the murder, admitted to being in Hays's apartment shortly before the murder. However, Reilly was inconsistent in her explanations for being at the apartment. The cold case detectives resubmitted evidence for testing. Reilly's blood was found along with Hays's blood on a washcloth. Reilly was convicted of murder on July 22, 2006, and sentenced to 20 years in prison (San Antonio Police Department, 2006).

Summary

The chapter began with the important concept of homicide clearance and clearance trends in the United States and other countries. Then the detailed major steps of a homicide investigation for the initial responder and the lead homicide investigator were presented. The importance of obtaining a search warrant and correctly proceeding with a search and the collection of evidence was emphasized. A review of several types of evidence, including blood splatter, fingerprints, and DNA, were also discussed. The chapter concluded with a review of academic research on homicide investigation, such as Puckett and Lundman's study of homicide investigators in Columbus, Ohio.

Chapter Questions

1. What does it mean to say a homicide is "cleared"?
2. What are the four criteria used in the NIBS to categorize a homicide as being "cleared exceptionally"?
3. What variables or characteristics are linked to higher homicide clearance?
4. What has been the trend in homicide clearance in the United States since 1976?
5. What are "dunkers"?
6. True or false: The likelihood of solving a homicide decreases with time.
7. Give a brief overview of the first responder's responsibilities at a homicide scene.
8. What does the acronym ADAPT stand for?
9. When may police search without a warrant?
10. Who was Flippo, and why is he included in this chapter?
11. Is there a "murder scene exception" to the warrant clause of the Fourth Amendment?
12. Why should witnesses be separated?
13. What are the seven guidelines for properly collecting evidence?
14. What is the difference between manner of death and cause of death?
15. List at least three indicators of time of death.
16. What type of evidence involves physics?
17. How might fingerprints help solve a case?
18. List and describe three types of fingerprints.
19. Briefly explain what the study of ballistics entails.
20. Where can police obtain DNA?
21. What are VICAP, CODIS, NIBIN, and AFIS?
22. What is a good major in college for an aspiring crime scene investigator?
23. What did Puckett and Lundman conclude about extralegal factors and homicide clearance?
24. Name and compare two types of lie detector tests.
25. Why are the Miranda warnings important?
26. What is Locard's exchange principle?
27. Name and compare the two types of profiling discussed in this chapter.
28. What have scientific studies suggested about profiling?

29. What are the four ways that investigators learn they should initiate a serial murder investigation?
30. What is a cold case squad, and what affects their success?

REFERENCES

ATF. 2005. *ATF's NIBIN Program.* Accessed online at http://www.nibin.gov/nibin.pdf

Alison, Laurence and David Canter. 1999. "Profiling in Policy and Practice." In David V. Canter and Laurence J. Alison (Eds.), *Offender Profiling Series: Vol. II. Profiling in Policy and Practice* (pp. 3–20). Aldershot: Ashgate.

Altoona.com. "Jury Hands Padilla Death Sentence." Accessed online at http://www.altoona.com/news/old_news.php3

Associated Press. 2006, October 10. "Bloody Fingerprint Leads to Murder Charge." *Associated Press State and Local Wire.*

Bass, Bill, and Jon Jefferson. 2003. *Death's Acre: Inside the Legendary Forensic Lab, the Body Farm Where the Dead Do Tell Tales.* New York: Berkley Books.

Biskupic, Joan. 1999, October 19. "Court Cites Need for Warrant at Murder Site." *Washington Post.* Accessed online at http://www.washingtonpost.com/wpsrv/national/longterm/supcourt/stories/court101899.htm

Bowes, Mark. 2006, February 24. "Coldest Case Heats Up." *Times-Dispatch.* Accessed at http://www.fbi.gov/hq/lab/codis/2006-02-24.htm.

Bureau of Justice Statistics. 2006. *Homicide Trends in the United States.* Washington, DC: U.S. Department of Justice.

Chisum, W. Jerry, and Brent Turvey. 2000. "Evidence Dynamics: Locard's Exchange Principle & Crime Reconstruction." *Journal of Behavioral Profiling,* 1(1). Accessed online at http://www.profiling.org/journal/vol1_no1/jbp_ed_january2000_1-1.html.

CNN.com. 2000, January 19. "Kennedy Kin Surrenders in Girl's 1975 Killing." Retrieved November 8, 2006, from http://archives.cnn.com/2000/US/01/19/moxley.arrest.06/index.html

Coleman, Clive and Clive Norris. 2000. *Introducing Criminology.* Devon: Willan Publishing.

Egger, Steven A. 1984. "A Working Definition of Serial Murder and the Reduction of Linkage Blindness." *Journal of Police Science and Administration,* 12: 348–357.

Egger, Steven A. 2002. *The Killers Among Us: An Examination of Serial Murder and Its Investigation.* Upper Saddle River, NJ: Prentice Hall.

FBI. 2000. *The FBI's Combined DNA Index System Program.* Washington, DC: U.S. Department of Justice.

FBI. 2005. *National Incident Based Reporting System Frequently Asked Questions.* Retrieved July 10, 2005, from www.fbi.gov/ucr/faqsinceidentspecific.htm

FBI. 2007. *NDIS Statistics Web Page.* Retrieved February 17, 2007, from http://www.fbi.gov/hq/lab/codis/clickmap.htm

Forensic Technology Inc. 2006. *History of Ballistics Web Page.* Accessed online at http://www.forensictechnologyinc.com/15/15year/history.html

Gaines, Larry K., and Roger Leroy Miller. 2004. *Criminal Justice in Action: The Core.* Belmont, CA: Wadsworth.

Geberth, Vernon J. 1996. *Practical Homicide Investigation: Tactics, Procedures, and Forensic Techniques.* Boca Raton, FL: CRC Press.

Hamill, Sean D. 2005, August 30. "Blair County DA: Homicide Suspect Says He Blacked Out During Shooting." *Post Gazette.com.* Retrieved November 8, 2006, from http://www.post-gazette.com/pg/05242/562268.stm

Hazelwood, Robert R. and Robert K. Ressler, Roger L. Depue, John E. Douglas. 1987. "Criminal Personality Profiling: An Overview." In Robert R. Hazelwood and Ann Wolbert Burgess (Eds.), *Practical Aspects of Rape Investigation: A Multidisciplinary Approach* (pp. 137–149). New York: Elsevier.

Horn, Stacy. 2005. "The First Cold Case Squad." *The Restless Sleep Web page.* Accessed online at http://www.echonyc.com/~horn/restless/cat_police_history.html

Keppel, Robert, and Joseph G. Weiss. 1994. "Time and Distance as Solvability Factors in Murder Cases." *Journal of Forensic Sciences,* 29(2): 386–400.

Litwin, Kenneth. 2004. "A Multilevel Multivariate Analysis of Factors Affecting Homicide Clearances." *Journal of Research in Crime & Delinquency,* 41(4): 327–352.

Lowe, Zach. 2006, April 26. "Controversial Lie Detector Used to Yield Confessions." *The Stamford Advocate.* Accessed at http://www.law.northwestern.edu/news/article_full.cfm?eventid=2567.

Montgomery, David. 1999, July 4. "William Bass Wants Your Body." *Washington Post,* p. F1.

Moore, Greg. 2006. "History of Fingerprints." Accessed online at http://www.onin.com/fp/fphistory.html

Mount, Steve. 2006, November 30. "Constitutional Topic: Martial Law." *USConstitution.net.* Accessed online at http://www.usconstitution.net/consttop_mlaw.html

Mouzos, Jenny, and Damon Muller. 2001. *Solvability Factors for Homicide in Australia: An Exploratory Analysis.* Canberra: Australian Institute of Criminology.

Muller, Damon A. 2000. "Criminal Profiling: Real Science or Just Wishful Thinking?" *Homicide Studies,* 4(3): 234–264.

National Institute of Justice. 2003. *Without a Trace? Advances in Detecting Trace Evidence.* Washington, DC: National Institute of Justice.

National Institute of Justice. 2004. *Crime Scene Investigation: A Reference of Law Enforcement Training.* Washington, DC: National Institute of Justice.

Office of Technology Assessment. 1983. *Scientific Validity of Polygraph Testing: A Research Review and Evaluation: A Technical Memorandum.* Washington, DC: U.S. Congress.

Osterburg, James W., and Richard H. Ward. 2004. *Criminal Investigation: A Method for Reconstructing the Past.* Cincinnati, OH: Anderson Publishing.

Puckett, Janice L., & Richard J. Lundman. 2003. "Factors Affecting Homicide Clearances: Multivariate Analysis of a More Complete Conceptual Framework." *Journal of Research in Crime and Delinquency,* 40(2): 171–193.

Regini, Charles L. 1997, August. "The Cold Case Concept." *FBI Law Enforcement Bulletin.*

Regoeczi, Wendy C., Leslie W. Kennedy, and Robert A. Silverman. 2000. "Uncleared Homicides: A Canada/United States Comparison." *Homicide Studies,* 4(2): 135–161.

Salfati, C. Gabrielle. 2000. "The Nature of Expressiveness and Instrumentality in Homicide," *Homicide Studies,* 4(3): 265–293.

Salfati, C. Gabrielle, and David V. Canter. 1999. "Differentiating Stranger Murders: Profiling Offender Characteristic from Behavioral Styles." *Behavioral Sciences and the Law,* 17: 391–406.

San Antonio Police Department. 2006. "Solved Cold Cases." San Antonio Police Department website.

Snow, Robert L. 2005. "Murder 101: Homicide and Its Investigation." Westport, CT: Praeger.

Spice, Linda. 2006, May 14. "Voice Stress Analyzer Helps Police Zero In on Homicide Suspect; Critics Question Reliability, But Others Praise Investigative Tool." *The Milwaukee Journal Sentinel.* Accessed at http://findarticles.com/p/articles/mi_qn4196/is_20060514/ai_n16366371

Summers, Chris. 2006. "Richard Ramirez, the Night Stalker." *BBC Crime Case Closed Infamous Criminals website.* Accessed at http://www.bbc.co.uk/crime/caseclosed/ramirez1.shtml

Washington State Attorney General. 2004. "Homicide Investigation Tracking System." Retrieved November 30, 2004, from www.atg.wa.gov/hits

Wilson, Thomas F., and Paul L. Woodard. 1987. *Automated Fingerprint Identification Systems: Technology and Policy Issues.* Washington, DC: U.S. Department of Justice, Bureau of Justice Statistics.

World Encyclopedia. 1980. "Ballistics." Oxford: Oxford University Press.

Chapter 15

HOMICIDE IN COURT

From *Perry Mason* to the more recent *Shark,* courtroom dramas have been very popular. However, the dramatic courtroom scenes portrayed in Perry Mason and other television programming are relatively rare. First of all, approximately half of the defendants charged with murder accept plea bargains to avoid the harshest penalties. Second, almost half of murder defendants in large urban counties have public defenders (Reaves, 2006). However, you may be surprised to learn that murder defendants are less likely to have public defenders than defendants charged with other violent crimes. Third, although some trials take just a day, they tend to be longer in real life and more mundane than they are on television.

Ideally, you are familiar with the administration of justice in the United States. This chapter focuses on each step of the process with particular attention to cases in which a defendant is accused of taking the life of another human being. You will read about the stages involved in processing a defendant through the U.S. court system after he or she has been arrested for murder or manslaughter. The chapter begins with the pretrial stages of the justice process. Initial appearance, bail, pretrial release, and grand juries are included in the discussions about the pretrial stages. There are also sections on the arraignment at which time the defendant enters a plea. You will learn about pleas and plea bargaining in this chapter before moving on to the trial. The steps of a criminal trial as they relate to murder cases make up the bulk of this chapter, beginning with pretrial motions and concluding with sentencing in cases where the defendant is convicted. Defenses to murder including self-defense are also discussed in detail.

After the arrest, the trial does not begin immediately as it may seem when you watch *Law & Order*. Instead, there are several stages between the arrest and the trial; if there is a trial. The next section briefly outlines these stages that you probably learned about in your introductory criminal justice course. However, as you read about the stages, you may realize that the names of the stages are called something different where you live. This is because different jurisdictions call the stages by different names. For the most part, however, the steps through the system are the same throughout the United States and similar in other Western societies.

Pretrial Stages

Once a suspect has been arrested, the case is in the hands of the prosecuting attorney, also known as the district attorney. The district attorney has an amazing amount of power through his or her discretion. He or she decides whether to charge the accused as well as what crimes to charge. The district attorney can decide to charge the accused with the most serious crime for which there may be evidence or a lesser charge. It is also common for the prosecuting attorney to charge murder defendants with several crimes when the evidence supports such charges. In 2003, 61% of defendants charged with murder in the 75 largest urban counties were charged with at least one felony in addition to the murder (Cohen & Reaves, 2006). The prosecutor may also decide there is not enough evidence to obtain a conviction and thus he or she may opt not to prosecute at all.

Initial Appearance

Within 48 hours of an arrest in the United States, the accused must be brought before the judge or magistrate to be formally advised of the charges he or she faces. If the defendant cannot afford an attorney, it is during this initial or first appearance that an attorney may be assigned. The judge may also decide whether the defendant will have the opportunity to be released on bail during the initial appearance. If the accused has been arrested without a warrant, a probable cause hearing also must take place within 24 hours to guarantee there was probable cause to make an arrest. In many jurisdictions, the probable cause hearing is included with the initial appearance hearing; in other jurisdictions the probable cause is included with a preliminary hearing. You may live in a state that skips the first appearance step and instead moves directly to an arraignment (Schmalleger, 2007).

Pretrial Release

In state courts, pretrial release on bail or on one's own recognizance is less likely in homicide cases than in other types of crimes. Nearly three fourths of those eventually convicted of murder were denied bail or had bail amounts of at least $100,000 (Reaves, 2006). In response to some high-profile cases in which defendants who were released awaiting trial committed other crimes, some state legislatures have instituted laws that do not allow the prerelease of those offenders who are believed to be a danger to society (Schmalleger, 2007).

Grand Jury

Grand juries are a part of the pretrial stage in federal criminal courts and in nearly half of state courts. Unlike court cases, which are public, grand juries meet in secret and the defendant has no right to attend or present evidence. The prosecutor presents evidence to support going forward with a case against the accused. If a majority of the grand jury believes there is enough evidence to proceed with the case, the defendant is indicted and the case is said to be a "true bill" (Schmalleger, 2007). It is the rare case in which a jury does not indict. It is so rare, in fact, that a popular saying attributed to Sol Wachtler, a former chief judge of New York, holds that any half decent prosecutor could indict a ham sandwich.

Instead of a grand jury, or in addition to a grand jury if you live in Tennessee or Georgia, the prosecutor in your state may be required to file a complaint against the accused in a preliminary hearing. At the preliminary hearing, a judge determines whether there is probable cause to continue the case against the accused. In contrast to a grand jury, defendants are permitted to testify and call witnesses during a preliminary hearing. It is also at the preliminary hearing that the defendant or prosecutor may question whether the defendant is competent to stand trial (Adler, Mueller, & Laufer, 2006; Schmalleger, 2007).

Arraignment

If it is determined that probable cause exists to justify continuing with the trial according to the grand jury or the preliminary hearing, the next step is the arraignment where the defendant enters his or her plea. The defendant may plead guilty, nolo contendere, not guilty, and, in some jurisdictions, not guilty by reason of insanity. With a guilty plea, the defender admits to the acts he or she is accused of committing and the judge schedules a sentencing hearing. Nolo contendere, or no contest, is a plea option in some jurisdictions. With a no contest plea, the accused admits criminal liability but does not actually admit guilt. If there is a civil suit, the offender has not admitted to any crime; however, he or she can still be convicted in criminal court and sentences as if he or she entered a guilty plea. A plea of not guilty is the defendant's way of saying that he or she wants the prosecution to make a case against them. A not guilty plea means there will be a trial (Adler et al., 2006; Schmalleger, 2007).

Offenders may plead not guilty even though they have confessed to the crime. In such cases, the accused may be taking his or her chances that a jury will see things differently than the prosecutor and treat the accused with leniency. For others, such as Reinaldo Rivera who admitted he had killed at least four women in Georgia and South Carolina, a plea of guilty seems to fulfill the accused's desire to be the center of attention. Several times during his 2004 trial, Rivera and his two attorneys admitted that Rivera was not denying he had killed army sergeant Marni Glista. His attorneys were attempting to show that Rivera was a sociopath. Rivera, who may have also been attempting to prove he was psychologically unbalanced, shouted and yelled he did not want to be found not guilty due to insanity. Although the judge forbade him from telling the jury, more than once in open court, Rivera claimed he wanted to be found guilty and sentenced to death for his crimes.

PLEA BARGAINING

Plea bargaining is usually a deal made between the prosecuting attorney and the defendant, although it must be approved by a judge. The defendant agrees to plead guilty to a lesser crime or to fewer crimes than he or she is charged with in exchange for a more lenient sentence than the defendant might receive by going to trial. Prosecutors who are certain the offender is guilty may prefer to plea-bargain if the case against the offender is weak or to avoid the expense and time of a trial and to guarantee a guilty plea (Adler et al., 2006; Schmalleger, 2007). Accused persons (sometimes even nonguilty individuals) may agree to plead guilty to avoid the risk of a harsh sentence.

It is no secret that plea bargaining is an everyday occurrence in the United States. In 2006, I taught a study abroad comparative criminal justice course. When we were told that plea bargains were uncommon in Australia, my students were dumbfounded. Plea bargaining is such a normalized part of the criminal justice system in the United States, the students could not fathom a system without plea bargaining. The students wondered how the system could handle all of the criminal cases brought forward. They considered whether the sentences would be more strict without plea bargaining or if there would be some other way for offenders to avoid the most strict of sentences.

Plea bargaining is common for those accused of murder, nonnegligent manslaughter, and other violent crimes in the United States. However, trials are more likely in murder and nonnegligent manslaughter cases than in other felony cases. Although 95% of all state felony convictions in 2002 were the result of guilty pleas, only two thirds (68%) of those convicted of homicide were convicted by a guilty plea (Durose & Langan, 2004). Data from the 75 largest U.S. counties indicate there were fewer murder trials than assault or drug trials in 2002. Still, the number of trials for robbery, burglary, and larceny were comparable to the number of homicide trials, making homicide trials a relatively common occurrence in the nation's courts. The next section reviews the basic steps of the trial.

Pretrial Motions

After an arraignment but before the trial begins, attorneys may file pretrial motions in which they make a request of the judge. Defense attorneys often make a motion for discovery, which asks that the prosecution reveal to the defense the evidence against him or her. Either side may also make a motion to have evidence suppressed. In the 2004 Reinaldo Rivera trial, the district attorney requested that the defense attorneys provide a copy of the psychological reports on Rivera they planned to use during the trial (Bohm & Haley, 2002).

THE HOMICIDE TRIAL

Like a sporting event, trials proceed in a particular way, with rituals, roles, and rules that those who are a part of the system understand well. For outsiders, including those who are being charged with a crime for the first time, all the rules and details

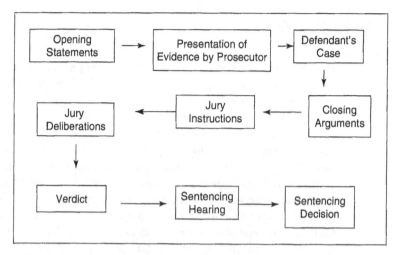

FIGURE 15.1
Stages in a Capital Murder Trial

can be daunting. Even for those who often watch Court TV, the reality of a homicide trial in person often has a sense of importance that is not always conveyed in television programs. Real trials are also often unbelievably slow and detailed in comparison to the fictionalized accounts we see on television. In the remainder of this chapter, the steps of a trial are reviewed along with issues related to the different steps. See Figure 15.1 for the usual order of a capital murder trial.

JURY SELECTION

If a murder defendant pleads not guilty, a date is set for trial. Each trial follows the same basic outline. First, a jury is selected. According to the Sixth Amendment, U.S. citizens accused of a serious crime are guaranteed the right to a trial by an impartial jury (see Box 15.2). For a jury to be impartial, according to the law, the jurors must be unbiased and selected from a *venire*, a group of potential jurors, that is representative of the community from which it is selected (FindLaw.com, 2006). Some call the jury selection process a "deselection process" because the goal is to excuse individuals with extreme views on either end of the spectrum in an attempt to assemble an impartial jury (Rice as quoted by Krupnik, 2006).

Juries in murder trials usually consist of 12 jurors and at least 2 alternates. If a trial is expected to be lengthy, additional alternate jurors may be selected. The process of jury selection is called *voir dire*, a French phrase that is translated as "to speak the truth." A panel of potential jurors, called a *venire*, are summoned to court for the *voir dire*. During the *voir dire*, the judge, and often defense and prosecution attorneys, asks potential jurors questions that are meant to discover whether there are reasons for excluding particular individuals from the jury (see Box 15.2). Each side has a certain number of peremptory challenges that they may use to exclude potential jurors

BOX 15.1

Trial Consultants

You may have never thought about working as a jury or trial consultant. However, if you have learned how to do correlation methods or conduct a focus group in your methods course, you have some of the important skills used by jury consultants. Jury consultants are used by both prosecuting and, more often, defense attorneys to select which potential jurors should be removed from the jury pool. These consultants use various social science methods, including the use of previous correlational research, to predict how individual jurors are likely to vote. For instance, research shows that those who work in criminal justice are more likely to side with the prosecution. Research also suggests that a juror is likely to decide on behalf of the defense or prosecution depending on their personality type, age, education, race, socioeconomic level, sex, or other characteristics (Schmalleger, 2007).

without having to give a reason. Each side may also make unlimited challenges for cause. Challenges for cause are used when it is believed the potential juror cannot be impartial or fair usually because of a conflict of interest. For example, challenges for cause would be used if a potential juror was related to the police officer who arrested the accused (Adler et al., 2006; Schmalleger, 2007).

SCIENTIFIC JURY SELECTION

In the early 1970s, relatively recently in the history of juries, sociologist Jay Schulman and other social scientists began the practice of scientific jury selection when they volunteered to help with jury selection in the Harrisburg Seven trial (Frederick, 1984; Miller, 2001). Schulman and the other social scientists conducted survey and interview research to develop demographic profiles of those most likely and least likely to side with the prosecution. The Harrisburg Seven were antiwar activists who were accused of a variety of crimes, including conspiring to destroy selective service records and kidnap Secretary of State Henry Kissinger. The Harrisburg Seven fared very well in court after the defense used Schulman's profiles to guide them during *voir dire:* The jury hung on all but one minor charge (Cleary, 2005).

Since its benevolent beginnings when academics volunteered to help defendants like the Harrisburg Seven and Joan Little, an African American woman charged with the murder of a white correctional officer in an "atypically racist" county, scientific jury selection has become a $400 million industry with hundreds of firms and even more practitioners who charge anywhere from $2,000 to over $100,000 for their services (Cleary, 2005: 2). The industry is definitely successful if measured by its growth and cost. However, its use remains controversial because of questions about its effectiveness and its fairness.

BOX 15.2

A Jury of Her Peers

Lena Driskell is the oldest woman incarcerated at Metro State Prison in Atlanta, Georgia. Driskell, who was born in 1927, is serving a life sentence for murdering her 85-year-old former boyfriend in June 2005. After she found out he was cheating on her, the couple broke up. However, she confronted him days later and shot him in the head. Officers who arrested Driskell testified that she said, "I did it and I'd do it again" (Associated Press, 2006a). Driskell's attorney, Deborah Poole, believed her client was deprived of her constitutional right to a fair trial because a "whole class of people" was not included on the jury. In Georgia, any person who is 70 years old or older is excused from jury duty if he or she makes a request. Reporters who picked up the story were questioning whether Driskell would have a jury of her peers if no elderly members were on the jury (Associated Press, 2006a).

Despite the common belief that U.S. citizens accused of crimes have the right to a jury of their peers, the U.S. Constitution makes no such guarantee. The Sixth Amendment of the Constitution states that U.S. citizens have the right to be tried by "an impartial jury of the State and district wherein the crime shall have been committed," but nothing is mentioned about a jury of "one's peers" (Constitutional Rights Foundation Chicago, National Endowment for the Humanities, 2006). However, historically there is support for the concept. The U.S. Supreme Court ruling *Duncan* v. *Louisiana* (1968) references the First Continental Congress, which stated in 1774 that the colonies were "entitled to the common law of England, and more especially to the great and inestimable privilege of being tried by their peers of the vicinage, according to the course of that law"(*Duncan* v. *Louisiana*, 1968). Furthermore, in this same decision, Justice White wrote,

> The framers of the constitutions strove to create an independent judiciary but insisted upon further protection against arbitrary action. Providing an accused with the right to be tried by a jury of his peers gave him an inestimable safeguard against the corrupt overzealous prosecutor and against the compliant, biased, or eccentric judge. (*Duncan* v. *Louisiana*, 1968)

Although there is no exact guarantee of a jury of "one's peers," the idea is that officers of the government would not sit in judgment over one accused of a crime but instead fellow citizens would be selected as a jury.

Critics of scientific jury selection are quick to point out that the successful results in the Harrisburg Seven and Joan Little trials do not prove that scientific jury selection is effective. Academic research suggests that personality and demographic variables that social scientists have studied account for no more than 15% of the variance in verdicts. In other words, the ability to predict juror decisions based solely on their demographic and personality characteristics increases only slightly with the use of scientific jury selection. Many other factors may affect the outcome of a trial.

Studies show that jurors report the nature and presentation of evidence is important in their decision making. Still, proponents of scientific jury selection argue that academic research on jury decision making is often flawed. The studies often use college student samples when typical-age college students rarely vote, and, as such, it is rare they are summoned for jury duty in many jurisdictions. Furthermore, some critics of the academic literature on scientific jury selection argue it is actually impossible to test because a true experiment in the field is impossible (Cleary, 2005).

Fairness is an also an issue with scientific jury selection. Jury consultants are more likely to be used by wealthy clients who can afford to pay a hefty sum for such services (Cleary, 2005). If only wealthy clients like O. J. Simpson, who was acquitted by a jury of killing his former wife Nicole Brown Simpson and Ronald Goldman, are able to hire jury consultants, is justice being served? If, in fact, jury consultants are an advantage, should every person accused of a serious crime have the right not only to a speedy trial by an impartial jury but also a right to a jury consultant?

Opening Statements

Following jury selection, the prosecution and then the defense have the opportunity to make an opening statement, essentially an outline of what each side intends to present during the trial. Attorneys are not required to present an opening statement, but they usually do. In some jurisdictions, the defense may opt to postpone their opening statement until after the prosecution finishes presenting the case in its entirety.

In his opening statement in the case against Yolanda Saldivar, who was eventually found guilty of killing Tejano singer Selena Quintanilla, Houston district attorney Carlos Valdez explained what an opening statement is:

> I am going to try and tell you where we are going and what we will prove. Nothing I say is evidence or anything Mr. Tinker has to say—we were not there. On March 31 of this year evidence will show that Selena Quintanilla was killed in a senseless and brutal act of violence in a Corpus Christi, Texas, motel and the person who performed this senseless tragedy is sitting in this courtroom today. That lady (pointing to Yolanda Saldivar) shot her in the back, severing an artery and causing Selena to bleed to death. What we are going to show is that this act did not just "occur," but we will show you exactly what happened and tell you of some of the acts that led up to the killing by calling several witnesses who will verify this act. (*Houston Chronicle*, 1995)

Presentation of Evidence

After opening statements are made, the heart of the trial begins. Each side, beginning with the prosecution, has the opportunity to present evidence to make its case. The prosecution has the onus of proving that the perpetrator committed the crime for which he or she has been charged. The defense does not have the same burden of proving the offender not guilty. However, the defense usually attempts to show through cross-examination of the prosecutor's witnesses and through evidence of their own that the defendant is not guilty. In some cases, the defense may admit the defendant has had a hand in the death of another but that he or she is guilty of no crime or a lesser crime.

Several examples of physical evidence were discussed in Chapter 14. Evidence as presented in a criminal trial may be divided into direct and circumstantial evidence. Direct evidence is evidence that proves a fact. The testimony from a witness who testifies witnessing a murder would be direct evidence. More common than in the past, perpetrators are providing direct evidence of their own crimes by filming them. A 16-year-old in Sparta, Michigan, for example, beat a man to death and then cut off his head. He filmed himself cutting the severed head with a butcher knife (Davis, 1998). Most murderers, however, still do not film themselves committing their crimes, and many are convicted with circumstantial evidence only.

Circumstantial evidence is indirect evidence. The jury or judge must deduce what happened from the evidence. There is nothing that directly links the offender to the crime. Scott Peterson was found guilty and sentenced to death for the murder of his wife Laci Peterson and their unborn baby Conner in a case that was built entirely of circumstantial evidence. Scott Peterson never confessed to anyone that he killed Laci. No one saw him kill her. A weapon was never found. Nevertheless, prosecutors built a case against Scott Peterson with the help of Amber Frey. Frey, who Peterson was dating at the time his wife went missing, told the jury that Scott said he was a widower. The jury also learned that the bodies of Laci and Conner were discovered washed up on the shore near where Peterson had reported he was fishing when Laci went missing around Christmas 2003. Additionally, a piece of Laci's hair was found on a pair of pliers on Scott's fishing boat. Finally, Peterson's cell phone records showed there were four hours in which he did not talk on his phone, extremely rare for Peterson whose phone records showed he usually used his phone several times every hour. The four hours he did not use the phone occurred during the time when Laci was believed to have disappeared. None of this evidence directly linked Scott to Laci's murder. However, together, this evidence and other details they learned during their five months as a jury, was enough to convince the jury in the Scott Peterson trial to find him guilty in 2004 (Finz, 2004; Walsh & Finz, 2004).

The trials you see on fictional television shows as well as reality programming such as *Court TV* reflect the reality of court cases. However, as you are likely aware, the homicide trials presented on television are often more dramatic, less tedious, and, not surprisingly, more entertaining than real trials. Nevertheless, the basics are there in television dramas. The prosecution presents evidence to show the defendant has committed the crime(s) for which he or she is accused. Once the prosecution completes its case, the defense has the option of presenting a case that they believe will show the defendant is not guilty of the offense(s) charged.

The prosecution and defense must follow strict rules in presenting their cases to the court. For example, it is likely you have heard of the no-hearsay rule, which stipulates that witnesses can only testify to what they have seen or heard directly and not what they have heard others say. You have probably heard less about who may be counted as an expert witness and what evidence an expert may testify about. Yet these are issues that must be decided in any trial in which an expert witness may testify.

In 1993, the Supreme Court made a ruling in *Daubert* v. *Merrill Dow* that gave more power to judges for determining what would be considered scientific evidence and whether such evidence would be admitted in a trial. However, for the most part, judges are using their discretionary power by continuing to follow the 1923 Supreme Court ruling in *Frye* v. *United States.* According to the *Frye* decision, to be permitted in court, scientific evidence must be based on accepted scientific techniques (Hickey, 2006).

As discussed in Chapter 14, expert witnesses testified in the capital murder trial of Reinaldo Rivera. Rivera's attorneys, Peter Johnson and Jacque Hawke, brought Gerald Blanchard, who had his master's degree in psychology and Thomas Sachy, a neuropsychiatrist, as expert witnesses in an attempt to convince the jury that Rivera had a brain deficiency called hypofrontality. The jury saw both of these men testify. Sachy showed colorful positron emission tomography (PET) scans of Rivera's brain, which he compared to a so-called normal brain. Observers of the trial saw what the jury saw, but we saw it twice. Even before jury selection began, the assistant district attorney Ashley Wright told the judge that she still had not received a report by defense experts explaining what she described as a "cartoon version of a PET scan." Then on January 21, the jury was sequestered for the morning while the defense and prosecution argued about whether the expert testimony would be permitted into the case. To determine whether the expert testimony should be permitted in court, the judge read peer reviewed journal articles about the scientific evidence that the defense wanted to present. In addition, Judge Pickett had the defense present what was in effect a preview of the expert witness testimony before he would allow it to be presented in court. As a result, everyone in the courtroom except the jury heard the same testimony twice.

After the prosecution has presented their case, the defense may present their own evidence and witnesses. The defense, however, may opt not to present a defense and simply to rest if they believe the prosecution has not proven every element of the crime. Usually when the defense chooses not to present any evidence or witnesses, and often even when they do decide to present evidence, they may make a motion for a mistrial. In the rare occasion that the judge finds the prosecution has not presented evidence to suggest the accused should be convicted, he or she may grant a mistrial or a redirected verdict. In a mistrial, the prosecutor has the option of retrying the case. If the judge orders a redirected verdict, he or she is ordering the jury to find the defendant not guilty. In this case, the offender may not be retried for the same crime (Bohm & Haley, 2002).

DEFENSES TO MURDER

Typically the defense does not rest after the prosecution presents its case. Instead, attorneys for the defendant usually present evidence and arguments to demonstrate the defendant is not guilty. The three general defenses to the charge of murder are alibi, justifications, and excuses (Schmalleger, 2007). More details for each of these types of defenses are discussed next.

Alibi

Some criminologists argue that an alibi is a denial instead of a defense; others include alibi as a defense (Schmalleger, 2007). Either way, when murder defendants use an alibi, they are arguing that they could not have killed the victim because they were somewhere else when the victim was killed. In Latin, *alibi* means "elsewhere." A person accused of a murder must prove that he or she was somewhere else when the murder was committed. It is not good enough to say, "It wasn't me. I was at home watching *Law & Order*." The accused needs to demonstrate that he or she was not where the murder occurred. However, the jury or judge deciding the case will determine whether the evidence of alibi is valid. If the defendant's wife says he was with her and three witnesses testify that they saw the defendant at the murder scene, it is quite likely the wife will not be believed over the three witnesses and he will be convicted (Klotter, 2001; Schmalleger, 2007).

Juan Catalan can tell you how difficult it is to prove an alibi. Catalan was accused of killing Martha Puebla in San Fernando Valley, California, on May 12, 2003. Catalan had ticket stubs from a Los Angeles Dodgers baseball game that he argued proved he could not have killed Puebla. The Atlanta Braves beat the Dodgers just minutes before Puebla was killed approximately 20 minutes away from the stadium. The case never made it to trial, but Catalan spent over five months in jail where he was being held on murder charges. Luckily for Catalan, the HBO show *Curb Your Enthusiasm* had been filming at Dodger stadium the same day that Puebla was murdered, and Catalan claimed to be at the ballpark with his 6-year-old daughter. The defense attorney was able to get the videotapes filmed for the show. In a corner of one shot Catalan could be seen eating a hot dog and talking to his daughter. With time codes on the videotape and cell phone records indicating Catalan was near the stadium after the game, Catalan's attorney, Todd Melnik, convinced the judge to order that the charges against Catalan be dropped.

Justifications

Murder defendants who employ a justification defense admit that they killed the victim, but they argue it was necessary to prevent great harm to themselves or another. A number of justifications may be used by a person accused of a crime, including consent, necessity, self-defense, defense of others, and defense of home and property. For the most part, necessity and consent do not work well for murder cases; the defense defenses, so to speak, work on occasion.

CONSENT

A defendant may use the defense of consent when any harm done occurred after the victim gave his or her permission for the harmful act. In relation to homicide and consent, you might think of Dr. Kevorkian who helped patients end their lives when they were suffering from an illness. Thomas Youk, for example, who was suffering from Lou Gehrig's disease, signed a written consent to the procedure that ended his life. But in most states, consent is not an acceptable defense to murder. After 130 assisted suicides, Kevorkian was convicted of second-degree murder in 1999 for administering a lethal injection to Youk. The 78-year-old Kevorkian, whose own health is failing, was released from prison in 2007 (Inciardi, 1996; Reuters, 2006).

NECESSITY

The defense of necessity may be used if a defendant commits a crime to prevent a greater harm. You may remember a case from Chapter 3 in which two shipwreck survivors killed a third survivor so they could eat him to survive. They argued it was necessary to kill him so they could survive. In this English case from the late 1800s, the court ruled that the two survivors were guilty of killing the third because he was not threatening their lives. Acceptable arguments of the necessity to commit murder are unlikely. A vigilante who kills sex offenders may attempt to use the defense of necessity. He may argue that he kills registered sex offenders to prevent the offenders from molesting any other children. This argument has yet to be accepted in a court of law, however. Most any situations you might imagine as possibly being appropriate for a defense of necessity are probably covered by the defenses of self-defense and defense of others (Schmalleger, 2007).

SELF-DEFENSE

Self-defense and defense of others are more appropriate defenses for murder than necessity or consent. As noted in Chapter 8 in most U.S. jurisdictions the law of self-defense states that an individual may use reasonable force against another when the individual reasonably believes the other person is threatening her or him with imminent and unlawful harm. Sometimes, self-defense cases have the same scenario as confrontational homicides, making it difficult for a jury to decide whether the incident was self-defense or an escalation of violence. It took a jury over 20 hours to decide that Ricky Senters Jr. acted in self-defense in Columbus, Ohio, on the last day of 1999. Senters stabbed three men outside of Coach's Tavern. According to news reports, all four men were intoxicated, and it was unclear who started the altercation. Witness testimony indicated that two of the men fighting Senters had crowbars or other weapons. Prosecutors argued that Senters should have retreated, but news reporters speculated that the jury decided he was not guilty because he was fighting three men (Doulin, 2000).

DEFENSE OF OTHERS

A defendant may be able to claim defense of others as a defense of murder. The force used against the other must be reasonable, and the person one is defending must be in imminent danger. However, a person will not be released of responsibility if he or she is defending a person who started the altercation. If, for example, you are hanging out at Coach's Tavern with your best friend Rob and he starts a fight with a couple of guys, you will be held responsible for the harm you do if you jump in to help him (Schmalleger, 2007).

DEFENSE OF HOME AND PROPERTY

In most jurisdictions, you do not have the right to kill to protect your property unless you are in imminent danger. Basically, if you kill someone and a jury or judge determines you could have retreated, you are likely to be found guilty. However, since 2005, several states in the South and Midwest have enacted what some call "stand your ground" laws. Most of these new laws are similar to Florida's law that became effective in October 2005. Florida's law allows individuals to use deadly force against intruders who enter their homes. According to the law, police are not permitted to arrest or detain an individual; nor may a person be prosecuted for killing an intruder who unlawfully and forcefully entered their home. Moreover, according to the law, an individual "has no duty to retreat and has the right to stand his or her ground and meet force with force, including deadly force." Critics of these types of laws call them "shoot first" laws and argue that they give citizens a "license to kill" (Liptak, 2006).

Excuses

Finally, excuses in murder cases are used by defendants who admit they committed a crime but argue they were not legally responsible at the time of the crime (Schmalleger, 2007). Legal excuses that may be used as a defense to homicide include age, involuntary intoxication, provocation, and insanity (Schmalleger, 2007). Each is discussed in turn.

AGE

As you may remember from Chapter 9, U.S. common law does not consider children younger than 7 years capable of *mens rea*. In other words, they are not believed to be capable of intending to commit a criminal act. Defendants older than 7 years but under age 14 may also attempt to employ age as a defense in murder cases. They are not considered guilty if they are found to be incapable of having criminal consent. However, a jury or judge may decide the youth is guilty if the prosecutor convincingly shows the child had *mens rea* (Klotter, 2001; Schmalleger, 2007).

INVOLUNTARY INTOXICATION

Although voluntary intoxication is not usually a viable or accepted defense to murder for anyone, including alcoholics and drug addicts, involuntary intoxication may be introduced as a defense. If a person is drugged against his or her will or tricked into taking a substance that results in intoxication, and the intoxication negates the individual's *mens rea*, the person may be found not guilty. You may be thinking this is unlikely in a murder case; however, there have been several cases in the news in which defendants have claimed they are not responsible for a murder because they were under the influence of pharmaceuticals prescribed by their physicians; however, in the United States, juries have not been convinced (see Chapter 2).

In 2005, 15-year-old Christopher Pittman was tried in South Carolina for the 2001 murders of his grandparents after his grandfather punished him. During the trial, a defense psychiatrist testified that Pittman did not have the ability to form criminal intent when he shot his grandparents to death because he was "intoxicated on Zoloft" (Polk, 2005). Then, in closing arguments, Pittman's attorney argued that "In this state, in this country, we do not convict children of murder when they've been ambushed by chemicals that have destroyed their ability to reason" (Polk, 2005). The prosecutors argued that the involuntary intoxication defense was a "smoke screen" used by defense attorneys. The jury sided with the prosecutors, finding Pittman guilty of two counts of murder. The judge sentenced Pittman to 30 years in prison (Polk, 2005). At the end of 2006, Pittman's attorneys were still appealing his case.

PROVOCATION

As you will recall from Chapter 2, provocation is a defense that may reduce a murder charge or conviction to a manslaughter charge or conviction. To prove provocation, the defense would have to prove the defendant, acting as any reasonable person would act, lost emotional control because of some provocation on the part of the victim. Furthermore, the killer could not have had time to cool off between the provocation by the victim and the killing. Note, however, that only a limited number of situations are considered provocation enough to provoke a killing. Insulting words are not sufficient provocations for a death to be considered manslaughter (Stacy, 2000). Rather, provocations for a killing to be deemed manslaughter include illegal arrest, adultery with offender's spouse, physical injury, or mutual combat.

BOX 15.3

Abuse Excuse or Environmental Hardship?

At the end of 1993, Colin Ferguson shot 25 people, killing 6 as they all rode on a Long Island commuter train. Before he fired William Kunstler as his attorney, the well-known defense attorney had been planning to use what he called the "black rage defense" to defend Ferguson. According to Paul Harris (1997) in his book *Black Rage Confronts the Law,* the black rage defense is a legal strategy that may be used to explain how a racist environment may help justify why some individuals commit crimes. Harris notes that the black rage defense is not an independent defense but is used to bolster accepted legal defenses such as insanity, self-defense, and provocation. Harris traces the black rage defense back to the mid-1800s when William Seward introduced evidence of racism along with the legal defense of insanity to explain why a young African American man went crazy and killed white people he believed to be responsible for his wrongful incarceration. Critics of the black rage defense and similar defenses agree with Alan Dershowitz (1994), who argues in his book, *The Abuse Excuse: and Other Cop-Outs, Sob Stories, and Evasions of Responsibility,* that such defenses are used by defendants as excuses for their behaviors as a way to avoid the responsibility for their actions.

More recently, defense attorneys have argued other defenses that Dershowitz is certain to find problematic, such as the "gay panic" defense in which a supposed homophobic man is so threatened by a sexual advance by another man that he freaks out and attacks the man who made the sexual advance. In 1995, Devin Moore's attorneys argued what has been called the "video game defense." Moore's attorneys claimed that he killed three police officers after stealing a car partially because of the influence of *Grand Theft Auto* video games (Associated Press, 2005).

What other so-called fad defenses have you heard about? What are your thoughts about them? Are some more relevant or less relevant than others?

INSANITY

Finally, as discussed previously in this chapter with regard to pleas, insanity refers to the mental state of defendants at the time of crime for which they are charged. Some people confuse insanity with competency to stand trial. Defendants are said to be competent to stand trial if they are capable of understanding the charges or proceedings against them and if they can aid counsel in their own defense at the time of the trial (Schmallenger, 2007).

Those who claim they are not guilty by reason of insanity are arguing that because they were mentally ill at the time of the crime, they could not have had a guilty mind. They were "out of their mind" and thus not capable of having a guilty mind. Very few individuals are found not guilty by reason of insanity, but importantly those who are found not guilty by reason of insanity are usually committed to a psychiatric facility (Adler et al., 2006).

As with other statutes discussed in this text, the standard used to determine whether an offender is considered to be legally insane at the time of their crime varies by state (and it is also different in the District of Columbia) (*Frontline*, 2005). Most states use the M'Naghten rule for determining legal insanity (see Box 15.4). Following the M'Naghten rule, a person is not guilty of a crime if at the time he or she committed a crime, the person had a mental defect or disability such that he or she did not know what he or she was doing or that it was wrong (Schmalleger, 2007).

BOX 15.4

M'Naghten Rule

Twenty-six states base their insanity rule on a British case from 1843. Daniel M'Naughten was a woodcutter who planned to assassinate Sir Robert Peel, the British prime minister at the time. M'Naughten believed that Peel was persecuting him. M'Naughten followed Peel, waiting for an opportunity to shoot him. On January 20, 1843, he spotted a man he thought was Peel and shot him in the back. The man he shot was Peel's assistant Edward Drummond, who died three months later from the wound on April 25, 1843. M'Naughten was charged with his murder but found not guilty by reason of insanity. Base on the ruling in this case, the M'Naghten rule was established, based on the premise that all offenders are to be considered sane unless proven otherwise. To prove insanity, then, "it must be clearly proved that, at the time of the committing of the act, the party accused as labouring under such a defect of reason, from disease of the mind, as not to know the nature and quality of the act he was doing; or, if he did know it, that he did not know he was doing what was wrong" (M'Naghten's Case, 1843). (Note that according to Diamond (1964), M'Naughten's name was misspelled as "M'Naghten" in the court ruling and thus the rule is known as the "M'Naghten" rule.)

In her first trial, Andrea Yates was found guilty in the drowning deaths of three of her five young children. (Yates killed all five of her children but was only charged in three of the deaths.) In this first trial, the jurors believed that although she was psychotic, she was aware her acts were illegal. However, an appeals court ruled there had been an error in Yates first trial. In the first trial, an expert witness for the state had wrongly testified that an episode of *Law & Order* showed a woman suffering from postpartum depression who drowned her children. As a result, Yates was retried, and on July 26, 2006, a jury found her not guilty by reason of insanity. At the time of this writing, Yates is still being held in a maximum security state mental institution. Doctors are evaluating her to determine whether she is a danger to society. Based on her physician's evaluation, Yates will either remain in the maximum security institution or be moved to another state hospital that is not maximum security (Associated Press, 2006b).

The substantial capacity test, which is part of the Model Penal Code discussed in Chapter 14, is used to determine sanity in 19 states (Schmalleger, 2007). Compared to the M'Naghten rule, the substantial capacity test is a more relaxed standard for determining a defendant not guilty by reason of insanity (Collins, Hinkebein, & Schorgl, 2006). The substantial capacity test is a combination of the M'Naghten test and what is known as an "irresistible impulse." This test allows a person to be found legally insane if it is proven that at the time of the crime, the individual because of a mental defect had a compulsion to commit the crime. Using this standard, an insane person may be aware that what he or she is doing is wrong, but he or she has an irresistible impulse to commit the act that is uncontrollable.

Attention to the insanity defense soared in 1982 after a jury found John Hinckley Jr. not guilty by reason of insanity. On March 30, 1981, Hinckley shot and wounded four men in his failed assassination attempt on President Ronald Reagan. The whole nation had seen the shooting over and over again on the news. James Brady, the White House press secretary, was left paralyzed for life. Still, after testimony from psychological experts about Hinckley's mental health, the jury found him not guilty. The public was outraged. Many believed Hinckley's not guilty verdict meant he would go free. Congress and the majority of state legislatures reacted by making changes to the insanity defense. Many states made changes that limited the use of the insanity defense, eight states introduced a new verdict of "guilty but mentally ill," and Utah removed the insanity defense altogether (Collins et al., 2006).

CLOSING ARGUMENTS

Regardless of which defense, if any, is presented by the defense attorneys, the closing arguments follow the presentation of evidence by both sides. During closing arguments, attorneys summarize their cases without presenting any new evidence. The prosecutor usually argues that they have proved beyond a reasonable doubt that the accused is guilty. The defense attorney uses the closing argument as a last chance to point out the weaknesses in the prosecution's case. Johnnie Cochran may have sealed O. J. Simpson's freedom with his now famous, "If it doesn't fit, you must acquit" closing arguments in the 1995 criminal trial in which Simpson was accused of killing

Nicole Brown Simpson and Ron Goldman. In murder trials where it is clear the defendant killed the victim, the defense attorney uses the closing argument to make a case for reduced charges and leniency in sentencing (Adler et al., 2006; Bohm & Haley, 2002).

JUDGE'S CHARGE TO JURY

In jury trials, after the closing argument, the judge gives the jury their instructions for deciding the case. The judge gives instructions regarding the law. This is a very critical part of a homicide trial. Cases are sometimes overturned because of the way the judge has given instructions. As such, a judge often has both the defense and prosecutor review or suggest instructions for the jurors. Once the judge is satisfied with the jury instructions, he or she officially charges the jury. If the defense is not satisfied with the final juror instructions, they object on the record in anticipation of future appeals if the defendant is found guilty.

JURY'S DECISION

The jury then must deliberate in private until they reach a verdict. The first step is to select a jury foreperson and determine how the jury will proceed. It is not unusual for deliberations to start with each juror discussing their take on the case against the accused. During the process of deliberations, the jurors may only speak about the case to one another. In high-profile cases, they may be sequestered to ensure that they do not speak to others. If they are not sequestered, the judge admonishes the jurors not to talk to others about the trial and to avoid any media coverage of the case. Most jurors take their duty very seriously and they refrain from violating the rules. There have been cases, however, where jurors have been removed from cases because of their actions while on the jury.

In the trial against Scott Peterson, for example, two alternate jurors had to join the jury when two original jurors were taken off the jury. According to news reports, the first juror was removed because she did some investigation on her own using the Internet. Jurors are supposed to make decisions about the case based on the presentation of evidence in court. They are not permitted to conduct their own research. Another juror was removed two days later, although there is no clear reason why except that he asked to be removed (Ryan, 2004).

VERDICT

In murder cases and other serious criminal trials, the jury usually must come to a unanimous decision about whether there is proof beyond a reasonable doubt that the accused committed the crime for which he or she is charged. If the decision is not unanimous, the jury is said to be a "hung jury." The judge must declare a mistrial and the district attorney will have to decide whether the case should be retried. If

BOX 15.5

Jury Decision Making and Race

Researchers who study jury decision making using mock juries have found that race, sex, and perceived attractiveness matter. In determining guilt and recommending sentences in a vehicular homicide case, two researchers at the State University of New York found that men treated attractive women more harshly than they treated unattractive women. In contrast, women treated attractive female defendants with more leniency than unattractive female defendants. African Americans were more lenient on African Americans, Latinos treated African Americans more harshly, and whites displayed no race-based leniency (Abwender & Hough, 2001).

The 240 mock jurors in this study were college students selected for a program to prepare good students from groups typically underrepresented in graduate schools (first-generation college students, low-income students, and ethnic minorities). Do you think the results may have been different if a different group of people was selected for the sample? Do you think attractiveness, race, and sex factor into jury decisions in real trials? In homicide trials, what factors about the victim and the offender do you think juries consider, and what factors do you think they should consider?

however, the jurors agree to a guilty or nonguilty verdict, the decision is read in court. A nonguilty verdict means the defendant is released unless he or she is charged with other crimes. With a verdict of guilty, the trial moves to the penalty phase (Adler et al., 2006).

SENTENCING

In death penalty cases, as discussed in the next section, the jury who found the defendant guilty is charged with the task of recommending a sentence to the judge. In noncapital cases, however, the sentencing decision is the responsibility of the judge in most U.S. jurisdictions including federal court. Judges follow the law in sentencing offenders; however, they often have some leeway in making their decision. Most every person convicted of murder is sentenced to some time in prison. The length of incarceration varies with the brutality of the murder and the offender's criminal history (Bohm & Haley, 2002). A 1999 study found that 95% of defendants convicted of murder or nonnegligent manslaughter in state or federal court were sentenced to incarceration. Only 5% were sentenced to probation. The average incarceration sentence was just over 20 years in 1996 (Brown & Langan, 1999). Data for 2003, however, showed a median sentence of 40 years with almost 40% of all those convicted of murder being sentenced to life (Cohen & Reaves, 2006).

Data indicate that those who are arrested for murder are far more likely to be convicted and sentenced to incarceration than those arrested for other felonies (Cohen & Reaves, 2006). The average time these offenders will serve is difficult to predict. A fourth of offenders who were sentenced in 1996 received life sentences, making it difficult to determine what the "going rate" is for murder currently in the United States. However, if the lifers are kept out of the calculations, the average time served for homicide is about 10 years (Brown & Langan, 1999).

DEATH PENALTY CASES

In the 1972 landmark case of *Furman* v. *Georgia,* the Supreme Court ruled that the administration of the death penalty in Georgia was cruel and unusual punishment because it was being administered arbitrarily and capriciously. In other words, no logic dictated when a convicted offender would be sentenced to death. Guidelines for the decision to sentence an individual to death were lacking. Georgia and other death penalty states instituted bifurcated trials to address the Supreme Court's concern and in their 1976 ruling in the case of *Gregg* v. *Georgia,* the Court ruled that bifurcated trials for capital punishment cases were acceptable. In a bifurcated trial, if a defendant is convicted of first-degree murder, the sentence for the crime is determined in a separate proceeding from the proceeding in which the offender was convicted. Most states follow a process similar to Georgia's procedure. In Georgia, the jury or judge must consider any mitigating or aggravating circumstances in determining whether the offender should be sentenced to death. Among other aggravating circumstances, Georgians consider whether the defendant has prior convictions, whether he or she committed other felonies at the time of the murder, whether there were multiple victims, and whether the murder was committed in a particularly horrific manner (Inciardi, 1996). Mitigating circumstances may include details about the offender's upbringing that may explain why he or she committed murder.

Although opinion polls show that most Americans support the death penalty, death penalty sentencing remains controversial. Besides issues about the morality of the death penalty, research indicates there is racial and gender disparity in death penalty sentencing. Researchers found that in Ohio, the odds of a death sentence were over 1.75 times greater in cases in which a white person was killed as compared to cases with nonwhite victims. Similarly, those in death penalty–eligible cases who killed women were 2.617 times more likely to be sentenced to death than those who killed men. Finally, offenders who killed white women were more likely to be sentenced to death than those who killed white men or African Americans of either sex (Holcomb, Williams, & Demuth, 2004). The researchers found this bias existed even when important factors such as weapon use, multiple victims, child victims, and urban area were considered.

Jury decisions are not the only point in the criminal justice system where sentencing disparity occurs in the United States. Prosecutors have almost complete discretion in determining who they will charge with capital murder (Sorensen & Wallace, 1995). Research indicates that the greatest racial disparity in criminal justice treatment occurs during the indictment or charging stage. Prosecutors are more likely to seek the death penalty when the victim is a white woman and least likely when the victim is an African American man (Paternoster, 1984). Further, the studies indicate that conscious discrimination does not explain these findings. Rather, prosecutors make decisions based on what cases are most likely to result in conviction (Radelet & Pierce, 1985).

Finally, recent decisions by the Supreme Court and by some state legislatures and politicians suggest that support for the death penalty in the United States remains controversial and ultimately unsettled. Supreme Court decisions in 2002 and 2005 put limits on the use of the death penalty. In *Atkins* v. *Virginia* (2002), the Supreme Court ruled that the execution of mentally retarded offenders was a violation of the Eighth Amendment's prohibition against cruel and unusual punishment. Then, in the 2005 case of *Roper* v. *Simmons,* the Court overruled their previous rulings and determined that a death sentence for those who committed crimes while younger than 18 years was a violation of the Eighth Amendment. In stating the Court's opinion, Justice Kennedy noted that the United States is the only country in the world that officially sanctions the juvenile death penalty (Adler et al., 2006). Additionally, in 2003, Governor George Ryan of Illinois, citing a flawed death penalty process, granted clemency to all 167 death row inmates in his state. In 2006, the New Jersey legislature placed a moratorium on executions. Whether the United States will continue to punish offenders with the death penalty remains an interest to those who study homicide and justice and to the Supreme Court, which agreed to hear a case in 2007 involving the execution of the mentally ill (Death Penalty Information Center, 2007).

BOX 15.6

Serial Killer's Freedom Due to Plea Bargain

Known as "The Sunday Morning Slasher," Coral Eugene Watts killed several women in Michigan in the 1970s and early 1980s. In 1981, Watts realized police had him under surveillance in Michigan so he moved to Houston, Texas, where he continued to kill. Eventually, the Houston police arrested him. However, the Texas district attorney was not sure there was enough evidence to convict Watts, so a plea bargain was instituted. Watts agreed to a plea bargain that allowed him to plead guilty to burglary and intent to commit murder. Watts was also given immunity for any of the 13 homicides he admitted to committing in Texas. The judge sentenced Watts to 60 years of incarceration. Texas authorities were relieved, believing Watts would remain incarcerated until 2042 if he lived to age 89. Unfortunately, however, overcrowding in the Texas prison system led to changes in the mandatory release of inmates incarcerated in Texas. As a result, Watts was scheduled to be released in May 2006 (Snow, 2005). Because he was given immunity for many of the murders he committed in Texas, it began to look like Watts would go free and there was nothing Texas could do about it. Furthermore, you may remember hearing in the news that even though Watts essentially promised he would kill again if he was released from prison, he was scheduled to be released without supervision. Fortunately, authorities in Michigan worked quickly because the immunity Watts received in Texas that allowed him freely to confess to 13 homicides only included one killing he committed in Michigan. Thus in late 2004, Coral Eugene Watts was convicted of the 1979 murder of Helen Dutcher in Detroit and sentenced to life in prison (Associated Press, 2004).

SUMMARY

This chapter used many examples to review the stages involved in prosecuting defendants for murder in the U.S. court system after they have been arrested for murder or manslaughter. The chapter began with the pretrial stages of the justice process, including the initial appearance, bail, pretrial release, and indictment. Murder defendants have various plea options depending on the jurisdiction in which they are tried. The plea options of guilty, not guilty, nolo contendere, and not guilty by reason of insanity were reviewed. The sometimes controversial practice of plea bargaining was also included. The bulk of the chapter focused on the different steps of a criminal murder trial. Defenses available to murder defendants, including alibis, justifications, and excuses, were also discussed with relevant cases. Finally, the chapter concluded with the special processes and issues involved in death penalty cases.

CHAPTER QUESTIONS

1. What power do district attorneys/prosecuting attorneys have?
2. List the steps involved in prosecuting a defendant accused of murder from the step of initial appearance to sentencing in a capital murder trial.
3. What occurs at an initial appearance?
4. True or false: Most defendants accused of murder are released on high bail so they may help with their defense.
5. What does a grand jury do?
6. List and briefly describe four possible pleas.
7. Are trials more or less common in murder trials or other felony trials?
8. Why might a prosecutor and a defendant agree to a plea bargain?
9. What is *voir dire*, and how does it work?
10. Explain scientific jury selection. Do you think it should be permitted? Why or why not?
11. What type of evidence is presented during the opening statements?
12. Explain the difference between circumstantial and indirect evidence.
13. What did the Supreme Court rule in *Daubert v. Merrill Dow*, and what is the general practice of judges following this decision?
14. According to the Sixth Amendment of the U.S. Constitution, to what type of jury do U.S. citizens have the right?
15. What are the three general defenses to murder according to this chapter?
16. What is an alibi?
17. Name the five possible justifications to murder. Which are most likely to be accepted?
18. What is a "stand your ground" law? Do you agree or disagree with such laws? Explain.
19. Name the four excuses for murder discussed in this chapter.
20. Explain the excuse of age for murder.
21. What is voluntary intoxication, and do you think it could ever be a viable excuse for murder?

22. What type of provocation do you believe should be relevant for murder?
23. Explain the difference between competency to stand trial and not guilty by reason of insanity.
24. What is the M'Naghten rule?
25. What is the substantial capacity test?
26. What are closing arguments?
27. Why is the judge's charge to the jury so important?
28. Who determines sentences for those found guilty of murder?
29. What is a bifurcated trial?
30. Does race or gender affect sentencing?

REFERENCES

Abwender, David A., and Kenyatta Hough. 2001. "Interactive Effects of Characteristics of Defendant and Mock Juror on U.S. Participants' Judgment and Sentencing Recommendations." *Journal of Social Psychology,* 141(5): 603–615.

Adler, Freda, Gerhard O. W. Mueller, and William S. Laufer. 2006. *Criminal Justice: An Introduction.* Boston: McGraw-Hill.

Associated Press. 2004, November 18. "New Conviction for Serial Killer." *Chicago Sun Times.* Accessed online at http://www.findarticles.com/p/articles/mi_qn4155/is_20041118/ai_n12568880

Associated Press. 2005, August 9. "Jury Doesn't Buy Video Game Defense." *Fox News.com.* Accessed online at http://www.foxnews.com/story/0,2933,165259,00.html

Associated Press. 2006a, June 19. "Defendant in Murder Case Too Old to Be Tried by Jury of Her Peers." Accessed at http://www.accessnorthga.com/news/ap_newfullstory.asp?ID=76699

Associated Press. 2006b, August 24. "Judges Grants 90-day Extension for Yates Hearing." *Houston Chronicle.* http://www.chron.com/disp/story.mpl/'special/drownings/4139556.html.

Bohm, Robert M., and Keith N. Haley. 2002. *Introduction to Criminal Justice.* New York: McGraw-Hill.

Brown, Jodi M., and Patrick A. Langan. 1999, July. "Felony Sentences in the U.S., 1996." Washington, DC: U.S. Department of Justice, Bureau of Justice Statistics Bulletin.

Cleary, Audrey. 2005, Spring. "Scientific Jury Selection: History, Practice, and Controversy." *Concepts: An Interdisciplinary Journal of Graduate Studies.* Accessed at http://www.publications.villanova.edu/Concept/2005.html

Cohen, Thomas H., and Brian A. Reaves. 2006, July. "Felony Defendants in Large Urban Counties, 2002." Washington, DC: United States Department of Justice, Bureau of Justice Statistics.

Collins, Kimberly, Gabe Hinkebein, and Staci Schorgl. 2006. "The John Hinckley Trial and Its Effect on the Insanity Defense." In Douglas O. Linder, *Famous Trials.* Accessed at www.law.umkc.edu/faculty/projects/ftrials/hinckley/hinckleyinsanity.htm

Constitutional Rights Foundation Chicago, National Endowment for the Humanities. 2006. *The American Jury: Bulwark of Democracy: An Online Resource.* Accessed at http://www.crfc.org/americanjury/index.html

Davis, Edward F. 1998, November. "Caught on Tape: Using Criminals' Videos Against Them." *FBI Law Enforcement Bulletin.* Accessed at http://findarticles.com/p/articles/mi_m2194/is_11_67/ai_53436002

Death Penalty Information Center. 2007. *Death Penalty Timeline.* Accessed at http://www.deathpenaltyinfo.org/GreggTimeline.pdf

Dershowitz, Alan. 1994. *The Abuse Excuse: And Other Cop-Outs, Sob Stories, and Evasions of Responsibility.* New York: Little, Brown.

Diamond, Bernard. 1964. "On the Spelling of Daniel M'Naughten's Name." *Ohio State Law Journal,* 25(1).

Doulin, Tim. 2000. "Jury Finds Man Not Guilty in Fatal Stabbing Outside Bar." *Columbus Dispatch,* p. 6b.

Duncan v. Louisiana. 1968. 391, U.S. 145, 155–156.

Durose, Matthew R., and Patrick A. Langan, 2004. "Felony Sentences in State Courts, 2000." Washington, DC: U.S. Department of Justice, Bureau of Justice Statistics Bulletin.

FindLaw.com. 2006. "Impartial Jury." FindLaw.com website.

Finz, Stacy. 2004, June 1. "The Peterson Trial: Can The Prosecutors Make Their Case Stick? The Problem: The Evidence on Hand Is Only Circumstantial." *San Francisco Chronicle.* Accessed at http://www.sfgate.com/cgi-bin/article.cgi?file=/c/a/2004/06/01/MNGEM6UQVR1.DTL

Frederick, Jeffrey T. 1984. "Social Science Involvement in Voir Dire: Preliminary Data on the Effectiveness of 'Scientific Jury Selection.'" *Behavioral Sciences & The Law,* 2(4): 375–394.

Frontline. 2005. "A Crime Of Insanity." Accessed at http://www.pbs.org/wgbh/pages/frontline/shows/crime/trial/states.html

Harris, Paul. 1999. *Black Rage Confronts the Law.* New York: NYU Press.

Hickey, Eric W. 2006. *Serial Murderers and Their Victims.* Belmont, CA: Thomson.

Holcomb, Jefferson E, Marian R. Williams, and Stephen Demuth. 2004. "White Female Victims and Death Penalty Disparity Research." *Justice Quarterly,* 21(4): 877–902.

Houston Chronicle. 1995. "October 11, 1995: Selena Murder Trial Opening Statements." Accessed at http://www.chron.com/content/chronicle/metropolitan/selena/transcripts/95/10/11/open.html

Inciardi, James. 1996. *Criminal Justice.* Fort Worth: Harcourt College Publishers.

Klotter, John C. 2001. *Criminal Law.* Cincinnati, OH: Anderson Publishing.

Krupnik, Matt. 2006, July 18. "Dyleski Trial Highlights Jury Selection Difficulties." *Contra Costa Times.* Accessed at http://www.contracostatimes.com/mld/cctimes/email/news/15063385.htm?template=contentModules/printstory.jsp.

Liptak, Adam. 2006, August 7. "15 States Expand Right to Shoot in Self-Defense." *New York Times.* Accessed at nytimes.com.

Miller, D. W. "Jury Consulting on Trial." *Chronicle of Higher Education,* 48(13): 15–16.

M'Naghten's Case. 1843. Available online at http://wings.buffalo.edu/law/bclc/web/mnaghten.htm.

Paternoster, Ray. 1984. "Prosecutorial Discretion in Requesting the Death Penalty: A Case of Victim-Based Racial Discrimination." *Law and Society Review,* 18: 437–478.

Polk, Jim. 2005, February 16. "Teen Gets 30 Years in Zoloft Case: Boy Found Guilty of Murder in Grandparents' Deaths." *CNN.com.* Accessed online at http://www.cnn.com/2005/LAW/02/15/zoloft.trial/index.html

Radelet, Michael L., and Glenn L. Pierce. 1985. "Race and Prosecutorial Discretion in Homicide Cases." *Law and Society Review,* 19: 587–621.

Reaves, Brian A. 2006, February. "State Court Processing Statistics, 1990–2002: Violent Felons in Large Urban Counties." Washington, DC: U.S. Department of Justice, Bureau of Justice Statistics.

Reuters. 2006. "Assisted Suicide Advocate Kevorkian Paroled." Boston.com. http://www.boston.com/news/nation/articles/2006/12/13/assisted_suicide_advocate_kevorkian_paroled/

Ryan, Harriet. 2004, November 11. "Jury Foreman Dismissed in Scott Peterson Murder Trial." Accessed at CourtTV.com.

Schmalleger, Frank. 2007. *Criminal Justice Today: An Introductory Text for the 21st Century.* Upper Saddle River, NJ: Prentice Hall.

Snow, Robert L. 2005. *Murder 101: Homicide and Its Investigation.* Westport, CT: Praeger.

Sorensen, Jonathan R., and Donald H. Wallace. 1995. "Capital Punishment in Missouri: Examining the Issue of Racial Disparity." *Behavioral Sciences and the Law*, 13: 61–80.

Stacy, Tom. 2000. "Changing Paradigms in the Law of Homicide." *The Ohio State Law Journal*. 62(3): 1–48 on-line (http://moritzlaw.osu.edu/lawjournal/stacy.htm).

Walsh, Diana, and Stacy Finz. 2004, December 16. "Behind Closed Doors: Two Jury Members Were Kicked Off, the Foreman Was Ousted, and the Case Was Nearly Deadlocked. Now Jurors in the Scott Peterson Case Tell the Story of Their Decision to Sentence Him to Death." *San Francisco Chronicle, p A1*. http://www.sfgate.com/cgi-bin/article.cgi?file=/c/a/2004/12/16/MNG80ACOTJ1.DTL

Chapter 16

THE IMPACT OF HOMICIDE

Images of murder are everywhere in our culture. My friends are "hosting a murder," a party in which the guests attempt to solve a murder mystery. As kids we played *Clue*, a game in which we had to determine whether Miss Scarlet or Professor Plum committed the murder in the ballroom or the study with the candlestick or the lead pipe. The *New York Times* bestseller list is filled with books about murder by writers who make a good living writing about homicide. Male teenagers and young adults spend much of their free time killing lifelike images of humans on their computers and video game consoles. Everywhere you turn, there are images of murder.

Murder is so common in today's society that you probably do not even think about how often words like *murder* and *killer* are used around you everyday. The word *murder* is a very common part of everyday language in the United States. We say things like "I'm gonna murder you" when we are talking to an opponent in sports or even in Scrabble. Sports teams have been known to "slaughter" their opponents. Someone can even "murder" the English language when they do not speak well. You may not even realize that a "murder" is the proper name of a group of crows in the same way that a group of cows is a herd. We also say things like "I'm going to kill you if you do that" when we certainly do not really mean we will kill another. Earlier today I was at the gym listening to *The Killers* on my MP3 player and my abs were 'killing' me because of the crunches I was doing. When you think about it, murder and images of murder are ubiquitous.

References to murder and killing are commonplace in today's society as is the slaughter of human beings for entertainment. Until you read this book, you may not have thought much about the ubiquity of murder in society today unless you have personally been touched by murder. If you are fortunate enough not to have been personally affected by murder, you may never have thought about what life might be like for those who have lost friends and loved ones to murder or for those whose family members or friends have committed murder. In fact, you may be quite callous when it comes to murder because you are, in all likelihood, exposed to it daily. In this chapter, you will learn about the challenges faced by those who have lost those they love to murder and those who live with the reality that someone they love has committed murder. From my own research, I will also include a discussion on the impact of serving as a juror in a homicide case. Finally, this chapter also has a section on the fascination with murder and killers in our society.

HOMICIDE SURVIVORS

Whether they are called "homicide survivors" or "co-victims," family members and friends of murder victims suffer immensely when their loved ones are taken away by murder. These co-victims, however, are not counted by the FBI or other organizations that keep track of the number of victimizations in the United States or other countries. If co-victims were included in national counts of victimization, the number of victims would increase astronomically. A national prevalence survey in the United States in 1991 found that 9.3% of those sampled were homicide survivors (Amick-McMullan, Kilpatrick, & Resnick, 1991). If we projected this finding to the adult population in the United States, estimated to be approximately 300 million people, that would mean there are approximately 28 million homicide survivors in the United States. This is a phenomenal number of people, who, according to research available, are likely to be suffering immensely from the tragic loss of their loved ones.

Although there are studies about grief and bereavement, very few of these studies focus on the effects of losing a close friend or family to murder (Armour, 2002). However, the sparse research on homicide survivors suggests there are unique problems faced by those whose loved ones are murdered. Even in comparison with people who lose loved ones unexpectedly through accidental deaths or car wrecks, homicide survivors experience deeper and longer lasting trauma. Homicide survivors face more than the unexpected deaths of their loved ones. Survivors must contend with the fact that their loved one died because someone willfully took his or her life (Armour, 2002; Horne, 2003; Mezey, Evans, & Hobdell, 2002). Additionally, survivors sometimes feel that the press invades their privacy or portrays their loved ones in an unfavorable light. Survivors also often must contend with the anger they have for the murderer of their loved one as well as the social stigma and isolation involved in having a loved one murdered. Moreover, survivors' experiences with the criminal justice system are often problematic; it is common for them to feel ignored or pushed out of the justice process altogether (Armour, 2002, 2003; Horne, 2003). Finally, as noted in Chapter 14, fewer homicides are cleared today than in the past. As a result, many survivors must face the reality that their loved one was murdered by someone who remains unpunished.

Homicide survivors are often traumatized by the murder of their loved one. Azim Khamisa describes the experience of learning that his son had been murdered as "a nuclear bomb going off in my heart" (Khamisa, 2006: 15). Although each survivor does not have the same experience, many find they are numb; others experience, fear, guilt, rage, and anxiety (Armour, 2002). Feelings of helplessness and apprehension are common as is survivor guilt. It is not uncommon for survivors to experience post-traumatic stress disorder (PTSD) (Beaton, 1999). In fact, research indicates that PTSD is more prevalent in murder survivors than in people who lose loved ones to other causes including accidents and suicide (Murphy et al., 1999). The trauma of losing a loved one may also be manifested in physical symptoms, such as headaches, sleep disturbances, gastrointestinal problems, and loss of appetite (Armour, 2002).

Interpersonal relationships are often affected by the murder of a loved one. Survivors sometimes believe that others do not understand what they are going through, and they feel isolated and alone. It is also not uncommon for family and friends to feel uncomfortable around survivors and thus avoid interaction with them, making them physically as well as emotionally isolated. The stress of losing a child often results in divorce for couples whose child is murdered (Armour, 2002). Families may also be torn apart when the murder offender and victim are related to one another (Asaro, 2001).

Research on homicide survivors indicates that many suffer from a "complicated bereavement," in which they cannot reconcile their loss (Armour, 2003: 522). Moreover, it is not clear what may help homicide survivors. Research indicates that prayer, church attendance, psychotherapy, and antidepressants fail to reduce the pain and trauma or decrease the PTSD experienced by most homicide survivors. For some survivors, support groups help make a difference (Armour, 2003).

In addition to the emotional turmoil experienced by homicide co-victims, survivors must also contend with extrapersonal losses. Survivors may have to pay medical bills if there were an effort to save their loved one. Some survivors lose their homes or have major social status changes related to the loss of the victim's income (Asaro, 2001). If there is a trial, survivors may find it difficult to maintain their own jobs or earn enough money to pay their bills while attending all of the criminal justice proceedings (Asaro, 2001).

The media may also present problems for survivors. Sometimes reporters are insensitive when they ask questions of survivors, who may not realize they are not required to talk to the media. Pictures of victims may be broadcast on the news or published in the newspaper without the survivor's consent. In sensational cases, family members may have to contend with media camping outside their houses, near constant news coverage, and unflattering or personal details about their loved ones' life or even their own lives (Asaro, 2001).

BOX 16.1

Murder Site Cleanup

Homicide survivors may have to contend with cleaning up the site where their loved one was killed. If you are not a homicide survivor, you may never have thought about who cleans the site of the murder. Crime scene companies such as Advanced Bio-Treatment (ABT) advertise the importance of using professional cleaners to clean crime scenes to protect those who come in contact with the scene. Noting that they are sensitive to the crime victim's family, ABT's website indicates the following: "Grout, cement, wood flooring and subflooring all have the potential to

continued

emanate death odors if they have been contaminated due to the decom-
position of human body fluids/blood, and tissue" (ABT, 2006). The price
of such a cleanup ranges between $400 and $10,000. If the murder
occurred in the survivor's or victim's home, the survivor will be responsible for arranging the cleanup and paying for the service. Many crime
scene cleanup companies offer to help work with insurance companies
that may cover the costs of cleanup services, and they also note that they
accept payment plans.

SURVIVORS AND THE CRIMINAL JUSTICE SYSTEM

Crimes in the United States and many other countries around the world are viewed
as crimes against the state instead of crimes against individual victims. Not only are
investigators, prosecutors, and judges taught to view crimes as crimes against the
state, the system is structured such that the victim's role is peripheral. Victims have
not traditionally been informed about the investigation of the murder of their loved
one, and often as family members, they may be considered suspects by the police
(Mezey et al., 2002). Finally, if law enforcement discovers a suspect, co-victims are
rarely if ever included in any decisions about prosecuting the accused.

Research indicates that interactions with the criminal justice system increase homicide survivors' feeling of powerlessness. Often the trauma for the survivor begins with
the death notification (Asaro, 2001). Even well-meaning police can seem insensitive to
survivors, and sometimes the media inform the survivors of their loss by asking them
intrusive questions. Many survivors also express frustration at the seemingly better treatment that the criminal justice system provides to offenders in comparison to the families
of the murdered victim (Mezey et al., 2002). Common practices such as plea bargaining,
not-guilty verdicts, and reduced sentences for good behavior or because of overcrowding
can also add to the helplessness and lack of control that survivors feel (Asaro, 2001).
Finally, although we might think that a trial would be cathartic for co-offenders, at least
one study indicated that family members who experienced a trial had higher depression
than family members whose cases were still unsolved (Goodrum & Stafford, 2001).

VICTIMS' RIGHTS MOVEMENT

During the 1970s, several social movements converged into what is now referred to
as the U.S. victims' rights movement. Feminists made progress in establishing battered women's shelters and encouraging legislatures to institute rape shield laws.
The National Organization for Victim Assistance was founded in 1975. In 1976, a
chief probation officer in California developed a victim impact statement to be used
by the criminal justice system. Robert and Charlotte Hullinger founded Parents of
Murdered Children (POMC) in 1978 after their 19-year-old daughter was murdered
by her former boyfriend. POMC and Mothers Against Drunk Driving (MADD)

began demanding that the criminal justice system pay attention to victims and see beyond the state and the defendant in criminal proceedings (Walker, 2000).

In 1982, President Reagan appointed the Task Force on Victims of Crime. The Task Force made 68 recommendations. This was followed in 1984 by what has been called the greatest event in the victims' rights movement: passage of the Victims of Crime Act (VOCA) (Walker, 2000). VOCA provides funding for victim assistance programs and state victim compensation. Although victims still have legitimate complaints with the criminal justice system, the victims' rights movement has greatly improved the treatment of victims by those in the criminal justice system. Victim compensation is commonplace, many district attorneys' offices now include victim assistance programs, and victim impact statements are now a part of the sentencing stage of criminal trials in most jurisdictions.

VICTIM ASSISTANCE PROGRAMS

In St. Louis in 1972, Carol Vittert witnessed an assault and robbery. She took the victim home and then established the first U.S. victim assistance program (Young, 1997a). Her voluntary organization, Aid for Victims of Crime, still provides services to victims in the St. Louis area today. Vittert's work was expanded in 1974 when the first government victim/witness programs were established with funds from the Law Enforcement Assistance Administration, a federal agency set up to study and fund crime prevention efforts. These victim/witness programs were created in district attorneys' offices in Brooklyn and Milwaukee (Young, 1997b).

The victim assistance programs were instituted to provide a better experience for crime victims and witnesses in the criminal justice system. Although problems still exist, much more care is taken in notifying survivors that someone has killed or injured their loved ones. Victims are also more likely to be notified about updates in the state's case against the offender (see Box 16.2). Victims may even be given a say or asked their opinions regarding the case in some jurisdictions. Additionally, victim assistance workers often inform victims about compensation programs and counseling available for them. During the Reinaldo Rivera trial in which Rivera was accused of killing Marni Glista, victim assistance workers were always in the court throughout the trial supporting Glista's family members and others who testified against Rivera (Young, 1997b).

BOX 16.2

Rights of Federal Crime Victims

Federal crime victims have the following eight rights:

1. The right to reasonable protection from the accused;
2. The right to notices of public court and parole proceedings involving the crime and notices if the accused is released or escapes;

continued

3. The right to be included in any public court proceeding unless the court determines that the victim's testimony would be materially altered if he or she were to attend the proceedings;
4. The right to speak at any public proceedings about the release, plea, sentencing, or parole of the accused;
5. The right to talk to the Government's attorney about the case;
6. The right to the timely payment of any restitution as provided by law;
7. The right to reasonably speedy proceedings;
8. The right to privacy and fair, respectful, and dignified treatment. (FBI, 2006)

BOX 16.3

Laura's Law

In September 2003, Bruce Lower was released from prison after serving 16 years of a 25-year sentence for the murder of 3-year-old Laura Skinner. According to news reports, evidence indicated that Laura had been sexually molested. Nevertheless, Lower pleaded guilty to manslaughter and was sentenced to 15 to 25 years of incarceration. When Lower came up for release in 2003, there was no opposition to his release. No one in the community knew Lower was to have a parole hearing. There was no one on Laura's victim list stipulating that they be informed of Lower's release. Brett Vinocur, who runs the website findmissingkids.com, stumbled onto the fact that Lower had been released, and he worked with the Ohio House of Representatives to introduce "Laura's law."

Laura's law (Ohio House Bill 15) mandates that the Ohio Parole Board make upcoming parole hearings public by posting them on an Internet site open to the community. The law also requires the Ohio Department of Corrections to update inmate information pages. Now community members can search for paroled inmate by zip code (Carmen, 2004; rememberinglaura.com, n.d.).

VICTIM COMPENSATION

One response to the victim's movement in the United States was the establishment of victim compensation funds to provide financial reimbursement to victims for the losses they incurred during a crime (Young, 1997b). The idea of victim compensation was initially proposed in the 1950s by English penal reformer Margery Fry. It was legislated into law in New Zealand and England in 1963. The first programs in the United States began in New York and California in 1965, but it took the victim's rights movement to see the institution of victim compensation programs throughout the states (NACVCB, 2006; Young, 1997b).

Victim compensation programs originally were established to provide monetary assistance to victims in need. However, today one need not be needy to receive victim compensation funds. Victims are considered deserving simply because they have been victimized. Nearly 200,000 victims are helped by victim compensation programs each year in the United States at a cost of approximately $450 million. Although the operation of compensation programs varies by jurisdiction, most are funded through offender fines and fees along with federal funding (NACVCB, 2006; Young, 1997b).

Victim compensation programs vary by state, but most often only victims of violent crimes who suffer physical injury or emotional trauma qualify for compensation. Family members of murder victims are among those eligible because they are considered to be victims of emotional trauma. Homicide victims' families may receive funding to pay for uninsured medical costs incurred in trying to save their loved one. Compensation funding may also be used to help pay funeral costs, crime scene cleanup, mental health counseling, and lost wages and support. Compensation, however, is often limited with $25,000 a typical maximum (NACVCB, 2006).

Victim assistance workers often make offenders aware of and help them apply for compensation funds. Most compensation programs require that victims report the crime and cooperate with the police to be eligible to receive funds. Additionally, to receive victim compensation funding, one must not have taken part in the crime (NACVCB, 2006; Young, 1997b).

VICTIM IMPACT STATEMENTS

As a result of the victim's crime movement, victim impact statements were introduced into the criminal trials as a way for victims to indicate the impact the crime has had on them. Beginning in the 1980s, criminal justice and mental health professionals began to recognize that victims who were informed about the criminal justice process and, moreover, those who felt they had a say in the process fared better than those who were not informed and were not included in the process (Alexander & Lord, 1994).

Every state in the United States allows homicide co-victims to present a victim impact statement during the sentencing phase of trials, and 44 states allow impact statements to be included as part of presentence reports. In this statement the victim tells the judge (or the jury in capital punishment cases) how the crime has affected him or her and others close to the murder victim. Impact statements may include details about emotional as well as financial suffering resulting from the murder. When an offender is found guilty or pleads guilty, the judge or jury may use the statement in determining the sentence the offender will receive. In most jurisdictions, victim impact statements may be presented orally in court, but even when they are presented orally, in many jurisdictions they must be written in advance of the oral presentation (National Center for Victims of Crime, 1999).

RESTORATIVE JUSTICE

Restorative justice has a long history that has been linked to Native American and aboriginal New Zealander customs, Anglo-Saxon tribal law, and the Bible (LeGardeur, 2003). The idea of retributive justice is to repair the wrong done to the victim and the community by bringing the offender, victim, and community members together. Restorative justice encourages communication between offenders and those they have hurt through victim/offender mediation. The goal is to allow the offender to work toward repairing the harm he or she has caused and to reintegrate him or her into society. Those in support of restorative justice argue that, especially for offenders who will return to society, it is important for them to recognize the pain they have caused. If offenders are to become a reintegrated contributing member of society, they must see the damage they have caused and work to repair it (LeGardeur, 2003; Umbreit & Vos, 2000).

Restorative justice is also seen as beneficial for victims. In fact, many victim advocates argue that the criminal justice system in the United States and many other countries revictimizes victims and co-victims by preventing them from having any input into the justice process. For example, because the state is seen as the wronged party, traditionally victims may be asked to testify, but they are only permitted to respond to questions posed by the attorneys. Victims are not asked what would be best for them or what would restore the damage done to them (LeGardeur, 2003). In contrast, restorative justice gives the victim a voice and some control. The victims have the opportunity to tell the perpetrator how his or her actions affected the co-victim. The process may be cathartic for the victim and help him or her begin to heal.

When murder is the crime, it may seem impossible that restorative justice could do any good. After all, how can anyone repair the damage done when the damage is the death of a loved one? Single mother Thomas Ann Hines may have asked this question herself at one time. Hines's 21-year-old son Paul, her only child, was murdered in Texas in 1985 by 17-year-old Charles White. Paul was just three months away from graduation when he agreed to give Charles a ride. Charles insisted that Paul give him the keys to Paul's Camaro, but Paul refused. Charles shot him once in the chest; killing him. Charles pleaded guilty and was sentenced to 40 years of incarceration (Evers, 1998).

Paul's mother, Thomas Ann, was furious. She believed Charles should have been sentenced to death. She spent the next several years working diligently to keep him in prison. She wrote the parole board regularly to express her pain. Hines felt empty; she could not get past her son's death. In 1998, however, she took part in the Texas Department of Victim Services' Victim Offender Mediation/Dialogue program. Hines and a mediator met with Charles, her son's killer.

The meeting was cathartic for both Charles and Thomas Ann. They talked for over five hours. Before the meeting, Charles did not think he could do anything about Paul's death. But Thomas Ann convinced him to start taking responsibility for his own life and future. Charles, who had grown up on the streets with little guidance, felt he had someone who cared about him. He agreed to work on his GED and vocational training in prison. Thomas Ann finally learned about the last minutes of her son's life and she began to heal. She still misses her son immensely, but she gained a sense of calmness that she did not have before she met with Charles. Hines was comforted by knowing that Charles now understands Paul was a real person and his death hurt her (Evers, 1998; Hines, n.d.). Studies show that Hines's experience is typical of victims who have participated in mediation with offenders. Victims report that after mediation, they no longer see the perpetrators as monsters. More importantly, after mediation, the victims feel more at peace, and they no longer feel as if the offender has any power over them (Umbreit & Vos, 2000).

BOX 16.4

May a Killer Receive Life Insurance Benefits from the Victim?

In Georgia in 1997, Kevin Spann opened his door where two young men stood. One of them shot him to death. Kevin's wife Gina had convinced her 18-year-old boyfriend and his three friends to shoot her husband for part of the $300,000 in insurance money she would receive after Kevin's death. The police quickly figured out the plot and arrested Gina Spann and the young men she had enlisted to kill her husband. The main players including Gina were sent to prison, but the $300,000 in insurance policies was still an issue.

There was no question that Spann, who was sentenced to life plus five years for Kevin's killing, was disqualified from receiving the insurance benefits. However, the policies named her blood relatives as the second beneficiaries. Should Gina Spann's blood relatives be awarded Kevin Spann's life insurance benefits when she was the reason he was dead?

Two policies both named Gina as primary beneficiary. A $200,000 policy named Gina's natural son as the second beneficiary, and a $100,000 policy listed Gina's sister as the beneficiary. Gina's 13-year-old son was never adopted by Kevin Spann, but he lived with the couple during their 11-year marriage and Kevin referred to him as "my son" in his will. As it turns out, Kevin had a minor daughter who he had never acknowledged while he was alive. However, postmortem DNA tests proved she was his daughter. Should Kevin's biological daughter receive the death benefits instead of his murderer's blood relatives? In district court, a judge determined that Gina's sister and son should receive the benefits; however, the daughter (and her mother) appealed and the case proceeded to the U.S. Court of Appeals in 1999.

The U.S. Appeals Court noted that a person cannot receive insurance benefits or inheritance if their wrongdoing led to the death that would benefit them. Moreover, the Court noted that because a murderer could indirectly benefit if the secondary beneficiary was awarded the benefits, the secondary beneficiary may also be barred from receiving the benefits in some U.S. jurisdictions. In this case, for example, if Gina was expected to be released from prison while her son was still a minor, she could easily have control over the benefits. In this particular case, Gina's entire family was estranged from her and she was serving a life sentence, so the likelihood she would benefit financially from the death was very low. Still, some states, including Georgia, disqualify murderers' relatives from receiving any death benefits to assure that the murderer cannot profit from his or her crimes. The only exception is that the murderer's children can receive insurance benefits but only if they are also the victim's children.

continued

Clearly, Gina's son and sister would not qualify for benefits in Georgia where Kevin was killed.

The court, however, indicated that they needed to consider which jurisdiction was relevant to determining this case. Both insurance policies were purchased in Germany while Kevin was in the army. Kevin was murdered in Georgia while he was posted at Fort Gordon army base. Yet Kevin was a permanent resident of Illinois.

To make a long story a bit shorter, the court ruled that Illinois law was the appropriate law to follow for two reasons. First, Kevin was a permanent resident of Illinois. Second, Kevin's daughter and her guardian had based the appeals on Illinois law, which allows the court to determine whether the murderer will benefit if the secondary beneficiary receives the benefits. As a result, the Appeals Court ruled there was no error made in determining that Gina's sister and son should receive the life insurance benefits. The court believed it was "exceedingly unlikely that Gina Spann will ever benefit significantly from the proceeds of her husband's life insurance policies in the hands of her son and her sister" (*Prudential* v. *Plaintiffs*, 178 F.3d 473).

THE COST OF HOMICIDE, LITERALLY

Have you ever thought about the economic cost of homicide? The Australian Institute of Criminology (AIC) assessed the cost of homicide in Australia in 2001 to be $930 million. They included medical costs (exclusive of mental health costs) and lost output as well as intangible costs calculated as the monetary value of pain, suffering, and lost quality of life (Mayhew, 2003). Lost output refers to the cost of paid and unpaid labor that victims can no longer do. The AIC determined that the medical costs of homicide in 2001 was $4.5 million. Lost output equaled $700 million, and the intangible costs were determined to be almost $225 million. In total, then, the cost for all the Australian homicides in 2001 according to the AIC equaled a little over $731 million U.S. (Mayhew, 2003). The Australian cost of homicide is based on 589 homicides for 2001. In 2001, the United States had 13,752 homicides. Assuming that the cost per homicide in the United States and Australia were the same in 2001, the U.S. cost would be $22 billion. This incredible figure, however, is less than the compensation paid to those impacted by the 9/11 attacks (see Box 13.4 in Chapter 13). According to a study by the RAND Corporation (2004), more than $38 billion has been paid to victims and businesses directly affected by the attack.

Amazingly, the high costs of homicide determined by AIC and by the Rand study do not include the criminal justice costs, such as the cost of investigating homicides, prosecuting offenders, and housing the convicted. These costs can be astronomical. Homicide investigation costs in the single state of Tennessee in 2005, for example, were estimated at approximately $14.2 million (Claxton, 2006a). Finally, the AIC figure that puts the cost of homicide in the United States in the $22 billion range also does not factor in the costs of supporting victim's dependents and the emotional and mental health costs to the survivors (Mayhew, 2003).

THE MURDERER'S FAMILY

When an offender murders another person, it is clear that the victim and his or her family suffer. However, many of us do not consider what murderers' families and friends experience when their loved one takes the life of another. Ironically, offenders' families deal with many of the same issues and emotions as victims' families. Both experience emotional stress, stigmatization, insensitive media, loss of income, and, to a lesser extent, the loss of a loved one. Although the loss is not the same as losing someone to death by murder, the murderer's family often loses their loved one to incarceration and occasionally to suicide. The murder may also affect the offender's family financially. Any income provided by the accused is often lost to the family as soon as there is an arrest. Family members may also lose income if they attend the trial of their loved one. Family finances may also be drained to help provide a defense.

Like victims' families, family and friends of offenders often also feel stigmatized. Often they are ostracized and isolated, or at the other end of the spectrum, some people seek them out because they are related to a murderer. Parents of murderers may be held responsible or blamed for the offender's behavior. Media are often insensitive, and they may camp out in front of the offender's home waiting to ask them questions or they may attempt to dig up information on the murderer's family. Especially in cases that capture the public's imagination, the offenders' family, like the victim's family, may feel a loss of control and privacy as their lives become fodder for the public.

Finally, finding out that a loved one has murdered another human being can be emotionally devastating. For family members of murderers, especially parents, denial may be the initial reaction when they learn that their loved ones are accused of murder. Although some may never get past denial, many family members realize that their loved one has committed the ultimate crime of taking the life of another. If they realize their loved one is guilty, relatives and friends may experience guilt, especially parents who may blame themselves for their child's behavior. Family members of an accused or convicted murderer may also experience anger or betrayal.

Unlike co-victims, the families of murderers may find it more difficult to find support. There are hundreds of groups and much sympathy for those whose family members have been murdered. Important national groups such as Parents of Murdered Children can be easily located on the Internet for those who lose their loved ones to murder. Similar groups for families of murderers are lacking. One might argue that these types of groups are needed. However, it is more likely that these groups do not exist because of the stigmatization, guilt, or denial that the family members of offenders face. Although neither would be easy, it would probably be much more difficult to be the public face for a group called "Parents of Murderers" as opposed to being the leader of Parents of Murdered Children. Still, there may be a group in your city or town.

A confidential support group in my city is called Beyond the Bars. The group is for people whose family members are incarcerated. The group is made up mostly of women who meet twice a month to talk about their experiences and help each other cope with having a loved one incarcerated. Beyond the Bars is not specifically for the family members of murderers; however, many group members have relatives who

> # BOX 16.5
>
> ## Grandmother Cares for Children of Murder Offender and Victim
>
> Marsha Scales is certainly not likely to be envied by many. Scales, who has a heart condition, is a retired nursing home worker. Since her son Marcus was murdered, Scales has been taking care of his two children, who each receive $116 in survivor benefits from social security. Scales's other son, Wendell, fathered a child in 2001 while out on parole for a 1985 murder. After a parole violation, Wendell was returned to prison, and then in 2005, the child's mother died. Scales told *The Tennessean* that she was too overwhelmed with Marcus's two kids to take care of Wendell's child, but she does what she can do to help with her care (Claxton, 2006b). Through Scales, we can see an example of children who suffer because of a family member's murder and because a family member has been convicted of murder.

have been incarcerated for murder. Gerry Nail, who founded the group, started it because of the isolation and stigmatization she felt. Nail wanted to talk to someone about her experiences and the hopelessness she felt. She found the experience of having a loved one who committed a crime humiliating (Weichman, 1997).

Others struggle alone, including young children whose parents are convicted murderers. The child of a murderer is also likely to suffer stigmatization along with a radical change of life. All that the child knew before the murder conviction may change.

If a child lived with his or her parent before he or she is convicted, the child may be placed in the custody of another family member or a foster family. The child has to deal with issues of abandonment as well as the stigmatization of being the child of an incarcerated felon. Often, the ripple effect on our society is felt for years as children of convicted murderers may also turn to crime because of lack of guidance, lack of financial resources, or out of anger.

CRIMINAL JUSTICE PERSONNEL AND REPORTERS

Like families of murderers, sometimes we forget the impact that violent crime may have on those who work in professions where they must deal with the reality of murder as frequently as daily. Law enforcement is a particularly stressful job, and research indicates that the stress is more pronounced for homicide investigators. Not only do they witness horrible murder scenes firsthand, but they often feel it is their personal responsibility to solve the murders and avenge the murder. Fatigue, long hours, and the inability to share the horrors they witness often result in relationship and emotional problems for those who investigate murder (Miller, 2006; Sewell, 1993).

Others, because of their jobs, may also experience stress related to murder. Court workers who must witness details of murders during trials may find themselves

BOX 16.6

Impact of Being Charged with Murder

In November 2002, Sharon Spangler shot and killed her estranged husband. According to Spangler, her husband Steven entered her house, took a gun from her night stand, and threatened to kill her. After a struggle, Sharon managed to grab the pistol and shoot him once in the side. Before Steven died, he told the police that Sharon had lured him to the house to kill him. Spangler was arrested and charged with murder.

At the time Sharon Spangler was arrested, she was on a medical leave from DaimlerChrysler where she had been working as an engineering supervisor earning $110,000 per year. While Sharon was awaiting trial in the county jail, DaimlerChrysler fired her for failing to attend an evaluation that was required for her to continue her medical absence. In early 2004, a jury believed that Sharon Spangler had acted in self-defense when she killed her estranged husband. They found her not guilty. Spangler then filed a wrongful termination suit against DaimlerChrysler. As this book goes to press, the attorneys on both sides are preparing for a trial scheduled in 2007. In most cases, employers may fire employees for any reason as long as they do not discriminate. However, in states such as Wisconsin and California, employers are not permitted to discriminate based on arrest records (Baldas, 2006; Berfield, 2006). Do you think DaimlerChrysler should be ordered to give Sharon Spangler her job back? Do you think they should have fired her?

either growing callous to descriptions of violence or, alternately, they may experience nightmares and find they are less trustful of others after learning the horrible details of some murders. Similarly, defense and prosecuting attorneys may struggle with the reality of murder at the level they must deal with it. Prosecuting attorneys are likely to share with homicide investigators a need to seek vengeance for the murder cases they try. Defense attorneys may face various psychological issues as they struggle with issues of justice and the reality that they may be helping free murderers. Finally, news reporters may be exposed to images that they find difficult to erase from their minds as they cover murder cases for various news outlets.

SERVING AS A JUROR IN A MURDER TRIAL

Jurors, especially those in homicide trials, usually take their duties very seriously. Although most judges are careful to tell jurors explicitly how important they are and to thank them in open court for their difficult work, the emotional toll of trials for jurors is rarely noted or studied. I had not thought about this myself until I interviewed a juror from the Reinaldo Rivera trial. Importantly, I did not seek out this juror. Rather, she had seen me as I attended the trial almost every day. When the trial was complete, she contacted me and asked me to meet with her to talk about the trial. While she asked me a few questions about the lack of DNA evidence presented in the case, most of her questions were about what could be done for the jurors who were suffering because of the trial. She noted that a few of her fellow jurors had told her they were having difficulty sleeping, and throughout the day, they found their thoughts drifting to details they had heard at the trial. It seemed that the horrible attacks on the victims would not leave their minds. Additionally, many of them were distraught about the decision they had to make regarding Rivera's sentence. Although they believed he was guilty—after all, he admitted he was guilty in court—they wondered whether a sentence of life in prison may have been better based on the information about Rivera's life presented in court, such as early exposure to pornography by his father.

The jurors in the Rivera case are not unique. In the few studies that have examined jurors' experiences, researchers have found that jurors who have served in trials of particularly brutal crimes suffer from anxiety, headaches, and even PTSD (Hafemeister, 1993). Judge James Williams told jurors before the Robert Pickton murder trial began in Canada that "I think this trial might expose the juror to something that might be as bad as a horror movie, and you don't have the option of turning off the TV" (CBS News, 2006). Pickton, a pig farmer, who is believed to have murdered 26 women, will be charged with the murder of six women in his 2007 trial scheduled to begin in January. You may remember hearing about Pickton, who is believed to have disposed of his victims' bodies by feeding them to his pigs.

FASCINATION WITH HOMICIDE

Tonight as I stood in line to check out at the grocery store, the customer asked the cashier a question to which the answer was "Union, South Carolina." The customer responded, "I know where that is; that crazy woman lived up there." The cashier answered, "Yes, Susan Smith," and she continued on to tell the customer that she attended the funeral for Alex and Michael. She reported that practically everyone in the town attended. The cashier talked about how the two boys were buried together in one casket and how sad it was at the funeral. She said she could not stop crying. Nothing that the cashier said indicated she knew the boys or their family before the funeral. However, their murders impacted her enough or piqued her interest enough that she attended the funeral for two young boys she did not know. Moreover, the cashier, the customer, and I each knew who the women were talking about immediately. You probably also know who the women at the grocery were talking about. Susan Smith claimed that an African American man had carjacked her car and abducted her two young boys, Alex and Michael, in October 1994. Days later, Smith confessed to strapping the boys in their car seats and letting her car go down a ramp into John D. Long Lake where both children drowned. Most murders do not get the attention or have the kind of impact that the well-publicized story of two young children drowned by their mother did, but plenty of evidence suggests that many people find murder fascinating.

As we noted at the beginning of this book, in the news business, a common operating principle about what to cover is subsumed by the saying "If it bleeds it leads." You probably only need to turn on your local news to find evidence of this, and the research also indicates that crime stories make up a good part of the news coverage we read and see. The Rocky Mountain Media Watch organization found that crime stories, particularly those on murder, dominated half the newscasts they monitored in 35 states for a study in the 1990s (Cohen & Solomon, 1995). Little has changed since this study in 1990s. Crime continues to sell and in ways you may have never imagined, as you will read about in the next section.

More than making money, some observers argue that this selling of murder desensitizes all of us to the reality of murder. Elaine and Gordon Rondeau, who lost their daughter, Renée, to murder in 1994, contend that the continual portrayal of murder for entertainment has made murder seem a normal part of society today. Through their group, Action Americans: Murder Must End Now! (AAMMEN!), the Rondeaus work to raise public awareness about the treatment of murder in the United States. They believe we should become more aware and work toward eradicating "the pleasurable aspects of murder as portrayed in games, TV, movies, etc" and "the profit motive associated with the unprincipled exploitation of society's fascination with murder" (AAMEN!, no date). AAMEN! also encourages the media to stop sensationalizing murder and portray more realistic presentations of murder in their everyday coverage. Finally, they not only advocate reasonable punishments for homicide offenders but they advocate a sociological view of homicide that considers the impact society has on murder as they look for community based solutions to prevent homicide (as will be discussed in Chapter 17) (AAMEN!, no date).

MURDERABILIA

In 1999, Andrew Kahan of the Houston Crime Victims Office started bringing attention to an issue he found troubling: murderabilia, serial killer memorabilia, are items sold by collectors, dealers, or the killers themselves. Much of the Murderabilia is artwork, but other items such as dirt from John Wayne Gacy's crawl space have been sold on online auctions (*BusinessWeek Online*, 2000; Schmid, 2004). Although you can no longer buy murderabilia on *EBay*, Kahan first discovered the market for murderabilia there. With the popular auction site out of the serial killer market, other websites, such as *Serial Killer Central and Murder Auction*, provide collectors the opportunity to buy original artwork by serial killers, serial killer action figures, calendars, clothing, autographs, and more. Victims' families and others are not only disgusted by the interest in these macabre collector's items but they are also outraged that people are making a profit from murderabilia. Particularly problematic for many is the fact that in some cases, the killers are those making the profit. Although one such website was banned in Houston and in California, and legislation has been enacted preventing serial killers from making money from murderabilia; other offenders still may be making a profit from the suffering of others (Stoney, 2004). Kahan, who first brought murderabilia to the public's attention, argues that murderabilia is another example of the glamorization of crime in our culture and the failure to recognize the suffering by victims and their families.

SON OF SAM LAWS

In 1977, the Son of Sam law was enacted by the New York State Legislature to keep convicted murderers such as David Berkowitz (the Son of Sam) from making any money from the sale of stories about the crimes they committed. The New York law did not violate First Amendment freedom of speech rights because it did not prohibit the sale of the murderer's story but instead required that any profit had to be paid to the state to be used to benefit crime victims. The federal government and 42 states enacted similar legislation. In 1991, however, the Supreme Court ruled that New York's Son of Sam law was too broad and thus unconstitutional. The Court indicated that the law applied not only to those convicted of crimes but to those who had been accused but not found guilty. Additionally, the New York law did not distinguish between accounts that focused on the crimes and those that mentioned the crimes in passing. As such, the court argued that St. Augustine and Malcolm X would not have profited from the books they wrote because their crimes were mentioned even though they were not the focus (National Center for Victims of Crime, 2004).

As a result of the 1991 Supreme Court decision in *Simon & Schuster, Inc.* v. *New York Crime Victims Board*, New York and other states have introduced new notoriety-for-profit statutes. The new statutes have been limited to convicted offenders, and they exclude written material in which any references to the crime are tangential. A few states have broadened their legislation to apply to what Iowa calls the "fruits of the crime," defined as any profit that was realized because of the crime. Iowa's legislation would, in all likelihood, count any profit made from a convicted murderer selling his or her artwork or locks of their hair on websites such as *Serial Killer.com.*

BOX 16.7

The Murder Wall

The Murder Wall is a traveling memorial to those lost to murder. Nancy Ruhe-Munch, the executive director of the National Organization of Parents of Murdered Children (POMC) created the memorial in 1987. Ann Reed, a survivor of her child's murder, designed the memorial, which currently consists of 26 walnut plaques that each contain names of 120 murdered victims with their birth and death dates. Survivors pay $50 to have a loved one's name engraved on a plaque. A booklet is available online at http://www.pomc.org/murderwall.cfm that lists each victim named on the wall, and several names are linked to touching memorials written by the family members about the murdered victim. Several also contain details about the murder and the offender (POMC, 2006).

SUMMARY

This chapter began by reemphasizing a point made throughout this book: Images of murder are everywhere in our society. As a result, it is easy to become callous to the reality of murder, which is the focus of much of this chapter. The reality of murder is often overwhelmingly traumatizing to victims' families and murderers' families and the economic cost to society is astronomical. Survivors face a myriad of problems, including emotional turmoil, relationship troubles, stigmatization, loss of income, and poor treatment by the criminal justice system. With the emergence of the victims' rights movement in the 1970s, some of the problems faced by survivors began to improve. Three main changes are discussed in this chapter, including victim assistance programs, victim compensation, and victim impact statements. The chapter also included an explanation of restorative justice and an example of the potential impact of mediation for some survivors. Murderers' family members are often overlooked when criminologists and others discuss the impact of homicide. Yet, as noted in this chapter, they face many of the same issues faced by homicide co-victims. Jurors who serve in murder trials are another group that we often do not consider when thinking about those who may suffer because of murder. Yet, as discussed in this chapter, research indicates that jurors may suffer tremendously from their experiences serving as jurors in particularly horrific murder cases. Finally, the chapter concluded by returning to the fascination with murder. Murderabilia and the issues that surround it were discussed including what are referred to as Son of Sam laws.

CHAPTER QUESTIONS

1. What do the terms *homicide survivor* and *co-victim* mean?
2. How do homicide survivors compare with individuals whose loved ones die of accidental deaths?
3. What are some of the unique challenges faced by homicide survivors?
4. What extrapersonal losses are experienced by homicide survivors?
5. What problems do the media present for homicide survivors?
6. Discuss the experience of survivors with the criminal justice system.
7. What changes might you propose in the criminal justice system to make the experience better for survivors?
8. What is the victims' rights movement?
9. What are some changes brought about by the victims' rights movement?
10. What are victim assistance programs, and how did they get their start?
11. What is Laura's law? Do you have a similar law in your state?
12. Who is entitled to receive victim compensation? What does it pay for and how is it funded?
13. What are victim impact statements? What purposes do you think they serve?
14. Explain restorative justice and how it might help a homicide survivor.
15. What are the estimated costs of homicide?
16. What are some of the issues faced by family members of murderers?

17. What are some of effects of serving as a juror in a murder trial? What do you think may make the experience less traumatic?
18. What other individuals because of their jobs may be greatly impacted by murder?
19. What is murderabilia? Do you think there should be any laws about murder-abilia sales?
20. What are Son of Sam laws?

REFERENCES

AAMEN!, No Date. "Action Americans: Murder Must End Now! (AAMMEN!)." Web page available at http://www.rorpf.org/Advocacy.htm.

ABT. 2006. *Crime Scene Clean Up*. Accessed online at http://www.traumacleaner.com/crime scene cleanup.htm

Alexander, Ellen K., and Janice Harris Lord. 1994. *Impact Statements: A Victim's Right to Speak*. Washington, DC: U.S. Department of Justice.

Amick-McMullan, Angelynne, Dean G. Kilpatrick, and Heidi S. Resnick. 1991. "Homicide as a Risk Factor for PTSD Among Surviving Family Members." *Behavior Modification*, 15(4): 545–559.

Armour, Marilyn Peterson. 2002. "Experiences of Covictims of Homicide: Implications for Research and Practice." *Trauma, Violence, & Abuse*, 3(2): 109–124.

Armour, Marilyn. 2003. "Meaning Making in the Aftermath of Homicide." *Death Studies*, 27: 519–540.

Asaro, M. Regina. 2001. "Working with Adult Homicide Survivors: Part 1. Impact and Sequelae of Murder." *Perspectives in Psychiatric Care*, 37(3): 95–101.

Baldas, Tresa. 2006. "On the Firing Line," *National Law Journal*. Accessed online at http://www.law.com/jsp/article.jsp?id=1153299922890

Beaton, Randal D. 1999. "PTSD Among Bereaved Parents Following the Violent Deaths of Their 12- to 28-Year-Old Children: A Longitudinal Prospective Analysis." *Journal of Traumatic Stress*, 12(2): 273–291.

Berfield, Susan. 2006. "Cleared of Murder But Out of a Job." *Business Week*, 4002: 102–104.

BusinessWeek Online. 2000, November 20. *Business Week*. Retrieved December 8, 2006, from http://www.businessweek.com/2000/00_47/b3708056.htm

Carmen, Barbara. 2004, October 4. "Knowing Girl's Killer Is Free Pushes Activists to Fight Harder." *The Columbus Dispatch*. Retrieved from http://www.findmissingkids.com/forum/viewtopic.php?p=254&sid=6cbbf4bc96b3752ff0e79a102a25173b.

CBS News. 2006, December 12. "Jury Selected to Hear Pickton Murder Trial." *CBS Canada British Columbia* Website. Accessed online at http://www.cbc.ca/canada/british-columbia/story/2006/12/12/pickton-jury.html?ref=rss

Claxton, Melvin. 2006a, June 27. "Tougher the Case, the Higher the Cost." Retrieved November 18, 2006, from Tennessean.com

Claxton, Melvin. 2006b, June 27. "Social Programs Pay Tab When Murder Hits Families." Retrieved December 9, 2006, from Tennessean.com

Cohen, Jeff, and Norman Solomon. 1995. "On Local TV News, If it Bleeds It (Still) Leads." *Media Beat*. Accessed online at http://www.fair.org/media-beat/951213.html

Evers, Tag. 1998, Fall. "Restorative Justice." *Yes! A Journal of Positive Futures*. Accessed online at http://www.yesmagazine.org/article.asp?ID=811

FBI. 2006. "Victim's Assistance." Accessed online at http://www.fbi.gov/hq/cid/victimassist/crimevictims.htm

Goodrum, Susan D., and Mark C. Stafford. 2001, August 6. *Homicide, Bereavement, and the Criminal Justice System, Final Report.* Accessed at http://www.ncjrs.gov/pdffiles1/nij/grants/189566.pdf

Hafemeister, Thomas L. 1993. "Juror Stress." *Violence and Victims,* 8: 177–186.

Hines, Thomas Ann. No date. "Working in the Verb Garden." Retrieved January 2, 2007, from http://www.n-spire.com/archives/100501.html

Horne, Christopher. 2003. "Families of Homicide Victims: Service Utilization Patterns of Extra- and Intrafamilial Homicide Survivors." *Journal of Family Violence,* 18(2): 75–82.

Khamisa, Azim. 2006. "A Father's Journey from Murder to Forgiveness." *Reclaiming Children and Youth,* 15(1): 15–18.

LeGardeur, Lili. 2003, May 30. "Restorative Justice: Mending the Fabric of Society." *National Catholic Reporter.* Accessed at http://ncronline.org/NCR_Online/archives2/2003b/053003/053003j.php

Mayhew, Pat. 2003. *Counting the Costs of Crime in Australia.* Canberra: Australian Institute of Criminology.

Mezey, Gill, Chris Evans, and Kathy Hobdell. 2002. "Families of Homicide Victims: Psychiatric Responses and Help-Seeking." *Psychology and Psychotherapy: Therapy, Research and Practice,* 75: 65–75.

Miller, Laurence. 2006. "Police Families: Stresses, Syndromes, and Solutions." *The American Journal of Family Therapy,* 35(1): 21–40.

Murphy, Shirley A., Tom Braun, Linda Tillery, Kevin C. Cain, L. Clark Johnson, and *Prudential Insurance Company* v. *Athmer and Athmer* v. *Hill & Pierce.* 1999. U.S. Court of Appeals for the Seventh Circuit. 178 F.3d 473.

National Center for Victims of Crime. 1999. *Victim Impact Statements.* Accessed online at http://www.ncvc.org/ncvc/main.aspx?dbName=DocumentViewer&DocumentID=32515

NACVCB. 2006. "Crime Victim Compensation: Resources for Recovery." *National Association of Crime Victim Compensation Boards Website.* Accessed at http://www.nacvcb.org/

National Center for Victims of Crime. 1999. "Victim Impact Statements," Retrieved December 7, 2006 from http://www.ncvc.org/ncvc/main.aspx?dbName=DocumentViewer&DocumentID=32515

National Center for Victims of Crime. 2004. "Notoriety for Profit/Son of Sam Legislation." National Center for Victims of Crime Website. Retrieved December 7, 2006, from www.ncvc.org.

POMC. 2006. "Murder Wall . . . Honoring Their Memory." *National Organization of Parents of Murdered Children Website.* Accessed at http://www.pomc.org/murderwall.cfm

RAND Corporation. 2004. "Rand Study Shows Compensation for 9/11 Terror Attacks Tops $38 Billion; Businesses Receive Biggest Share." News release available at http://www.rand.org/news/press.04/11.08b.html

Rememberinglaura.com. No date. "About Laura's Law." Accessed online at www.rememberinglarua.com/LarasLawabout.htm.

Schmid, David. 2004. "Murderabilia: Consuming Fame." *M/C Journal,* 7(5). Retrieved December 8, 2006, from http://journal.media-culture.org.au/0411/10-schmid.php

Sewell, James D. 1993. "Traumatic Stress of Multiple Murder Investigations." *Journal of Traumatic Stress,* 6, 103–118.

Stoney, Mellina. 2004. "Murder, She Bought: Crime Item Collectors Face Heat." *The Lowell on the Web.* Retrieved December 7, 2006, from http://www.thelowell.org/content/view/399/27/

Umbreit, Mark S., and Betty Vos. 2000. "Homicide Survivors Meet the Offender Prior to Execution." *Homicide Studies,* 4(1): 63–87.

Walker, Steven D. 2000. "History of the Victim's Movement in the United States." *Perspectives: Electronic Journal of the American Association of Behavioral and Social Sciences,* 3(Fall). Accessed at http://aabss.org/journa12000/

Wiechman, Lori. 1997. "Group Helps Families Get Beyond the Bars." *The Augusta Chronicle,* January 4, 1997. Accessed at http://chronicle.augusta.com/stories/010597/beyondbars.html

Young, Marlene A. 1997a. "The Victims Movement: A Confluence of Forces." Paper presented at the National Symposium on Victims of Federal Crime, February 10, 1997. Available from the National Organization for Victim Assistance.

Young, Marlene A. 1997b. "Victim Rights and Services: A Modern Saga." In Arthur J. Lurigio, Robert C. Davis, and Wesley G. Skogan, eds., *Victims of Crime.* Thousand Oaks, CA: Sage.

Chapter 17

STOPPING MURDER

The future can be seen. Murder can be prevented. The guilty punished before the crime is committed. The system is perfect. It's never wrong. Until it comes after you. —Minority Report film advertisement

In the film *Minority Report*, Tom Cruise plays a law enforcement officer in Washington's "precrime division." It is the future, and law enforcement officials have found a way to learn about murders before they happen. Even before the would-be offender considers committing a murder, the murder is predicted and the special precrime police force snaps into action and goes after the would-be murderer. Once the would-be offender is arrested, he or she is locked up in the "Hall of Containment." Another life is saved; a murder is prevented. Of course, this is fiction, and law enforcement cannot accurately predict who will commit murder and prevent it. Moreover, in the United States and other democratic societies, we are not supposed to be punished for crimes we have yet to commit.

If the methods used in the *Minority Report* were possible and determined to be ethically sound, the murder rate would surely drop. But the reality is that preventing or at least reducing murder is a laudable goal but an extremely difficult issue. If we are logical, the approach we would take to stopping homicide would be predicated on what we believe are the causes of homicide. However, this approach is complicated by the fact that different types of homicide might have different etiology, and moreover, any particular type of homicide is likely to have several causes. This chapter presents several approaches and programs that have been introduced to prevent, stop, or reduce murder in the United States and other countries. Crime control efforts aimed at reducing crime generally are omitted in favor of approaches and programs directed at curbing murder or specific types of murder. Approaches focusing on specific at-risk populations, including juvenile gangs and individuals in battering relationships, are included along with the more controversial approaches of gun control and capital punishment. When available, appropriate theoretical explanations for and empirical research on the different approaches are included throughout the chapter.

DETERRENCE

As mentioned in Chapter 6, deterrence theory is based on the premise that punishment will dissuade would-be offenders from committing crimes. In other words, you are unlikely to kill someone (or commit some lesser offense) if you believe you are certain to be punished and the punishment is something so severe that you wish to avoid it. Although there are also other reasons, such as retribution, for instituting harsh penalties for murder, one way we attempt to prevent (or deter) murder throughout the world is by instituting strong penalties for those who commit homicide. Whether such penalties work is a point of debate and, to some extent, an issue of study. Moreover, criminologists may argue that various penalties for murder may fill the role of general or specific deterrence. A penalty is said to be a general deterrent to murder if it successfully prevents the masses from committing murder. A specific deterrent is aimed at a particular offender. Following this logic, if an offender is incarcerated, he or she should be less likely to consider further criminal offending because the penalty was so unpleasant as to be a deterrent. In later sections of this chapter, "striking out" and capital punishment are discussed with regard to their possible deterrent and incapacitating effects.

INCAPACITATION

Incapacitation, like deterrence, is also predicated on the idea that penalties or punishments for crimes are necessary. However, selective incapacitation is intended for those who are believed to be very likely to offend because they have offended in the past. If they are incapacitated, they are literally prevented from continuing to kill. As such, another reason for the incarceration of convicted murderers is to prevent them from killing again. Of course, incarceration does not completely incapacitate offenders; inmates do occasionally commit murder while they are incarcerated. For this reason, particularly heinous murderers may be locked away in solitary confinement where they have very little opportunity to interact with, let alone murder, another individual. For the same reasons, some murderers are sentenced to death. If a convicted murderer is put to death, it is certain that he or she can not commit further murders.

In the recent history of the United States, the idea of incarcerating offenders has become evermore popular. Although there is much argument over whether incarceration makes sense for various crimes, a number of criminologists have attempted to determine whether incarceration reduces homicide. Marvell and Moody (1997), for example, found that a 10% increase in the prison population was associated with nearly 13% fewer homicides from 1930 to 1994. Another study that looked at the issue of incarceration and homicide by studying prison populations and homicide from 1975 to 1999 also concluded that increases in prison population were significantly related to decreases in homicide (Kovandzic, Sloan, Vieraitis, et al., 2004a). In contrast, however, this second study also found no significant relationship between the numbers of inmates released and the number of homicides (Kovandzic et al., 2004a). We cannot be certain what these results mean for incarceration and murder. It could be that incapacitation works and prisons rehabilitate or it could be that those being released are nonviolent offenders. It may be important to consider whether those who are locked up and those who are released are likely to be violent offenders.

Incarcerating individuals solely to prevent them from committing crimes, however, is troubling in a democratic society. In the United States and other democratic societies, citizens are not supposed to be incarcerated without due process of law. Ideally, persons are not incarcerated for crimes they have not committed. Even if we thought it was reasonable to lock up a person we believed would commit crimes, there is no sound way to predict who will commit murder. Criminologists have completed thousands of studies of criminals, and we still cannot predict with great accuracy who is likely and who is not likely to commit crime, let alone a particular crime. Homicide, in particular, is difficult to predict.

Criminologist Richard Berk has been working with the Philadelphia probation department to develop a computer model that could be used to predict who is likely to commit murder. Using 30 to 40 variables shown to be related to homicide offending, Berk uses a computer program to generate a score for probationers. Factors such as youth, being male, having committed serious crime at an early age, and committing previous acts of violence would gain individuals a higher score than not having these factors. If Berk's program or others like it would work, probation boards may be less likely to release those with high scores. At worst, probation officers, then, could watch the probationers with higher scores more closely than those with lower scores (Matza, 2006).

The problems of false negatives and false positives, however, are always an issue with predicting who will commit homicide or any other crime. If we predict that someone is not likely to commit a crime but they do, we would have a false negative. The Philadelphia Probation office, for example, may use Berk's model to predict that Robert Smith is unlikely to commit a murder and thus not watch him closely. When Smith kills his neighbor, the probation office is likely to be upset that someone died when he or she may have prevented the death. Less important but nevertheless a problem, they probably will not enjoy the media attention focused on their organization when Smith kills. If, however, we predict that someone is likely to commit murder and they do not and would not even if we did not watch them closely, we have a false positive. Although false positives may be less troubling because there is no murder, we have focused our resources and energy on preventing something that never would have happened. False positives can be costly both monetarily and in terms of democratic freedom. For now, criminologists are not perfect, or even close to perfect, in predicting who will murder. Thus the issue of using models to predict crime for determining who should be incapacitated will continue to be controversial but is likely to be an issue that criminologists continue to study (Matza, 2006).

BOX 17.1

Why Did Homicide Decrease?

U.S. homicide rates decreased noticeably in the 1990s. It would seem that knowing what caused this decrease could help us learn how to deliberately reduce homicides. The difficulty, however, lies in the fact that we are not certain why this decrease occurred. Criminologists have considered many possibilities, and they have found that a handful of factors may be related to the homicide decrease. Importantly, economists point out that the economy may be linked to homicide. During the 1990s, the unemployment rate dropped and so did homicide. With a better economy, individuals may be less stressed, and they may be less likely to turn to crimes to provide for themselves and their families. The 1990s also saw changes in the crack cocaine market and gang wars. Reductions in gang turf wars are very likely to have contributed to reductions in homicide. Others have argued that tough criminal justice policies and gun laws may explain the homicide decrease. Policies such as mandatory sentencing, truth in sentencing, penalty enhancements for gun crimes, and "three strikes and you're out" policies certainly increased the numbers of individuals incarcerated in the United States in the 1990s. Some research suggests that the increased prison population explains the decrease in homicide (*The Lancet*, 2000).

TARGETING YOUTH GANGS REDUCTION THROUGH LEVER-PULLING STRATEGIES

As you can see in Figure 17.1, U.S. murder rates began increasing in the 1960s, and by the early 1990s it did not seem they were going to level off anytime soon. It was at this time that researchers and criminal justice officials in Boston began working together in an attempt to reduce the number of murders in their cities. Community leaders, state, local, and federal law enforcement officials and parole and probation workers began meeting together to look at the possible causes of violence in Boston with a mind to reducing it. When the officials studied homicide cases, they found that a small portion of the population was responsible for much of the homicide in their city. Analyses of homicide and gun violence in Boston, for example, indicated that as few as 1% of the city's youth population was responsible for at least 60% of the homicides involving young people as victims or offenders. This 1% tended to be gang members with previous arrests if not convictions (McGarrell, Chermak, Wilson, et al., 2006).

Boston officials responded to what they had learned by implementing Project Ceasefire, a so-called lever-pulling strategy that aims to stop violent crime by being extremely tough on crime. The plan is to pull every lever, or, in other words, use every strategy that can be employed to prosecute and punish anyone who uses a gun in the commission of a crime. Federal and local law enforcement officials work together using local and federal laws to prosecute those who illegally use guns to ensure they

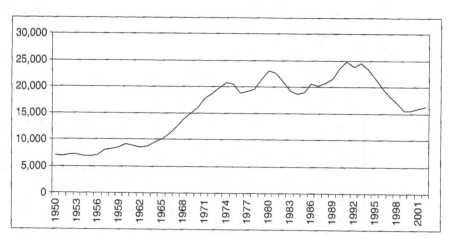

FIGURE 17.1

Homicides Known to the Police, 1995–2002

Source: Fox and Zawitz, 2004.

will spend a long time in prison. Although this plan may work to incapacitate offenders, the focus of Project Ceasefire and the programs that followed it was deterrence (Dalton, 2003; McGarrell et al., 2006).

Ceasefire brought gang members, parolees, and probationers together in town meetings where the new approach to gun crimes was emphasized (Dalton, 2003; McGarrell et al., 2006). Community leaders explained to offenders at these town meetings that zero tolerance was being put in place to make their community safer for everyone. Convicted offenders and gang members believed to be at risk for homicide victimization or offending were encouraged to take advantage of social programs to improve their lives. They were told that if they did not stop the violence and they continued to involve themselves in criminal acts, they would be caught and they would be punished harshly (Dalton, 2003; McGarrell et al., 2006).

Importantly, criminal justice agencies reinforced their message by doing what they said they would do: They prosecuted offenders to the fullest. Law enforcement cracked down on gangs who continued to operate as usual, and these crackdowns were well publicized. Many adult gang members were prosecuted in federal courts where they were sentenced to hard time in federal prison (McGarrell et al., 2006). To the relief of many who had to live with the daily violence of neighborhood gangs, Project Ceasefire's results were impressive. Violent gang offending and youth violence decreased dramatically after the implementation of the program.

Moreover, research indicates that the Ceasefire approach to reducing youth gun violence also worked in Minneapolis and Indianapolis. McGarrell et al. (2006) compared youth homicide before and after the implementation of the Indianapolis Violence Reduction Partnership (IVRP) in the fall of 1998. In the year prior to the IVRP lever-pulling program, there were 149 homicides in Indianapolis as compared to 101 in the year after the implementation of the program. As you can see in Figure 17.1, U.S. homicide rates began decreasing in the mid-1990s, leading one to question whether the reduction in homicides seen in Indianapolis is a result of the lever-pulling strategy employed by IVRP or something else. To answer this question, McGarrell and his colleagues compared the reduction in homicide in Indianapolis to six other mid-western cities. The comparisons indicated that the 34% decrease in homicide in Indianapolis was unique. The six comparison cities did not experience comparable drops during the same time periods. They concluded that IVRP very likely contributed to the reduction in homicides in Indiana.

STRIKING OUT

U.S. crime rates soared in the 1980s, and politicians and the public reacted with calls for tough criminal justice policies. One popular policy known as "three strikes and you're out" was instituted to incapacitate and deter offenders from making a career out of crime. By 1996, the federal government and 25 states enacted strike-out policies that mandated sentence enhancements for individuals who were convicted of a serious crime for the second or third time. With the passage of these policies, government officials believed individuals would either refrain from further offenses to avoid long-term incarceration or those who "struck out" would be incarcerated and thus incapacitated from committing further crimes (Kovandzic, Sloan, & Vieraitis, 2004b).

Studies that examine the impact of three-strike laws, however, have failed to demonstrate their success. More specifically with regard to homicide, three studies found that three-strike laws did not work. Worse yet, these studies found that cities and states with strike laws saw increases in homicide as high as 29% greater than those without strike laws (Kovandzic et al., 2002, 2004b; Marvell & Moody, 2001). Kovandzic (2004b) theorized that the positive association between strike laws and homicide rates could be explained in a number of ways. First, research on criminals suggests they do not believe they will be caught and thus deterrence does not work. Second, and particularly relevant to homicide offenders, is that perpetrators may be under the influence of drugs or alcohol and thus not thinking about the consequences of their actions when they kill. Third, the strikes law may have made it more likely for offenders to kill witnesses so the perpetrators would not be identified and arrested (Kovandzic et al., 2004b).

CAPITAL PUNISHMENT AS A DETERRENT

Some death penalty advocates argue that the death penalty deters would-be murderers from committing homicide. There is a rich tradition of criminological research about the possible deterrent effects of capital punishment dating back to the 1700s and Cesare Beccaria's *Essay on Crime and Punishment* (Bailey & Peterson, 1989). Most research, however, supports the contention that capital punishment fails to deter murder. The research shows that death penalty states do not have lower homicide rates than non–death penalty states as would be expected if capital punishment is a deterrent.

Some scholars, however, have questioned whether execution publicity is important in determining whether the death penalty is a deterrent. In other words, if the death penalty is on the books but no evidence indicates it is actually used, how could it deter? To answer this question, some scholars compared the numbers of murders before and after executions that were publicized. Initial research on the issue showed that when executions were known to the public, they had a deterrent effect on the numbers of murders (Erhlich, 1975; Stack, 1987). More recent research using more rigorous methods, however, consistently finds that capital punishment and its attendant publicity fails to deter murder (Bailey & Peterson, 1997).

If you think about what you have been reading about murder throughout this text, it should not be surprising that capital punishment is not a deterrent. Often murder is a crime of passion—the offender does not stop to consider the punishment. People who deal with crime regularly understand this reality. Surveys of criminologists and criminal justice officials find that over two thirds of both academic criminologists and criminal justice officials agree that the death penalty is not a significant deterrent to murder (Radelet & Borg, 2000).

GUN CONTROL IN THE UNITED STATES

Gun control is one of the most controversial solutions for reducing homicide. There are strong voices and opinions on both sides of the gun control issue. Moreover, both proponents and opponents of gun control use scholarly research to support their contentions. There is no doubt that guns can be used to kill humans. Nevertheless, the debate continues with proponents of gun control arguing that gun availability increases serious violence and murder. Opponents of gun control argue that, at the very least, guns do not cause violence and, moreover, gun ownership by law-abiding citizens may even deter violence (Duggan, 2001; Kleck, 1997; Stolzenberg & D'Alessio, 2000).

Unfortunately, even though many empirical studies have considered the possible deterrent or exacerbating effects of gun availability on violent crime including homicide, there is no consensus within the field of criminology. Scholars have attempted to determine if levels of gun ownership in a nation, state, or county are significantly related to the levels of violence in these geographical areas with both cross-sectional and longitudinal studies. The findings have been mixed, with some studies finding a positive relationship between gun ownership and violence and others finding a negative relationship. There have even been studies that have found mixed results (Duggan, 2001). As social science methods have evolved, so too have studies about guns and violence and criticisms about the previous studies. Still, the results remain contradictory.

Because of the contradictory findings, strong ideas about guns and violence, and the ever-present high levels of violence in the United States (even at our lowest levels), scholars continue to examine the possible link between guns and violence. Duggan (2001), for example, made the argument that many of the studies about guns and crime are flawed because there is not a reliable measure of gun ownership in a particular geographical area. Instead of data on gun ownership, then, Duggan used *Guns & Ammo* sales data as a proxy for gun ownership. *Guns & Ammo* is one of the nation's foremost gun magazines, and according to Duggan, the magazine's sales figures are a way to measure the level of gun ownership and changes in gun ownership within an area over time. After he showed that other data such as membership in the National

Rifle Association (NRA) and death rates from gun accidents in an area correspond to sales of *Guns & Ammo*, Duggan examined the relationship between *Guns & Ammo* sales and homicide.

Duggan found that there was a significant positive relationship between gun ownership and homicide. Moreover, he found the relationship was "lagged," such that increases in gun ownership measured as *Guns & Ammo* sales were followed by increases in homicide committed with guns. In other words, homicide rates did not increase gun ownership, but instead increasing gun ownership preceded increases in gun homicide rates. Importantly, Duggan reported that non–gun homicide was not related to gun ownership as he measured it. As with any other study about guns and violence, Duggan's study is likely to have critics. Nonetheless, it serves as an example of the interesting ways scholars are examining the link between gun ownership and homicide.

Stolzenberg and D'Alessio (2000) also attempted to overcome a weakness in the existing research about the connection between gun ownership and violent crime with their South Carolina study. They argued that a weakness in nearly all studies about gun ownership and crime is the use of Uniform Crime Report (UCR) data and data on legal gun ownership. As you learned in Chapter 3, the National Incident-Based Reporting System (NIBRS) was developed to overcome weaknesses in the UCR. Using NIBRS data, Stolzenberg and D'Alessio were able to include data on the numbers of guns reported stolen and the number of crimes in which an offender used a gun. Their results indicated that legal gun ownership did not affect violent crimes either positively or negatively. Gun ownership did not appear to have a deterrent effect on crime as gun proponents argue, nor did they find evidence that overall gun ownership increased violent crime. However, Stolzenberg and D'Alessio found that illegal gun availability was related to violent crime. In particular, youth gun violence was linked to reports of stolen guns. Based on their findings, the researchers suggest homicide could be prevented by preventing gun theft. Gun owners should be encouraged to store their guns securely, and law enforcement should institute policies aimed at reducing firearm theft.

GUN CONTROL AND GUN BUYBACKS IN AUSTRALIA

As discussed in Chapter 11, on April 28, 1996, Australians witnessed one of the worst mass murders in their history. Twenty-nine-year-old Martin Bryant killed 35 people and wounded 18 others with an AR15 rifle. In the aftermath of this horrific massacre, Australia instituted some of the strictest gun control laws in the world. By the end of 1997, the Australian National Firearms Agreement (NFA) had been enacted throughout the country. The NFA prohibited semiautomatic rifles and shot guns, made legal ownership difficult to obtain, and required all gun owners to be registered and licensed. Finally, the Australian government instituted a gun buyback program to remove as many guns as possible from the Australian public. Although the Australian government successfully purchased over 600,000 firearms through the buyback program, controversial research by Jeanine Baker and Samara McPhedran (2006) shows that the NFA may have reduced gun suicides, but it had no effect on gun homicides and accidental shooting deaths. Examining the period from 1979 to 2004, Baker and

---

BOX 17.2

Are Gun Owners More Likely to Be Murdered?

The debate over gun ownership is one of the most contentious debates within criminology and in society at large. Kellermann et al.'s (1993) article on the risk of homicide to gun owners generated much discussion and further studies about the possible relationship between gun ownership and risk of homicide. They found that individuals who live in households in which at least one person owns a gun are 2.7 times more likely to become homicide victims than individuals who lived in non-gun-owning households. Supporters of gun control touted this finding as proof that gun ownership is dangerous. Gary Kleck (2001) and other critics, however, noted that the relationship between gun ownership and homicide victimization could be spurious. In other words, it may be that the same factors that increase the likelihood for homicide victimization also motivate people to own guns. Those who sell drugs or who join gangs may be more likely to own guns and more likely to be killed whether they own guns or not. Kleck also reported that a reanalysis of Kellermann et al.'s 1993 data found that approximately 1 in 21 homicide victims were likely to have been killed by the gun in their own home. Unfortunately, the data did not indicate whether the victim was actually shot by his or her own gun. Kleck bases his conclusions on the fact that only 88 out of 1,860 victims were killed with a gun in or near their own home or by someone who resided in the victim's household, making the use of a household gun unlikely.

McPhedran found that homicides decreased after the implementation of the NFA. However, the decline in homicides was part of a decline that had begun before the NFA was instituted, suggesting that factors other than the NFA accounted for the decline (Baker & McPhedran, 2006).

CONCEALED WEAPON LAWS

In stark contrast to the argument that gun ownership increases murder is the argument that concealed handgun laws may reduce violent crimes including murder. The idea is that the potential cost to those who perpetrate crimes will increase when more people are armed. In other words, those motivated to commit crimes may be less likely to take a chance in attacking another person because that person may be armed. Many states have right-to-carry concealed firearm laws that allow adults to obtain permits to carry concealed handguns. Not surprisingly, specifications in these laws bar felons from obtaining such permits, but for the most part, any other citizen is granted a permit (Kovandzic, Marvell, & Vieraitis, 2005).

It is very difficult to determine whether concealed weapon laws work to reduce violent crime as some predict. The study results are mixed, with some showing that violent crimes are lower in jurisdictions after such laws are enacted, others showing increases, and even a few showing no effects at all (Kovandzic et al., 2005). The results may differ depending on what other factors are considered in the studies or because the impact of such laws varies by jurisdiction. An examination of the effects of concealed weapons laws in 24 states found that the laws do not reduce homicide or other violent crimes. However, the authors of the study were cautious to point out that the focus of the study was the enactment of gun permit laws themselves. The research did not measure whether people actually armed themselves after concealed weapons laws were passed, nor was it clear whether would-be murderers knew about such laws (Kovandzic et al., 2005).

IT'S THE ECONOMY, STUPID

As Figure 17.1 shows and as discussed elsewhere, U.S. homicide rates fell dramatically in the 1990s. Explanations for this decrease may help point us toward structural (or sociological) factors that will help prevent or stop homicide. At the same time homicide and other crime was decreasing, the U.S. economy grew as measured by the GDP (gross domestic product) per capita, and importantly, the unemployment rate decreased from an annual average of 6.8% in 1991 to 4.8% in 2001. Several economic studies show a link between increases in unemployment and increases in crime (Levitt, 2004). Theoretically, if individuals commit crime because of economic need, we would expect decreases in crime when the economy is good. But it may be less likely that this would be the case for homicide, especially homicide not linked to economic crime, unless we consider how economic crimes and homicide may be linked. For example, in the 1980s, much youth violence was linked to gangs and territorial battles during the crack epidemic. It may be that increases in legitimate avenues for making a living decrease the need to sell drugs, and thus the battle for territory is lessened. However, if homicide is not economically driven, it is still possible to imagine that low unemployment could be linked to low homicide rates. Altercations within families and outside of families may be fueled by stress that is connected to unemployment.

If unemployment is related to homicide, policies for decreasing homicide should consider increasing the employability of potential offenders. Education and vocational training as well as policies that improve the economy may help decrease homicide. Levitt (2004), however, argues that the economy has a minor effect on crime rates, and this effect is, for the most part, limited to property crimes. He contends that the economy may impact homicide rates only because governments increase their spending on crime control measures during economic booms, which in turn may decrease homicide through their incapacitation effects (Levitt, 2004).

DEATH REVIEWS

A more recent innovation for decreasing homicide is the use of fatality reviews. Similar to a review of an airplane crash, fatality reviews attempt to figure out what may have led to a death and what may have prevented it. Law enforcement officers and community service providers work together on homicide fatality reviews. The thought is that these reviews may result in the discovery of patterns contributing to murders that may be staved off with the introduction of new policies and practices (Websdale, 2003). Fatality reviews are most commonly employed to help social services and criminal justice agencies learn more about what they may do to prevent intimate partner homicide and child abuse homicide. Although those involved in these reviews believe they are helping prevent violence by encouraging interagency cooperation and increasing knowledge about factors related to homicide, there are no published studies examining the effectiveness of such reviews for the prevention of homicide.

IMPROVING MEDICAL RESPONSES AND TECHNOLOGICAL ADVANCES

Although it would be best to prevent violence overall, research suggests that homicide may be reduced by improving emergency medical response. As early as the 1950s, Wolfgang (1958) suggested that medical and technological advances might possibly explain decreases in U.S. homicide rates from the 1930s to the 1950s. Similar explanations may work today to explain decreases in homicide in the 1990s. The ever-increasing availability of cell phones and improved cell phone service, as well as improvements in medical care, could explain decreasing murder rates throughout the United States. With these ideas in mind, another approach to preventing homicide may be to increase emergency response times, improve trauma centers, and perhaps increase the number of medical facilities capable of handling trauma cases.

A medical approach of this type will not reduce violence, but it may prevent homicides by preventing aggravated assaults from turning into murders. A study published in 1988, for example, found that emergency transportation was linked to

---

BOX 17.3

Access to Medical Transportation, Race, and Homicide Convictions

In a study of Alabama female homicide offender records from the 1930s to 1985 and 1988 homicide victims in the United States, Hanke and Gundlach (1995) found a connection between a victim's time of death and the race of the offender. Access to medical care and emergency transportation differed by race such that African American assault victims were more likely to die than white victims. In addition to this troubling fact is the outcome this has for offenders. In the United States when we kill, we are far more likely to kill those who are the same race as we are. Thus, as Hanke and Gundlach (1995) report, racial inequalities in the delivery of medical care may exacerbate the racial inequalities that are already occurring in the administration of justice in the United States.

lower homicide in Florida during the 1980s (Doerner, 1988). Other studies over time have also supported the finding that emergency medical advances reduce homicide (Harris, Thomas, Fisher, et al., 2002).

What about other technological advances. such as the great increase in surveillance cameras? Following the ideas of routine activities theory, it is possible that surveillance cameras could prevent murder. As you may recall, routine activities theory asserts that three factors are required for criminal activity: motivated offenders; suitable targets; and the absence of effective guardians (Cohen & Felson, 1979). If would-be offenders are aware that cameras are present, they may refrain from attacking another, or, at the very least, they may be more careful about where they attempt to victimize another. As discussed in the final chapter, surveillance cameras are helping law enforcement officers to solve crimes, and their use is likely to increase.

EARLY INTERVENTION

A number of violence prevention programs focus on teaching elementary or middle school children how to solve conflicts without resorting to violence. Although homicide prevention is not an explicit goal of most of these programs, as discussed throughout this text, murder is often the result of a disagreement or a confrontation. Successful violence prevention programs, then, should help reduce homicide. A major difficulty, however, is determining whether the programs reduce violence or homicide over the long term. Most studies of such programs are limited to relatively short evaluation periods (Flannery et al., 2003).

The PeaceBuilders Universal School-Based Violence Prevention Program is a fairly typical violence prevention program for children. Noting that young people are at greater risk for both violence victimization and perpetration when they do not have the skills to resolve conflicts, PeaceBuilders teaches students and teachers prosocial behaviors and social skills that help students deal with conflict. An experiment that compared teacher's reports and student's self-reports of children's prosocial and aggressive behavior in schools with and without PeaceBuilders after one year and two years of the program, found that the children in school's with PeaceBuilders were less aggressive and more prosocial than children not involved in the program. PeaceBuilders appeared to have the greatest affect on first and second graders, although third, fourth, and fifth graders also benefited from the program. Time will tell whether PeaceBuilders and similar programs have a long-lasting effect in reducing violence (Flannery et al., 2003).

There are hundreds of programs aimed at reducing violence, and some see their mission as homicide reduction specifically. Azim Khamisa, a father whose 20-year-old son was gunned down by a 14-year-old gang member, started a foundation named in his son's memory. The mission of the Tariq Khamisa Foundation (TKF) is to stop kids from killing other kids. Through prevention programs in elementary and middle schools, the foundation works to get children to realize that violence is real and it hurts everyone. Moreover, the program emphasizes forgiveness rather than revenge in an attempt to stave off confrontational homicides. To make the message stick with students, the TKF focuses not only on Tariq's murder but the consequences it had for Tariq and his family as well as for Tariq's 14-year old murderer, Tony Hicks. The importance of forgiveness is emphasized by Ples Felix's role in the organization. Felix is Hicks's guardian and grandfather. Tariq's dad and Hicks's guardian talk about the impact of Tariq's murder but also the importance of forgiveness and working together (Khamisa, 2006).

DOMESTIC VIOLENCE INTERVENTION

Most domestic violence does not lead to murder, but the majority of intimate partner murders are the culmination of violent relationships. Hence criminologists have argued that one way to reduce murder is to reduce domestic violence. Vernon Geberth, the former commander of the Bronx homicide division, argues that early intervention by social services and those in the criminal justice system is necessary to prevent future violence. But he cautions that it takes more than law enforcement to end domestic violence; a community must not tolerate any domestic violence if it is to be prevented. Schools must play their part in teaching kids that domestic violence is intolerable, members of the clergy must make it clear that domestic violence is wrong, and anyone who interacts with a victim of domestic violence must be aware of the danger so domestic violence will be taken seriously (Geberth, 1998).

As discussed in Chapter 8, other researchers, although not disagreeing with Geberth, have identified risk factors for homicide in domestic violent situations. These risk factors, including firearm availability, marital separation, depression, abuser's drug or alcohol abuse, may be used by social service personnel, law enforcement, and criminal justice workers to help identify specific cases that warrant intervention (Block & Christakos, 1995; Campbell et al., 2003; Davies, Block, & Campbell, 2007; Lindgren, 2006). It is really difficult to determine how well intervention works overall because we cannot know for sure if an intervention has prevented a homicide. But there are indications that intervention works. First, research presented in Chapter 8 indicated that domestic homicides are lower when there are more options for battered women (Dugan, Nagin, & Rosenfeld, 2003). Second, individual testimonials by women who have survived battering relationships with the help of shelters indicate that they believe intervention saved their lives (Anonymous, 2006).

REDUCING CONFRONTATIONAL HOMICIDE

Studies indicate that in over half of all homicides involving adult males in England and Wales, either the victim or offender had consumed alcohol (Brookman & Maguire, 2003). Many of these homicides could be classified as confrontational homicides. With these statistics in mind, there have been attempts in the UK to reduce violence in establishments where alcohol is served. One approach, often called environmental design, involves the physical designs of pubs and clubs to make them seem more spacious. For example, furniture is arranged so there is less likelihood that individuals will inadvertently bump into each other. Another approach involves training staff so they are more likely to reduce potential violence than escalate it (Brookman & Maguire, 2003). Finally, Brookman and Maguire note that pubs and clubs with high violence rates are threatened with liquor licenses withdrawal to encourage the businesses to discourage violence. Although we have not seen similar approaches discussed in the United States to reduce confrontational homicides, other approaches used to reduce confrontational homicide such as lever-pulling strategies were discussed earlier in this chapter. Additionally, as noted in the final chapter, researchers and criminal justice officials are beginning to talk about the importance of reducing confrontational homicide in the United States because it appears that homicide rates are again increasing in some cities.

Summary

Although there is no clear certain policy we can put in place to stop murder, this chapter highlighted a number of approaches. Beginning with traditional reasons given for punishment, you read about deterrence and incapacitation in this chapter. In the section about incapacitation, the issue of false negatives and false positives was addressed. This chapter also included approaches to homicide reduction believed by some to have worked in the 1990s, including lever-pulling strategies and so-called striking-out legislation. Research about capital punishment and gun control, both controversial approaches to murder prevention, are given considerable attention. We also considered the possibility that the economy and medical care are linked to homicide rates. Finally, early intervention with children, domestic violence intervention, and ways to prevent confrontational homicide through environmental design round out this chapter about stopping homicide.

Chapter Questions

1. What is the difference between general and specific deterrence?
2. What is incapacitation? How could it reduce murder?
3. What is the relationship between the prison population and the number of homicides? What about the number of inmates released and the number of homicides?
4. Explain what is meant by "false negatives" and "false positives."
5. How could early intervention programs such as PeaceBuilders potentially reduce murder?
6. How does the Tariq Khamisa Foundation attempt to prevent violence?
7. What is meant by the phrase "lever-pulling strategies"?
8. The creators of Project Ceasefire focused on deterrence rather than incapacitation. Explain how Project Ceasefire could work as either incapacitation or deterrence.
9. According to the research, has Project Ceasefire been successful? What do you think explains these results?
10. What did the studies about the three-strike laws find? What might explain these results?

11. Is capital punishment a deterrent to murder? How do you know?

12. What do studies about the connection between gun availability and homicide find?

13. How did Duggan measure gun ownership in his study, and what do you think about his measure?

14. How is Stolzenberg and D'Alessio's study about guns and crime different than other studies, and what do they suggest as a policy implication of their study?

15. What are gun buybacks and how are they supposed to work?

16. What did Baker and McPhedran find in their study about the Australian National Firearms Agreement?

17. What are right-to-carry laws and how are they supposed to lower crime?

18. What do the studies suggest about right-to-carry laws?

19. How might the economy be linked to homicide?

20. What does Vernon Geberth suggest will end domestic violence and how is this related to murder?

21. What are fatality reviews and how might they help decrease murder?

22. How might technology be related to decreases in homicide?

23. What does race and access to medical care have to do with homicide victims and offenders?

24. How does routine activities theory explain the role of surveillance cameras in preventing murder?

25. What is being done in the UK to prevent confrontational homicide in clubs and pubs?

REFERENCES

Anonymous. 2006, December 3. "One Woman Shares Story of How the Guardian Shelter Saved Her Life." *Natchez Democrat.* Accessed at http://www.natchezdemocrat.com/articles/2006/12/30/news/news177.txt

Bailey, William C., and Ruth D. Peterson. 1997. "Murder, Capital Punishment, and Deterrence: A Review of the Literature." In H. A. Bedau, ed., *The Death Penalty in America: Current Controversies.* New York: Oxford University Press.

Bailey, William C. and Ruth C. Peterson. 1989. "Murder and Capital Punishment: A Monthly Time-Series Analysis of Execution Publicity." *American Sociological Review,* 54(5): 722–743.

Bailey, William C. and Ruth D. Peterson. 1987. "Police Killings and Capital Punishment: The Post-Furman Period." *Criminology,* 25:1–25.

Baker, Jeanine, and Samara McPhedran. 2006. "Gun Laws and Sudden Death: Did the Australian Firearms Legislation of 1996 Make a Difference?" *British Journal of Criminology,* 47: 455–469.

Block, Carolyn Rebecca, and Antigone Christakos. 1995. "Intimate Partner Homicide in Chicago over 29 Years." *Crime & Delinquency,* 41(4): 496–526.

Brookman, Fiona, and Mike Maguire. 2003. *Reducing Homicide: Summary of a Review of the Possibilities.* RDS Occasional Paper No. 84. London: Home Office.

Campbell, Jacquelyn C., Daniel Webster, Jane Koziol-McLain, Carolyn Block, Doris Campbell, Mary Ann Curry, Faye Gary, Nancy Glass, Judith McFarlane, Carolyn Sachs, Phyllis Sharps, Yvonne Ulrich, PhD, Susan A. Wilt,, Jennifer Manganello, Xiao Xu, Janet Schollenberger, Victoria Frye, and Kathryn Laughon. 2003. "Risk Factors for Femicide in Abusive

Relationships: Results from a Multisite Case Control Study." *American Journal of Public Health*, 93(7): 1089–1097.

Cohen, Larry, and Marcus Felson. 1979. "Social Change and Crime Rates." *American Sociological Review*, 44: 588–608.

Dalton, Erin. 2003. *Lessons in Preventing Homicide.* A Project Safe Neighborhoods Report. East Lansing: Michigan State University, School of Criminal Justice. Assessed online at www.cj .msu.edu/~outreach/psn/erins_report_jan_2004.pdf

Davies, Kim, Carolyn Rebecca Block, and Jacquelyn Campbell. 2007. "Seeking Help from the Police: Battered Women's Decisions and Experiences." *Criminal Justice Studies: Critical Journal of Crime, Law and Society*. Forthcoming.

Doerner, William G. 1988. "The Impact of Medical Resources Upon Criminally Induced Lethality: A Further Examination." *Criminology*, 26: 171–179.

Dugan, Laura, Daniel S. Nagin, and Richard Rosenfeld. 2003. "Exposure Reduction or Retaliation? The Effects of Domestic Violence Resources on Intimate-Partner Homicide." *Law & Society*, 37(1): 169–198.

Duggan, Mark. 2001. "More Guns, More Crime." *The Journal of Political Economy*, 109(5): 1086–1114.

Erhlich, Isaac. 1975. "The Deterrent Effect of Capital Punishment: A Question of Life or Death." *American Economic Review*, 65: 397–417.

Flannery, Daniel J., Albert K. Liau, Kenneth E. Powell, Wendy Vesterdal, Alexander T. Vazsonyi, Shenyang Guo, Henry Atha, and Dennis Embry. 2003. *Developmental Psychology*, 39(2): 292–308.

Fox, James Alan and Marianne W. Zawitz. 2004. *Homicide Trends in the U.S.* Washington D.C.: Bureau of Justice Statistics. http://www.ojp.usdoj.gov/bjs/pub/ascii/htus02.txt

Geberth, Vernon J. 1998. "Domestic Violence Homicides." *Law and Order Magazine*, 46(112): 51–54.

Hanke, Penelope J., and James H. Gundlach. 1995. "Damned on Arrival: A Preliminary Study of the Relationship Between Homicide, Emergency Medical Care, and Race." *Journal of Criminal Justice*, 23(4): 313–323.

Harris, Anthony R., Stephen H. Thomas, Gene A. Fisher, and David J. Hirsch. 2002. "Murder and Medicine: The Lethality of Criminal Assault 1960–1999." *Homicide Studies*, 6(2): 128–166.

Kellerman, Arthur, Frederick P. Rivara, Norman B. Rushforth, Joyce G. Banton, Donald T. Reay, Jerry T. Francisco, Ana B. Locci, Janice Prodzinski, Bela B. Hackman, and Grant Somes. 1993. "Gun Ownership as a Risk Factor for Homicide in the Home." *New England Journal of Medicine*, 329: 1084–1091.

Khamisa, Azim. 2006. "A Father's Journey from Murder to Forgiveness." *Reclaiming Children and Youth*, 15(1): 15–18.

Kleck, Gary. 1997. *Targeting Guns: Firearms and Their Control.* New York: Aldine de Gruyter.

Kleck, Gary. 2001. "Can Owning a Gun Really Triple the Owner's Chances of Being Murdered?" *Homicide Studies*, 5(1): 64–77.

Kovandzic, Tomislav V., John J. Sloan III, and Lynne M. Vieraitis. 2002. "Unintended Consequences of Politically Popular Sentencing Policy: The Homicide Promoting Effects of 'Three Strikes' Laws in U.S. Cities. (1980–1999)." *Criminology and Public Policy*, 1(3): 399–424.

Kovandzic, Tomislav V., Thomas B. Marvell, Lynne M. Vieraitis, and Carlisle E. Moody. 2004a. "When Prisoners Get Out: The Impact of Prison Releases on Homicide Rates, 1975–1999." *Criminal Justice Policy Review*, 15(2): 212–228.

Kovandzic, Tomislav V., John J. Sloan III, and Lynne M. Vieraitis. 2004b. " 'Striking Out' as Crime Reduction Policy: The Impact of 'Three Strikes' Laws on Crime Rates in U.S. Cities." *Justice Quarterly*, 21(2): 207–239.

Kovandzic, Tomislav V., Thomas B. Marvell, and Lynne M. Vieraitis. 2005. "The Impact of "Shall-Issue" Concealed Handgun Laws on Violent Crime Rates: Evidence from Panel Data for Large Urban Cities." *Homicide Studies*, 9(4): 292–323.

The Lancet. 2000, October 21. "Reducing Gun Deaths in the USA." *The Lancet*, 356 (9239): 1367–1367.

Levitt, Steven D. 2004. "Understanding Why Crime Fell in the 1990s: Four Factors That Explain the Decline and Six That Do Not." *Journal of Economic Perspectives*, 18(1): 163–190.

Lindgren, April. 2006, June 21. "Domestic Violence Death Toll Remains High." *Kingston Whig-Standard*, p. 11.

Marvell, Thomas B., and Carlisle E. Moody. 1997. "The Impact of Prison Growth on Homicide." *Homicide Studies*, 1(3): 205–233.

Marvell, Thomas B., and Carlisle E. Moody. 2001. "The Lethal Effects of Three Strikes Laws." *Journal of Legal Studies*, 30(1): 89–106.

Matza, Michael. 2006, December 3. "Software Used to Predict Who Might Kill." *Philadelphia Inquirer.* Accessed at http://www.kansascity.com/mld/kansascity/news/breaking_news/16155226.htm

McGarrell, Edmund F., Steven M. Chermak, Jeremy M. Wilson, and Nicholas Corsaro. 2006. *Justice Quarterly*, 23(2): 214–229.

Radelet, Michael L., and Marian J. Borg. 2000. "The Changing Nature of Death Penalty Debates." *Annual Review of Sociology*, 26: 43–61.

Stack, Steven. 1987. "Publicized Executions and Homicide, 1950–1980." *American Sociological Review*, 52: 532–540.

Stolzenberg, Lisa, and Stewart J. D'Alessio. 2000. "Gun Availability and Violent Crime: New Evidence from the National Incident-Based Reporting System." *Social Forces*, 78(4): 1461–1482.

Websdale, Neil. 2003, November. "Reviewing Domestic Violence Deaths." *National Institute of Justice Journal*, 250. Available at http://www.ncjrs.gov/pdffiles1/jr000250g.pdf.

Wolfgang, Marvin. 1958. *Patterns in Criminal Homicide.* Philadelphia: University of Pennsylvania.

Chapter 18

Future of Homicide in the United States

Chapter 17 began with a quote from *Minority Report,* a film that suggests in the future there will be a way for criminal justice officials to know who is going to commit a murder so they can be stopped before they kill. It is seems highly unlikely that the criminal justice system will ever have such capabilities. But it is likely that advances in technology will change the way murders are solved, how we study homicide, and perhaps even how offenders commit homicide. This final chapter is dedicated to the future of homicide. Here you will find predictions for the future with regard to homicide trends, criminal justice responses to homicide, and future studies of homicide.

Future Homicide Trends

As this book goes to press, the headlines across the United States report that homicide is increasing again in some cities after the reduction trend noted in Chapter 4. At the end of 2006, an Associated Press article indicated that murder rates had increased to "their highest rates in a decade after many years of decline" (Matthews, 2006). City officials in New York City, however, noted that 35 of the 579 deaths recorded in their city in 2006 through December 24 suffered their fatal wounds before 2006. Even if these deaths were not included in the 2006 New York statistics, the city would have recorded a 6% increase from 2005 when the number of murders was at the lowest the city had seen in over 40 years (Matthews, 2006).

New York, however, was not the only city to see increases between 2005 and 2006. Preliminary 2006 crime data released by the FBI on December 18, 2006, indicated that many cities recorded more murders in 2006 than in 2005. The city of Indianapolis had 68 murders in the first six months of 2006, an increase over the 44

BOX 18.1

Offsetting Trends

Although confrontational murders may increase, especially in large cities, improved medical care may prevent some assaults from turning into homicides. Confrontational homicides are the result of an offender or victim attempting to "maintain face." As such, they often occur in front of others and in public, making it theoretically more likely that emergency services will be contacted. Moreover, emergency services continue to improve, making survival of would-be murder victims more likely. In Seattle's Harborview Medical Center, for example, gunshot victims in 2006 had a greater than 90% chance of living if they arrived at the hospital alive. Just two years before, gunshot victims had an 80% chance of surviving their injury. As surgery and postsurgery care improves, the survival rate may increase even more (Green, 2006).

---

reported during the first six months of 2005. Detroit increased during this same time period from 290 to 349; Cincinnati's numbers increased from 37 to 41. Orlando's murders more than quadrupled in the same six months from 7 in 2005 to 30 in 2006. Other cities, however, saw declines in the first six months of the year, including Cleveland and Columbus that decreased from 56 and 47 to 43 and 37, respectively. Gary, Indiana, once infamous for being the murder capital of the United States, reported 26 murders in the first six months of both 2005 and 2006 (FBI, 2006).

Criminal justice practitioners and criminologists alike may attempt to predict increases or decreases in murder. However, as discussed in Chapter 17, we are still not certain why we saw decreases in the 1990s. We certainly have reasonable hypotheses to explain the decrease, such as changes in the crack cocaine market, economic changes, and changes in criminal justice practices. However, as I tell students in my statistics courses, humans are complex. A multitude of factors influence what humans do. Figuring out why they do what they do is much more difficult than explaining mitosis (how cells multiply). We think we understand mitosis, but homicide remains a mystery. Moreover, as noted in Chapters 5 and 6, a multitude of theories attempts to explain why humans commit murder.

Knowing all the theories, hypotheses, and factors that may be related to murder, it would be very bold to believe one could predict whether we will see increases or decreases in murder in the United States or anywhere else over the next year, decade, or more. Nevertheless, it is possible to make what we might call "educated guesses." Looking at recent homicide patterns and trends and listening to criminal justice officials, we certainly do not expect the end of murder anytime soon. Moreover, we may expect that the number of murders and the murder rate will increase in large urban areas. Large urban areas that are densely populated with youth are likely to continue to battle increasing homicide rates without radical interventions. Confrontational homicides, as discussed in Chapter 7, are likely to increase, and these types of homicide appear to be driving the increases in homicide in many areas (Zernike, 2006).

As reported by Kate Zernike in a *New York Times* article, petty disputes are increasingly the explanation police officers are finding for the murders they investigate. In Milwaukee, the number of homicides attributed to arguments rose from 17 in 2004 to 45 in 2005, making it the largest circumstance category. Disputes were also cited as the leading reason for murder in both Houston and Philadelphia, two cities that are facing increasing numbers of murders. In many, but not all of the disputes, the offenders and victims knew each other, and previous criminal records were not uncommon for either (Zernike, 2006).

Other criminal justice officials, noting that many of the murders are occurring in poor neighborhoods, explain the killings as a "lack of hope" (Zernike, 2006). As discussed in Chapters 6 and 7, many of the youngsters living in these neighborhoods who are just beginning to reach the crime-prone teen years face particularly difficult lives as children born to single teenage mothers (Blumstein, 1993). Criminal justice officials and criminologists note that many of the youngsters involved in the murders are young men living in desperation with few viable options for employment. The only thing many of these young men believe they have is their manhood. If anyone disrespects them, they have to prove their manhood with violence, and more often than in the past, the violence involves guns (Zernike, 2006). As a result, many large cities that have neighborhoods with a high concentration of disadvantaged people are likely to continue to see growth in their homicide numbers because, according to demographers, the number of youths in these neighborhoods is expected to increase (Fox & Piquero, 2003).

Although the future of youth violence and confrontational homicide appears somewhat bleak, particularly in large urban cities with areas of concentrated disadvantage, the aging of our population, according to demographers, is likely to be at least partially offset by the growing numbers of violence-prone youth. In the United States, baby boomers make up such a large percentage of the population that their behavior drives, to some extent, the trends for the nation. Over 30% of the total U.S. population is age 50 or older. As you may remember from Chapter 4, in 2004, less than 5% of murder offenders were older than 54 years. Thus, as the largest cohort in our population, the baby boomer generation, ages, we can expect decreasing violent crime. In other words, even if young males continue to solve disputes with guns, baby boomers are less likely to commit murder each year as they grow older. As a result, any increase among teens is not likely to send the murder rate skyrocketing to the numbers we witnessed in the 1980s because the contribution of the largest age groups is likely to continue to decrease (Fox & Piquero, 2003).

BOX 18.2
Katrina Contributes to Houston's Murder Numbers

The Houston Police Department recorded 379 homicides in 2006, reflecting a 13.5% increase in homicides from the 334 reported in 2005. The overall rate of homicide, however, increased less than 1% from 16.33 per

continued

100,000 in 2005 to 17.24 in 2006. As the title of this box indicates, a national disaster contributed to the homicide increase. Because of the population increase due to as many as 150,000 evacuees moving to Houston from New Orleans, the Houston murder rate barely changed at all (Goodwyn, 2006; O'Hare, 2007). The denominator for determining the murder rate increased as much as 7.5% when Houston's population grew tremendously in a matter of days.

During the first six months of 2006, the number of homicides in Houston surged to 202; nearly 28% over the 158 in the first half of 2005. With Katrina evacuees from New Orleans; a city which Houston mayor Bill White noted had a homicide rate eight times the national average before Katrina, Houston expected to deal with a horrendous homicide problem (O'Hare, 2007). In reaction to what promised to be a tremendous murder increase, the Houston police department increased overtime, added police academy classes, and initiated a zero tolerance policy on narcotics. Officials credited these policies for the modest increase in the overall homicide rate they saw during 2006 instead of the phenomenal increase they expected.

HOMICIDE PREDICTIONS AROUND THE WORLD

Although many other countries do not contend with gun homicides to the same extent that we do in the United States, it is no easier to predict the future of homicide outside the United States. In 2005, year-end murder counts in Ireland not only indicated a rising murder rate but also that more individuals were murdered by assault or stabbing than with guns. Just over half (54%) of the murders in Ireland in 2005 were the result of stabbings or assaults. To Irish criminal justice officials, this pattern is the result of late-night violence most likely growing out of disputes much like we see in the United States (but to a lesser degree) (Rice & Burke, 2006). The murder rate in Russia, in contrast, appears to be on a downward slide. Since 2002, the numbers of homicides have been decreasing, according to police officials in Russia, although serial killing and murders in Moscow appear to be increasing (Nowak, 2006; RIA Novosti, 2006).

HIGH-TECH CRIME FIGHTING

Regardless of whether murder increases or decreases, DNA evidence, as reported in Chapter 14, is likely to remain a valuable crime-solving tool. The importance of DNA evidence, however, is not likely to be as important for everyday homicides as crime shows like *CSI* may have us believe. If confrontational homicide predominates, homicide investigators will, in all likelihood, rely on witnesses as opposed to DNA evidence for locating perpetrators.

This is not to say that the value of DNA evidence is likely to vanish. The availability of DNA testing and expanding DNA databases are likely to continue to help law enforcement investigate more difficult cases. In murder cases in which there are no witnesses and in cold cases, homicide investigators are likely to increasingly use a new type of arrest warrant called a "DNA" warrant or a "John Doe" warrant. Rather than warrants that name individuals, these are warrants issued for a person by their genetic code. Finally, DNA analyses will be used increasingly by individuals who claim they are wrongly convicted to help prove their innocence. In 2004, President Bush signed the *Justice for All Act*, which makes it easier for convicted murderers to obtain DNA testing of evidence if it may prove they are innocent (Cormier, Calandro, & Reeder, 2005).

Surveillance cameras and technological advances in video imaging are already helping homicide detectives solve murder cases, and their value is likely to increase as the technology evolves. In May 2005, Patricia McDermott was murdered in Philadelphia. Detectives used more than 50 cameras, both private and public, to trace McDermott's steps during the day she went missing. Amazingly, a post office camera had recorded the murderer as he followed McDermott off a bus and then shot her in the head. The images were fuzzy but clear enough for members of the public to identify Juan Covington as the killer. With this lead, detectives returned to their use of surveillance tapes where they found a video of Covington arriving at work the day of McDermott's death wearing the same clothes he was wearing in the video of the murder. The videos and good police work made this a "dunker" case, and Covington is now serving a life sentence for McDermott's murder (Jones, 2007).

Technology also provides many valuable records that we are likely to see law enforcement officials continue to use. Cell phone, credit card, and electronic toll collection records have helped detectives solve murders, and we can expect that they will continue to use such records and expand the records they use in the future. Law enforcement is also likely to expand their use of the Internet. We already see missing persons and most wanted bulletins on the Internet. At the end of 2006, police in Canada took another step by posting a surveillance video of a murder suspect on YouTube. According to news reports, the suspect, George Gallo, turned himself in after the police posted a 72-second clip from a murder scene outside a club in Toronto. No witnesses came forward, but the attention brought about by the YouTube posting was believed to have contributed to Gallo turning himself in to the police. The video had more than 34,000 hits by the time Gallo was in police custody (Associated Press, 2006). We are seeing detectives on television shows like *The Wire* and *Law and Order* use these types of technology because these shows reflect what actual police are doing. Of course, the real-life work is often much more tedious and time consuming than we see on these shows.

It is unlikely that we will be able to predict who will commit murder as portrayed in the science fiction film *Minority Report*. As computer technology has evolved, however, computer scientists have developed computer systems that aid law enforcement officers in fighting crime. Recently, computer scientists at DePaul University developed the Classification System for Serial Criminal Patterns (CSSCP). Like sociologists who seek out patterns in human behavior, CSSCP works to find patterns among different crimes. CSSCP, which runs twenty-four hours a day, seven days a week, is able to detect more nuanced connections than humans looking at the same crime data. Although CSSCP is likely to be particularly helpful for solving robberies, it may be a valuable tool for law enforcement to use to detect serial killing patterns and, more importantly, apprehend the offender (Graham-Rowe, 2004).

BOX 18.3

Pregnant Women and Homicide

In March 2004, Melissa Rowland, a 28-eight-year-old woman, was arrested in Salt Lake City, Utah, for the death of her son. Rowland's son, however, was never born. Unlike the cases noted in Chapter 10 of this book, Rowland was not arrested because she had taken illegal drugs while pregnant. She was arrested and charged with homicide because she failed to undergo a cesarean delivery (commonly called a C-section) as doctors advised her. Rowland went into labor on January 13, 2004, and gave birth to a baby girl, but the girl's twin brother was stillborn. An autopsy suggested that the boy had died after physicians had advised Rowland she should have a cesarean. Rowland decided not to fight the charges but instead pleaded guilty to two counts of child endangerment, and the prosecutor dropped the homicide charge (Miller, 2006).

It will be interesting to see if this trend to arrest woman who have stillborn or unhealthy babies will continue. Moreover, if the trend does continue, is it likely to deter women from seeking prenatal care or a physician's care or will it encourage or force women to act against their will by electing medical treatment they would prefer not to risk? These are questions that time will answer for us.

FUTURE STUDIES OF HOMICIDE

Predicting the future direction of research about homicide is as difficult as predicting homicide trends. Asking those who study homicide what we do not know about homicide may be a place to start. Luckily, as the year 2000 approached, Dwayne Smith asked the editorial board of *Homicide Studies* what else could be learned about homicide. In the resultant article published in the February 2000 issue of the journal, several of the leading experts in the study of homicide from around the globe shared their ideas for the future of homicide research (Smith, 2000). The 16 experts wrote about a variety of topics, and many are likely to be the focus of future research about homicide. Anyone wishing to generate ideas for research on homicide would be best served by reading Smith's compilation of answers to his question. Nevertheless, three ideas for the future study of homicide stand out because they were noted by more than one of the experts.

First, the study of homicide would benefit from an examination of the connections between nonlethal violence and murder, questions such as how often is the difference between nonlethal and lethal violence the intention of the offender, the weapon chosen, or the availability of medical services. If we can determine the sometimes subtle differences between near-lethal violence and lethal violence, we may be able to make great steps toward preventing murder. Second, many of the experts believed that we should continue to examine offenders, victims, and homicide events to enhance our understanding and theory development. Importantly, we may want to consider whether the current categorizations as discussed in several chapters of this text are valuable in our studies. Polk, in particular, noted that categorizations such as stranger homicide could be further broken into various categories such as bar fights, predatory crime, and honor encounters. Third, cross cultural and international homicide research is likely to teach us much about murder in the United States and elsewhere. Comparisons between countries with similar exposure to media violence and gun access with different murder rates promise to help us better understand the etiology of homicide offending. Comparisons among different countries and issues of race and class may also prove fruitful (Smith, 2000).

In addition to the ideas generated by the editorial board of *Homicide Studies*, Fox and Piquero (2003) were smart to point out that it will be relevant to consider the growing Latino population in studies of homicide as the nation's demographics shift. Ramiro Martinez Jr. (2002) is driving much of the research in the area. Martinez is likely to be continually joined by others because the Latino population has overtaken the African American population as the largest minority in the United States and issues of immigration are still a focus of our politicians.

SUMMARY

Predicting human behavior is extremely challenging. Nonetheless, in this chapter an educated guess about homicide is put forth. It is likely that homicide rates, especially among young males, will continue to increase in the near future. Because of the great number of baby boomers in our population, the numbers are not expected to soar as much as they have in the past. Technological advances are much more certain than murder rates, and we are likely to continue to see the use of technology for solving homicide cases and prosecuting offenders. Finally, research on homicide is likely to continue. The direction of the study of homicide may be more predictable than homicide itself. In the future, we are likely to see a focus on the connections between lethal and nonlethal violence, attention to various murder categorization, comparative studies, and attention to the Latino/a populations in the United States as we continue to see criminologists search for ways to understand and ideally prevent homicide in the future.

CHAPTER QUESTIONS

1. According to this chapter, is homicide likely to increase or decrease?
2. Explain why homicide may increase or decrease according to this chapter.
3. Do the predictions in this chapter about homicide trends appear to be coming true? Why or why not?
4. What type of homicide appears to be increasing?
5. How is the baby boomer generation likely to affect future homicide trends?
6. How do homicides in other parts of the world appear to be similar to the United States?
7. Explain the role DNA is likely to play in solving homicides in the near future.

8. What do surveillance cameras have to do with homicide?
9. What type of technology is being used by law enforcement to solve murder?
10. List the four directions for homicide study we are likely to see in the near future.

REFERENCES

Associated Press. 2006, December 21. "Canadian Police Arrest Murder Suspect After Surveillance Tape Shown on YouTube." Accessed at http://www.foxnews.com/story/0,2933,238029,00.html

Blumstein, Albert. 1993. "Making Rationality Relevant." *Criminology,* 31: 1–16.

Cormier, Karen, Lisa Calandro, and Dennis Reeder. 2005. "Evolution of DNA Evidence for Crime Solving—a Judicial and Legislative History." *Forensic Magazine,* 2(4): 1–3.

FBI. 2006. *2006 Preliminary Semiannual Uniform Crime Report.* Accessed at http://www.fbi.gov/ucr/prelim06/index.html

Fox, James Alan, and Alex R. Piquero. 2003. "Deadly Demographics: Population Characteristics and Forecasting Homicide Trends." *Crime & Delinquency,* 49(3): 339–359.

Goodwyn, Wade. 2006, August 30. "Houston Shines in First Year with Katrina Evacuees." *NPR Morning Edition.*

Graham-Rowe, Duncan. 2004. "Cyber Detective Links Up Crime." *NewScientist.com.* Accessed at http://www.newscientist.com/article.ns?id=dn6734

Green, Sara Jean. 2006, December 19. "Gun Violence Rising, But Homicide Rate Only Slightly Up in Seattle." *The Seattle Times.* Accessed at http://seattletimes.nwsource.com/html/localnews/2003484510_violence19m.html.

Jones, K. C. 2007. "Technology Helps Catch Serial Killer." Accessed at http://www.techweb.com/wire/196801477

Martinez, Ramiro Jr. 2002. *Latino Homicide.* New York: Routledge.

Matthews, Karen. 2006, December 28. "Murder Rate Up In Several U.S. Cities for 2006." *Associated Press State & Local Wire.*

Miller, Monica K. 2006. "Refusal to Undergo a Cesarean Section: A Woman's Right or a Criminal Act?" *Health Matrix Journal of Law and Medicine,* 15: 383–400.

Nowak, David. 2006, December 15. "Murder Rate on the Rise in Moscow." *The Moscow Times,* p. 2.

O'Hare, Peggy. 2007, January. "City Sees 13.5% Rise in Slayings for 2006." *The Houston Chronicle.* Accessed at http://www.highbeam.com/doc/1G1-156557387.html.

RIA Novosti. 2006, December 14. "Russia's Murder Rate Down 10% But 15% Remain Unsolved—Ministry." *Russia News and Information Agency.*

Rice, Eoghan, and John Burke. 2006, December 31. "More People Died in Assaults and Knife Attacks Than Were Shot in 2006." *Sunday Tribune.* Accessed at http://www.tribune.ie/2006/12/31/80656.html

Smith, M. Dwayne. 2000. "A New Era of Homicide Studies? Visions of a Research Agenda for the New Decade." *Homicide Studies,* 4:3–17.

Zernike, Kate. 2006, February 12. "Violent Crime Rising Sharply in Some Cities." *New York Times.* Accessed online at http://www.nytimes.com/2006/02/12/national/12homicide.html?ex=1297400400&en=cdb21abf99ff0c1b&ei=5088

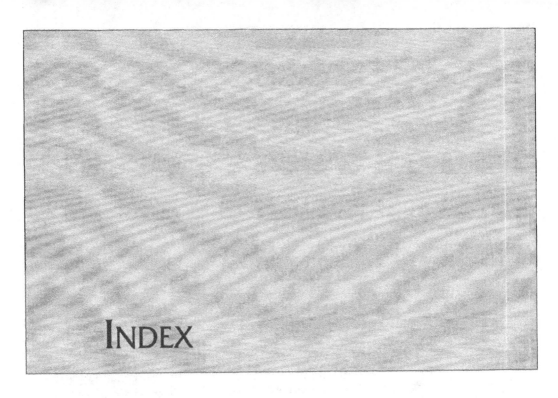

INDEX